VIRGIL'S PASTORAL ART

VIRGIL'S PASTORAL ART

Studies in the Eclogues

MICHAEL C. J. PUTNAM

PRINCETON UNIVERSITY PRESS
PRINCETON, N.J. 1970

Copyright © 1970 by Princeton University Press
Library of Congress Card: 77-90956
ISBN: 0-691-06178-5

Publication of this book has been
aided by the Whitney Darrow Publication Reserve Fund of
Princeton University Press

This book is composed in Linotype Granjon
Printed by Princeton University Press
Princeton, New Jersey

For Anne, Cedric, and Peter

But for all this I do deny that the *Eclogue* should be the
first and most auncient forme of artificiall Poesie, being
persuaded that the Poet devised the *Eclogue* long after
the other *dramatick* poems, not of purpose to counterfait
or represent the rusticall manner of loves and communica-
tion, but under the vaile of homely persons and in rude
speeches to insinuate and glaunce at greater matters, and
such as perchaunce had not bene safe to have beene disclosed in any other sort, which may be perceived by the
Eclogues of *Virgill*, in which are treated by figure matters
of greater importance than the loves of *Titirus* and
Corydon.

George Puttenham, *The Arte of
English Poesie*

Preface

If any excuse for an additional book on Virgil is defensible, it is its limitation to the pastoral poems. We have had in English no critical work of book length dealing solely with them since H. J. Rose published his Sather Lectures on *The Eclogues of Virgil* in 1942. Professor Rose, though he attacked many of the problems with which they abound, did not offer literary expositions—nor was such his aim.

The present volume, though it follows in the tradition of Cartault and others, is an effort to fill this gap. I have made as full a use of previous discussion of the *Eclogues* as sheer bulk, and human fallibility, will allow. Especially in recent years there has been, happily, an increase in the number of careful elucidations of individual poems. Likewise the idea of pastoralism itself has received renewed attention, with benefit to the student of ancient, as well as modern, poetry. The following chapters have tried to take advantage of each, in the search for an approach which, like the poems themselves, leavens unity with diversity.

Since this book is a series of critical studies and not a line-by-line commentary, I have made no attempt to accept the challenge of every controversial difficulty, or even to defend in full my stand on every critical matter. Nevertheless, my position on most issues will, I hope, be clear. Though undoubtedly worshiping false divinities of my own, I have striven not to bow blindly before the gods of past criticism. For instance, I am not convinced that Daphnis in *Eclogue* 5 must be an allegory for Julius Caesar (more important, I cannot see how such an equation in any way increases our respect for the poem). *Eclogues* 1 and 9 do not appear to me to be poems conceived in even partial optimism. *Eclogue* 4

Preface

is not so deliberately cryptic—and hence superficial—a document that humorous lightness must be the critic's only recourse. To some, such views will seem upsetting, not to say heretical. They arise, however, not from any conscious preconceptions but from an honest attempt to face the meaning and tone of each poem without obscuring or suppressing any of its essential ideas.

My purpose is to present a structural analysis of each of the ten eclogues. With one exception, where *Eclogues* 2 and 3 are treated together, each chapter discusses the sense and strategy of one poem. Hopefully, however, the whole book of *Eclogues* is never out of sight. In working with the symbolic value of words, my principal guide has been the poet's total vocabulary. I have endeavored to keep my interpretation of the meanings of words within the possible ken of a master craftsman of the Latin language in the 40's and 30's B.C.

I have relied heavily on analogy as a critical tool. It is my firm belief that Virgil, more than any other ancient poet, was fully aware of the effect of word or phrase repetitions within a poem or group of poems. This is not to maintain (as I hope I do not presume to do) that one word in any context equals another elsewhere but only that the reverberations should not be denied. When, in the first eclogue, Virgil uses the adjective *lentus* to describe both Tityrus at his ease and the landscape's bending osiers, he makes us see the one in terms of the other.

I am as much indebted to Virgil's ancient commentators as to the works of more recent literary criticism. The translations of Virgil are my own and seek as close a literal rendering of the Latin as the prose of another tongue will allow. For the text and translations of Theocritus I have used the edition of A.S.F. Gow.

The book was begun at the American Academy in Rome during 1963-64. I owe much to stimulating discussions there with Professor Frank E. Brown, now Director of the Acad-

Preface

emy, and with my colleagues. I am deeply grateful to the trustees and President of the Guggenheim Memorial Foundation for an award which afforded me the leisure to complete the book and to President Emeritus Barnaby C. Keeney of Brown University for granting me a leave of absence at that time. An early draft benefited from the counsel of Sir Roger Mynors. I have also profited from the close critical readings of the manuscript by Professors Palmer Bovie of Rutgers and J. William Hunt of the University of Massachusetts. Many friends and colleagues, in particular Professors Charles Babcock and Charles Fornara, have given freely of their time. My family, especially my parents and Charles and Polly Chatfield, have been helpful in a variety of ways. I am also obliged to Sarah George of Princeton University Press for her careful and sympathetic editing. The greatest debt is acknowledged elsewhere. Despite this assistance, no one but the author bears responsibility for the falterings and shortcomings in the pages which follow.

Michael C. J. Putnam

Petersham, Massachusetts

Contents

Abbreviations Used in the Notes

AJP	American Journal of Philology
Cal. Pub. in Class. Phil.	University of California Publications in Classical Philology
CJ	Classical Journal
CP	Classical Philology
CQ	Classical Quarterly
CR	Classical Review
CW	Classical World
HSCP	Harvard Studies in Classical Philology
JRS	Journal of Roman Studies
Journ. War. and Court. Inst.	Journal of the Warburg and Courtauld Institutes
Mem. Am. Aca. Rome	Memoirs of the American Academy in Rome
P.-W.	Pauly-Wissowa-Kroll Realencyclopädie der classischen Altertumswissenschaft
REL	Revue des Études Latines
REA	Revue des Études Anciennes
RhM	Rheinisches Museum für Philologie
Sitz. Heid.	Sitzungsberichte der Heidelberger Akademie der Wissenschaften, Philos.-Hist. Klasse
TAPA	Transactions and Proceedings of the American Philological Association
WS	Wiener Studien

VIRGIL'S PASTORAL ART

Introduction

The notion of Virgil as gentle poet of simple charm has been slow to die.[1] We accept melancholy as the poet's dominant characteristic, yet we assume its incorporation in a stance which is poised, reserved, aloof—"classical," in a word. Though evil continues to scheme and life remains charged with passions, though man be forced into a not always kindly dialogue with nature, his fellow creatures, and himself, Virgil somehow manages (we are assured) to bathe all suffering in a magic glow which reconciles opposites and leaves a sense of virtue and justice triumphant. The ten poems which comprise Virgil's first major work, the *Eclogues*, have been most subjected to this devitalizing approach. Since the publication of Horace's first book of *Satires* a few years after the *Eclogues* were completed, readers have been schooled to characterize Virgil's work—in the words of his great contemporary—as *molle atque facetum*, smooth and elegant.[2] We presume the judgment applies to content as well as to the rhetoric of expression.

The *Eclogues* are pastorals, and poetry of this form, perhaps more than any other kind of poetry, stands open to easy abuse. It is, by convention, a fantasy: a countryside with singing shepherds and their loves, with heroes like Daphnis (once human, now divine), with epiphanic gods and demi-gods. But Virgil's is no rugged, bleak, literal Arcadia. The closest he comes to projecting his dream upon a real landscape is in

---

[1] A writer in the *Times Literary Supplement* of August 23, 1963 (p. 640) remarks: "The charm, and *significance*, of the *Eclogues* lies . . . in their tenderness and in their feeling for the countryside, the qualities which were later to flower into the Georgics" (italics mine).

[2] Horace *Sat.* I. 10. 44.

Introduction

the seventh eclogue where the banks of his beloved Mincius offer the hospitable setting for a contest. Even there, however, the shepherds are twice styled *Arcades*, not to shatter the spell; so it is easy to see how the *Eclogues* can be labeled "escapist" verses, witnesses of responsibilities evaded and of studied withdrawal from the pressures of society into a "rustic," simple life.

Other definitions accommodate an allied, nostalgic yearning for the distant in space or time, for a situation of stable perfection, far removed from anything odd or evil, tragic or transitory, a situation impossible to achieve but inspirational or mesmeric to contemplate. I am referring not to the many different shapes the pastoral myth may take but to formal poetry which assumes a deliberately bucolic guise.[3] The history of pastoral poetry from Theocritus through the Renaissance to Milton and Arnold shows that its use as a vehicle for ideas, for social comment, for "involvement" while maintaining a detached pose, is the exception rather than the rule. Especially in the Renaissance it is the exceptions like Spenser who, because they resisted easy satire, kept vital the best aspects of what was for more than fifteen hundred years a highly creative tradition.[4]

Virgil's *Eclogues* are the first, and in many ways the greatest, example of pastoral poetry used to convey a message as well as to delight. Nevertheless certain misconceptions about them, some of which are superficial, persist. Though filled with problems which we still cannot solve, the *Eclogues* are not veiled allegories whose mysterious references to contemporary affairs in the fourth and third decades of the last cen-

[3] For a suggestive treatment of bucolic elements in works which do not stay strictly within the pastoral convention, see William Empson, *Some Versions of Pastoral* (London, 1935).

[4] On the importance and achievement of pastoral poetry in the Renaissance, see Hallett Smith, *Elizabethan Poetry* (Cambridge, Mass., 1952), pp. 1-63, esp. 41.

4

Introduction

tury before Christ cannot be understood today.[5] Virgil does use disguises—the first eclogue offers a notable instance in the young god living at Rome—and understatement is the essence of his art. However, when a clue is necessary—for example, in the third and fourth poems the mention of the soldier and man of letters Pollio—it is usually forthcoming.

The *Eclogues* are no more mere variations on Theocritean themes than they are veiled allegories. It is true that the relationship between the Alexandrian master and his Roman disciple is an intricate one: Virgil has often absorbed the matter and wording of his predecessor.[6] But a close analysis of the parallels reveals that Theocritus was only a stepping-stone for Virgil's new approach, which pays little attention to Theocritus' ethical and aesthetic ideas. In Theocritus the city still represents civilization and society complements rather than challenges nature. The pains of love to which Theocritus' shepherds submit are pleasantly ephemeral when compared to the horror which the bucolic life faces in some of the *Eclogues*. Even in the "lighter" eclogues Virgil expands upon his master. Compare *Eclogue* 2 with its model in Theocritus, *Idyl* 11, a lovesong of the cyclops Polyphemus to the sea nymph Galatea. Juxtaposition brings out a twofold meaning in Virgil's work. There is a "rhetorical" side in which the poet

[5] The allegorical approach is taken by Leon Herrmann (*Les masques et les visages dans les Bucoliques de Virgile* [Brussels, 1930]) and, more recently, in a series of articles by J.J.H. Savage (*TAPA* 91 [1960]: 353-75 and *TAPA* 94 [1963]: 248-67). See the just strictures on this method of criticism by H. J. Rose, *The Eclogues of Vergil* (Berkeley, 1942), pp. 71ff.

[6] The influence of Theocritus on the *Eclogues* has been much discussed, though a reappraisal is long overdue. See especially G. Rohde, "De Vergili Eclogarum forma et indole" (Ph.D. diss., University of Marburg, Berlin, 1925) and the review of it by Friedrich Klingner, *Gnomon* 3 (1927): 576-83. Klingner's chapter "Virgil" in *L'influence grecque sur la poésie latine de Catulle à Ovide*, Entretiens II (Geneva: Fondation Hardt, 1956), pp. 131-55, is of great value. See also his *Römische Geisteswelt* (Munich, 1961), p. 265.

proves, with engaging humor, how one must *not* sing if he is to succeed as a lover. Such *incondita*, such rude uncouthness as Corydon mouths—and the deprecatory word is common in Cicero's vocabulary of oratorical criticism[7]—can scarcely effect the desired result. Yet a distinct implication in the shepherd's words confirms that nature postulates an unswerving rationale whereas man's emotions defy logic and ruin the harmony with his surroundings, which is one justification of the shepherd's lot. In *Idyl* 11, Polyphemus apparently loses Galatea, but in *Eclogue* 2, Corydon's lack of success causes him to regain a higher and tougher reasoning.

The structural interrelationship of the ten poems is also still debated. Since poems 3 and 7 are amoebean, or poems 5 and 8 have two long, separate songs, one common argument runs that we are meant by Virgil to view them in pairs. But the superficial resemblances which abound among these poems are no defense of their quality as literature and should not receive undue stress. The seventh eclogue may have technical similarities with the third; its force largely results from conjunction with poems 6 and 8. That the application of any system of balances to the *Eclogues* as a group cannot help but project one or more poems for focal consideration[8] and that the number of differing proposals is considerable is reasonable evidence that none in particular fulfills the poet's intention. It is more economical to argue that he would have wished us to read the poems in the order the manuscripts assign them, watching the ideas progress and interact from one poem to the next in a culminating design.

One reason for the *Eclogues'* having gained the epithet "escapist" derives from a more basic misinterpretation. Only a trite reading can see in these poems the delineation of a

---

[7] See below, chap. 2, notes 3 and 5.

[8] See, for instance, Brooks Otis, *Virgil: A Study in Civilized Poetry* (Oxford, 1963), chap. 4, "The Young Virgil." Otis sees *Eclogue* 5 receiving particular emphasis from the book's structure. Cf. Carl Becker, "Virgils Eklogenbuch," *Hermes* 83 (1955): 314-49, esp. 320ff.

Introduction

"pastoral" way of life in its literal, agrarian sense—as if they were pieces written to distract the citified Roman from his urban cares or, to put it more romantically (and borrow a traditional distinction), as if they described some more lasting, model value to be found in "emotional" rural man than in the practical city-dweller. In this formulation the first is somehow associated with intelligence, the second with matter; the one, an inhabitant in a "sophisticated," private nirvana, the other, mired in the slough of vulgar reality. The *Eclogues*, however, are not an obscure espousal of an Emersonian triumph of mind over artifice.

This is not to deny the hold of the actual countryside on the imagination of the Roman people, indeed on its most important poets. Rural landscape did provide a necessary foil to the elaborateness and difficulties of city life. As the responsibilities of empire grew, the countryside came more and more to symbolize simplicity and other evaporating virtues of a once essentially agricultural populace.[9]

Certainly this moral and intellectual dialogue between city and country is a topic of Latin literature at least from the time of Lucilius on.[10] It is a constant theme in the works of Cicero. At the opening of *De Oratore* (1. 24), for instance, Crassus, spokesman for the great orator in the subsequent dialogue, withdraws from the press of Roman political life to Tusculum for the sake of "collecting" himself (*quasi conligendi sui causa*). Yet however much Cicero, philosopher and litterateur, depends on the country for the quiet of renewal, Cicero, advocate and statesman, cherishes, indeed requires, the bustle of the forum.

There is no doubt on which side of the fence Catullus stands: *rusticitas* in all its forms is anathema. He, too, has a villa which lovingly receives him after a bout of flu (*Carmen*

[9] See Viktor Pöschl, "Horaz und die Politik," *Sitz. Heid.*, Abhandlung 4 (1956): 14 and 17ff.
[10] See chap. 2, n. 2.

44), but its location near Tibur was a matter of humorous concern to him because it reflected on his social standing and intellectual attitudes (lines 2-4):

> nam te esse Tiburtem autumant, quibus non est
> cordi Catullum laedere; at quibus cordi est,
> quovis Sabinum pignore esse contendunt, . . .

For those who do not wish to harm Catullus affirm that you are Tiburtine; those who do, maintain on any terms that you are Sabine.

Catullus' detractors, he tells us, put his villa in the Sabine country and, accordingly, accuse master and house of boorishness. If, on the other hand, it is near enough to Tibur (and Rome) to earn the epithet *suburbana*, then Catullus is happy. The villa is civilized, like himself.

Lucretius can even go so far as to satirize the constant flitting back and forth between city and villa in which the well-to-do Roman indulges (*De Rerum Natura* 3, lines 1053-1075). There is no question here of any higher, curative value in country life: the bored Roman is only seeking forgetfulness through change. This restless ennui would not be such a besetting trial, the Epicurean poet claims, if men could analyze their burdens and, other concerns put aside, devote themselves to learning "the nature of things."

On the contrary, the countryside for Virgil is only in a secondary sense to be viewed either literally or as a garden of Eden. His shepherds are no symbols of youth and innocence, dwelling in a paradise in danger of being lost to that epitome of vice and crime, the city. Rather "pastoral," for Virgil, has significance on a still deeper level: it means, at least during this decade in his career, the life of the imagination and the poet's concerned search for freedom to order experience. The landscape and its inhabitants are a realization in tangible form of the poetic mind at work. The shepherds are his voices.

Introduction

Their debates are his thoughts on poetry and life in the process of formulation. This is the sense in which "pastoral" will be used in the pages which follow.

The poet and his fictitious world, the creator and the created, uninvolved with reality as they may at first seem, are, in Virgil's view of bucolic poetry, open to the challenges any writer of poetry must face from a sometimes narrow, often alien milieu in which he must exist. In this regard the *Eclogues* have as much in common with fifth-century tragedy as with Theocritus. Not only is Virgil writing of the spiritual world of the artist, he is emphasizing the need for preserving individual freedom if the highest human values are to survive.

If pastoral poetry delineates the imagination at work, it depends upon a concomitant personal liberty to create in an atmosphere of integrity and order. Virgil evokes the challenges of the complex world of power to his shepherds' retreat not to suggest escape from the battle of life or to depict a charming image of evasion into a magical golden age. His purpose is to show what is at stake in Rome if the life of the imagination loses, and what could be gained if the two opposing conceptions of "pastoral" and power, poetry and history, were to live in harmony. That the notion is idealistic does not detract from the force of either those poems which claim it as true or their pessimistic counterparts which acknowledge the vanity of the search.

Part of the appeal and pertinence of the *Eclogues* lies in following the poet's search to define the place and status of the individual in an increasingly intricate and more restrictive society, victimized by civil disturbance for almost a hundred years. Virgil is the observer of a people in transition, whose old institutions were decaying but whose power, by astute employment of political and technological acumen, not to speak of military strength, was unparalleled in ancient civilization. This tension forced upon Virgil a question the varying answers to which were to become one of the intellectual con-

9

Introduction

cerns of the Augustan literary scene, a question which, though it is allied to the conflict of *physis* and *nomos* in fifth-century Greek thought, remains one of the few original formulations of the Roman mind. What is the relationship of society and "nature," of the institutions which impose an apparent order on life and the landscape which, at the opposite extreme, has come to symbolize freedom from such restraints as well as, paradoxically, a higher form of morality?

The one instance of such an implied comparison usually cited as an example from Greek literature—Socrates' choice of the banks of the Ilissus instead of the city of Athens itself as a setting for discussion in the *Phaedrus*[11]—is a far cry, say, from Horace's admonition to Maecenas to abandon the *fumum et opes strepitumque Romae*, the smoke and commercialism and noise of Rome, for the simplicity of the Sabine farm. This reflects, in part, a basic difference between Socratic and Stoic ethics. For the Stoics, the wise and just man, far from accepting his soul as a microcosm of the state and participating in civic life accordingly, should seek an order beyond mere political convention and detach himself from *Realien* to achieve morality and wisdom. In Horace's specific case the countryside offers a chance for the integrity of poetry as well. Horace's prayer is, to him, the only way to sanity as well as the only way to remain a poet. For Socrates, lover of his polis, to withdraw from the city is an act of whimsy which can scarcely endure for any length of time: "Country spots and trees will not teach me a thing. Men in the city do" (*Phaedrus* 230d).

Dr. Johnson, according to Boswell, would have agreed: "Our conversation turned upon living in the country, which Johnson, whose melancholy mind required the dissipation of quick successive variety, had habituated himself to consider as

[11] On the *Phaedrus* and pastoral tradition, see Clyde Murley, "Plato's *Phaedrus* and Theocritean Pastoral," *TAPA* 71 (1940): 281-95; Adam Parry, "Landscape in Greek Poetry," *Yale Classical Studies* 15 (1957): 3-29; C. P. Segal, "Nature and the World of Man in Greek Literature," *Arion* 2 (1963): 45ff.

Introduction

a kind of mental imprisonment. 'Yet, Sir (said I), there are many people who are content to live in the country.' Johnson: 'Sir, it is in the intellectual world as in the physical world; we are told by natural philosophers that a body is at rest in the place that is fit for it; they who are content to live in the country are *fit* for the country.'" Or, as he says elsewhere, "When a man is tired of London he is tired of life." The Johnsonian manner is amusing and typical of the eighteenth century. Yet the glorification of the city is the other side of the coin from the bucolic mode and anticipates, paradoxically (for Johnson was no lover of "vulgarity"), the succeeding century's search to free the proletariat, the urban mob, from the shackles which, according to Marx and Engels, had long held it.

But Horace and Virgil were in no sense "unurbane" or unaware that their lives were closely involved with the affairs of Rome, however far away their thoughts might flee. As the republic changed to empire, the pressures of society—indeed the artificiality imposed on life by society as it grew—expanded to such a point that the poets reacted against it. They reversed the mode of thinking we have seen in Cicero, Lucretius, and Catullus and returned to what was partially a traditional stance. One must, however, emphasize again that the countryside of Virgil's *Eclogues* is not to be interpreted objectively as the habitat of woolly sheep and piping shepherds. Nor is it the territory worked by the sturdy ploughman, that primitive nobleman, outdistanced by culture albeit representative of a Saturnian age long past. Virgil's landscape takes on virtually the opposite of the rustic, though morally upright, role it ordinarily plays as foil to the cultured grace of the metropolis. Even in a poem such as *Eclogue* 2, which seems at first to deal with the traditional dichotomy, the levels of meaning are still more complex.

In part the *Eclogues* are meditations on the position of the human personality, always caught in the turmoil of conflicting

11

Introduction

values and attempting to make "nature" meaningful, to create a rationale for life. They pose for the thoughtful reader many of the same problems as the tragedies of Shakespeare, and demand that he ponder the place of traditional ethical values in a fluctuating, disordered world subject to the necessities of time and death. In some poems the matter is treated gently and the poet withdraws through the lightness of the particular aspect under discussion (*Eclogues* 2 and 3) or the imaginative virtuosity which emblazons his theme (*Eclogue* 4). In other, more matter of fact poems the tone borders on despair in the realization that politics and morality are rarely reconcilable or in contemplation of the poet's apparently losing battle against society and history.

Even Tityrus' seemingly ideal happiness in the first eclogue leaves the reader wondering: What about Meliboeus? Is that god who can dispose of things physical and spiritual with something approaching unfair nonchalance really so divine? Will the monolithic state ever understand the plight, not to say rights, of the loser? Can the position of Tityrus be called perfect when it is created and bestowed by a higher power, or stable when Tityrus can allow himself to make only a passing and ineffectual bow to the suffering of Meliboeus? Can callousness or even indifference toward another's grief be a possible characteristic of a true singer of songs, pastoral idyls though they be? Tityrus is Virgil's symbolic victim before his time of that harmful, even evil, aspect of Romanticism which depends upon "a severance of mind from world, soul from circumstance, human inwardness from external condition."[12]

Too often in the criticism of Latin literature, a flatly literal interpretation of poetry does the poet the gravest disservice. To see Virgil as Tityrus alone, the happy shepherd-bard, beloved by Rome, with his land restored, is to burden Virgil with a false piece of common criticism: that the poet is himself

---

[12] Erich Heller, *The Artist's Journey into the Interior* (New York, 1965), p. 103, summarizes Hegel's diagnosis of his age.

words. With his *carmen* he "soothes" the stricken Pasiphaë and with verse controls her madness, which is a complete reversal of life's natural processes. Then, turning directly to poetry per se, he initiates Gallus, former devotee of an "errant" type of verse, into a possibly loftier realm of poetry than elegy. Once purged of direct emotional involvement with his theme, Gallus can sing of *origines* and define through poetry the world of experience and knowledge. All these songs Apollo approves and reiterates, pastoral, unbacchic god though he is.

Both sides of the *Eclogues*, exploring the form of pastoral poetry and the meaning of "pastoral" life in general, meet most directly in the ninth and tenth poems. The first of these poems asks and answers a question never before directly posed in the *Eclogues*, though the reader has been subtly prepared for it: Assuming that the happiness of nature is an essential backdrop for song, how can poetry be written under such conditions as presently prevail in Mantua, a mirror for Italy? When soldiers (and the politicians behind them) impose themselves on the poet's land, not only is freedom lost but the ability to create departs as well.

The tenth eclogue changes the perspective but not the theme. This time the challenge to "pastoral" comes not from armed might but from the person of Gallus, who is not only an historical figure, a soldier and statesman of repute, but also the writer of subjective love elegy, a genre of poetry whose axioms threaten those of the pastoral to the core. Virgil presents him as lovesick, in an almost conventional bucolic setting, craving relief first in death and then in acceptance by the company of shepherds. His reorientation out of the countryside back to the world of elegiac love, where to die is to delight in living, comes ironically, though not unexpectedly. Whatever his reasons (beginning with the disharmony in reality), Virgil's own stand does not survive unscathed. This time the loss to the bucolic life is, if anything, more disastrous than the destruction of the landscape. Now the poet himself, the imaginer of the

involved in only one part of his poem while the other part is merely a convenient foil for his own felicity. We tend to decide in advance what we think Virgil wants to do—to perform his first act of homage to Octavian—rather than to consider objectively what he accomplishes.

The opposite view, which sees the figure of Tityrus as pure artifice, entirely false to reality, unresponding and aloof to the tragedy of life, is perhaps too bitter and severe—though we may remember Nietzsche's dictum: "We have art in order not to perish of truth." Nevertheless *Eclogues* 1 and 9 are poems which almost "make pessimism seem a hopeful evasion."[13] Yet such is the poet's mastery of the art of restraint that his strongest thoughts are conveyed in an atmosphere of spiritual generosity and external quiet.

The *Eclogues* postulate the search for an order which is only rarely attained but is, nevertheless, a prerequisite for happiness. Lack of order can be caused by unrequited love, by death, by some indefinable outside force inimical to the bucolic "retreat," by the violent pressures of political reality. The search for reconciliation between these adverse elements and the pastoral dream is a basic theme in the *Eclogues*. An idealistic vision such as *Eclogue* 4 can propose such an exalted union. Poetry itself—the magic incantation of song or the power of disciplined verse—can sometimes harmonize opposites, but although the poet in his own person may try his luck, the result is often irrational passion or terror. Finally, the poet may be forced to acknowledge in himself the tense union of reason and emotion which is his inheritance from Orpheus.

[13] The phrase is that of Randall Jarrell, talking of Robert Frost ("The Other Frost" in *Poetry and the Age* [New York, 1955], p. 27), a poet who shares much in common with Virgil and whose power, until recent decades, has been equally misinterpreted. Frost once remarked that he "first heard the speaking voice in poetry in Virgil's *Eclogues*" (see R. A. Brower, *The Poetry of Robert Frost* [New York, 1963], pp. 156-57).

Here, too, Theocritus is only partially a prototype. We often sense that the Alexandrian poet aims to define the power of verse as well as to scrutinize the poet's motivation to sing. Nevertheless, in the *Idyls* there seems an almost deliberate unconcern with deep issues, as if the poet believed that the chief value of his verse was to entertain, to attract his readers by beauty of setting or richness of sound. The *Eclogues* are not poems that flee from life, diverting, artificial masquerades for "nature," soothing antidotes to urban elaborateness. Virgil's poetry is no ritual aimed at turning "complex into simple," but rather one of deep involvement in issues just as important now as they were in Rome in the decade after Caesar's assassination.

Similar discussions of the relationship of the individual to society and of man to nature, of the world of institutions to a world which parallels Virgil's conception of the poet and his landscape, are not unknown in American literature. In the nineteenth century, in *Walden, Huckleberry Finn,* or Melville's *Typee* (which fabricates and then destroys a perfect pastoral dream), these discussions regularly take the form of the claims which a society grown increasingly more machine-oriented and industrialized makes upon a quasi-idealized agricultural existence of oneness with nature. In the twentieth century Frost is one champion of individual man's experiences, feelings, desires—for good or evil, or purely for self-knowledge—against the increasing threat of impersonal, fragmentizing scientific schemata which reduce humanity and its purposes to little more than abstractions. Yet even nature herself, for Frost as for Virgil, is not without menace.

In the Rome of the last half of the first century B.C. the steady expansion of city and empire forced similar considerations upon the two chief poets and their colleagues. How is the individual to survive—or the poet to create—when his freedom remains unconfirmed? What of a government which relies on force (or the possible use of force) and appeals to the

14

populace with hollow slogans, while material and more displace humane values as the yards achievement? The answers which Horace a larly supply are as damning of the present as future. We might summarize this side of th "social commentary," a poetry of ideas dealing and mankind at large, the confrontation of stable life of the free imagination and the for be they represented by an urban Alexis (*Eclo* the grandest progress of the ages (*Eclogue* 4).

There is another kindred aspect to the *Eclog* lection is also an informal *ars poetica* which se ened definition of pastoral as a form, often by bri conjunction with other poetic modes. We are ma ine the appropriate setting for song and the p expression as well as to contemplate contents of variety than in the *Idyls* of Theocritus.

In the sixth eclogue the figure of Silenus and th sings illustrate well the added dimensions of Vi toral poetry: while serving as the promulgator of bucolic song, he is also poetry itself. The drunke part god, part animal, is omniscient; he is an e knowledge and of inspiration, both of which are pr sities for the poet at work but of no value without pline of expression. Just as he must be physically his garlands before he can sing, so too the content must first be confined by form—infused by madness jected to craft—before it can become a true *carme* enchants by mere utterance and moves the tangible spiritual. He is a poetic Proteus who from his chain themes of varied sorts to charm his listeners and crea well as to "free" himself.

Silenus' songs, which Virgil quotes only in summary embrace one basic topic in different patterns. Amorph disordered nature is fashioned and confined by the

15

Introduction

whole fabric, instead of being forced to leave in search of a way to return (as in *Eclogue* 9), abandons the shepherd-poet's life of his own volition.

Yet, at the end of the tenth eclogue Virgil is far from denying the validity of his work; rather, he admits the necessity of moving on to another genre of writing, more suitable to his maturing outlook. If in the *Georgics*, which follow, Virgil appears to embrace a more practical subject and approach, the poetry itself, instead of negating the ideas of the *Eclogues*, carefully reaffirms their force while expanding their horizon. The *Georgics* discuss the obstructions nature puts in the path of man, forcing upon him the necessity of trial and hardship to make life viable. If the actual death of the poet is adumbrated in *Eclogue* 9 and his disavowal of bucolic poetry stressed at the conclusion of 10, the myth of Orpheus, which virtually ends *Georgic* 4, treats the same topic in a new guise. Human emotion again destroys the ideal. It kills love and the poet, and ruins the possibility of poetry, though the farmer's existence itself is renewed.

The *Aeneid* is the culmination of the sequence. It, too, starts, as the *Eclogues* at first seem to do, as poetry of uninvolvement. In this case the hero's commitment is necessary only to an ideal mission. Allegiance to fate's progress precludes immediate submission to suffering or emotion, but gradually Aeneas is forced to confront the humanity which is at first easier to ignore. The supposedly simple heroism of establishing an allegorical model for the greatness of a future empire becomes a much more real struggle entailing carnage and violence which the hero must take part in as well as cause. Finally the power struggle centers on a defeated opponent who should be spared but is not, and emotion once more triumphs over reason.

The basic problems the *Aeneid* explores—the confrontation of history and the individual, of progress and freedom, of practical action and idealistic pose, of passion and poetry, to name

17

Introduction

only a few areas of concern—are all suggested to the observant reader not many lines after the start of the first eclogue. In their search for meaning in human life, the *Eclogues* are in the profoundest sense ethical poems. They do not so much deny "progress" as aver that society can only survive if the moral quality of each of its members is preserved and fortified. Even following the "shepherd's life" man may be subject to the vagaries and pressures of existence, to love and to death. He may yearn by nature for that very social fabric which contains the seeds of his undoing, but there is an immutable element of grandeur within him—call it what you will, the soul, or poetry, or heroism—which cannot be suppressed, much less denied. This forces him to break away from the society which he has helped to create and seek what the existentialists would term his own essence with its challenging union of flesh and spirit, formed by, yet rising above, social *mores*.

But the fifth and fourth eclogues are visions which claim that this ideal reconciliation between man and society through poetry is possible. The former asserts that Daphnis, poet-shepherd whose presence is essential to the landscape, though claimed by death, is nevertheless raised to the stature of divinity. Thence he can bless a pastoral world whose processes have been regularized by his apotheosis. The fourth has a still more idealistic notion. It affirms that the value of history lies precisely in those decisive moments which, by assertion of the superhuman, allow us to see beyond the prison of ourselves as creatures of society to a vista of timeless beauty. *Virtus*, as the word is used in the fourth eclogue, has its common double sense: it is literally that aspect of heroism which suffers present violence for future peace, that creates (or recreates) spiritual order through physical action. It also symbolizes that power to initiate an era of perfect morality in which mankind is victimized by no crime (*scelus*). Human nature is envisioned by Virgil above the struggles that derange existence, even above the labor necessary to exist.

Yet the fantasy of the fourth eclogue, by its very unreality, conjures up its opposite. Such a poetic dream, by denying life the drama of striving for the ideal, becomes ineffectual, if fascinating, banter—perhaps deliberately so. By imagining life as it is not, the poet destroys not only suffering but that heroism which makes of suffering an aesthetic as well as a moral act. This division was very much with Virgil in all his works. Nevertheless by accepting Gallus' world of history and the turmoil of love at the end of *Eclogue* 10, and by emphasizing not the courage of an idealistic, triumphant Aeneas but the anguish of his beaten rival, Turnus, at the conclusion of the *Aeneid*, Virgil sides, as he does from the start of *Eclogue* 1, with troubled humanity. The quest for the ideal has no happy conclusion except in the poet's fancy.

M. Tityre, tu patulae recubans sub tegmine fagi
   silvestrem tenui musam meditaris avena:
   nos patriae finis et dulcia linquimus arva.
   nos patriam fugimus: tu, Tityre, lentus in umbra
   formosam resonare doces Amaryllida silvas.
T. O Meliboee, deus nobis haec otia fecit.
   namque erit ille mihi semper deus, illius aram
   saepe tener nostris ab ovilibus imbuet agnus.
   ille meas errare boves, ut cernis, et ipsum
   ludere quae vellem calamo permisit agresti.

M. Tityrus, you, reclining under the protection of a spreading beech, woo the pastoral muse on slender pipe. We
are leaving the bounds of our fatherland and our sweet
fields. We are exiled from our fatherland. You, Tityrus,
at ease in the shade, teach the woods to resound "beautiful Amaryllis."
T. O Meliboeus, a god has created this leisure for us. For
he will always be a god for me; a tender lamb from our
folds will often dye his altar. As you observe, he has
allowed my cattle to wander and me myself to play what
I wish on rustic pipe. (lines 1-10)

Virgil's first eclogue takes the form of a dialogue between
two shepherds, Meliboeus and Tityrus, the one forced to leave
the bucolic life, the other allowed to remain in his idyllic
existence.[1] The dispossessed Meliboeus puts the difference

---

[1] I have benefited from two recent articles on *Eclogue* I—C. P. Segal,
"*Tamen Cantabitis, Arcades*—Exile and Arcadia in *Eclogues One* and
Nine," *Arion* 4 (1965): 237-66; and E. A. Fredricksmeyer, "Octavian
and the Unity of Virgil's First Eclogue," *Hermes* 94 (1966): 208-18—

Introduction

involved in only one part of his poem while the other part is merely a convenient foil for his own felicity. We tend to decide in advance what we think Virgil wants to do—to perform his first act of homage to Octavian—rather than to consider objectively what he accomplishes.

The opposite view, which sees the figure of Tityrus as pure artifice, entirely false to reality, unresponding and aloof to the tragedy of life, is perhaps too bitter and severe—though we may remember Nietzsche's dictum: "We have art in order not to perish of truth." Nevertheless *Eclogues* 1 and 9 are poems which almost "make pessimism seem a hopeful evasion."[13] Yet such is the poet's mastery of the art of restraint that his strongest thoughts are conveyed in an atmosphere of spiritual generosity and external quiet.

The *Eclogues* postulate the search for an order which is only rarely attained but is, nevertheless, a prerequisite for happiness. Lack of order can be caused by unrequited love, by death, by some indefinable outside force inimical to the bucolic "retreat," by the violent pressures of political reality. The search for reconciliation between these adverse elements and the pastoral dream is a basic theme in the *Eclogues*. An idealistic vision such as *Eclogue* 4 can propose such an exalted union. Poetry itself—the magic incantation of song or the power of disciplined verse—can sometimes harmonize opposites, but although the poet in his own person may try his luck, the result is often irrational passion or terror. Finally, the poet may be forced to acknowledge in himself the tense union of reason and emotion which is his inheritance from Orpheus.

[13] The phrase is that of Randall Jarrell, talking of Robert Frost ("The Other Frost" in *Poetry and the Age* [New York, 1955], p. 27), a poet who shares much in common with Virgil and whose power, until recent decades, has been equally misinterpreted. Frost once remarked that he "first heard the speaking voice in poetry in Virgil's *Eclogues*" (see R. A. Brower, *The Poetry of Robert Frost* [New York, 1963], pp. 156-57).

Introduction

Here, too, Theocritus is only partially a prototype. We often sense that the Alexandrian poet aims to define the power of verse as well as to scrutinize the poet's motivation to sing. Nevertheless, in the *Idyls* there seems an almost deliberate unconcern with deep issues, as if the poet believed that the chief value of his verse was to entertain, to attract his readers by beauty of setting or richness of sound. The *Eclogues* are not poems that flee from life, diverting, artificial masquerades for "nature," soothing antidotes to urban elaborateness. Virgil's poetry is no ritual aimed at turning "complex into simple," but rather one of deep involvement in issues just as important now as they were in Rome in the decade after Caesar's assassination.

Similar discussions of the relationship of the individual to society and of man to nature, of the world of institutions to a world which parallels Virgil's conception of the poet and his landscape, are not unknown in American literature. In the nineteenth century, in *Walden*, *Huckleberry Finn*, or Melville's *Typee* (which fabricates and then destroys a perfect pastoral dream), these discussions regularly take the form of the claims which a society grown increasingly more machine-oriented and industrialized makes upon a quasi-idealized agricultural existence of oneness with nature. In the twentieth century Frost is one champion of individual man's experiences, feelings, desires—for good or evil, or purely for self-knowledge—against the increasing threat of impersonal, fragmentizing scientific schemata which reduce humanity and its purposes to little more than abstractions. Yet even nature herself, for Frost as for Virgil, is not without menace.

In the Rome of the last half of the first century B.C. the steady expansion of city and empire forced similar considerations upon the two chief poets and their colleagues. How is the individual to survive—or the poet to create—when his freedom remains unconfirmed? What of a government which relies on force (or the possible use of force) and appeals to the

Introduction

only a few areas of concern—are all suggested to the observant reader not many lines after the start of the first eclogue. In their search for meaning in human life, the *Eclogues* are in the profoundest sense ethical poems. They do not so much deny "progress" as aver that society can only survive if the moral quality of each of its members is preserved and fortified. Even following the "shepherd's life" man may be subject to the vagaries and pressures of existence, to love and to death. He may yearn by nature for that very social fabric which contains the seeds of his undoing, but there is an immutable element of grandeur within him—call it what you will, the soul, or poetry, or heroism—which cannot be suppressed, much less denied. This forces him to break away from the society which he has helped to create and seek what the existentialists would term his own essence with its challenging union of flesh and spirit, formed by, yet rising above, social *mores*.

But the fifth and fourth eclogues are visions which claim that this ideal reconciliation between man and society through poetry is possible. The former asserts that Daphnis, poet-shepherd whose presence is essential to the landscape, though claimed by death, is nevertheless raised to the stature of divinity. Thence he can bless a pastoral world whose processes have been regularized by his apotheosis. The fourth has a still more idealistic notion. It affirms that the value of history lies precisely in those decisive moments which, by assertion of the superhuman, allow us to see beyond the prison of ourselves as creatures of society to a vista of timeless beauty. *Virtus*, as the word is used in the fourth eclogue, has its common double sense: it is literally that aspect of heroism which suffers present violence for future peace, that creates (or recreates) spiritual order through physical action. It also symbolizes that power to initiate an era of perfect morality in which mankind is victimized by no crime (*scelus*). Human nature is envi-

Introduction

whole fabric, instead of being forced to leave in search of a way to return (as in *Eclogue* 9), abandons the shepherd-poet's life of his own volition.

Yet, at the end of the tenth eclogue Virgil is far from denying the validity of his work; rather, he admits the necessity of moving on to another genre of writing, more suitable to his maturing outlook. If in the *Georgics*, which follow, Virgil appears to embrace a more practical subject and approach, the poetry itself, instead of negating the ideas of the *Eclogues,* carefully reaffirms their force while expanding their horizon. The *Georgics* discuss the obstructions nature puts in the path of man, forcing upon him the necessity of trial and hardship to make life viable. If the actual death of the poet is adumbrated in *Eclogue* 9 and his disavowal of bucolic poetry stressed at the conclusion of 10, the myth of Orpheus, which virtually ends *Georgic* 4, treats the same topic in a new guise. Human emotion again destroys the ideal. It kills love and the poet, and ruins the possibility of poetry, though the farmer's existence itself is renewed.

The *Aeneid* is the culmination of the sequence. It, too, starts, as the *Eclogues* at first seem to do, as poetry of uninvolvement. In this case the hero's commitment is necessary only to an ideal mission. Allegiance to fate's progress precludes immediate submission to suffering or emotion, but gradually Aeneas is forced to confront the humanity which is at first easier to ignore. The supposedly simple heroism of establishing an allegorical model for the greatness of a future empire becomes a much more real struggle entailing carnage and violence which the hero must take part in as well as cause. Finally the power struggle centers on a defeated opponent who should be spared but is not, and emotion once more triumphs over reason.

The basic problems the *Aeneid* explores—the confrontation of history and the individual, of progress and freedom, of practical action and idealistic pose, of passion and poetry, to name

17

Introduction

populace with hollow slogans, while materialistic goals more and more displace humane values as the yardstick to measure achievement? The answers which Horace and Virgil regularly supply are as damning of the present as ominous for the future. We might summarize this side of the *Eclogues* as "social commentary," a poetry of ideas dealing with the writer and mankind at large, the confrontation of the essentially stable life of the free imagination and the forces of history, be they represented by an urban Alexis (*Eclogue* 2) or by the grandest progress of the ages (*Eclogue* 4).

There is another kindred aspect to the *Eclogues*: the collection is also an informal *ars poetica* which seeks a broadened definition of pastoral as a form, often by bringing it into conjunction with other poetic modes. We are made to examine the appropriate setting for song and the proprieties of expression as well as to contemplate contents of far greater variety than in the *Idyls* of Theocritus.

In the sixth eclogue the figure of Silenus and the songs he sings illustrate well the added dimensions of Virgilian pastoral poetry: while serving as the promulgator of novelty in bucolic song, he is also poetry itself. The drunken Silenus, part god, part animal, is omniscient; he is an emblem of knowledge and of inspiration, both of which are prime necessities for the poet at work but of no value without the discipline of expression. Just as he must be physically bound by his garlands before he can sing, so too the content of poetry must first be confined by form—infused by madness, yet subjected to craft—before it can become a true *carmen*, which enchants by mere utterance and moves the tangible with the spiritual. He is a poetic Proteus who from his chains shapes themes of varied sorts to charm his listeners and creations as well as to "free" himself.

Silenus' songs, which Virgil quotes only in summary fashion, embrace one basic topic in different patterns. Amorphous and disordered nature is fashioned and confined by the singer's

15

words. With his *carmen* he "soothes" the stricken Pasiphaë and with verse controls her madness, which is a complete reversal of life's natural processes. Then, turning directly to poetry per se, he initiates Gallus, former devotee of an "errant" type of verse, into a possibly loftier realm of poetry than elegy. Once purged of direct emotional involvement with his theme, Gallus can sing of *origines* and define through poetry the world of experience and knowledge. All these songs Apollo approves and reiterates, pastoral, unbacchic god though he is.

Both sides of the *Eclogues*, exploring the form of pastoral poetry and the meaning of "pastoral" life in general, meet most directly in the ninth and tenth poems. The first of these poems asks and answers a question never before directly posed in the *Eclogues*, though the reader has been subtly prepared for it: Assuming that the happiness of nature is an essential backdrop for song, how can poetry be written under such conditions as presently prevail in Mantua, a mirror for Italy? When soldiers (and the politicians behind them) impose themselves on the poet's land, not only is freedom lost but the ability to create departs as well.

The tenth eclogue changes the perspective but not the theme. This time the challenge to "pastoral" comes not from armed might but from the person of Gallus, who is not only an historical figure, a soldier and statesman of repute, but also the writer of subjective love elegy, a genre of poetry whose axioms threaten those of the pastoral to the core. Virgil presents him as lovesick, in an almost conventional bucolic setting, craving relief first in death and then in acceptance by the company of shepherds. His reorientation out of the countryside back to the world of elegiac love, where to die is to delight in living, comes ironically, though not unexpectedly. Whatever his reasons (beginning with the disharmony in reality), Virgil's own stand does not survive unscathed. This time the loss to the bucolic life is, if anything, more disastrous than the destruction of the landscape. Now the poet himself, the imaginer of the

carefully. Tityrus, in his eyes, is at one with the landscape and its muse. The sounds of his name reverberate through Meliboeus' first words, sketching the spreading beech. Verbal structure, too, reflects the actual description. The phrase *patulae . . . fagi* "surrounds" the reclining bard.[2] *Tegmen* and *meditaris* are strong words. The first, with its quasi-military overtones, implies that the beech tree shields Tityrus. In this retreat he may apparently sing at will. Tityrus' existence, we already assume, is essentially intellectual. He lives, in fact, in an exclusive and imaginary world, free from the disruptions of ordinary life.

Virgil describes Tityrus as "wooing" the sylvan muse, that is, pondering the meaning of and then "writing" pastoral poetry. The muse is the personification of what she provokes her poet to create. This suggests a secondary meaning for *tenui avena*. Literally it is the slender reed on which the shepherd pipes—the *calamo agresti* of line 10. Beyond that, however, it betokens a style of writing as well, the inheritance of the Alexandrian poet Callimachus. It is the "slim," elegant man-

---

though I do not always share their conclusions. Fredricksmeyer gives an excellent summary of scholarship on the poem which need not be duplicated here. Of special note among past articles is Friedrich Klingner, "Virgils erste Ekloge," *Hermes* 62 (1927): 129-53, the essence of which is now reprinted in *Römische Geisteswelt* (Munich, 1961), pp. 312-26.

The first eclogue, more than any other in the collection, has attracted the attention of critics of more recent literature. See, in particular, Philip Damon, "Modes of Analogy in Ancient and Medieval Verse," *Cal. Pub. in Class. Phil.* 15 (1961): 261-334 (esp. 281-90); Leo Marx, "Two Kingdoms of Force," *Massachusetts Review* 1 (1959): 62-95 (esp. 90ff.), and *The Machine in the Garden* (New York, 1964), pp. 19-24; Renato Poggioli, "Naboth's Vineyard or the Pastoral View of the Social Order," *Journal of the History of Ideas* 24 (1963): 3-24, esp. 5ff.

[2] On the sound of the opening line and its relationship to Theocritus, see Damon, "Modes of Analogy," p. 281. On the verbal pattern of the first five lines, and on the importance of the chiastic order, see Karl Büchner, *P. Vergilius Maro* (Stuttgart, 1961), col. 160. On *recubans* and the posture of the reclining bard, cf. Propertius 3. 3. 1.

ner of expression appropriate to bucolic ideas and, in particular, to making love to a *formosam Amaryllida*—the visible counterpart of the more impersonal *silvestrem musam*. Though
the spreading beech offers broad protection from the world's
pressures, the delicate, graceful fashion of song practised in
this refuge is anything but grand. The setting and the song
are the necessary complements of each other.[3]

These lines summarize a perfection which embraces not
only the requisite beauty of setting but the form of pastoral
poetry—its style, slender and delicate, and its content, the
beauty of Amaryllis. Ordinarily, in thinking of bucolic verse,
we postulate the happy union of the literal landscape and
poetry, its figurative counterpart: one fails without the other.
Here, at the opening of the first eclogue, with all country
dwellers in peril, the future of the spiritual entity of which
they are emblematic is at stake.

Meliboeus' situation is quite opposite from Tityrus', and the
divergence informs the poem's dialectic. From the *tu* of
Tityrus' singular happiness we pass to *nos* (lines 3 and 4),
meaning those sharing a common misfortune of which Meliboeus is the spokesman. From the limited, exclusive compass of the spreading beech and the sanctuary of a sylvan muse
we travel, by way of Meliboeus' thoughts, to a different world,
one of *patriae finis* and *dulcia arva*. This is no idyllic dream.
Meliboeus is worried about the land itself. No mythical
Amaryllis mesmerizes his leisured attention. His life involves
real fields and people, and, above all, thoughts the weight of
which cannot be borne by pastoral's fragile myth. As protected

---

[3] On *tenui avena*, see the definition of Servius: "stili genus humilis
latenter ostendit, quo . . . in bucolicis utitur" ("he shows through
symbol the type of 'humble' style which he uses in the bucolic poems");
quoted by Viktor Pöschl in his important discussion of these lines
(*Die Hirtendichtung Virgils* [Heidelberg, 1964], p. 11). For a brief
but enlightening discussion of the *Eclogues* and the "slender" style,
see W. V. Clausen, "Callimachus and Latin Poetry," *Greek, Roman
and Byzantine Studies* 5 (1964): 181-96, esp. 193ff.

rest yields to disruptive motion, the contrast in the two lives grows gradually more distinct. The poet introduces a broader sphere of ideas which offer a marked contrast to the light-heartedness which is often pastoral poetry's trademark.

The word *patria*, for example, conveys not only a specific place reference, unusual in bucolic poetry, but also a series of values foreign to it—patriotism, devotion, justice and the like —concepts with which Tityrus is apparently not concerned.[4] We may say the same for the words *finis* and *arva*.[5] Both imply practical considerations more georgic than pastoral, and, because they postulate direct, affectionate involvement with the land, both clash with the detached, exclusive implications of *silvestrem musam* and *silvas*, which verbally enclose them. *Finis*, especially, connotes a specific geographical distribution and delimitation of property unlike the vision of Tityrus' retreat. If *tegmen* suggests a defense of the poet and *umbra* a bastion against the harsh brightness of life itself, *finis* delimits the fields of afflicted Italy, which Meliboeus loves as his fatherland.

We should be prepared, then, for the shock of the verbs *linquimus* and *fugimus*. Suddenly we are in a land, physically near and intellectually remote, wherein violence rules. Idealism yields to contact with the painful necessities of life. The

[4] The classic Roman definitions of *patria* are to be found in Cicero's *De Or.* 1. 44. 196, and *Cat.* 1. 7. 17. Cicero elsewhere emphasizes that the idea of *patria* transcends any individual's emotions and affections (e.g., *Fin.* 3. 19. 64). Three of the five uses of *patrius* in the *Eclogues* occur in this poem. In sound alone the anaphora *"nos patriae, nos patriam"* forces the reader to think back to Tityrus, protected under his spreading beech (*patulae fagi*).

[5] *Arva*, for instance, is a word used only once elsewhere in the *Eclogues* (5. 33) but common in the *Georgics*. *Finis* appears later in this poem (lines 61 and 67) but never again in the *Eclogues*. On the phrase *patrios fines* in particular, see Hendrik Wagenvoort, "Virgil's Eclogues I and IX" in *Studies in Roman Literature, Culture, and Religion* (Leiden, 1956): 264-65; and H. J. Rose, "Some Second Thoughts on Vergil's Eclogues," *Mnemosyne*, n.s. 7 (1954): 57-68, esp. 64-66.

reflective *meditaris* gives place to the sudden force of *linqui-mus* and *fugimus* and these in turn submit to *doces*. Pondering poetry and teaching song in a sylvan setting are far from the menace of flight.

The suppressed martial tone of the language Meliboeus applies to Tityrus—he is "shielded" after all, though only, as far as we know hitherto, by a shadowy beech—is released by the reference to the actualities of his sorrow. He has not only left his fatherland in the company of his fellows, he has been expelled from it: there is no mistaking the technical force of *fugimus*. Meliboeus' thoughts, as Virgil wishes to convey them, have nothing to do with Tityrus' unconcern but betray the passionate involvement of the shepherd-farmer in his acres and, more generally, of the citizen in his country. It may even be that this trial led him to a realization of his relationship to the land, and to the knowledge that *pietas* must exist between a man and the earth he lives on.

Within this intellectual framework, Meliboeus' change from *tu* to *nos* also raises the question of justice. It places a problem before the reader for the remainder of the poem: Is it right for one man to possess a landscape wherein complete disinterest in practical affairs (*otium*) is possible when another dweller in the land suffers exile imposed by a potent enemy? One person uniquely possesses that ideal we might offer as visual definition of the pastoral myth: leisure and undisturbed intellectual freedom. This individual's life is wholly his own. Another, who speaks for at least a plurality of his fellow citizens, is driven from the land. These situations have as little to do with each other as the different roles which the shepherds assume—the one emblematic of the world of the imagination, of that liberty for which spreading beeches and resounding woods are tangible evidence, the other symbolic of the troubles of rural affairs, vulnerable now to the whims of power politics and military might. What, then, brings Tityrus his good fortune, Meliboeus his bad luck?

Eclogue I

Before attempting an answer, the poet, still speaking through Meliboeus, gives, in lines 4-5, one last summary of Tityrus' happiness. *Tityre, tu* in line 1 leads to *nos patriae* in 3. The same contrast is reversed here with *nos patriam* in line 4 anticipating *tu, Tityre* in line 5. Through verbal symmetry, the generalized suffering of mankind, figured in Meliboeus, is enclosed for a moment within the refuge of Tityrus. In lines 4 and 5 we are once again part of Tityrus' escape; *recubans* leads to *lentus*. The threat of exile and the possible destruction of the earth are momentarily forgotten with reiteration of his happiness. The practical concerns of fields and property yield to *otium*. The shepherd-farmer's love for his dear fields shifts again to the unreal, to the mythical beauty of lovely Amaryllis (*formosam*) in a world free from care.[6]

Tityrus, in reply, offers neither a general analysis of this sad turnabout in rural affairs nor any particular words of sympathy to Meliboeus. Instead he explains the reason for his happiness. There is the same interaction of realistic description and metaphor with which the poem began in lines 9-10 where the wandering of the cattle at will (*errare*) is the visible counterpart of Tityrus' freedom to play (*ludere*) what he would on his rustic pipe. This is no ordinary *otium*, the assumed leisure without which the pastoral idyll cannot exist, the opposite of the *discordia* which is abroad in the land; it is a special creation of a *deus*, an *otium* unique to Tityrus. A god has made this beauty possible (*fecit*) for Tityrus and has allowed it (*permisit*) to continue.

There are two points in this passage which, perhaps from their obviousness, have not received the emphasis they deserve. The first is that the shepherd's world has now reached such a pass that it takes a god to "create" the *otia* which are a prerequisite for its existence and to "permit" its prosperity. This is a tragic admission of how dependent the myth has

[6] On the structure of these lines, see Pöschl, *Die Hirtendichtung Virgils*, p. 13.

become on external conditions. It is easy enough to prove the impotence and vulnerability of the shepherd's world by stating that there are other worlds which create havoc merely by announcing their existence, not to speak of imposing their presence. To suggest in a "bucolic" poem that there are opposing ways of life is to court disaster for the myth; to suggest that the pastoral scene is accountable to something else is to destroy it. Destroying the myth is the same as suppressing the imagination and those whose lives depend upon it, even though it seems to endure in the idealism bestowed on a chosen few.

Much of this idea of power is conveyed through the verb *fecit*, which is all the more forceful for being prosaic. Whatever the impression Tityrus wishes to convey of his *deus, fecit* is an objective, impersonal word, suggesting that the pastoral life is something to be created or destroyed according to the fancy of a higher power, something to be tolerated or dismissed on a purely utilitarian basis. We, if not Tityrus, realize the implication of stating that *otium* is the "creation" of anyone—even be he divine!

Thus far we know nothing else of this benign, saving *deus*, but it is already a jarring sign for a mythic landscape when it relies on external backing for survival. Meliboeus' opening words make clear that it is no longer possible to assume the idyll. Rather we must stand, like Meliboeus, on the border line between dream and reality, and behold the idyll's essence by watching someone else's happiness. Meliboeus is a spectator in a land whose survival is now an object of awe to him.

Meliboeus stresses his tragic circumstances. From Tityrus, on the other hand, we perceive—what is perhaps more disquieting for the landscape of poetry—that it is not due to luck that "pastoral" is possessed by one and not the other, but due to the deliberate granting of a privilege. And the reader, because of the conflicting lives of the protagonists, cannot himself enter the shepherds' existence as he does in later eclogues, but must stand outside it, a detached spectator watching the advent of disintegration. Though *otium* may be conceded to one man, it is in fact destroyed by the implicit grip of foreign rule on its supposedly sacred quality.[7]

The second point which Tityrus' words raise concerns the divinity himself and his connections with Tityrus. Though Tityrus considers the purveyor of this beauty to be a god, his language indicates that he may not seem so to others. The implication of the phrase *namque erit ille mihi semper deus*, with its stress on *mihi*, is ambiguous. Also, it is possible that Tityrus' use of *nobis* in line 6 and *nostris* in line 8 is meant to imply that this unspecified benefactor came to the aid of more shepherds than the lucky Tityrus. Each time he uses the first person in a sense which could be plural, however, he negates the effect, first with *mihi* in line 7, then with *meus* in line 9, and most explicitly in the final phrase of line 10. The god allows Tityrus himself (*ipsum*) to play on the shepherd's pipe, in his words, *quae vellem*, "what I like."

He who through his good offices seems a god to Tityrus may, the poet insinuates, appear mortal and human to others. That Tityrus considers himself in a special position increases our apprehension. It intimates that the *deus* has granted the prerogatives of *otium* to Tityrus alone. The cloud which looms on the bucolic horizon darkens as we realize that the whole myth can, apparently, be made and unmade by one man. The pastoral dream, the freedom of the cattle to wander at will and the complementary leisure of the shepherd to create, is shattered when subjected to arbitrary control.[8]

---

[7] There is patent irony in the sacrifice of an *agnus* to the god: some could charge him with the obliteration of the landscape (and, in particular, the death of the *gemelli*). That the pastoral world must be kept alive by the slaughter of sheep implies more than Tityrus states or possibly realizes.

[8] Again, one need scarcely point out the artistic construction of the lines, this time centering around a unity (Tityrus and his god) rather than a contrast (Tityrus and Meliboeus). Line 6 (*fecit*) balances line 10 (*permisit*); line 7 (*ille mihi*), line 9 (*ille meas*), etc.

Eclogue 1

Tityrus has defined the reason for his happiness. Meliboeus' role, here and for the remainder of the poem, is to describe his sufferings of which Tityrus does not, perhaps cannot, betray awareness (lines 11-18):

> Non equidem invideo, miror magis; undique totis
> usque adeo turbatur agris. en, ipse capellas
> protinus aeger ago; hanc etiam vix, Tityre, duco.
> hic inter densas corylos modo namque gemellos,
> spem gregis, a, silice in nuda conixa reliquit.
> saepe malum hoc nobis, si mens non laeva fuisset,
> de caelo tactas memini praedicere quercus.
> sed tamen iste deus qui sit, da, Tityre, nobis.

Indeed I am not envious. Rather I stand in amazement. Everywhereabouts in all the fields things are in turmoil to such an extent. Look how I, ill though I am, drive the goats further on. This one, Tityrus, I scarcely even lead. For here among the thick hazels she just now gave birth to twins, hope of the flock, and abandoned them, alas, on the open rock. I remember that the oaks, struck from heaven, often foretold this evil to us, if our mind had not been dull. But nevertheless tell us, Tityrus, who is this god of yours.

We have learned the position of Meliboeus from Tityrus' *ut cernis* of line 9: he is watching Tityrus in disbelief. But Meliboeus is no ordinary shepherd seeking in song a moment of quiet from his daily concerns nor is he, unlike his colleague of the same name in the seventh eclogue, escaping from his cares through song. At the opening of the *Eclogues*, the psychological position is quite the reverse of what it is in *Eclogue* 7 where, as we shall see, Meliboeus' trials matter little in the magical presence of Daphnis and the two singers over whose competition he presides. Here Meliboeus' troubles directly contrast with Tityrus' singularly fortunate position.

Eclogue 1

Retreat into poetry is no longer feasible. Greater trials than pasturing one's flock and protecting one's myrtles have come upon the land. When Tityrus does finally extend an invitation to Meliboeus, it is delivered for one night only, and in the past tense, courteous but with a touch of dubiety. The first lines of the poem already preclude the possibility of acceptance.

Meliboeus begins his response by elaborating the hint of *ut cernis* and acknowledging that he is on the far side of the pastoral scene, standing in amazement (*miror*), mesmerized by the enchantment of a sight which for him now seems impossible—the actual view of a poet in a poet's land. Having every right to be jealous, he could put a curse on the scene with his eyes (*invideo* has a double meaning); instead, he only looks, stupefied at a landscape which he thought could no longer survive.[9] The realities of his life have led him not to trust in a renewal of the dream.

Meliboeus' words increase the effect of the preceding hyperbolic description. All else, save Tityrus' blessed isle, must be included in the temporal and spatial breadth of *undique* and *usque adeo*. Tityrus may lie quietly at his ease, but everywhere about him nature is exposed to turmoil. Ironically, he is allowed to play on his rustic pipe (*calamo agresti*) while in all the fields (*totis agris*), in the setting which should be undisturbed and able to grant the inspiration of song to every shepherd, there is only commotion. A peaceful landscape has apparently become the exclusive property of one man.

The cause we need not know yet; the effect, however, is observed closely. After his generalized statement on the universal disorder, Meliboeus appeals to Tityrus (and to the reader) to look out and to see how the disturbing forces abroad have affected another individual who symbolizes grief common to all rather than private felicity. *En* makes the invitation explicit, and the sound of *agris* leads directly to the harsh *aeger ago*. Helped by both *ago* and *duco*, we are now made

[9] On *miror* and its associations with magic, see *Ecl.* 8. 2.

to visualize a state of existence where all is disturbed. Instead of the generalized, plural utterance of his earlier, equally emotional, *linquimus* and *fugimus*, Meliboeus now looks at his private sorrow. Sick though he is—the torture of the landscape is the shepherd's illness—he cannot rest but is forced to move on. The word *ipse*, which he applies to himself in line 12, subtly contrasts with Tityrus' *ipsum* in line 9: the one forlornly urging his flock along, the other singing at will. The sudden, ironic reappearance of the vocative *Tityre* in line 13 adds to the formal distinction.

Aeger ago applies to the shepherd himself. The verb *duco* acknowledges that movement is also necessary in the life of the animals. Here, as with Meliboeus, one goat and her offspring are singled out as a symbol for many, to show how the trials of the land and the shepherd affect the beasts as well. The perfect young lamb is sacrificed to the ideal god. The twin goats, hope of the flock, are born and abandoned, victims of a widespread, uncontrollable disaster.

Appearances, for a brief moment, are deceptive: the phrase *hic inter densas corylos* could perfectly well prepare for a description of the countryside at its happiest and most carefree, when song is not only possible but essential.[10] We may think ahead, to *Eclogue* 2 for instance, with Corydon singing to Alexis among the thick beeches with their shady tops (*inter densas, umbrosa cacumina, fagos*), or to Menalcas' suggestion to Mopsus at the opening (line 3) of *Eclogue* 5 that they sit and sing among the elms mixed with hazels (*corylis mixtas inter . . . ulmos*). In such a setting the she-goat has borne twins. Normally this would be an augury of future prosperity and hence, in the poet's words, the hope of the flock. But the hope has been blasted immediately. She has left them abandoned (to die, we assume) on the open rock, *nuda in silice*. Nature, at least the nature that now thrusts itself upon Meliboeus, is more brutal than protective to the helpless shepherd.

[10] The use of *hic* is especially important at *Ecl.* 9. 40ff.

Eclogue I

The whole picture, writ large, is that of disease within the land, foisted upon the unknowing beasts and their keepers. The goat has forsaken her twins (*reliquit*), symbols of youth and continuity. The shepherds themselves are forced to withdraw from the countryside (*linquimus*, line 3). The landscape and the abandoned goats are one; their mother's desertion is but a small reflection of the general disaster.

The change in the setting, from the thick hazels (*densae coryli*) where the goat bears her offspring, to the naked rock (*nuda silex*) where she leaves them, acknowledges the larger malaise. Nature's beauty is especially associated with the protective cover of the hazels (or Tityrus' beech); its serenity is broken by the appearance of the flint which bespeaks death. The land is now exposed, hard and bleak.[11] The occurrence of death upon bare rock is nothing Tityrus could understand. The lot of Meliboeus, as of his flock, is exposure; Tityrus holds the life-giving imperatives of shade and song.

Meliboeus adds that, if their wits had not been dull, the oaks struck by lightning from heaven would have foretold the disaster to them often. Virgil uses the phrase *si mens non laeva fuisset* again in line 54 of *Aeneid* 2 when Laocoön fruitlessly throws his spear at the side of the wooden horse. Aeneas assures Dido that, had they listened to Laocoön and allowed him to expose the horse's hidden deceit, Troy would now stand. An appreciation of the full potentiality of the wooden horse as a *monstrum* is as significant to the Trojans as perception of the stricken oaks' meaning to the dwellers of the land. Yet there is a difference: a correct interpretation of the omen, according to Meliboeus, would only predict the advent of the evil (*malum hoc*) before it happened, not ward it off.

There is further sadness to Meliboeus' words. He and his fellow shepherds are dependent on the traditional means of divination. The oak is the tree sacred to Jupiter, and it is only natural that as an expression of his displeasure and an omen

[11] On *silice*, see *Aen.* 6. 471.

31

of evil to come he would blast its top with his thunderbolt.[12]
The oaks forebode future misfortune, but only as a sign sent
from heaven. This is the closest the shepherds now come to
having any converse with divinity—an impersonal and reserved, if conventional, display of wrath through symbol.[13] For
this reason Meliboeus' command at line 18 is particularly forceful: Tell us, Tityrus, he says, tell us, the suffering shepherds
(the double use of *nobis* in lines 16 and 18 recalls the anaphora in 3 and 4) who is that god of yours (*iste deus*). What is
this strange new divinity? What sorts are there, he naïvely
asks, save those which deal in the primitive ways known to
shepherds, ordinary mortals not blessed with visions of the
supernatural? Theirs is a god who may have shown them the
approaching evil often (*saepe*) without their seeing. For
Tityrus' god the altar is often (*saepe*, line 8) stained with the
blood of a lamb, an offering from his grateful devotee. His
god, who is present and visible and alive, creates then and
there the leisure (*haec otia*) that is so important for the preservation of the idyll. The shepherd's traditional divinity sends
only an easily misunderstood sign of evil to come—not future
happiness—and that from the remote distance of the heights
of heaven. Meliboeus has every right to inquire concerning a
god who has the power to make Tityrus' private world serene
when his is collapsing.

The indirectness of Tityrus' reply is surprising and eluci-
dating (lines 19-25):

Urbem quam dicunt Romam, Meliboee, putavi
stultus ego huic nostrae similem, quo saepe solemus
pastores ovium teneros depellere fetus.
sic canibus catulos similis, sic matribus haedos

---

[12] See, e.g., Horace *Carm.* 3. 5. 1.
[13] It is a wrath, nevertheless, which destroys the trees (and oaks
are the home of bees, for instance, at *Ecl.* 7. 13) as an omen of a more
extensive disruption soon to appear. With *tactas quercus*, cf. *fracta cacumina* (*Ecl.* 9. 9).

noram, sic parvis componere magna solebam.
verum haec tantum alias inter caput extulit urbes
quantum lenta solent inter viburna cupressi.

The city which they call Rome, Meliboeus, I thought in
my folly was like this one of ours whither we shepherds
are often wont to drive the tender offspring of our ewes.
Thus I knew whelps were like dogs, goats like their
mothers; thus I was wont to compare large with small.
But this city has raised its head among other cities as much
as cypresses are wont to do among bending osiers.

In the first place, it is a shock to the pastoral myth to admit
that cities exist, that Tityrus' life of unconcern is involved
with such material necessities as the raising of sheep for purposes of commerce; but this in itself is bearable as part of that
complex of references to hunting, farming, and other practical pursuits whereby the shepherds' retreat merges with
reality. It is proper to think of sending or driving the lambs,
teneros fetus, into the city. What comes as a surprise is that
the shepherd Tityrus should be concerned not with some
anonymous town which always hovers on the verge of the
dream to serve its more practical needs but with the city of
cities, Rome, either because the all-powerful metropolis literally is his god or because it is there that his special *deus*
dwells. Whatever the answer (and we soon learn it), merely
to have the name mentioned further shatters the spell.

Tityrus may henceforth have no need to pursue such chores
as driving his flocks into the town or to be concerned with the
afflictions which are the lot of Meliboeus. Paradoxically, he
lives in a fantasy but has associated himself with Rome, the
focal point of practical affairs. The reader marvels with Meliboeus at the still inexplicit tension between Tityrus' idealism
and its practical source. This causal relationship is surprising
and fraught with potential. It raises the question of whether
or not "pastoral" is viable under such circumstances.

Eclogue 1

Through Tityrus, the poet offers an analogy of the relationship Rome bears to the town which the shepherds regularly visit. The comparison of their village to Rome is not like that of a whelp to a dog or of a small goat to its mother, but of a bending osier to a majestic cypress. Going to Rome is like entering into a brave new world so different from theirs that the regular human comparison of large to small within its kind is no longer operative. We may even hear in the phrase *caput extulit* a tone of menace, though the speaker still is Tityrus,[14] who, with apparent naïveté, still uses the present tense in line 20 to describe the processes of nature. Fortune continues on.

Tityrus' comparison is carefully chosen. It conveys the notion of physical inequity: the osier is flexible by nature and bends toward the ground, whereas the cypress shoots sturdily upward. There is an implied spiritual contrast as well. The use of *lenta* to describe the pliant osier recalls the position of Tityrus at ease in the shade (*lentus in umbra*). Though there is an obvious difference in meaning, the verbal repetition is crucial. The tree is a parallel in nature of the shepherd-poet's *otium*. When, in *Eclogue* 10, line 40, Gallus suggests to his love that she might lie with him amidst the willow trees under a pliant vine (*lenta sub vite*), he comes close to a direct equation between the bending vine and the leisure of his imagined love.

The spiritual and physical implications of *lentus* are similar to those of *humilis*, and the two appear together on occasion in comparisons.[15] There is a forceful instance in *Eclogue* 5, lines 16-18, where Menalcas draws a reassuring contrast between Mopsus' song and the verses of his rival Amyntas:

> Lenta salix quantum pallenti cedit olivae,
> puniceis humilis quantum saliunca rosetis,
> iudicio nostro tantum tibi cedit Amyntas.

---

[14] On *extulit*, cf. *Aen.* 3. 215; 8. 2. Lucretius has the phrase *caput . . . ostendebat* (*De Re. Nat.* 1. 64), describing religion's threatening mien.
[15] See Servius' definition of bucolic poetry quoted above, n. 3.

Eclogue 1

As much as the bending willow yields before the glisten-ing olive, as much as the lowly reed to the crimson rose-trees, so much, in our opinion, does Amyntas give place to you.

Without even reading ahead, we could conclude from these analogies that the novelty and forcefulness and breadth of Mopsus' subsequent song will contrast with Amyntas' regu-lar themes as the victor's olive and festive rose challenge the *lenta salix* and *humilis saliunca*. Here, however, the com-parison applies only to a contrast of topics within the re-strictions of pastoral song. At the opening of the fourth eclogue, in grander tones, the poet announces that his themes are about to depart from regular bucolic procedure (*Eclogue* 4, lines 2-3):

> non omnis arbusta iuvant humilesque myricae;
> si canimus silvas, silvae sint consule dignae.

Hedge and lowly tamarisk do not delight everyone. If we sing of woods, let the woods be worthy of a consul.

The *arbusta* and *humiles myricae* are symbols of the inglori-ous existence of the rustic, inglorious not in itself, but by jux-taposition with the proud, heroic stance of the consul.

Returning to *Eclogue* 1, the opposition of osier to cypress contains several levels of meaning, but it chiefly establishes a mood of tension: What happens when Rome and the village come into conjunction? Or more specifically: What has Tityrus, dweller in the yielding, humble land, to do with the lofty, proud, urban life of Rome? A more ominous note is sounded if we reverse the question and ask that which we can-not without assuming the ruin of "pastoral": What will be Rome's ultimate effect upon him? The practical sphere of organized politics has the power to make or break myth be-cause it has the opportunity to mold or destroy the imagina-tion. It would therefore seem the course of folly to think that two such dissociable worlds could form a viable connection. Making a juxtaposition like this is one of Virgil's strokes of genius. Here it poses the significant question: How does an intellectual idea suffer when suddenly confronted with Roman practicality, law, power? Virgil chooses to illustrate the conjunction of the bucolic life and reality by showing the tangible reaction it produces in the landscape and the shepherd-singers.

The ambiguities the poet uses to describe Tityrus indicate the essence of pastoral as poetry as well as *otium*. The *tenuis avena*, we have seen, denotes poetic style as well as the literal means of making music; the wandering of the cattle is but a visible symbol for the spiritual "play" of the poet. No such happy double-meanings enrich Virgil's presentation of Meliboeus' life. The suffering, which disturbs the landscape as well as the shepherds, not only precludes the possibility of song for Meliboeus but forces him to reorient his life—now one completely of motion, with no *otium* whatsoever—outward and to exist beyond Tityrus' exclusive confines. Even now, however, Virgil's art is such that there is no confrontation, only two blueprints placed side by side with any comparison left to the reader.

It is ironic that Tityrus is the one who has been outside this paradise before, not Meliboeus. Tityrus has seen glorious Rome. Meliboeus knows nothing at all of her actual power, whether for good or evil, and even as the poem continues, Virgil never states—nor does Meliboeus seem to realize—that Rome could be the source of misfortune as well as bounty.

We have learned at line 19, from Tityrus' answer to Meliboeus' inquiry, that the city of Rome harbors a *deus*. The poet, still deliberately fostering the impression of Meliboeus' inexperience, has him ask at line 26:

Et quae tanta fuit Romam tibi causa videndi?[16]

[16] The image of "seeing" is of special importance throughout the poem. Here Meliboeus asks what was the reason for Tityrus' seeing

Eclogue 1

And what was the great reason for your seeing Rome?

The exactness of Tityrus' reply comes the more forcefully for the indirection of the preceding exchange (lines 27-35):

> Libertas, quae sera tamen respexit inertem,
> candidior postquam tondenti barba cadebat,
> respexit tamen et longo post tempore venit,
> postquam nos Amaryllis habet, Galatea reliquit,
> namque, fatebor enim, dum me Galatea tenebat,
> nec spes libertatis erat, nec cura peculi.
> quamvis multa meis exiret victima saeptis,
> pinguis et ingratae premeretur caseus urbi,
> non umquam gravis aere domum mihi dextra redibat.

Liberty, though in my laziness she looked at me late, after my beard fell white from the clippers, nevertheless looked at me and came after a long time, after Amaryllis held me and Galatea had left. For I will confess that while Galatea was my love I had neither hope of liberty nor care for my savings. Though many a victim left my folds and rich cheese was pressed for the unresponding city, never did my palm return home heavy with bronze.

Here a god is associated with Rome and both in turn with the personification of *libertas*. In fact *libertas* in line 27 balances *urbem* in line 19, and each receives strong emphasis. We have previously sensed that the concept of liberty with its concomitant tensions—between justice and injustice, law and anarchy, peace and unrest, and so on—was of importance to an interpretation of the anomalous relationship of Tityrus to Meliboeus. It is curious, then, to watch what interpretation Tityrus

---

Rome. Tityrus replies—again with apparent indirection—that Liberty, though late, looked at him. But is *Roma* to be equated directly with *Libertas* in his mind? Also, *video* is coupled with *miror* at line 69 (describing another event which would be a marvel to behold, should it ever occur).

places on the word. The construction of the poem, with the *tamen respexit* of line 27 reflected in *respexit tamen*, and *postquam* repeated in lines 28 and 30, gives us two separate though parallel views of the time and means of Liberty's epiphany in his life. In spite of, perhaps even because of, Liberty's advent (through contact with the city of Rome), his is a narrow view, limited to shepherding and sylvan love.

The goddess looked at him, though late, and came to him, though his beard had already grown white. Literally, Tityrus went to Rome: symbolically, she came to him. Two reasons are given for her tardy arrival. One is that he himself was *iners*. Speaking in practical terms, this could mean that Tityrus had an aversion toward labor which might have helped him on the road to freedom. Even before his present piece of good fortune he had been *lentus* and possessed the *otium* which is now dispensed by Rome.

The second reason is that for Tityrus *spes libertatis* has a distinguishable goal, the *cura peculi* the accumulation of which has taken time. *Libertas* lies in the *peculium* itself, the money laid by so that the shepherd, who is really a slave, can buy his autonomy. A necessary stage in this process was the departure of Galatea, who apparently squandered Tityrus' savings, and the subsequent arrival of Amaryllis. Yet even this description shows how Tityrus' intellectual horizon is constricted to rustic concerns, whereas Virgil has already made the reader look beyond this.

The idea of "possession" appears in two bucolic guises in these lines. The one involves Tityrus' love, first for Galatea and then for Amaryllis (the names themselves confine us to fantasy). *Habet* and *reliquit*, in the sense in which they are used in line 30, have amatory connotations. By contrast, we may look back at the use of the verb *reliquit* in line 15 where the mother goat's abandonment of her twins helps symbolize the coming of death to Meliboeus' land. It is also worth looking back to the verb *linquimus* in line 3 where we are clearly shown Meliboeus' concern not for any idyllic love but for the land itself, for his *patria* and his beloved acres (*dulcia arva*). The other idea of possession may be seen in a glance ahead to the use of *habebit* in line 70: "impius haec tam culta novalia miles habebit . . . ?" ("Will a blasphemous soldier possess these fields I have so nurtured?"). Here is the idea of possession in a broader sense: the impiety of the soldier who lords it over fields so cherished that they might seem to have been worshipped as divine. Again it is Meliboeus' words that point up the challenge which force presents to the land. Meliboeus' conception of love (for the reality of the land, not for insubstantial Amaryllis), as well as his awareness of the meaning of human liberty, even though it be learned from grief, is both broader and deeper than that of Tityrus. The latter's, even though he has seen Rome, is only a sheltered search for shallow perfection within the myth. In the double vision of *Eclogue* I, Tityrus is scarcely a poet.

This time it is Meliboeus' turn to offer an apparent *non sequitur* as reply to Tityrus' remarks. He returns to the absence of Tityrus in Rome (lines 36-39):

> Mirabar quid maesta deos, Amarylli, vocares,
> cui pendere sua patereris in arbore poma;
> Tityrus hinc aberat. ipsae te, Tityre, pinus,
> ipsi te fontes, ipsa haec arbusta vocabant.

I wondered, Amaryllis, why you called sadly upon the gods and for whom you allowed the fruit to hang on its trees. Tityrus was away from here. The very pines, Tityrus, the very fountains, these bushes themselves called you.

The poet uses the word *miror*, we remember, in line 11 to indicate Meliboeus' amazement at Tityrus' present good fortune. Now with the same verb in the past tense, *mirabar*, Virgil conveys Meliboeus' reaction to a previous event in Tityrus' life, which is equally idealized. Tityrus' absence proves, to

Meliboeus at least, that he is one of the essential spirits of the sylvan world, without whose presence it languishes.

One of the pleasures of the rustic life is to sing happy songs to the heavens. Likewise, nature's ideal is to have all the trees give freely of their fruits in due season. In this respect we may compare line 37 with the similar line 54 of *Eclogue* 7 (lines 53-56):

> Stant et iuniperi et castaneae hirsutae,
> strata iacent passim sua quaeque sub arbore poma,
> omnia nunc rident: at si formosus Alexis
> montibus his abeat, videas et flumina sicca.

Here are juniper and shaggy chestnuts. Everywhere fruit lies strewn beneath its own tree. Now everything smiles. But if beautiful Alexis were to leave these hills, you would see the streams go dry.

Were beautiful Alexis to be away, nature's productivity would be halted and the streams become dry. In *Eclogue* 1 the symbolic value of Tityrus is virtually the same: his absence, too, causes a concerned reaction in the land. It is specifically Amaryllis, however, who is distressed and who seems, by the effort of her sadness, to slow the workings of nature and make the fruit, whose fall would ordinarily mean nature's rejoicing in her abundance, stay on the boughs.

Amaryllis, then, becomes emblematic of a perfect but fragile union which is ruined by death or even absence. She grieves, along with the landscape, at her lover's momentary but necessary withdrawal. We hear an echo of Meliboeus' words in *Eclogue* 5 as Mopsus describes the universal lamentation for the death of Daphnis whose mother embraced the pitiful body of her son and cried out at the cruelty of gods and the heavens: *atque deos atque astra vocat crudelia* (line 23). Here the reaction in nature—Mopsus tells how even the lions mourned Daphnis' passing—is equally strong.

Eclogue 1

And so Tityrus suddenly appears, at least to Meliboeus, the contemplative, still idealistic, spectator of the situation around him; he seems a Daphnis figure, one of the semi-divine creatures upon whose well-being the landscape depends. Meliboeus visualizes this first in the reaction of Amaryllis and then in that of her surroundings, the pines, founts, and shrubs. Perhaps it is partially an echo of Amaryllis' cries, but the threefold use of *ipsae, ipsi, ipsa* is also the affirmation of nature's own spontaneous cries of grief at Tityrus' departure.[17] Hence, though he now voices his amazement at time past, Meliboeus once again establishes Tityrus as a necessary representative of the "pastoral" ideal, living in a perfect landscape which is at one with his joys and sorrows. His existence is ideal, now as then, but he has been forced, for whatever reason, to abdicate his role as a focal figure and submit to domination by a young, new deity.

Though he has seen Rome, Tityrus is still treated by the poet in strictly pastoral terms, as if the journey away were only a brief interruption to reassure the continued endurance of his idyll. Since he is an indispensable spirit of creativity and love, nature should weep for his absence and thrive upon his return. But does it actually? Even in these lines there is a note of sorrow which, with compelling directness, shifts the reader's attention to Meliboeus. This stems particularly from the word *hinc.* Though the landscape grieved for the absent Tityrus, nevertheless that was still a time when he, Meliboeus, was a part of the same world, where he was a witness to Amaryllis' sorrow and himself heard nature's cries.

In response to Meliboeus' exclamation, Tityrus spells out in clearer terms the reason for his journey (lines 40-45):

> Quid facerem? neque servitio me exire licebat
> nec tam praesentis alibi cognoscere divos.
> hic illum vidi iuvenem, Meliboee, quotannis

[17] See, e.g., *Ecl.* 4. 21-23; and 5. 62, 64.

41

Eclogue I

bis senos cui nostra dies altaria fumant.
hic mihi responsum primus dedit ille petenti:
'pascite ut ante boves, pueri; summittite tauros.'

What was I to do? Elsewhere I could not escape my servitude nor come to know gods in person. Here, Meliboeus, I
saw that youth for whom my altars smoke twelve days
yearly. Here to my suit he first gave a response: "Feed, as
before, your cattle, youths; breed your bulls."

Nowhere but in Rome was it permitted for him to put off the
yoke of *servitium* or to contemplate *praesentis divos*, gods to
be worshipped not in the abstract and from a distance but as
living beings.[18] The *hic* repeated in lines 42 and 44 takes us
emphatically out of the rural context and face to face with the
power of Rome—a setting important to Tityrus, if un-pastoral.
The divine youth he met in Rome is presumably the same *deus*
he had mentioned in lines 6-7, whose altar is often dyed with
the blood of a tender lamb as an offering of thanks for the
bestowal of *otium*.

There is a splendid richness in the language. *Cognoscere*
means to become intellectually aware of a fact, in this case

---

[18] On *praesens deus*, see P. Riewald, "De imperatorum Romanorum
cum certis diis et comparatione et aequatione" (Ph.D. diss., Martin
Luther University, Halle, 1912), esp. pp. 266-67. See also Franz Altheim,
A History of Roman Religion (London, 1938), pp. 339-49; Franz
Bömer, "Tityrus und sein Gott," *Würz. Jahr. für die Altertumswissen-
schaft* 4 (1949-50): 60-70; Rudolf Hanslik, "Nachlese zu Vergils
Eclogen 1 und 9," *WS* 68 (1955): 5-19; Werner Hartke, *Römische
Kinderkaiser* (Berlin, 1951), chap. 8, part B: ("Vergil und die Prägung
des römischen Imperialismus").
On Octavian as the *deus*, see Büchner, *P. Vergilius Maro*, col. 164;
Pöschl, *Die Hirtendichtung Virgils*, pp. 91-92; L. R. Taylor, *The
Divinity of the Roman Emperor* (Middletown, 1931), pp. 111-12;
C. G. Starr, "Virgil's Acceptance of Octavian," *AJP* 76 (1955): 34-36,
and *Civilization and the Caesars* (Ithaca, 1954), pp. 36-39, 171-74,
though I cannot agree that Virgil identified peace with Octavian and
made Meliboeus "a symbol of the dying Republic"; and Ronald Syme,
The Roman Revolution (Oxford, 1938), p. 253.

previously unperceived by the person involved.[19] But the poet turns straightway to the direct *vidi* (line 42), following up the implications of the phrase *praesentis divos*. This is no unseen divinity whose message is to be interpreted through signs and omens, but a human divinity. The force of the passage is enhanced by a comparison with the way Meliboeus previously sensed destruction coming to the countryside, through the omen of the ruined oak: his gods and their ways are as opposite to Tityrus' as heaven-sent signs are from Roman.

Tityrus has witnessed an epiphany of the god at whose shrine he went to worship. Within the pastoral convention this is more unusual than, say, the shepherds' sight, electrifying as it must have been, of Pan come to see the suffering Gallus in *Eclogue* 10, line 26 (*quem vidimus ipsi*). Indeed at first this *praesens divus* would seem to have nothing to do with rustic matters. In the crowning addition to the shepherd's disbelief the oracle, the god in person, spoke "first" (*primus*), which probably means that he was expected to give an eagerly awaited answer. Yet, instead of responding to Tityrus' particular wants (namely release from his *servitium*), he pronounced a formula that would seem to deal, in suitably oracular terms, with a situation affecting the whole rural world.[20] The god appears to know more about the needs of the country than the shepherd who has come to Rome. The lucky Tityrus is so oriented toward himself and his sequestered life that he is either unmoved by or—more ironic still—un-

[19] On *cognoscere*, see Altheim, *A History of Roman Religion*, pp. 348f.

[20] On *primus*, see the commentary on *Aen.* 7. 118 in P. Vergili Maronis *Opera*, ed. J. Conington, H. Nettleship, and E. Haverfield (London, 1883-98); Hanslik, "Nachlese zu Vergils Eclogen 1 und 9," pp. 15-18; and I. S. Ryberg, "Vergil's Golden Age." *TAPA* 89 (1958): 118, though the relevance of *Theogony* 24-26 to *Eclogue* 1 would seem debatable. It would be ironic if the oracle did speak first in time (treating *primus* as *prior*). On the oracular language, see *Aen.* 7. 86, 92; also Josef Martin, "Vergil und die Landanweisungen," *Würz. Jahr. für die Altertumswissenschaft* 1 (1946): 103.

aware of the trials to which the rest of the countryside is subject. It is toward remedying these ills that the god's response seems directed.

There are several enigmas about the god's terse statement in line 45: " 'pascite ut ante boves, pueri; summittite tauros.' " One is that, although Tityrus speaks of himself in the singular (*mihi*, line 44), the god replies in the plural (*pueri*, line 45). Also, the apostrophe is particularly striking because, as we learn twice in succeeding lines (46 and 51), Tityrus is a *senex*, an old man. Finally the god's command to feed cattle and rear bulls as before has little to do with Tityrus' excuse for a Roman journey.

What the oracle may mean to do is to assure Tityrus that he could return to his life as it was in the past, that is, as it was before trouble came to the fields. If this is the case, however, there is a grave discrepancy between the god's terse general commands and the facts the poem presents. I do not refer now to the minor points noted above but to something of more importance to the poem's meaning as it gradually becomes clearer. The discrepancy might best be phrased in terms of a question: How is it that the oracle's statement is in the plural whereas the stress in the earlier part of the poem is on Tityrus' private *otium*? Or, to put the problem more directly: Why is it that the youthful god-man in Rome can, according to his will, promise the essence of nature to all, but in fact bestow it only on one? To Tityrus the god does grant *libertas*, which to him—his view being as narrow as the efficacy of the god's command is limited—is release from slavery and acquisition of the shepherd's *otium*. Yet even this, the goal which Tityrus has attained by the poem's start, is at variance with the almost georgic quality of the young god's command, with its practical concern for feeding and raising cattle. There is inconcinnity in the spectacle of a human god, powerful and omniscient, who could be expected to implement his words but does not. In this poem at least, no relief is imminent in the future, only a sham command to revive normality.

All these considerations, which raise more questions regarding the god's role for good or evil to be discussed later, underline further the variance between Tityrus' happiness and the plight of Meliboeus. Meliboeus draws the distinction in terms of the landscape after first looking at Tityrus (lines 46-58):

> Fortunate senex, ergo tua rura manebunt.
> et tibi magna satis, quamvis lapis omnia nudus
> limosoque palus obducat pascua iunco:
> non insueta gravis temptabunt pabula fetas,
> nec mala vicini pecoris contagia laedent.
> fortunate senex, hic inter flumina nota
> et fontis sacros frigus captabis opacum.
> hinc tibi quae semper vicino ab limite saepes
> Hyblaeis apibus florem depasta salicti
> saepe levi somnum suadebit inire susurro:
> hinc alta sub rupe canet frondator ad auras;
> nec tamen interea raucae, tua cura, palumbes,
> nec gemere aeria cessabit turtur ab ulmo.

Fortunate old man, and so your lands will remain. And for you they are large enough, even were naked rock and swamp with marshy reed to cover all the pasture. No unusual fodder will tempt your breeding ewes, no evil diseases from a neighboring flock will harm them. Fortunate old man, here among streams you know and holy founts you will find cool shade. Here, as it always has done, the hedge along your neighbor's border, whose willow flowers are fed upon by bees of Hybla, will often induce you by its gentle buzzing to fall asleep. Here, under a lofty rock, the pruner will sing to the heavens. Nor then, too, will your pets, the cooing pigeons, and the turtle-doves cease to moan from the lofty elm.

Eclogue I

Since certain aspects of this description of an ideal landscape recur often in the *Eclogues*, it is worth looking at in detail. One of the emphatic words in the first line is *tua*. The idea of possession is contradictory to the pastoral myth, as we have noted. Things are held freely in common: private property is not familiar to the shepherd. Tityrus need not worry about such conceptualization, but Meliboeus, having lost his lands, must now realize what it is to have something to call one's own. Even were Tityrus' pasture lands covered with open rocks and choked with slimy reeds—and from the next lines we learn that this is far from the case—still they would be his.[21] Simply by remaining on the land, by the providential gift of a god, Tityrus can forget about the idea of "mine" and "thine" and recreate a private sanctuary.

There can be no bucolic poetry without perfection of setting and this Meliboeus now visualizes as Tityrus' lot. There will be no temptation for his sheep, no exposure to anything which is not customary (*insueta*). Nothing violent will happen to his breeding ewes as just occurred to Meliboeus' flock. Above all—and this is of primary importance to Meliboeus' point— there will be no contact, especially evil contact, with a neighboring flock.[22] By this Meliboeus may be referring to the disease that has struck himself and his goats. He is, we recall, characterized as *aeger* in line 14. His illness is a symbolic reflection of the calamity which has befallen all nature and, with the land as paradigm, all areas prey to civil war.

With the repetition of *fortunate senex* in line 51 the orientation of Meliboeus' words changes from the suffering which Tityrus' lands lack to a more positive view of the beauty which he actually enjoys. From the first eclogue to the last, the use of the word *hic* and its kindred *hinc*, as in lines 53 and 56, sig-

---

[21] On *quamvis*, see Friedrich Leo, "Vergils Erste und Neunte Ecloge," *Hermes* 38 (1903): 10, n. 2.

[22] On *tempto*, see *Ecl.* 4. 32.

46

nals the beginning of an idealized vision of the countryside.[23] We may compare, for instance, Gallus' succinct summary for Lycoris of certain aspects of natural beauty at *Eclogue* 10, lines 42-43:

> hic gelidi fontes, hic mollia prata, Lycori,
> hic nemus; hic ipso tecum consumerer aevo.

Here are cool springs, Lycoris, here soft meadows, here a grove; here with you I would be eaten away (by love) for my whole life.

What Meliboeus chooses to emphasize first is the shady coolness bestowed by fountain and stream. The phrase *captare frigus* recurs in the next poem (*Eclogue* 2, line 8) in a contrast between the refuge which the herds take from the noonday heat and the fire of love in Corydon's heart which he is unable to quench, even by singing among the beeches with their thick tops. Nature's harshness mirrors, in fact symbolizes, his suffering; he is unable to return to her cool comfort until unhappy love leaves his soul. In *Eclogue* 1, Meliboeus indulges in no specific comparisons. He has no hatred or enmity, he simply states the situation firmly. Yet it is Tityrus who rests while Meliboeus must move along, enduring the blight on nature.

Tityrus' *frigus* is real. Under his spreading beech, perhaps by a river bank, he may enjoy a chill retreat from the sun's heat. *Frigus*, however, is also figurative for one aspect of the pastoral myth—the soul's absorption by poetry and spiritual calm. We feel some such essential meaning in Horace's ode on the *fons Bandusiae* (*Carmina* 3. 13), with its welcome cold and its immunity from the evil touch of the Dog Star (which is

---

[23] On the "pastoral oasis" see E. R. Curtius, *European Literature and the Latin Middle Ages* (New York, 1953), pp. 195-200; Renato Poggioli, "The Oaten Flute," *Harvard Library Bulletin* 11 (1957): 147-84, esp. 154ff.

to Horace what the *mala vicini pecoris contagia* are here to Virgil):

> te flagrantis atrox hora caniculae
> nescit tangere, tu frigus amabile
>   fessis vomere tauris
>   praebes et pecori vago; . . .

The harsh advent of the burning Dog Star knows not how to taint you. You furnish loving coolness to bulls tired from the plough and to the roaming flock. (lines 9-12)

In his hymn to Faunus from the first book of *Odes*, Horace makes more explicit the connection between protected landscape and poetry (*Carmina* 1. 17. 17-20):

> hic in reducta valle caniculae
> vitabis aestus et fide Teia
>   dices laborantis in uno
>   Penelopen vitreamque Circen; . . .

Here in a hidden vale you will shun the swirling heat of the Dog Star and, on Teian lyre, tell of Penelope and gleaming Circe yearning for one man.

Tityrus' domain, too, is one of *fontis sacros*, of fountains sacred to the water nymphs, but also sources, perhaps, of that song which forms, with the landscape, an extended metaphor for the imagination itself.

One word disturbs this happy spectacle—*nota*. Virgil has mentioned the privilege granted to Tityrus in Rome before: *praesentis . . . cognoscere divos*, to know the gods at first hand. Now it is Meliboeus' turn to remark on a similar closeness between Tityrus and the landscape. In so doing he calls attention again to his own plight, to the fact that he must now depart to places with which he has no familiarity and is in no way personally involved. The word *nota*, otiose from

Tityrus' point of view, is poignant coming from the mouth of Meliboeus.

Meliboeus has pictured Tityrus' world from without and from within: it will not be encroached upon by any external evil, and at the same time it will possess the streams and shade central to "pastoral."[24] He now turns to the dividing hedge. Ordinarily, even on a literal level, the mention of a *limes*, which could bound anything from fields to countries, would be unnecessary. The pastoral myth abhors the distinctions of property and possession, hence the appearance of a boundary here in *Eclogue* 1 is significant. It means that the landscape, which once was free—needing hedges for clarification, not confinement—has been torn into two parts. This is something unheard-of and forbidding, not only because of the concepts it introduces but also because of the particular manner of the division indicated here.

The phrase *vicino ab limite* urges upon the reader a direct comparison with line 50 and the reference to the *mala vicini pecoris contagia*. The flock (perhaps Meliboeus' sick animals, perhaps another's) beyond the boundary is diseased, but this, like the abandoned baby goats, is symptomatic of more general ills. Tityrus' private preserve is apparently the only place where *otium* remains undisturbed. The careful use of *semper* and *saepe* in lines 53 and 55, implying unceasing continuity of Tityrus' good fortune, recalls their appearance in lines 7 and 8 where Tityrus promises everlasting worship to his self-styled god, who has given him his land.[25] Meliboeus carefully, albeit indirectly, reminds us that the maintenance of Tityrus' idealism is at the pleasure, one might say mercy, of Rome.

Though the reason for the discrepancy between the two

[24] The reference to neighboring fields intimates that division of property has been imposed on the lands beyond Tityrus' preserve. The principle is destructive but, by itself, need not imply personal suffering.
[25] Cf. the uses of *saepe* in lines 16 and 20.

fields may have occurred to Meliboeus and its existence have been a worry, it is on Tityrus' side of the hedge that his thoughts center. The description of the *saepes* itself makes a beautiful transition from one place to the other. Each detail renders the spot more idyllic—the bees, the willow and its fostering flowers, the sleep into which the shepherd easily falls. Line 55, with its soothing sibilants, must have especially pleased Virgil for he offers a variation of *somnum suadebit* in the famous phrase *suadentque cadentia sidera somnos* which occurs twice in the *Aeneid*.[26]

Above all, by drawing our attention to the music of the line, Virgil emphasizes the importance of the idea of "sound."[27] Meliboeus realizes that it is neither the willow flowers nor the bees themselves but the buzzing of the bees which is of primary importance in the landscape. They are the means to one of the chief purposes of the pastoral life, the creation of song, and this is the point of the lines which follow. If the group of three lines introduced by *hinc* at line 53 accents the music of the *saepes* itself, the second set, beginning with *hinc* at line 56, broadens the idea.

Within the bucolic landscape there is an infinite variety of songs, be it the cooing of the wood-pigeon and turtle-doves or the happy singing of the pruner as he goes about his work.[28] All is alive with music, the natural world and its creatures as well as man himself. There seems to be no limitation to the extent which sound can reach within this perfect land, where all the horror beyond the hedge is forgotten. It is under a lofty rock that the pruner sits, sending his words toward the breezes of heaven, and the doves moan from elms as tall as they are timeless. Under the spreading beech and within the enclosure of the *saepes*, which keeps out pain and whatever causes it

[26] *Aen.* 2. 9, and 4. 81.
[27] On the importance of "sound," see Damon, "Modes of Analogy," passim.
[28] On the tenses and the word *interea*, cf. *Ecl.* 10. 55.

and where all thought of a literal boundary is cast aside, there is no limitation to the possibilities of song.[29]

Meliboeus' beautiful exposition of Tityrus' happiness causes the latter to exclaim about his unfailing devotion to the god-man in Rome (lines 59-63):

> Ante leves ergo pascentur in aethere cervi,
> et freta destituent nudos in litore piscis,
> ante pererratis amborum finibus exsul
> aut Ararim Parthus bibet aut Germania Tigrim,
> quam nostro illius labatur pectore voltus.

Sooner therefore shall nimble stags feed in the air and seas desert their fish naked on the shore, or the Parthian drink of the Saône or Germany the Tigris, with each wandering in exile across the boundaries of the other, than his features will slip from my heart.

Tityrus may mean to imply that it would be an absolute impossibility for him to forget the face of the divine Roman youth. One anticipates an expression of unceasing gratitude. Indeed, had he followed the usual catalogue of "impossibilities" (*adunata*)—and said, for instance, "Sooner shall stags fly, fish live happily on dry land and men readily exchange countries with one another, than I shall forget his visage"— then we would have no reason to pause further on the lines.[30] They could be taken merely as a compliment, heartfelt if hyperbolic, coming at a logical point in the poem. The fact that the paraphrase offered above is correct neither as a whole nor in part urges further scrutiny.

---

[29] For a fine elucidation of these lines when compared to one of their literary ancestors (Theocritus *Id.* 7), see Pöschl, *Die Hirtendichtung Virgils*, pp. 44ff. The only other use of *saepes* in the *Eclogues* is at 8. 37, where they fence off apple trees into an orchard (cf. *G.* 1. 270; 2. 371, 436).

[30] On the *adunaton*, see Ernest Dutoit, "Le thème de l'adynaton dans la poésie antique" (Ph.D. diss., University of Fribourg, Paris, 1936); G. O. Rowe, "The *Adynaton* as a Stylistic Device," *AJP* 86 (1965): 387-96.

Any statement that stags exist in the air at all, much less fly, is, of course, an impossibility, but Virgil uses the word *pascentur*. It is not the idea of their flying but of feeding in the air that the poet chooses to stress. The necessity for the creatures of nature to eat is a recurring theme in the poem. Part of the oracle's command, we recall, is *pascite, ut ante, boves, pueri*. It is not long since Meliboeus has mentioned the flowery hedge inside Tityrus' happy boundary, fed upon (*depasta*) by Hyblaean bees. Soon Meliboeus will cry out in his sorrow (lines 77-78):

> non me pascente, capellae,
> florentem cytisum et salices carpetis amaras.

Not while I lead you to pasture, my goats, will you crop the flowering clover and bitter willows.

Things are nourished, as we would expect, in Tityrus' utopia, but the two other uses of *pasco* quoted above offer scant comfort. From the first instance we assume that the cattle, for a while at least, had not been fed as usual and that it takes a god's order to renew even the simplest functions for the shepherds. The last example, though sad as far as Meliboeus is concerned, has ominous overtones for the animals themselves: Who will feed them in the future? Will the soldier taking over the land have any care at all for their welfare? The time may soon come, it may already be at hand, when stags will feed in the air. This means, in a more disquieting sense, that they may soon have nothing to eat on earth so they may as well feed on air—which is to say virtually the same thing.

The next example is less impossible; it is, in fact, a common occurrence. There is no question of fish surviving in a medium which is not theirs. Rather the natural inference is that the seas, in which they ordinarily live, have deserted them on the shore (*destituent*), exposed and vulnerable (*nudos*). We may

well say that, in spite of the implications of death in Tityrus'
words, this is a situation which the poet means will never
occur. The creatures of the sea will never be forsaken by their
native milieu for something foreign and destructive. Yet here,
more than in the previous instance, it is the context of the
poem itself which urges upon the reader a less reassuring interpretation. Worlds now are being thrust upon each other
which ordinarily would be as distinct as land from water.
When Rome and the pastoral life clash, the power of war will
inevitably be victorious over the spirit's fallible retreat.

In the poem thus far, the effects of Rome's victory have been
twofold: both animals and men have been afflicted. We have
seen its results in the animal world symbolized by the desertion of the twin, new-born goats (lines 15-16): "hic inter
densas corylos modo namque gemellos, / spem gregis, a, silice
in nuda conixa reliquit." If *reliquit* and *destituent* are allied
in meaning only, there is strong likelihood of a connection
between *silice in nuda* and *nudos in litore*. Far from being impossible, the disease in the countryside has reached the
point where a mother goat will abandon her offspring to die
in an exposed spot. And this, as we have seen, is a reflection
into nature of the trials which the shepherds must now face.
In other words, far from being impossible, Tityrus' second
analogy is probable. The shepherds are to be like the fish,
forced to depart from the security of their rural setting to accept the brutal exposure of exile.

We are by now prepared for the otherwise startling realism
of the third *adunaton*. This one is concerned with the idea of
exile, as the natives of one country drink from the waters of
another far away. It is true that, taken literally, no Parthian
tastes the Saône nor German the Tigris in the course of the
first *Eclogue*. But the necessity of exile (and here the poet
uses the word *exul* for the first time) is one of the significant
themes of the poem—not from Germany to Parthia, or vice
versa, but something more terrifying, from dream world to

lands both real and distant. The theme is first stated, we recall, by Meliboeus at line 3: "nos patriae finis et dulcia linquimus arva." It is reiterated, with significant verbal repetition, at line 67 as he asks himself if he will ever see again his
patrios finis. The word *finis* is stressed in each instance. At one
time Meliboeus uses it to stand for the land enclosed within
his boundaries, yet it also grows to mean, as it does in Tityrus'
analogy, the actual borders themselves which one crosses going into exile. The synonymous *limes* of line 53 has a similar import.

Hence the idea of exile, even of the most final sort, is essential to the whole poem. Virgil is not just talking of an exchange
of countries, of relocation by force of circumstances to another
spot, hard as this might be. Meliboeus' loss is more difficult,
and, in fact, more of an *adunaton* than the ones Tityrus offers.
We are not dealing with two geographically separated land
masses but with two opposite spheres, as incapable of comparison or union as earth with air or water with earth. The
one is poetry, whose visible element is the landscape with
flocks and founts. The other is the actuality of enforced exile
in lands as remote as Britain and Scythia. In other words,
the example of an "impossibility" which Tityrus offers last,
in the place of greatest importance, has been realized even
more terrifyingly in the life of Meliboeus.

We may pause on one detail in Tityrus' words. The motif
of "drinking" is of special significance. The instance of seemingly impossible exile is to have the Parthian drink the waters
of the Arar and the German the Tigris. We may contrast this
with Tityrus' own life, *inter flumina nota / et fontis sacros.*
It is well, also, to anticipate the opening of Meliboeus' reply
where, among the places of exile he names, two are directly
connected with unpastoral aspects of water, the Afri, because
they have no water at all (*sitientis*), and the Oaxes, because
it rushes thickly along.

If these supposed "impossibilities" are closely related to

present conditions, why does Tityrus use them as if they could never happen? We may dismiss any idea that Tityrus, in his simplicity, is telling Meliboeus (and Virgil warning his reader) that the face of the god-man in Rome will be forgotten by him forthwith. This would be a nonsensical statement on his part and impute to Virgil an unwonted directness of expression. One answer to the questions posed above is obvious, however. By his use of these analogies, Tityrus betrays little or no comprehension of what is afflicting mankind. The reader's major source of orientation in the poem has been the eyes of Meliboeus. He has told us of his trials and of the happiness of Tityrus. The latter, while confirming Meliboeus' sketch of his idyllic state, has made no attempt to understand, much less sympathize with, the lot of Meliboeus. He betrays no knowledge of suffering.[31]

There is another implication of the old shepherd's use of these *adunata* to be dealt with in detail later. Tityrus considers that his words could never find fulfillment, and associates these good things—stags that will never have to feed in air, fish that will not be left destitute, men who need not fear exile—with the face of the young god in Rome. For Meliboeus, the "impossible" horrors have become true. Some might come again to the conclusion that the Roman youth, divine to Tityrus, could appear differently to others and might even be held responsible for Meliboeus' misfortune. He might conceivably be playing two antithetical roles at once which it would take a poet with extreme finesse to expose. Virgil has so arranged his poem that his thoughts are not directly stated. Tityrus adores his Roman god, and Meliboeus, who does not envy Tityrus, has never been outside the pastoral world. Only an examination of the following lines will tell whether or not such an opinion is prejudged.

[31] Tityrus, in all his utterances, seems to remain oblivious and unaware. Virgil is not so much parodying as deprecating the "pastoral" poet's lack of interest in or conflict with external affairs.

Meliboeus continues with a contrasting description of his
sad future, almost as if Tityrus' exclamation of gratitude had
been an interruption (lines 64-78):

> At nos hinc alii sitientis ibimus Afros,
> pars Scythiam et rapidum cretae veniemus Oaxen
> et penitus toto divisos orbe Britannos.
> en umquam patrios longo post tempore finis,
> pauperis et tuguri congestum caespite culmen,
> post aliquot, mea regna, videns mirabor aristas?
> impius haec tam culta novalia miles habebit,
> barbarus has segetes? en quo discordia civis
> produxit miseros: his nos consevimus agros!
> insere nunc, Meliboee, piros, pone ordine vitis.
> ite meae, quondam felix pecus, ite capellae.
> non ego vos posthac viridi proiectus in antro
> dumosa pendere procul de rupe videbo;
> carmina nulla canam; non me pascente, capellae,
> florentem cytisum et salices carpetis amaras.

But we others will go from here to the thirsty Afri. Some
of us will come to Scythia and the Oaxes, turbulent with
mud, and to the Britons, sundered afar off from the whole
world. Lo, will I ever after a long time marvel at my pa-
ternal lands and the roof of my lowly hut, piled high with
sod, looking hereafter at those few ears of corn, my kingdom? Will a blasphemous soldier possess these fields I
have so nurtured, a barbarian, these crops? Behold whither
strife has led hapless citizens! For these we have sown
our fields! Graft now your pears, Meliboeus; put your
vines in a row. On, on, my goats, once happy flock. Hereafter, stretched in a green grot, I will not see you from
afar, hanging from a bushy rock. I will sing no songs.
Not while I lead you to pasture, my goats, will you crop
the flowery clover and bitter willows.

If *hinc* refers back to lines 53 and 56, it serves the more to underscore a distinction, a distinction which takes the form of a tension between movement (*ibimus*) and stability (*manebunt*, line 46, for example). The quiet land will always remain for Tityrus whereas Meliboeus' exile is part of its dissolution and the scattering of its inhabitants to the points of the compass. And the powerful *nos alii* implies that it is a dissolution in which all his colleagues take part.

In line 55, Tityrus, within his landscape, will enter (*inire*) nothing but a sleep lulled by song. Meliboeus and the rest will go (*ibimus*) not further into a realm of beauty but out of it entirely. There is a sad irony in Meliboeus' command to his goats at line 74: "ite meae, quondam felix pecus, ite capellae." Ordinarily this would be the shepherd's order for the flock to make its way to the stables and folds at nightfall. We may anticipate the poet's command to his goats, who have had their fill of browsing, as has he of song, at the end of *Eclogue* 10: "ite domum saturae, venit Hesperus, ite capellae" ("Homeward, goats, homeward, filled from browsing. Hesperus has come.") Night is falling at the end of the first eclogue as well. Hence the situations at the conclusion of both poems are parallel to a degree, but the word *domum* is conspicuously absent from Meliboeus' cry. The flock may apparently remain in the land but will never again be fed under his guidance. He has no home toward which to direct them; it has been rent from him along with them. They were once *felix* and lived under a happy star, but it is Tityrus alone who remains *fortunatus* in this troubled time.

Tityrus' figurative life needs nothing factual save a romantic reference to the bees of Hybla to complete its splendor. But Meliboeus and his companions must look forward to the hard reality of place names which embrace nearly the geographical limits a Roman might know. We jump via Meliboeus' sorrow from the private realm of flocks, streams and songs, of which everything is known and assumed (*nota*), to far away spots which, ironically, must be named because they border on the unknown.

There are other points of contrast as well. As we observed, the *Afri* are *sitientis*, thirsty, ignorant of the streams and founts inherent in the shepherd's landscape. And when we do come to a river, the Oaxes on the eastern boundary of Roman lands, it is rushing and (if we may follow the interpretation of Servius) muddy.[32] For the final name on the list, the *Britanni,* Virgil uses an image which is an extreme form of the recurrent theme of division. The Britons, remote as they are, physically and spiritually, from the bucolic life, are even separated from known places. In other words, Tityrus' confinement within the ideal, a poet's sphere and creation of the imagination alone, is contrasted with the prospect of Meliboeus' relegation to something so literal and barbarous as to be without civilized society, beyond Scythia and Africa in distance, the implication is, a world beyond our world.

Even though the pattern of thought initiated at line 64 refers back to the description of Tityrus' landscape beginning at 46, it has a clearer, more devastating purpose as well. It shows that the horror of exile from one clime to another, which seemed as impossible to Tityrus as to forget the face of the Roman god, is a part of Meliboeus' future life. Meliboeus passes over Tityrus' remarks, but the poet nevertheless asks his reader, now more strongly, to ponder their implications. Will Tityrus forget the face of his god because of what he sees to be Meliboeus' ill fortune? Will the god in fact no longer remain divine if the most violent form of exile, from a land of dream to the farthest margins of the earth, is forced upon Meliboeus, who fulfills the potentiality of Tityrus' expression? Tityrus never does accept the hint his words provide.

Meliboeus' realization of what Tityrus had deemed impos-

[32] The reading of most MSS is *cretae* which Servius glosses "hoc est lutulentum, quod rapit cretam" ("that is muddy, because it carries clay with it").

sible creates at this point in the poem another contrast between vision and reality, between imaginary escape and the brutalities of life. This brings with it the same tensions which the opening lines create: those of a narrow, confined "ideal" opposing a broad, geographical extent; of inner peace versus external motion; of the apparently timeless versus a sphere subject to the processes of history.

Meliboeus now turns his thoughts, as he had in the opening lines of the poem, to his lands, visualizing them first through the eyes of an exile, returned home at last.[33] The use of the phrase *longo post tempore* in 67 and *post* in 69 turns the reader's attention back to the earlier appearance of the same phrase in line 29 in conjunction with a double employment of *postquam* in lines 28 and 30. The earlier passage, it will be remembered, tells how *libertas* came to Tityrus in his old age. Again no bitterness need, or should, be directly imputed to Meliboeus' words, but the irony inherent in Virgil's characteristic understatement must not be dismissed. *Libertas* came to Tityrus, slothful though he had been, within the already happy context of his lands and his girl. His only barrier to full freedom is the *servitium* of a shepherd. The grace he gains is the complete leisure to sing at will.

As for Meliboeus, all liberty has been taken from him: the rights of citizenship, the right to love the land that had nourished him, the right to his own unpretentious home and scanty ears of corn. With the advent of slavery comes the realization of the qualities of real freedom. What Meliboeus speaks of is not an essential part of the pastoral myth: his references to the *patrios fines* and the rooftop heaped up with turf are only an elaboration of all that he implies in the phrase *dulcia arva*. Meliboeus has a practical, georgic involvement with the earth and affection for its detail. If only because his life now bridges the gap between the sylvan utopia of Tityrus and the harsh realities of Rome-centered civil war, he has

[33] On *patrios fines*, see note 5 above.

experienced pain and a deeper love. No pastoral dalliance balances the loss of that for which a man has lived and worked. Meliboeus' corn is, in his eyes, as well as in the reader's, a kingdom through the affection he lavishes upon it.

Tityrus' life turns from the minor troubles of a shepherd's existence to an ideal of peace and security. Meliboeus, though leaving little doubt about his former poverty, moves in the opposite direction, toward the worst servitude. It is Meliboeus' portrayal of the loss of all freedom, even the freedom to love, that forms the final, most significant, distinction between the two shepherds. With this we are forced not only to contemplate two men's varying fortunes in life but also to acknowledge how varying interpretations of the idea of liberty and justice can affect individuals and lands. When these interpretations are the products of different occasions, peoples or times, we need only compare them. When a double standard of liberty emanates from a single source, the problem should become the concern of more than poetry and poets. Superficially, however, the comparison still rests on the grounds of fact rather than inner value. Here Meliboeus, pondering the possibility of his return, uses the same verb, *miror* (now in its future tense), that he had in line 11, contemplating Tityrus' happy spot. Yet even a factual comparison such as this is left to the reader.

Meliboeus' next remark (at line 70) reveals a fact which the reader may have sensed before but which has never been made explicit: civil war, dissension among the people themselves, has caused this tragedy. Disagreements in the world of war and politics have consequences even in the countryside. What Meliboeus had said of himself before—"en, ipse capellas / protinus aeger ago; hanc etiam vix, Tityre, duco"—has proved to be emblematic of "pastoral" as a whole and then of life at large—"en quo discordia civis / produxit miseros."

The instrument imposing the disaster is a soldier who is *impius* and *barbarus*. The adjectives, perhaps the most force-

Eclogue 1

ful words in the poem, are important in their specific context, first of all. The soldier is *impius* primarily because he has no piety for fields and no special bonds of affection toward the lands he is about to seize, whereas *tam culta,* as an attribute of *novalia,* implies not only the regular pursuits of agriculture but also something akin to reverence and love, parallel to the phrase *dulcia arva. Barbarus,* too, contrasts with *culta*: the unkempt soldier knows nothing of the cherished land. It is ironic that Meliboeus, himself about to leave for the farthest segments of the earth, should be driven to characterize a Roman soldier as "barbarous."

The power of the passage, however, does not depend simply on the fact that the landscape is suddenly swept into the *Realpolitik* of the 40's B.C. In the strife that followed upon the death of Julius Caesar, veterans of one campaign or another, one side or another, were indeed compensated for their services with lands which had to be wrenched on occasion from those innocent of complicity with either party. But to leave an interpretation of *Eclogue* 1 thus is to treat it only as an exposition of good fortune versus ill luck or, more misleading still, justice versus injustice, though these tensions are present in the poem.

It is well to remember that the soldier upon whom Meliboeus in his anger heaps the abusive *impius* and *barbarus* is depicted not so much as a Roman as a minion of the powers that be in Rome, a symbol of the encroachment of civil war upon the countryside. The lands which he receives, which Meliboeus is forced to give over to him, are the generous manifestation of Rome's debt to its soldiery. Still, the emotional focus of the poem is not Rome in particular but the suppressed pain of the shepherd Meliboeus as he contemplates Tityrus' happiness. Both the pain and the happiness are caused by Rome. The power of Rome, the central idea behind the surface beauties and tensions of the poem, is depicted with irony.

On the one hand, Rome can be envisioned personified as a young god, devoted to *libertas*, who grants a life of *otium* to Tityrus even before he is asked. On the other hand, Rome is visualized as something brutal, domineering, ignorant of human needs, imposing the trials of proscription and exile on the poorest of its members. The medium and symbol of this aspect of Rome is no aloof, awe-inspiring oracular man-god, ideal in an ideal city, but a soldier so lacking in the qualities of divinity as to seem *impius*, so given to the ways of brutality as to seem uncivilized, Roman citizen though he be. In Meliboeus' life, barbarity and irreverence are imposed on civilization and love. He need not see Rome to visualize its less happy aspects.

Rome can work two ways, Virgil is telling his reader. It can convey, with brilliant awareness, that freedom to live apart, essential to the imaginative life and indispensable for the perfecting growth of any civilized society. Yet apparently at the same time, Rome can subject the spirit to ruthless and savage examples of physical compulsion. In destroying the landscape, it destroys the poetry that subsists on it.

We may sense, then, the weight of Meliboeus' irony in line 73, a command to himself: "insere nunc, Meliboee, piros, pone ordine vitis." In spite of difference in detail, there is enough similarity in expression to suggest that Meliboeus is parodying the divine oracle's words to Tityrus—"'pascite ut ante boves, pueri; summittite tauros'"—and measuring the ideal he announces against the trials that have come to afflict his existence. Since he did not happen to be among the fortunate *pueri* to whom the youth addressed his words, he must give the command to himself. His words are in the singular albeit he stands for *nos alii*, and though the oracle's utterance is in the plural, there is some evidence, previously mentioned, that the poet wished his reader to see it as affecting Tityrus alone. *Nunc*, in Meliboeus' command, offers a sarcastic counterpart to the oracle's *ante*; there is continuity of happiness in

Tityrus' life. Meliboeus may give himself a false order to continue living as he once did, but to contemplate a mock exactness in the placing of his vines is to ignore the chaos of his existence and of the pastoral world in general. One cannot plant vines or graft pears under such circumstances in Italy any more than in the extreme cold of Scythia or in Africa's dry heat.

As the ironic *nunc* yields to the realistic *quondam* of the past, Meliboeus, balancing his future life against that of Tityrus, bases his final comparison on the landscape. Meliboeus, *viridi proiectus in antro*, echoes Tityrus, *patulae recubans sub tegmine fagi*, and the spectacle of the far away goats hanging from a shaggy rock is not unlike the pruner in line 56, singing to the breezes, *alta sub rupe*. The further emphasis on the idea of seeing (*videbo*) reminds us that once the life of Meliboeus was graced with the same happy vision that will always remain for Tityrus. Tityrus can now sing whatever he wishes. His domain is alive with the music of man and nature. In Meliboeus' new life there is to be no song —*carmina nulla canam*—for singing is impossible in exile, away from the bucolic landscape. The final vignette from this happy former life concerns the goats which will continue to feed without his guidance. The spectacle has verbal likenesses to Tityrus' magic hedge: *pascente* (line 77) recalls the hedge, *saepes depasta* (lines 53-54), and the flowering clover and bitter willow shoots upon which the goats will graze resemble the willow flower of the hedgerow, fed upon by the bees.

Meliboeus has had, until this moment, the landscape that will ever belong to Tityrus. Starting from this landscape, the roads of the two shepherds diverge, the one into a reassured idyll, the other to its complete renunciation. This discrepancy, though it is the result of civil war, shows the countryside and its creatures as the chessboard and pawns by means of which mighty Rome plays its unpredictable, double game.

Even to mention Rome is to intrude upon the retreat from

Eclogue I

reality always implicit in the pastoral myth. To show the fragile creation of poetic fancy subject to the powerful whim of such an antagonist is to verge upon the acknowledgment that "pastoral"—which in this poem becomes as much a symbol of human freedom and individual liberty as it does of poetry and of the poet's inalienable, if ideal, privilege to create freely and at leisure—is doomed. But even here, as he raises the greatest issue in the poem, Virgil acts with characteristic subtlety. He never states the problem in black and white. Tityrus and Meliboeus, and parallel to them, the two sides of Rome, never collide. Meliboeus steadfastly eschews the envy that might cause a clash. Virgil accomplishes a major tour de force by brilliantly evoking his ambivalent subject, quietly demonstrating its meaning in any appreciation or interpretation of "pastoral," and then allowing the reader to draw his own conclusion.

The ending of the poem has the effect of seeming to smooth over rough edges (lines 79-83):

Hic tamen hanc mecum poteras requiescere noctem
fronde super viridi: sunt nobis mitia poma,
castaneae molles et pressi copia lactis,
et iam summa procul villarum culmina fumant,
maioresque cadunt altis de montibus umbrae.

Here, nevertheless, you could rest this night with me upon the green leaves. I have ripe apples, soft chestnuts and a supply of cheese. And now afar off the high peaks of the farm houses are sending up smoke, and deeper shadows are falling from the lofty hills.

Tityrus' final words, introduced by the characteristic *hic* and proceeding to details of graphic power and beauty, are an invitation to Meliboeus to spend one last night in the country. With lines 79-80 we may compare Daphnis' invitation to a shepherd, either the same or another Meliboeus, to come into his ideal world of song in *Eclogue* 7 (lines 9-13):

64

'nunc ades, O Meliboee; caper tibi salvus et haedi;
et, si quid cessare potes, requiesce sub umbra.
huc ipsi potum venient per prata iuvenci,
hic viridis tenera praetexit harundine ripas
Mincius, eque sacra resonant examina quercu.'

Come over here, Meliboeus; your ram is safe and your
kids. And, if you can relax a while, rest in the shade. Hither
the bullocks of their own accord come through the meadows to drink. Here the Mincius interweaves its green
banks with tender reed and the swarms buzz in the sacred
oak.

There is not only the same striking repetition of the verb
requiesco preceded by *possum* in each instance, but also a similar feeling for flocks feeding by water and the happy noise
of bees, trademarks of Tityrus' version of pastoral.

Tityrus in *Eclogue* 1 is, of course, akin to Daphnis, the
quasi-mythical shepherd, symbol of the perfect singer in a
perfect setting. What differentiates the two passages, however,
is that in 7 the concerns of Meliboeus, which might have kept
him from enjoying the contest over which Daphnis presides,
are only the trifling preoccupations of any shepherd. The
limited cares of the shepherd in 7 are expanded in the case of
the Meliboeus of *Eclogue* 1, to something ominous of ruin:
there will be no further enjoyment of song. The details of
Tityrus' offer are seductive and the coming of nightfall alone
might have urged him to accept, but Tityrus' request that he
spend the night *fronde super viridi* might well have served
as a sad reminder to Meliboeus who has just mentioned how
he once watched his flocks while stretched out in a green grot
(*viridi sub antro*). Indeed we may see in the darkening gloom
and greater shadows of evening one final symbol of disruption.

For Tityrus the coming of night is the cause of an invitation. His words are meant as a positive enticement to renew
contact with the beauty of the land as the darkness brings

obscurity to the visible world and supposedly obliviates future sorrow. As we have seen, the form of the invitation is particularly pastoral. If the word *hic* recalls Daphnis' request in 7, there are other details which anticipate *Eclogue* 2 where the unhappy shepherd Corydon invites the urbane, careless Alexis into his world. Twice, in connection with Alexis, he uses the word *mecum* (lines 28 and 31). The inevitable *hic* of the catalogue of beauty to be found in the pastoral *locus amoenus* takes the form of the prayer *huc ades* (line 45). Finally, among the gifts which Corydon offers to Alexis we find the same chestnuts and fruits which are a part of Tityrus' catalogue of attractions. All these parallels merely underscore the fact that Tityrus no longer considers Meliboeus a part of the land.

In night's gloom there is no possibility for Meliboeus of enduring the sorrow of seeing Tityrus' happiness and therefore of comparing it with the prospects of his own future. But, from a negative point of view, the obliteration of the land by the growing shadows of evening betokens the irrevocable end of the pastoral life for Meliboeus. It is his death to the setting that Tityrus so persuasively recreates in the nightfall seen from a vantage point at some ideal distance between the far-off rooftops of a village (the workaday world) and the lofty mountains whence the shadows descend, where ordered land yields to rugged wilderness. The happiness caused by any momentary renewal by Meliboeus of his former associations, were he to give in to Tityrus' inducements (and we never learn the outcome), is immediately dampened by remembrance that night also brings with it the finality of exile.

Meliboeus might find quiet, but only for this night. The predictable part of his life is exactly what he has told us it would be, chaos. The shadows which now fall are not those which provide shelter against the day's bright sun and are so necessary for song. They are more powerful and sinister, descending with a heavy weight like the *umbrae* which the poet-shepherd at the end of the tenth eclogue acknowledges are deadly for the singer and his song. They embrace both Tityrus and Meliboeus in sadness because the counterfeit happiness of one is as grievous to the myth as the direct suffering of the other.

There is much about these final lines which brings the poem full circle and recalls the opening lines. The invitation to rest (*requiescere*) is but a reminder that, throughout the poem, Tityrus has been reclining at his ease in the shadow of his beech. It is the privilege of Tityrus to proffer to Meliboeus one last look at his surroundings and his words may at first be greeted as the poet's way of achieving a reconciliation, fleeting though it be, between two lives once similar and now grown suddenly apart. But Tityrus, as Virgil chooses to portray him, always has the easy way; he is ignorant of the burdens of others and unsympathetic to their needs, in spite or because of his striking good fortune. Unstated though it is, inevitable bitterness aroused in Meliboeus by the beauty of Tityrus' description is enhanced by the latter's bald statement that any further involvement of Meliboeus with the land can be for the present night only. Meliboeus is not given a chance to answer. The reader is left with the ring of Tityrus' lovely words in his ears and, at first, with some soothing notion that Meliboeus' momentarily renewed association with Tityrus can somehow piece together his shattered life.

At the beginning of the poem Meliboeus stands on the outside and looks in, but the poet verbally "surrounds" the lines devoted to his plight with the first glimpse of Tityrus' haven. At the end Tityrus invites his friend to step within and share his life. We are allowed to imagine Meliboeus' reply as the poet's hold over our imagination dictates. However, it could well be the voice of Meliboeus' unspoken grief that remains with us long after the shadows of nightfall have covered Tityrus' perfect land.

Eclogue I

CRITICS OF this poem have followed several general lines of interpretation. One has a markedly practical bent.[34] It sees the poem as another document in the history of the late 40's B.C., a document which can shed light not only on the proscriptions which accompanied the struggles consequent to Caesar's death but also on the specific misfortunes which Virgil himself may have suffered during these years. The ancient commentators assure us that Virgil endured the loss of an ancestral estate near Mantua as a result of land division and allotments. They may well be right. Even though, as seems likely, the chief evidence stems from the *Eclogues* themselves, there is no denying that the poet is responding to difficulties that had come to the territory around Mantua as an aftermath of civil war.

There is a parallel approach to *Eclogue* 1, also much travelled, opened by those who see the poem primarily as an historical document which is illustrative of its time and which takes us into the tortuous ways of allegory. It is a prevalent opinion that the god of lines 6-7, both youthful (*iuvenis*, line 42) and living in Rome, is Octavian, the future Augustus, rejuvenator of the Roman race, disguised hero of the *Aeneid*. This view is worth closer inspection. It has much to commend it and indeed may well have been the poet's chief concern.[35] However, merely reading Virgil's future admiration for Augustus (limited though this might become) into a poem of the late 40's, when Octavian was still a youth in his early twen-

---

[34] The "practical" aspects of the poem have been the chief subject of discussion since Servius. This is now rightly giving way to more "literary" appreciations (see the just criticism of Segal, "*Tamen Cantabitis, Arcades,*" pp. 237ff.). The two are occasionally combined. See, e.g., L. A. MacKay, "On Two Eclogues of Virgil," *Phoenix* 15 (1961): 156-58, who sees *Eclogue* 1 as an indictment of Augustus' agrarian policy and condemns Tityrus accordingly.

[35] On Octavian as the *deus*, see note 18 above. Others have had their champions; e.g., L. Antonius by Josef Liegle, "Die Tityruskloge," *Hermes* 78 (1943): 209-31.

ties, gifted but generally untried, is not adequate support for this approach. It is well to recall the words from Cicero's fifth phillipic delivered on the first day of the year 43 B.C. "Quis tum nobis, quis populo Romano obtulit hunc divinum adulescentem deus?"[36] To some, even then, Octavian was the preserver of the state. Yet, to generalize for a moment, extreme care must be taken before acknowledging direct allegory in any work which does not explicitly accept such a mask at the start. To overstress allegory cramps and inhibits a generous interpretation of any poem by placing the poet in an intellectual strait jacket while his work becomes a series of correlations and nothing more.

The initial trouble with this view of *Eclogue* 1, or with any allegorical interpretation of the *Eclogues*, right though it may be in part, is that we simply do not have any basis for certainty. There is always present the disquieting fact that, however devious or vague his references on occasion, when Virgil wants to name a specific place or mention a person directly he does so. It is true that, for obvious reasons of discretion, Virgil might not have wished to mention Octavian's name openly. There could even be the possibility of doubt that a specific person is meant. When Meliboeus asks Tityrus, in line 18, "sed tamen iste deus qui sit, da, Tityre, nobis," he receives the abrupt and apparently unconnected answer *urbem Romam*. That reply, however much of a shock it may be to the reader who expects a direct response, is assuredly what Virgil means. The awesome power which presides over the first eclogue is exactly what Virgil makes Tityrus reveal: the city of Rome. It happens that Tityrus has seen an idealistic side of Rome, personified in the young god who commands a return to pastoral normality. There is another side as well, a side from which Meliboeus suffers though, ironically, he has no com-

[36] *Phil.* 5. 43: "What god offered to us, what god offered to the Roman people this immortal youth?"

prehension at all of Rome's appearance or of the sentiments of its rulers.

Those critics who see in the poem Virgil's first, almost prophetic, glorification of the future Augustus are often forced, as a corollary of their stand, to see Tityrus as the mouthpiece of Virgil's ideas, in fact a symbol of the poet himself. The reader, one then supposes, is tacitly requested to forget Meliboeus' sufferings in favor of the beauty and idealism bestowed on Virgil-Tityrus by Octavian because they make Meliboeus' trials seem temporary and individual. The ending of the poem becomes, according to such a happy view, a reconciliation of opposing forces, a final invitation into "pastoral"—in spite of the tense of *poteras* (used more than for mere politeness' sake), the implications of nightfall and, most important, the reader's awareness of the course Meliboeus' life must take on the morrow. Yet Tityrus could not even proffer the invitation were he not allowed to do so by a higher power, and if his existence seems without drawback, he is nevertheless an old man, fortunate in being sponsored by a young god.

Aside from the manifest difficulties that lie in the path of any such Virgil-Tityrus allegory—for example, the poet himself was far from a *senex* at the time the poem was written—it is the injustice that this approach does to the poem as a whole which is troublesome. The reader is asked to believe that the feelings of Virgil are engaged only when he is dealing with the figure of Tityrus. By implication, therefore, the sections of the poem which describe Meliboeus serve only as a foil to set off the felicity of Tityrus, which itself is merely emblematic of the divine attributes and human sympathies of the young Octavian. To treat the poem as if it belonged to Tityrus alone is to wrong the poet and his artistry; in fact, to give either Tityrus or Meliboeus a place of pre-eminence violates one of the essential laws of poetic unity. Rather, we may only marvel again at the subtle manner of presentation whereby two divergent situations can be reviewed, perhaps with irony on the poet's part, but never with malice from the protagonists.

That our response to the *iuvenis deus* is of crucial importance here, there is no doubt, but our final impression of the poet's feeling toward him must be judged not only in the light of his treatment of Tityrus but in relation to the poem as a whole. Although Virgil's art never precipitates a clash between Tityrus and Meliboeus, the mind of the reader tends always to see where their two roads meet. They meet in the past where both apparently shared the life of an ordinary shepherd. They also meet in the idea of Rome, which affects each disparately but which nevertheless dominates the poem.

Herein lies another irony. Tityrus, though he has visited the city itself and compared its monumentality with the pastoral life's humility, knows only one aspect of Rome, the oracular god-man who offers generalized utterances for a return to order. But, as seen through Meliboeus' sad but unenvious eyes, this god-man actually bestows order upon few or even one alone. Tityrus defines Rome by the person of a young god. Meliboeus, though he apparently knows nothing explicit of Rome, must suffer the results of Rome's present situation. The *impius* and *barbarus miles*, the savage soldier who has no piety toward the land, has come to impose himself and shatter, not help rebuild, the dream. Virgil never mentions Rome in this connection—the words are Meliboeus', after all, and he is ignorant of the city—but the reader is not unaware of the implications.

By implication then, there are two contradictory aspects of the anomaly called Rome. The one preaches the creation and maintenance of the bucolic fantasy. For Tityrus, Rome and its god are both awe-inspiring and perfect; their existence complements the good they bestow. The other Rome, unmentioned by name but not unfelt, takes the form, neither urban nor divine, of a soldier forcing an era of devastation on the land. The aloofness of Tityrus' god is emphasized by contrast with the threatening advent of the *miles*. In sum, the one seems an ideal Rome, bestowing an ideal milieu on the lucky Tityrus. The other, cogent for the poet's understatement, is a more realistic depiction with a more realistic purpose.

As if these intimations about Rome were not sufficient, it is well to ponder for a moment the specific situation of Tityrus. There is little doubt that, taken in and of itself, his position is to be visualized as perfect. For him "pastoral," an expansive metaphor for a way of living and writing, is preserved unharmed. Yet by this very perfection Virgil forces his reader to inquire further. Can such a man who knows nothing of suffering (his most grievous trial is his *servitium*) be a true poet? Could he really be meant, in the situation where Virgil places him, to stand as surrogate for poetry and the imagination's struggle for perfection? In the context of *Eclogue* I, there is no reality to Tityrus: he is a wraith as empty as his god's promises and the poem's greatest irony. Ideal as his status may at first seem, ultimately it is false; it mirrors artifice, not truth.[37]

Once we are past momentary contemplation of Rome's limited beneficence, any acknowledgment that the existence of the bucolic life is subject to the generosity of a higher power (be it Rome or anything else) is tantamount to an announcement that this essential freedom is in fact no longer viable. For *otium* to be the lot of one person alone, or even of a few, is strange in itself. To have the life of the imagination subject to the caprice of Rome—representative of power politics, of the human context of men's loves and hates, and of peace and war—is to admit that, at least under present circumstances, poetic values are no longer of primary concern. Dictatorship over the world of the spirit means that its essence is destroyed at the core. In Rome's present state, Virgil seems to say, there is no liberty, no matter how idealistically bestowed

[37] On the ineptitude of Tityrus' rhetoric see Segal, "*Tamen Cantabitis, Arcades,*" p. 242. For a perhaps too strong denunciation of Tityrus' character, see Jacques Perret, *Les Bucoliques* (Paris, 1961), p. 18.

and cherished, which is not balanced by a contingent *servitium*. The beauty of Tityrus' existence forces a realization of how much is actually subject to another's whim. Tityrus sings apart, happy in his *otium*, forgetful that his life is direct proof that the poet has now become completely dependent upon asking for freedom to write. The essential substratum for poetry, far from being strengthened, is gradually being undermined and destroyed.

This is but one part of the whole apparent infliction of modern life upon traditional beliefs and values, best exemplified here in the relationship each shepherd bears toward his gods. The one is remote and traditional, the other alive and responsive; yet this god, too, receives sacrifice in the old-fashioned manner, as befits the supposed preserver of the landscape. Tityrus views him only as an epiphany of the divine in human form, and not specifically as a vital force which brings evil along with good. But while Tityrus is pondering his ever-enduring god and proposing the frequent offering of a lamb to him, the goats of Meliboeus, which ordinarily would have been sold or used for sacrifice, are dying. There is a large discrepancy between Tityrus' lamb, taken willingly from his sheepfold and slain for his new divinity, and the twin goats, hope of the flock, caught along with their shepherd in an uncontrollable disturbance. The twins are the greater victims of the same power. Tityrus' naïveté may court the new god in an old way. Meliboeus' loss does the god's other self scant credit.

We may well feel that the poem's chief emotional impact stems from the sufferings of Meliboeus. Tityrus describes his personal god and his bountiful Roman journey, but it is through Meliboeus' eyes that the beauty of Tityrus' life is seen and the inevitable comparison made. The result of this comparison is, for some, to see in the poem the challenge of justice by injustice and to treat the poem as if it were a dialogue between right and wrong. Yet here again such a judg-

ment virtually necessitates the equation of justice and righteous-
ness with the life of Tityrus as bestowed by the power of
Rome. Though Tityrus appears a paragon and is himself
guilty of nothing untoward, there is on the poet's part no
implication whatsoever that the god's treatment of Tityrus
was in any sense just. Conversely, anonymous as the soldier
remains, the treatment of Meliboeus is manifestly brutal.
And, as for the *deus*, why does he salvage the ideal world for
Tityrus and not offer succor to Meliboeus? Why does one
singer succeed and not another? How can a distinction ever
be made when it is human freedom, *libertas*, which is at stake?

Rather than centering on the specific problem of justice, the
poem is concerned with something of greater impact. It is, in
part, a meditation on the meaning of *libertas*.[38] This begins,
on the simplest level, with freedom from the servitude of
slavery, which is all Tityrus knows, and with the freedom
which Meliboeus lacks, to have and love one's land. It extends
to the most complex problems, involving both the necessity of
"pastoral" to be free from external despotism and the poet's
imperative to create. This extension in turn suggests the power of government to make or break the fragile fabric of the
mind, to impose itself or remain aloof, to bestow freedom or to
obstruct it by imposing its will on something that should remain untouched. *Libertas*, to a shepherd-poet, assumes complete leisure. He should not be forced even to engage in a discussion of his sacrosanct rights.

---

[38] On the Roman conception of *libertas*, see H. Kloesel, "Libertas"
(Ph.D. diss., University of Breslau, 1935); Syme, *The Roman Revolu-
tion*, pp. 155-56; Chaim Wirszubski, *Libertas as a Political Idea at
Rome* (Cambridge, 1950), and its review by Arnaldo Momigliano,
JRS 41 (1951): 146-53; M. Hammond, "Res olim dissociabiles: Princi-
patus ac Libertas," *HSCP* 67 (1963): 93-113. See also Harold Fuchs,
"Augustus und der antike Friedensgedanke," *Neue Philologische
Untersuchungen* 3 (Berlin, 1920), Appendix 3 ("Der Begriff des
Friedens"), pp. 167-223; J. H. Oliver, *Demokratia, the Gods and the
Free World* (Baltimore, 1960), pp. 152ff.

Around this focal problem further tensions are developed. The poet's use of abstracts, which were of great moment in contemporary Roman thought on the philosophy of government, is of special importance. The *otium* of Tityrus is allied to *pax* and *concordia*, and these, in turn, are opposed to *discordia*, rebellion, civil war or any irrational violence which destroys the *status quo*. Cicero's conception of *otium* as peace common to all has recently been defined as "public tranquillity born of undisturbed political order."[39] It is to the opposite of this, to the *discordia* (line 71) which ruins the lives of hapless citizens (the word *civis* is intentionally stressed at the end of 71), that Meliboeus falls victim.

The irony of the use of the word *otium* by Tityrus—especially because it is bestowed by Rome itself—is that, far from being something *commune* as the idealist Cicero would prefer, it is only a personal, private freedom, the inner peace of a dream world. Rome's bounty is an imagined fiction, easily bestowed on one lucky individual. Only in a special context can the slogans be operative, says the poet. At least in the present state of things no general peace is possible. The affliction which Meliboeus endures offers a contrast with this perfection all the more impressive because Meliboeus does not stand for himself alone. He is a symbol of universal ruin, whereas Tityrus symbolizes an individual, exclusive idyll.

Yet the two sides cannot meet in the characters which exemplify them. The poem does not seek to bestow a simple resolution of its many tensions: timelessness versus time, quiet versus motion, peace versus war, happiness versus sadness,

[39] Chaim Wirszubski, "Cicero's *cum dignitate otium*: A Reconsideration," *JRS* 44 (1954): 4. On *otium*, see also E. Bernert, "Otium," *Würz. Jahr. für die Altertumswissenschaft* 4 (1949-50): 89-99. On *pax* and *concordia*, see Syme, *The Roman Revolution*, p. 304; Arnaldo Momigliano, "Camillus and Concord," *CQ* 36 (1942): 111-20, and "The Peace of the *Ara Pacis*," *Jour. War. and Court. Inst.* 5 (1942): 228-31; Stefan Weinstock, "Pax and the 'Ara Pacis,'" *JRS* 50 (1960): 44-58.

stability versus exile, and so on.[40] Rather, its point, which is of deeper import, more thought-provoking and revelatory of the poet's feelings regarding the contemporary civic affairs of Rome, is that the personal, private, secluded *otium* of Tityrus is something which should be universalized and become the property of everyone, whereas here it belongs to just one man. It is deliberate on Virgil's part that Tityrus' conception of *libertas* never gets beyond an equation with freedom from a shepherd's slavery, never beyond the leisure to sing at will. The challenges caused by the absence of that larger liberty, centered on universal, human concerns, as presented in the life of Meliboeus, are never realized by Tityrus.

The *tumultus* which besets the rural world is a reaction in nature to the civil *discordia* which afflicts all contemporary mankind save Tityrus. The irony of such a paradox cannot be dismissed. For Virgil as he writes the first eclogue, true peace does not exist any more than does true liberty. It follows that poetry must suffer accordingly; Virgil himself may write, but it is only to denounce. It becomes clear as the poem progresses that the way Meliboeus uses the word *patria* may give it a more general meaning than the mere acres he once called his own. His *patria* is Virgil's *patria*—Italy and its land. The disease that now afflicts it cannot be cured by the bestowal of freedom on one lucky shepherd. In sum, the *otium* granted by the Roman god means private serenity; world peace appears virtually impossible because of the spirit of civil strife emanating from that most un-pastoral of cities.

Other tensions must also be isolated in visualizing the poet's ideas on *libertas*. This is virtually the first time in Roman poetry that the city, as a focal symbol of certain clearly defined values, enters on the literary scene. For one man, a poet and a dweller in paradise, Rome poses as guardian, but for all

---

[40] For a detailed discussion of what he calls the "principle of contrast" operative in the poem, see Pöschl, *Die Hirtendichtung Virgils*, pp. 71-73.

others, *nos alii*, the challenge of the city over the country, which here also has overtones of society opposing the private individual, cannot be met. Whatever social forces are at work in the city, the pastoral world, the land of flocks and fields and poetic fancy, is at its mercy. The flocks and fields are subject to a soldier's might, while poetic fancy is the plaything of a god's whim.[41] Both sources of power are part of the city, that strange new phenomenon which seems easily to encroach on an old world, which believes in *pietas* even toward the land and relies on methods of divination long antiquated to pick out the intentions of a remote and unconcerned god. Yet no epiphany is granted to Meliboeus: the city controls his destiny through the medium of its emissary.

The complex of Rome with its god and civil war with its terror stands as an incubus over the whole poem. Yet the traditional opposition of city to country, of society to the individual, of progress and history to the timeless realm of poetry and the imagination, are only elements of a grander design which Virgil expressed most fully in the *Aeneid* and which occupied him for the remainder of his life: *libertas* and the double standard of leadership. The tension which mounts throughout the poem begins with a straightforward statement of the present relationship of poetry to reality and grows to suggest a difference between the imaginative world, as represented by one man whose haven is protected by a living god, and the world of brutal reality wherein all others are subjected to a display of force.

In the *Aeneid* virtually the same problem is realized as an examination of the effects of implementing a dictatorial government, however unerring it is envisioned as being in theory.

[41] The problem of progress versus primitivism, city versus country versus nature is of overriding concern during the Augustan period (see above, pp. 9-10). Of the many recent discussions of the same theme I have learned much from M. L. White, *The Intellectual versus the City* (Cambridge, Mass., 1962).

Eclogue I

To maintain that the progress of empire, or the advance of history in any form, can exist without the loss of individual rights is to fancy the impossible. The hero Aeneas, burdened with the allegory of a future ideal Roman state, must himself prove the folly of such a conception as he battles his story to a conclusion, man for man, with the tragic madness of personal vendetta. Every human god is subject to human reactions; paper divinities alone can achieve a perfected form to create, or recreate, a perfect, paper world.

The same double standard of leadership apparently exists in the first eclogue, proposing and disposing with whim and sometimes cruelty. Perhaps as early as the late 40's Virgil recognized the two sides of Rome and, more specifically, the two roles which any revolutionary leader must play in order to survive. He perceived that airy statements condoning attractive escapism carry little weight in the face of social imperatives which produce only human sorrow. Few great poets are seduced by idealism, though they may use it as a mask. The *Aeneid* has its definition of empire mouthed by Jupiter in heaven and Anchises in hell. The first eclogue has its young man-god, oracular and, even more awesome, visible to his devotee. Yet Virgil is careful to show that this *deus* commits no wrong and is never directly associated with mankind's folly. The god can no more be explicitly connected with the horrors of civil war, death and exile, than Tityrus can directly clash with Meliboeus. To have either level meet would spoil the delicate balance the poet has created and lessen his poem's force.

THIS IS NOT an easy poem. There is a mood of crisis about it connected with the revolution taking place in Rome during the decades preceding and following the death of Julius Caesar. As in all periods of social upheaval, the literature reflects a growing tension between ideal and real, between things as the author would wish them to be and life as it actually is.

78

We may think, for instance, of the contrast in early sixteenth-century thought between Thomas More's utopian fancies and the pessimism of Machiavelli and sometimes More himself. It is a major accomplishment of Virgil in the first eclogue to reflect, in one poem, this divergence between Rome as it might be, all-powerful but benign, and the realities of a harsh and gloomy context where traditional values are collapsing and where the realm of the spirit is enslaved, where civil discord destroys the *pietas* men bear the gods, themselves, and their land. It is perhaps an even greater tour de force of poetic refinement and indirection to say so much about what it means to have the two worlds existing side by side.

The poem is a milestone in the history of ancient pastoral poetry and a focal point in Virgil's own development. In terms of style and content it is trailblazing. Theocritus' verse, rich as it is, knows nothing of this machine of political structure suddenly thrust upon a quiet land. It would be an oversimplification—and a disservice to Theocritus' greatness—to say that the difference between the Alexandrian poet and his Roman successor, at least as exemplified in *Eclogue* I, is illustrated by the change from idyllic dream to reality, from pastoral as a self-sufficient imagined retreat from an oversophisticated urban society to pastoral as an emblem of spiritual freedom now become the prey of forces beyond the poet's control. Such generalizations, however, do suggest one inescapable fact: the pastoral, in Virgil's hands, has been turned into a poetry of ideas.

At the end of the fourth georgic, Virgil reviews his past and, quoting part of the first line of *Eclogue* I, states that he once in youthful boldness played at the songs of shepherds (lines 563-66):

> illo Vergilium me tempore dulcis alebat
> Parthenope, studiis florentem ignobilis oti,
> carmina qui lusi pastorum audaxque iuventa,
> Tityre, te patulae cecini sub tegmine fagi.

Eclogue 1

> At that time sweet Parthenope nourished me, Virgil, flourishing, zealous for humble leisure, while I played at the songs of shepherds and, with youthful boldness, sang of you, Tityrus, under the protection of the spreading beech.

Such a statement could be (and has been) taken merely as a suggestion of the difficulties of the "translator's" art. It could imply, as well, that the poet introduced something new and challenging into his inherited poetic tradition.

Perhaps, however, as the quotation implies, the poet's boldness may be specifically related to the thought of *Eclogue* 1 and only through it to the poems which follow. In spite of Tityrus' happy life and protecting divinity and in spite of the enticing detail of his final invitation, the poem as a whole is a design of darkness, the lines of which are drawn with distinct but never bold strokes. This is no pleasant masquerade, with life's problems put aside or elegantly disguised in refined dialogue, but a confrontation between two violently opposed ways of life whose outcome is the life or death of "pastoral."

In terms of "pastoral" as an expanded metaphor for the world of poetry, imagination, *pietas*, love, and freedom, Virgil confronts the problem of evil for the first and not least impressive time in his literary career. Traditionally, pastoral may have had its petty trials—the lovesick shepherd is a familiar figure in Virgil and elsewhere—but never before has it been forced to confront Rome, the kindly god become autocratic government and brutal soldier. Private *otium* yields to universal *discordia*, private *libertas* to universal *servitium*. Suffering is the rule, happiness the exception, and the bucolic life survives only in a protective shell, an admitted ideal, small and secluded, in a real world upon which it is now dependent. Pastoral can no longer assume its dream state; in this poem, at least, it is destroyed as a myth.

The only direct hint of the poet's sympathies is that all the basic elements in the poem save Tityrus' trip are seen through the eyes of Meliboeus, dispossessed and preparing for exile. Tityrus may explain his happiness but he is never allowed by the poet, in spite of his Roman connections, to see beyond his hedge and to express sympathy for Meliboeus' loss. Hence in revealing the tension through the words (though not thoughts) of Meliboeus, Virgil sides with the sufferer, deliberately underscores the callow, sheltered idealism of Tityrus, and allows the reader to see the meaning of the juxtaposition. At the start of his poetic career, Virgil is already master of an allusive strength which beggars final analysis for its forceful combination of emotion and restraint, and has already succeeded in transforming pastoral poetry from a mask for idyllic escape to one for tragedy.

Formosum pastor Corydon ardebat Alexim,
delicias domini; nec quid speraret habebat.
tantum inter densas, umbrosa cacumina, fagos
adsidue veniebat. ibi haec incondita solus
montibus et silvis studio iactabat inani: . . .

The shepherd Corydon burned for handsome Alexis, the
delight of his master. He did not know what to hope for.
He just kept going back again and again to the thick
beeches with their shady tops. There, alone, he hurled
these unformed strains to the mountains and woods with
futile eagerness: . . . (*Eclogue* 2, lines 1-5)

From the deep and universal disorder of the first eclogue we
turn to the restricted, private sphere of a lovesick shepherd.[1]
The juxtaposition of the two poems is purposeful—and a relief—but the change is deceptive. The trouble at first seems
simple because general grief is now limited to the trials which
afflict one man. This much we learn from lines 1 and 2:
Corydon burns for Alexis (*Corydon ardebat Alexim*), but
the flame has not been quenched and does not seem likely to
be in the future (*nec quid speraret habebat*).

Each of these lines, however, also reveals something else.
The plot is announced at the end of the first line where the
gap between the initial adjective and final noun makes the

---

[1] On connections between *Eclogues* 1 and 2, see Büchner, *P. Vergilius
Maro*, col. 170. On the second eclogue, in particular its relationship to
Theocritus, see Antonio La Penna, "La seconda ecloga e la poesia
bucolica di Virgilio," *Maia* 15 (1963): 484-92. On the poem as a whole,
see now E. W. Leach, "Nature and Art in Vergil's Second Eclogue,"
AJP 87 (1966): 427-45.

beauty of Alexis of primary concern. Corydon is verbally "caught" by *formosum Alexim*, though the middle section of the line is reserved for him alone. The sounds of the line are worked out in such a way as to hint at unity between the two protagonists. The "o" sounds (often combined with "r") lead from *formosum* to *pastor* to *Corydon*; and the sound of "a," first appearing in *pastor*, runs, via *ardebat*, to the first syllable of *Alexim*.

Yet suspicions of order through niceties of sound and verbal arrangement are already undercut by the challenge which the first two words present to each other, initiating the tension of the poem. Before the name of either character is mentioned, we have a succinct delineation of each. The one is beautiful, the other is a shepherd. Alexis is charming, the *deliciae* of someone else, symbol of love and the sophisticated (to a shepherd, perhaps hypercivilized) society of city life. Corydon is a shepherd (*pastor*), which is ordinarily no insult in a pastoral poem, but here the *pastor* is juxtaposed with *formosum* suggesting the challenge beauty per se could present to any rustic.

There is, in addition, a more negative side. Alexis is the plaything of the master of Corydon. Corydon, apparently, must pasture the flocks of his owner while the latter (a city dweller, if we may rely on a reference later in the poem) possesses the person Corydon loves. It is hard enough to have to admit that *domini* exist who control the shepherd and his doings, to whom the pastoral world, ideally free, is actually subject. To say that this *dominus* also impinges upon pastoral love is to add another element of uncertainty, leading to suffering and restraint. It also offers evidence of a stability in the outside world that the pastoral world should but does not have, at least for Corydon at the poem's start. Corydon's love is not even an unhappy bucolic love, like that to which one of the shepherds in *Eclogue* 8 falls victim; the beauty he yearns for is outside, under external authority. The irony is

that the same power which governs love governs Corydon as
well. Corydon is its special victim at the moment, but the
land is also subject to this power as Corydon later realizes to
his sorrow.

Within these lines, then, the overarching tension between
happy and unhappy love, between possession and its lack,
embraces subsidiary themes which raise the superficial struggle between city and country into an intellectual dialogue between *rusticitas* and *urbanitas*, rural boorishness and the polish
of civilization. By the poem's conclusion this dialogue forces
the reader to view the two opening words as an oxymoron,
pinpointing two ways of existence which, in this setting at
least, cannot meet.[2] The ideas of the second eclogue are different from the first, and the possible love-death of one shepherd
is perhaps of less moment than universal ruin. But the reader already senses that the battle between two antagonistic societies—where the outer, unpastoral, real world has the power
to control the happiness and values of the supposedly ideal
land—is common to both poems.

Accordingly, Corydon's life is turned upside-down. The
setting of his song presents the essence of pastoral beauty, but
that he comes to the spot again and again (*adsidue veniebat*)
does not augur well, for motion and journey are alien to the
leisure which forms such a vital part of the pastoral retreat.
Ideally the shepherd should be like Tityrus, at his ease, piping
of or to his beloved. Restless activity betokens unfulfilled desire. Still, the setting itself—thick beeches with shady tops—

[2] On *urbanitas*, see E. S. Ramage, "Early Roman Urbanity," *AJP* 81
(1960): 65-72; and "*Urbanitas*: Cicero and Quintilian, A Contrast in
Attitudes," *AJP* 84 (1963): 390-414. In the first article, Ramage shows
that the favorite Roman contrast of city and country may appear as
early as the work of Naevius.

The contrast between *urbanitas* and *rusticitas* is a Catullian commonplace (see Introduction, pp. 7-8) and is of special significance in *Carm.*
22 and 36. There is also an implied contrast here between *deliciae* and
the "rudeness" which *inane* and *inconditum* suggest.

is perfect, abstractly because shade is a *sine qua non* of the idyllic landscape, and specifically because the "darkness" of the shady boughs might be expected to give some assuaging coolness to the burning of Corydon's love.

The landscape seems literal, while love's ardor is metaphysical. The beeches, both real and symbolic at the same time, would bestow escape from the sun's burning heat to the ordinary shepherd; to Corydon they offer a setting for the song which could bring his beloved to him. The shade facilitates song, since setting and poetry should be inseparable to the shepherd. For Corydon, at the moment, they are not, because the unhappiness of his love, as *ardebat* first makes clear, forces his personal stance to be at odds with the landscape. Song may reconstruct the shepherd's world, either by granting him the love he needs or by allowing him to think himself back into a union with the land. Which turn the poem will take we can only guess at this point, but the next lines provide a series of hints.

The song which in his loneliness he sings to the mountains and the forest is formed of a series of *incondita*, ill-conceived things, hurled out *studio inani*, with hopeless eagerness. The latter phrase, especially, seems to have bearing on the uselessness of his words. Yet it is well to note Servius' first definition of *incondita*: "id est incomposita, subito dicta, agrestia" ("that is: unformed, spoken impromptu, boorish"). Virgil is using a familiar word from Cicero for the rhetorically uncouth. A noteworthy instance of the orator's use of the word appears in *Orator* 44. 150: "quamvis enim suaves gravesve sententiae tamen, si inconditis verbis efferuntur, offendent aures, quorum est iudicium superbissimum" ("for though the thoughts are agreeable or weighty, if they are delivered in ill-thought-out words, they will trouble the ears of those whose judgment is the most acute"). Cicero uses *incondita* again at *Brutus* 69. 242, where he speaks of *oppidano quodam et incondito genere dicendi* ("a certain rustic and ill-conceived manner of speaking"); here *oppidanus* implies a contrast with *urbanus*.³ It is not surprising that the same word figures in Quintilian's definition of *urbanitas*: "nam meo quidem iudicio illa est urbanitas, in qua nihil obsonum, nihil agreste, nihil inconditum, nihil peregrinum neque sensu neque verbis neque ore gestuve possit deprendi" ("indeed in my opinion 'urbanity' is that in which nothing inconsonant, nothing rustic, nothing unformed, nothing exotic can be discerned, either in meaning or vocabulary, delivery or gesture").⁴ The word is the opposite of *meditor* as used in the *Eclogues* and in works on rhetoric. When Meliboeus says to Tityrus (in *Eclogue* 1) *silvestrem musam meditaris* or Virgil says of himself (in *Eclogue* 6) *agrestem meditabor Musam*, they are acknowledging the practice and study necessary to write a successful poem. By his use of *incondita*, therefore, Virgil comments not only upon what the shepherd sings but also upon the manner of its delivery.⁵ Corydon will reveal himself the rustic both in content and in rhetorical construction, doubly assuring an unfavorable outcome to his suit.

The phrase *studio inani* has a similarly ambiguous sense. Certainly its foremost meaning must be that paraphrased by Servius: "pro 'nihil sibi procurans contra absentem loquebatur'" ("instead of 'he directed his words toward the absent [Alexis] to no avail for himself'"). The *studium* is Corydon's fruitless passion for Alexis, but the fact remains that both these words frequently appear in technical rhetorical vocabulary as well. *Studium*, in a metaphor for the poet's eagerness in composition, even comes on occasion to mean the poem itself.⁶ More usually it is a synonym for *ars*, to be weighed with

³ See Otto Jahn (ed.) on *Brut.* 69. 242, in Marcus Tullius Cicero *Brutus*, 5th edn. (Berlin, 1908). Cf. also *Orat.* 70. 233; *De Or.* 3. 44. 173.

⁴ Quintilian *Inst.* 6. 3. 107.

⁵ To give *incondita* the meaning "unpremeditated" (as does Otis, *Virgil*, p. 120) is to weaken the rhetorical side of Virgil's phraseology here. We may contrast *incondita* with the appearances of *condere* at *Ecl.* 6. 7 and 10. 50.

⁶ See, e.g., Catullus 68. 26.

ingenium in the discussion of a poem's worth. Horace uses *studium* in this sense at *Ars Poetica*, lines 408-10:

> natura fieret laudabile carmen an arte,
> quaesitum est: ego nec studium sine divite vena
> nec rude quid prosit video ingenium.

The question is whether a poem becomes praiseworthy by nature or design. I myself observe that study is unavailing without a vein of innate richness or wit without training.

Perhaps Corydon's work is meant as an example of that *rude ingenium*, untaught wit, which Horace claims cannot stand alone. Certainly his song lacks that combination of simplicity and unity which the Augustan poet considered vital for success.[7] We also find the word *inanis* in Cicero with the sense of rhetorically "inadequate." It is joined with *inconditum*, for example, at *Orator* 51. 173: "nihilne eis inane videtur, nihil inconditum, nihil curtum, nihil claudicans, nihil redundans?" ("Does nothing seem empty to them, nothing ill-conceived, stunted, lame or overelaborate?").[8]

Hence even before Corydon begins to sing, Virgil announces that the shepherd's song, like the shepherd himself, is to be found wanting. Though taking his stand amid beeches, he addresses his song to the mountains, not to Alexis, who could not be expected to hear him anyway. Moreover, though his song might be his road to success with Alexis, we must not expect of Corydon any of the particularly urbane forms of poetic expression, Catullian lyrics or Propertian elegiacs. Rather, he must be visualized as a rustic shepherd attempting to charm his love in his own uncouth versions of traditional bucolic formulae. Rustic in his person and rude in his wit, he cannot hope to compete for *deliciae*. His song is as much an expression of the failure of poetry as of love's despair. Only poetry

---

[7] On *Ars P.* 409, see C. O. Brink, *Horace on Poetry* (Cambridge, 1963), pp. 255-56; 258.
[8] See also Cicero *Brut.* 8. 34.

perfect enough to charm could perform the impossible feats these lines suggest and create love when it should not exist.

The first segment of these *incondita* lasts but two lines and accents this theme (lines 6-7):

> O crudelis Alexi, nihil mea carmina curas?
> nil nostri miserere? mori me denique cogis?

> O cruel Alexis, do you care nothing for my songs? Do you have no pity on me? Are you compelling me at last to die?

Crudelis, curas, miserere, and *mori* are all standard parts of the unhappy lover's stock-in-trade vocabulary, whether he is working in the elegiac or the pastoral convention.[9] Alexis is cruel. He has no pity on the poor shepherd and hence may force him to commit suicide. At the start Corydon's song already goes in spurts, its disorder the echo of a fevered brain. All the more effective, then, is the position of *mea carmina* in line 6. Alexis is cruel, first and foremost, not so much because he has no pity on Corydon himself but because he has no care—no love, that is—for the shepherd's songs.

The Orphic quality of song to charm is a motif which recurs frequently in the *Eclogues*. Through the magic of his poetry the shepherd had hoped to rouse Alexis' affection for him. It is the one aspect of his life which might have sufficient immediate appeal to bridge the gap between two hostile worlds and turn indifference into love and Corydon, instead of his master, into the *dominus*. Pastoral song is a reflection of one's self; the poet and his verses are one. The spurning of one is the death of the other. Song can, in fact should, create order just as it is a sign of order in itself. If it does not, there seems

---

[9] *Cogo* is curious in this regard. It is very much an elegiac word (in the *Monobiblos* of Propertius alone it appears thirteen times). In the *Eclogues*, with one other exception (6. 31), it is used for the herding of a flock (and the "shepherding" of a poem): see 3. 20, 98; and 6. 85. This, too, would seem part of the power Alexis has over Corydon.

no recourse to the shepherd but to die since his unhappiness
has forced him away from his ordinary duties (that he is *solus*
might imply not only lack of a beloved but also of a flock!)
to sing of his trials to the mountains. He has reached an im-
passe which must lead either to a complete withdrawal from
the land, which is death, or else to a return to the uses of ordered pastoral. The landscape is the man himself and becomes
the focus of one of the poem's chief tensions, that between
loneliness and love, between isolation and the fulfilling presence of beauty.

There is order in nature, order which Corydon fully com-
prehends and against which he must be measured (lines 8-13):

> nunc etiam pecudes umbras et frigora captant;
> nunc viridis etiam occultant spineta lacertos,
> Thestylis et rapido fessis messoribus aestu
> alia serpyllumque herbas contundit olentis.
> at mecum raucis, tua dum vestigia lustro,
> sole sub ardenti resonant arbusta cicadis.

Now even the flocks find shade and coolness. Now the
brakes shelter even the green lizards, and Thestylis concocts pungent herbs of garlic and thyme for the reapers,
tired from the raging heat. But with me, while I scan
your tracks, the bushes echo under the burning sun from
the shrill cicadas.

The first two lines deal with the animal world of flocks and
lizards. In the noonday heat nature follows the prescribed
rationale and resorts to her own remedies. Without shade
and coolness, nothing in the natural world can survive. Not
even the lizards can retain their greenness, the implication is,
unless the brakes grant them protection from the sun's elemental glare. If the creatures in nature which can most readily
stand the sun's force must retreat from it, how much more
violent must be the love which Corydon bears! We recall
Tityrus *lentus in umbra* or, verbally closer still, Meliboeus'

sad words to him that "hic inter flumina nota / et fontis sacros frigus captabis opacum." Tityrus possesses by good fortune what the animals crave by instinct. For a moment Corydon becomes an echo of Meliboeus, forced by suffering out of that regular system which is a necessity of bucolic life and the lack of which spells exile and sometimes death.

The tired reapers also find relief in the salad of herbs which Thestylis mixes. With the human analogy Virgil makes explicit the present difference (emphasized by the anaphora of *nunc etiam*) between Corydon and ordinary life. The reapers have been worn down by exposure to the sun's swirly heat (*rapido aestu*) and can find, in a salad of herbs, the same relief that the cattle discover in the shade. Man and nature conspire to bring order to man as well as beast. But the burning inside Corydon is unlike the sun's heat, and no normal remedy is available. We are drawn beyond the practical aspects of rural life, where, though the sun is hot, nature counteracts it, into the metaphysical world of love which, if unhappy, can easily destroy the shepherd's vital contact with reality. Corydon's spiritual state finds its analogue in the sun itself. The rushing swirl of its heat parallels his continuous coming and going.[10] The animals and the reapers win the battle against nature; Corydon remains at odds with her.

Corydon is so far withdrawn from his normal pursuits that alleviation of his suffering must come not from the literal medicine of shade or salad but only from the spiritual magic of song. He must gauge his poetry to meet the challenge Alexis provides, a challenge both literally and spiritually beyond the trials of the countryside. It is only at the end of his song that Corydon realizes how much easier it is to weave the humble baskets of bucolic song than proclaim verses of elegiac distress, portent of disaster to the shepherd.

[10] On the erotic connotations of *aestus*, see René Pichon, *De sermone amatorio* (Paris, 1902), pp. 81-82. The verbal parallels with Propertius 3. 24. 17-18 are striking.

Exactly how much his present life is disordered the next
lines make clear. Instead of Alexis, Corydon's company is the
screeching cicadas which alone remain active in the noonday
heat. The full potential of the word *mecum* is not felt until
we come upon it again in lines 28 and 31, where the presence
of Alexis is visualized as the prime necessity of the shepherd's
happy reunion with life. Here it is the negative quality of
the word which remains paramount. Corydon is, in fact, *solus*,
his only company being the locusts who are especially fit companions. Restless when nature is at peace, they, too, are singers,
yet *rauci*, as little likely to have a soothing effect on nature as
Corydon's *incondita* are to charm Alexis. At odds with nature and spiritually restive, Corydon is about to lose both rationality and rationale.

The phrase *tua dum vestigia lustro* implies a still broader
concept of disorder.[11] *Adsidue veniebat* reveals only that con-
tinuing motion symptomatic of Corydon's disquiet, whereas
vestigia lustro specifies his role as tracker or hunter. In the
"tracking" sense, *lustro* is the antonym of *captant* at line 8:
the cattle, escaping from the heat, "grasp" and "hold" the
coolness they need. It is the lot of Corydon, on the other hand,
to be always seeking for a completeness which never comes.
The suggestion of violence inherent in a hunting metaphor
should not be dismissed. Though hunting may be a necessity
mentioned several times in the *Eclogues*, it forms no regular part of Virgil's pastoral idyll. The active labor necessary to
obtain life's staples, the destruction of animal life, the wildness of scenery beyond the bounds of shadowed fountain,
and even the notion of search itself are all foreign to the stability on which the pastoral myth relies.

The simile of pursuer and pursued is, to be sure, a common
one in Latin poetry. It is the basic idea of one of Horace's
most charming odes (*Carmina* 1. 23), which begins: "Vitas

[11] With *vestigia lustro*, cf. *Aen.* 12. 467 (Aeneas, searching for Turnus, *vestigat lustrans*).

hinnuleo me similis, Chloe, / quaerenti pavidam montibus aviis / matrem" ("You shun me, Chloe, like a doe, seeking its frightened mother on pathless mountains"). Horace smooths the force of the metaphor by protesting that his role is not to follow her (*persequor*) like a tiger or lion. Rather, it is time for the tables to be reversed, for her to follow him (*sequi*).[12] No such sentiment relieves Corydon's directness here. For a moment he is the hunter or beast, following in the tracks of his prey, and he should therefore appear all the more *rusticus* to Alexis.

The final line which Corydon devotes to describing his setting reinforces these thoughts. *Sole sub ardenti* makes explicit the connection already drawn between the burning of the sun and Corydon's ardor. The phrase also stresses the fact that the *umbrosa cacumina*, especially when taken in conjunction with the *umbras* of line 8, are literal and figurative at the same time. The comfort shade provides the cattle is protection against the heat. For Corydon the beeches provide the setting for song's comfort as well, a double solace against double *ardor*. What remains disturbing is that, even then, the noise which fills the land is not Corydon's song but merely the cicadas' shrill accompaniment to his turmoil.

One of the chief reasons that any shepherd sings to forest and hill is so that the trees can memorize his words and the mountains return a reassuring echo. Meliboeus, we recall, in telling of Tityrus' singing in the shade, attributes to him the almost didactic purpose of teaching the woods to resound "beautiful Amaryllis": "formosam resonare doces Amaryllida silvas." But Tityrus' is a happy love. Corydon's grows sadder still because, far from giving a sympathetic echo, nature provides only the companionship of those creatures whose cry reflects and reiterates his own expression of tortured love, just as the sun is an emblem of its fire. Worse still, nature echoes

[12] For other occurrences of the motif in Horace, see *Carm.* 2. 5. and 3. 11.

not his song but the screeching of the locusts; nature, too, is aware of the folly of Corydon's design, both in purpose and in workmanship.[13]

Nature's, and secondarily Alexis', unsatisfactory reaction forces Corydon to another change of topic; this time it is a further meditation on unhappiness in love (lines 14-18):

> nonne fuit satius tristis Amaryllidis iras
> atque superba pati fastidia? nonne Menalcan,
> quamvis ille niger, quamvis tu candidus esses?
> o formose puer, nimium ne crede colori!
> alba ligustra cadunt, vaccinia nigra leguntur.

Was it not better to endure the bitter wrath and proud disdain of Amaryllis? Was it not better to endure Menalcas, though he is swarthy, though you fair? Beautiful youth, do not trust too much in your bloom. White privets fall, black hyacinths are plucked.

Corydon is reversing, for his own purposes, a theme to be made much of by the Roman elegists: it is better to endure the harshness of love than to attempt an escape. Though suffering is present, the stability of the trials of ordinary love, *pati fastidia*, forms a marked contrast with *vestigia lustro*, for example. For the elegist, unrequited love and infidelity are essential to the poet and poetry. Any thought of retiring from the fray proves less satisfactory than the agony upon which the elegist battens.[14] For Corydon thoughts of enduring the

---

[13] On Corydon and the cicada, see Damon, "Modes of Analogy," p. 293. The singing of the locust or cricket in the heat is, of course, a commonplace. For a modern example, see *The Waste Land*, line 23 (with Eliot's note thereto).

[14] The parallels with Propertius 1. 17. 15 and 2. 25. 11 are instructive. The elegist claims that it is better to bear the harshness of love than to attempt escape from it. The introduction of the elegiac *topos* into *Eclogue* 2 betokens special disorder. Propertius is searching for momentary relief. Corydon is seeking stability, but through search.

On *tristis Amaryllidis iras*, cf. *Ecl.* 3. 80-81. Angry love is as destructive of harmony as a wolf attacking sheep. But, in *Eclogue* 3 at least,

wrath and disdain of Amaryllis are only second best. His life, at least at this moment in his song, seems to demand the search for permanence which in turn necessitates that he look beyond his own purview to make it more perfect.

His words are consoling when looked at from another point of view, for his unhappiness in the relationships he had with Amaryllis and Menalcas was at least within the rural world. Lovers' feuds may still exist in a perfect setting, but there is a difference between the search outside the bounds of "pastoral" which *vestigia lustro* implies in this case and the stability of *pati fastidia*, even though it means endurance and some bitterness. For Corydon the difference is between Menalcas, the rustic love, *niger*, and the brightness of Alexis, *candidus*. The rest of the song will prove that the designation of Menalcas as "black" is perhaps not innocent of irony even here. The shepherd's main point, however, is to remind Alexis that beauty (the word *formosus* is reiterated with a purpose) is not everlasting but a passing thing. Alexis and his particular charm bring not only a special form of love but also the idea of "time" into the pastoral myth. For Corydon, unhappy love shatters the eternal idyll, constraining him to a realization of death. This death is not just the sham of the "elegiac" love-death but the real suicide that lack of alignment between his life and the landscape could cause. At lines 17-18 it is Corydon's turn to warn Alexis of the same thing: that time, the destroyer, threatens him as well. Just as the brightest flowers wither, fall, or are plucked, so beauty fades.[15] Change, in the form of time passing and age, can

---

all of this is within the land and the shepherd in his desire is not going beyond the bounds.

On the relationship of the *Eclogues* to elegy, see C. Fantazzi, "Virgilian Pastoral and Roman Love Poetry," *AJP* 87 (1966): 171-91.

[15] The motif is stock. See A.S.F. Gow (ed.) on *Id.* 7. 120ff in Theocritus *Poems*, 2 vols. (Cambridge, England, 1952). See also *Id.* 10. 28-29; 23. 28ff; 27. 8ff. It is central to several Horatian odes (e.g., *Carm.* 2. 11; 4. 10).

ruin Alexis; change, in the form of sad love, can bring sufficient instability to shatter Corydon's life.

In brief, Corydon is establishing Alexis in the elegiac pattern of *deliciae*, of beauty joined with time, of love possessed
or lost. Although strange and inimical to the pastoral myth,
the passage of time is a common elegiac fancy. For a shepherd to state that he is aware of time could spell disaster were
he to embrace the prospect of change this implies. The idea
of *cadunt*, the flowers' fall, is echoed in the word Virgil gives
Corydon to describe the setting of the sun at the poem's end
(*decedens*, line 67). The full power of the reflection can be
felt only then, but the irony looks back to this moment. The
daily rise and fall of the sun is, to Corydon, an example of apparent "change" in the rural world, but in fact it only typifies
its eternally unchanging pattern. At that point Corydon
realizes with horror that what remains stable in his life is unhappy love, that he is out of the order which is crucial to
his survival. Thus, he reminds Alexis (and perhaps himself,
too) that the conventions of the elegiac stance demand and
thrive on fickle alternation: permanence of any sort is
anathema.

Line 19 brings another complete change of topic and
perspective:

> despectus tibi sum, nec qui sim quaeris, Alexi,
> quam dives pecoris, nivei quam lactis abundans.
> mille meae Siculis errant in montibus agnae,
> lac mihi non aestate novum, non frigore defit.
> canto quae solitus, si quando armenta vocabat,
> Amphion Dircaeus in Actaeo Aracyntho.
> nec sum adeo informis: nuper me in litore vidi,
> cum placidum ventis staret mare. non ego Daphnim
> iudice te metuam, si numquam fallit imago.

I am scorned by you, Alexis. You do not even inquire
who I am, how rich in herds, how wealthy in snow-white

95

milk. A thousand lambs of mine wander on the mountains of Sicily. I lack fresh milk neither in summer nor
in winter. I sing songs such as Amphion of Dirce was wont
on Attic Aracynthus, whenever he called his herds. And
I am not so ugly. The other day I saw myself on the shore
while the sea stood in windless calm. I would not fear
Daphnis, with you as judge, if the mirror never lies.

Now Corydon means to put us in the position of Alexis
looking at him. It is amazing, he suggests, that their roles are
not reversed and that Alexis does not seek him (*quaeris*). The
charms which he offers, part of the enduring bucolic world,
are threefold: possessions, song, and personal beauty. Since
each example has elements of exaggeration bordering on hyperbole, the humorous result is a further epitome of the shepherd's *rusticitas*.

So rich in flocks does Corydon claim to be that a thousand
of his lambs wander on the hillsides of Sicily. A reference to
Sicily, especially as if it were a foreign land, sounds strange
coming from the mouth of a shepherd singing *incondita*.[16]
Moreover such a boast would sound very peculiar indeed
should it happen to reach the ears of the *deliciae domini*. No
sheep, not to speak of Sicilian sheep, distant property of
some aristocratic landowner, belong to this humble shepherd-
slave.

That Corydon is the proud possessor of abundant fresh,
snowy milk at all seasons of the year, even winter and summer, and apparently never has to make cheese against those

---

[16] The reference is oriented to Rome, not to Theocritean Sicily,
though line 19 is, in part, modelled on Theocritus *Id.* 11. 34. The
words *dives* and *meae* suggest possessions of which Theocritus' cyclops
need not boast ("tend" is the word he uses, not "own"). Flocks of
Sicilian sheep are an example of richness for a Roman (see, e.g., Horace
Epode 1. 27-28; *Carm.* 1. 31. 56 and 2. 16. 33ff; *Ep.* 2. 2. 177-78).
The implications of the word *dives* are anti-pastoral. (This is the only
place it appears in the *Eclogues*.) For a moment Corydon imagines
himself the *dominus*, not the *pastor*.

times when the milk might fail[17] is even more magical and improbable than the possession of many flocks. It was one of any ordinary shepherd's constant worries that the seasons might cut off the flow of milk, as we may see from *Eclogue* 3 (lines 98-99) where Menalcas commands

> Cogite ovis, pueri: si lac praeceperit aestus,
> ut nuper, frustra pressabimus ubera palmis.

Pen the sheep, boys. If the heat forestalls the milk, as recently, we will press the udders in vain with our palms.

This threat explains why, when speaking of the golden age which will come about at the birth of the boy in *Eclogue* 4 (lines 21-22), Virgil can say "ipsae lacte domum referent distenta capellae / ubera" ("Of their own accord the goats will bring home udders swollen with milk"). The spontaneity of the goats' return and their ever-bursting udders are both parts of an age of make-believe. Actually life in the rural world was much less ideal. Rustic Corydon's golden age exists only in his imagination.

Corydon's claim to the prowess of an Amphion is just as magical.[18] Here, too, affected learning comes abruptly from the lips of an uncouth swain; the inaccurate position of Mount Aracynthus in Attica only makes matters worse. The point of Corydon's reference is that Amphion is one of the select few in mythology gifted with the ability to move material objects by the power of song: he built the walls of Thebes through the sound of his lyre. And if Amphion's music could charm the stones into bastions, think of how beautiful must have been the songs he sang as he pastured his sheep! Though Corydon here imagines himself into the Orphic tradition, the

[17] See Theocritus *Id.* 11. 36ff.

That Alexis' milk is snowy may be because he is *candidus*, like *alba ligustra*.

[18] On Amphion, see Marie Desport, *L'Incantation Virgilienne* (Bordeaux, 1952), pp. 173-81.

reader cannot help but think back to his initial cry: *nihil mea carmina curas?* Whatever the momentary change of mood, it is obvious that the shepherd's songs do not, in fact cannot, have the effect he desires, no matter what he claims to the contrary.

Finally there is the matter of Corydon's appearance. The phrase *nec sum adeo informis* is meant to be a direct challenge to the *formosus puer,* but in the context of exaggeration already established its use compounds the error. It should make Alexis, as it does the reader, shudder before the picture of Corydon's ugly features, so much does he protest to the contrary. Besides, what is a shepherd of Corydon's inconsequence doing gazing at himself in the sea? What has the sea to do with the life of an ordinary shepherd anyway? This final piece of bravado becomes almost laughable. Not only does Corydon boast of a flock in Sicily, which would indicate great wealth to the average Roman, and of a song powerful enough to move the world around him, he also expects Alexis to see in him beauty surpassing that of Daphnis, the spirit of love upon whom the land depends.

Hence, looking at lines 19-27 through the eyes of Corydon, the rustic shepherd has performed for himself a momentary miracle, special privilege of the poet. He has recreated, if only through the medium of his verse and in his mind's eye, a vision of what constitutes perfection for him: a large flock with ever-flowing milk, the magical voice of Amphion, and a beauty beyond that of Daphnis. And ideal it all would be if Corydon did not undercut his whole picture with the phrase *si numquam fallit imago.* Once more his rhetoric turns in on itself and propounds the opposite of what he intends. Of course the image does deceive, especially Corydon. The *imagines* in his life are not only the literal reflections he sees of himself in the water but also the fictitious depiction of his circumstances and prowess with which he hopes to deceive Alexis, as he does himself. It might be wise for Alexis to think care-

fully about Corydon's admonition *nimium ne crede colori*,
but Corydon himself would do well to ponder the interrelationship of belief, trust, and deceit in his own life. Alexis
might be duped into thinking that beauty can endure. There
is no doubt, however, that Corydon's beauty has little to compare with that of Daphnis and that his songs, far from being
able to fortify Thebes, could not even draw Alexis into the
country.

All this Corydon must have realized since he turns forthwith from dream to reality, from wishful thinking to a more
objective view of his existence (lines 28-35):

> o tantum libeat mecum tibi sordida rura
> atque humilis habitare casas et figere cervos,
> haedorumque gregem viridi compellere hibisco!
> mecum una in silvis imitabere Pana canendo
> (Pan primum calamos cera coniungere pluris
> instituit, Pan curat ovis oviumque magistros),
> nec te paeniteat calamo trivisse labellum:
> haec eadem ut sciret, quid non faciebat Amyntas?

Would that you would only live with me in the dingy
countryside and in lowly cottages, shoot deer and drive
the flocks of kids with green hibiscus. In the woods with
me you will imitate Pan with song (Pan first taught man
to join together many reeds with wax. Pan cares for flocks
and their masters). Nor should it trouble you to rub
your lips against a reed. What did not Amyntas do to
learn these very things?

Corydon now admits that life in the countryside, at least his
life, is different from the idealized portrayal of lines 19-27.
Instead of complementing the brightness of *candidus* Alexis,
the country is really *sordida*, squalid and dreary, as grim as
Alexis, or the privets, or the snowy milk of Corydon's dream
sheep are white. No rich flocks with abundant milk now come

99

before Corydon's more honest eyes, but rather lowly huts and the necessity to live the life of an ordinary serf, hunting and ordering a flock about with an hibiscus rod. To make matters worse (or at best more realistic), Corydon is no Amphion, no shepherd whose music is magic, but only someone who can imitate Pan in the woods, someone whose poetry depends on rehearsing songs already heard.

Nevertheless there is a certain completeness in Corydon's vision of "pastoral" which depends on the influence of Pan and the constant presence of song. The shepherding of one's flock with an hibiscus stave and the singing of poetry are occupations so inseparable as to become interchangeable metaphors, and it is the mythical Pan who presides over both. Poetry is essential to the shepherd's world and when Corydon cries *nihil mea carmina curas* he already prophesies the poem's conclusion. It is Pan, on the other hand, who does care (*curat*) for rustics by teaching song and by keeping a watchful eye on the creators of this song as they go about their tasks. The only thing that keeps Corydon's life from being perfect is the absence of Alexis, who, Corydon hopes, would find pleasure (*libeat*) in the shepherd's ordinary occupations just as he would not disdain (*paeniteat*) playing their necessary accompaniment on the Pan-pipes.

Unity becomes a major theme. First and foremost, of course, it is on the personal level. Corydon appeals to the compound *mecum* twice as he prays for Alexis to become the companion of his shepherding and his song. *Mecum* is one of the usual phrases to express that happy conjunction of disparate elements within the pastoral frame. When Gallus, in the tenth eclogue, prays that his love would lie with him midst willows under a pliant vine (*mecum inter salices lenta sub vite iaceret*), he is only outlining what he considers an ideal vision of the landscape. Tityrus' use of *mecum* at the end of *Eclogue* I (line 79) is much less satisfactory, whatever his intent. Since Corydon's double recourse to *mecum* here is closely

connected with what might come about rather than what
actually is, the reader feels (what Corydon cannot yet admit)
an ironic reference back to his previous use of *mecum* in line
12, where Corydon's real companion is shown to be not Alexis,
but the screeching locusts.

The idea of "unity" persists in the smaller details which
strengthen Corydon's wish. It is with a green shoot—green as
the lizards who hide from the sun at its zenith—that they will
hopefully drive together the flock (*compellere*). It is Pan who
taught the shepherds how to join together (*coniungere*) many
reeds with wax to make the shepherd's pipe. And, as Corydon
again alters his theme in line 36 and turns to the gifts he will
offer Alexis, it is a pipe formed together (*compacta*) out of
seven reeds that he puts first and foremost (lines 36-44):

> est mihi disparibus septem compacta cicutis
> fistula, Damoetas dono mihi quam dedit olim,
> et dixit moriens: 'te nunc habet ista secundum':
> dixit Damoetas, invidit stultus Amyntas.
> praeterea duo nec tuta mihi valle reperti
> capreoli, sparsis etiam nunc pellibus albo;
> bina die siccant ovis ubera: quos tibi servo.
> iam pridem a me illos abducere Thestylis orat;
> et faciet, quoniam sordent tibi munera nostra.

I have a pipe formed of seven reeds of different lengths,
which Damoetas once gave me as a gift. He said as he
died: "You are now its second owner." These were
Damoetas' words, and foolish Amyntas was envious.
Moreover I have two roebucks, happened upon in a dangerous valley, their coats still sprinkled with white. They
drain a ewe's udders twice a day. These I am saving for
you. For a long time Thestylis has been begging to take
them from me, and she will do so, because my gifts appear
unseemly to you.

Again music is the chief inducement which Corydon has to offer: if anything should succeed as a *munus* it is that which produces song, just as the song itself should mesmerize. Like the music of the *fistula*, which is made of seven reeds of uneven length, all music must reconcile opposites. It may even bring Alexis out of the city. Should it succeed, Alexis will immediately become part of a tradition of bucolic song extending from Damoetas to Corydon and then to him.

Tradition in song is another part of the permanent structure of "pastoral." Ironically, it was on his deathbed (*moriens*) that Damoetas had presented the pipe to Corydon as the poet who could take his place. Corydon, on the other hand, presents the pipe as a lover's offering to someone who would condemn him to a love-death. Alexis may own the pipe, but for a different reason from that which gives Corydon his priority of ownership: the use of *habet*, coming after *nec habebat* in line 2, amounts to an acknowledgement of the difference. Here everything is out of joint because of love, and customs of ordinary procedure have broken down. It is the wrong kind of "death" which induces Corydon to present the gift, breaking tradition and suggesting an impossible role for Alexis. If the pastoral Amyntas can have no such aspirations, why Alexis?

The other offering is a pair of roebucks. If the *fistula* followed easily after the mention of Amphion and Pan, the *capreoli* seem the counterpart of the exaggerated and then more rational glimpses Corydon has given the reader into his life. Yet there is a change which makes them unusual. In one sense their mention breaks the ordinarily idyllic spell of bucolic song because, in spite of *figere cervos* (line 29), hunting is not only a part of the "practical" world, which regularly goes unmentioned, but unpastoral in itself. It involves things beyond the bounds of the shepherd's life, the other extreme from the city, as it were, typifying a ruggedness which is not a part of the shepherd's quiet life. For this reason

Corydon adds that they were found *nec tuta valle*, in a treacherous, out of the way vale. They have, however, been successfully caught and kept as an inducement to Alexis. Thestylis envies them, as Amyntas does the pipes. They are things of wonder to shepherds, yet, within any realistic view of pastoral, a possible but special gift.[19]

Just as hyperbole and more reasoned prayers for companionship are failures, so are the *munera*, as Corydon well knows. Just as the countryside is *sordida*, so the presents that the countryman offers *sordent*. They appear dull and dirty to the pampered eyes of the city dweller. Once more, the idealism of a lover's hopes gives way before a realistic appraisal of the possibilities. No more than his songs can his *munera* be expected to reconcile such antagonistic ways of life.

Yet even now Corydon does not relent or despair (lines 45-55):

huc ades, o formose puer: tibi lilia plenis
ecce ferunt Nymphae calathis; tibi candida Nais,
pallentis violas et summa papavera carpens,
narcissum et florem iungit bene olentis anethi;
tum casia atque aliis intexens suavibus herbis
mollia luteola pingit vaccinia calta.
ipse ego cana legam tenera lanugine mala
castaneasque nuces, mea quas Amaryllis amabat.
addam cerea pruna (honos erit huic quoque pomo);
et vos, o lauri, carpam, et te, proxima myrte:
sic positae quoniam suavis miscetis odores.

Come hither, beautiful youth. See, for you the Nymphs bring baskets filled with lilies. For you the fair naiad, plucking pale violets and the heads of poppies, joins narcissus with the blossom of sweet-smelling fennel. Then, interweaving cassia and other sweet herbs, she paints the delicate hyacinth with yellow marigold. I myself will

19 On the special beauty of the roebuck, see Columella 9. 1. 1.

gather quinces, white with soft down, and chestnuts,
which my Amaryllis loved. Waxen plums I will add
(honor will be given to this fruit, too). You also, laurels,
I will pluck, and you, neighboring myrtle. Set thus you
blend your sweet perfumes.

Rather, he begins anew with the phrase *huc ades* which, along
with *mecum*, regularly introduces an invitation to the pastoral life. This invitation is comparable to that at the beginning
of Moeris' song in *Eclogue* 9, line 39: " 'huc ades, o Galatea;
quis est nam ludus in undis?' " (" 'Come hither, Galatea; for
what sport is there in the waves?' "). Alexis is a type of
Galatea, living in a world distinct from, even hostile to, the
shepherd's and yet necessary for it—in one person's eyes. Now
at last Corydon turns to reasons for a link both real and imaginative between Alexis and "pastoral," namely his beauty. In
line 17, where the phrase *o formose puer* occurs for the first
time, Corydon visualizes Alexis' charm first in terms of color
and then in terms of a flower that represents that color. Flowers also form the first offerings in his final invitation.

The epiphany of the nymphs and the naiad, announced by
ecce, is particularly graceful. The nymphs bring in person
what the earth pours forth of its own accord for another *puer*
in *Eclogue* 4. There the spirit of beauty is already present in the
land, and the *munuscula* that the land offers are one of several spontaneous gestures of affection. But flowers, mentioned in passing in the fourth eclogue, become the center of
attraction here: the lilies, violets, poppies, and so on, are all
emblems of love. They are intended to appeal to Alexis as a
reflection of himself in Corydon's world.[20] This is why the
nymphs carry lilies in their baskets and why the naiad, who
brings the rest, is *candida*, like *candidus* Alexis. The new con-

[20] On flowers and the ideal landscape, see, e.g., Propertius 1. 20. 37-38;
3. 13. 28ff; Tibullus 1. 3. 61-62; *Copa* 13-16; Columella 10. 99ff. The
latter two passages have much in common with *Eclogue* 2.

text is also the reason why, when *vaccinia* reappear at line 50, they have no association with time's passing, as at line 18, but become simply *mollia*, another link of Alexis' beauty with the aspects of the pastoral world which Corydon imagines might be charming to him. The recollection of *herbas olentis* (line 11) in *olentis anethi* (line 48) and *aliis herbis* (line 49) serves a parallel purpose. Corydon can now unite himself and Alexis by means of the ordinary beauty of the rural scene, perhaps specifically by means of those herbs which refresh the reapers after their labors.

Underlying the main theme is still the idea of unity. Most things seem to go in pairs, the nymphs and the naiad, the violet and the poppy, narcissus and fennel, cassia and other herbs, hyacinth and marigold. Verbally *intexens* balances *carpens*, and *pingit, iungit*. The essential point is not just the gifts themselves, but their union. The naiad joins together (*iungit*) narcissus and fennel and interweaves (*intexens*) the cassia with other herbs, as Pan had taught the shepherd to join (*coniungere*) many sticks into a pipe. Nevertheless, though these new herbs are meant to give "relief" to Corydon's love by charming Alexis, they, too, are doomed to failure.

With *ipse* at line 51 we are introduced to Corydon and his special gifts, as if he were one of the mythical, semidivine nymphs, part of spontaneous nature, making offerings to some new god. Though his catalogue has a slightly more practical, georgic hue than that of the nymphs and seems to come from a world where cultivation is a requirement, nevertheless the same themes run through his words. White (*cana*) is the first color to be mentioned, and there is a tendency to stress the softness and tenderness of nature at her most alluring. Again things go in pairs: plums are joined with nuts, laurels with myrtles.

It is curious that both *poma* and *castaneae* form part of the list of attractions which Tityrus puts before the departing Meliboeus, at the end of the previous eclogue, as an inducement to remain one more night. But Corydon's final gift is more symbolic still. He joins together the laurel of Apollo with Venus' myrtle, poetry with love, a union which would come about in his life if the pastoral world of Pan-pipes and shepherds' songs were to become attractive to Alexis.[21] It is for the blending of poetry with love as much as for any conjunction of flowers and herbs, fruits and nuts, that he expresses the hope in line 55.

Once masks are off, however, he does not possess (or indeed think he possesses) that idealized side of the myth which is always assumed, along with nymphs for playthings and gift-bringers. He is fooling himself with this, his finest dream so far, but at line 56 he takes us summarily back into the world of reality and contradicts all the *incondita* he has been uttering since line 19:

> rusticus es, Corydon; nec munera curat Alexis,
> nec, si muneribus certes, concedat Iollas.

Boorish you are, Corydon. Alexis does not care for your gifts. Nor, were you to vie with gifts, would Iollas yield.

Corydon is, of course, *rusticus* in several senses, all implied in the poem before this: he inhabits *sordida rura*. But merely the fact that he applies such an adjective to what is regularly deemed perfect proves that he is looking at the bucolic world more often than not from the vantage point of Alexis. What should seem to him to be without blemish is ruined because it cannot for the moment be made complete. As the visions of idealism pass, the countryside becomes ordinary when Corydon juxtaposes himself with Alexis, the rustic boor with the urbane sophisticate who cares for a shepherd's gifts (*munera curat*) as little as he is pleased by his songs (*carmina curas,* line 6). In Alexis' eyes, as Corydon imagines himself, he is rustic both physically—because of his person,

[21] On laurels and myrtles together, see *Ecl.* 7. 61-64.

his surroundings, and his gifts—and spiritually—because his songs deal with rustic topics and are delivered in a manner as inane as it is inept.

Again at line 58 there is a change of theme:

> heu heu, quid volui misero mihi? floribus Austrum
> perditus et liquidis immisi fontibus apros.

> Alas, alas, what have I asked for, in my pitiable state? Madman, I have let in the south wind to my flowers, wild boars to my clear fountains.

This time Corydon emits a cry of woe as Alexis now appears, from another angle, the bane of the landscape. The words Corydon applies to himself (*miser, perditus*) are "elegiac." He is dying of love, but by finally equating himself with the essence of pastoral beauty, its flowers and fountains, he sees in his collapse the ruin of life around him as well. This paradise of flowers belongs to Corydon, not Alexis who, quite the contrary from any light in which we have seen him before, has thoroughly upset Corydon's vision of himself. By putting him out of step with life he has forced Corydon to view it in a more realistic light or, at very best, from an unpastoral perspective. Corydon may offer flowers to Alexis as a symbol of the landscape's beauty, but the previous analogies between Alexis and flowers are now seen by Corydon as patently false. Alexis' flowers will fade; the flowers of pastoral are permanent, capable of being ruined only by the interruption of destructive madness.

Fontibus reminds the reader of the shade (*umbras*) and coolness (*frigora*) of line 8 and is the equivalent of the *frigus opacum* of *Eclogue* 1, with its streams and sacred founts. At line 8, Corydon has no share in the coolness the cattle possess. By line 59 he realizes that these fountains are his but that by his folly he is spoiling his relationship with them. Alexis and the world he represents are fraught with menace for Corydon's preserve. Alexis is the spiritual equivalent of the dark, rainy south wind or a boar—both emblems of nature's wildness encroaching on the shepherd's retreat. Again the levels of meaning are both physical and metaphysical. The streams and flowers are as real as the poet and his love, but they are also, on another level, products of the mind itself. As Lycidas says of the absent poet Menalcas and his songs at lines 19-20 of *Eclogue* 9: "quis caneret Nymphas? quis humum florentibus herbis / spargeret aut viridi fontis induceret umbra?" ("Who would sing the Nymphs? Who would strew the ground with flowery grasses or cover the fountains with green shade?"). The pastoral myth remains a living thing in the imagination because the poet-shepherd, necessary for its survival, is still alive. We have a clear example here, realized in the simple terms of a personal drama between two people, of how easily the shepherd's paradise is antagonized and destroyed. Writ large, it can be seen, as in the preceding poem, as the challenge of Rome to the imaginative life. Here love alone could be the shepherd's undoing.

Even now Alexis is not forgotten (lines 60-65):

> quem fugis, a, demens? habitarunt di quoque silvas
> Dardaniusque Paris. Pallas quas condidit arces
> ipsa colat; nobis placeant ante omnia silvae.
> torva leaena lupum sequitur, lupus ipse capellam,
> florentem cytisum sequitur lasciva capella,
> te Corydon, o Alexi: trahit sua quemque voluptas.

Whom are you fleeing, madman? Even the gods and Trojan Paris have dwelt in the woods. Let Athena herself live in the cities she has built. Let the woods be my delight before all else. The fierce lioness follows the wolf, the wolf himself the goat, the wanton goat the flowering clover. Corydon follows you, Alexis. His desire draws each along.

Again Corydon uses a series of *incondita*, picking up, first, the hint of line 12, *tua dum vestigia lustro*. Corydon considers Alexis mad because he flees, not because he is in love. The word *quem* itself is strange: like *nec qui sim quaeris, Alexi* (line 19), it suggests that Alexis does not know his pursuer and would not flee if he possessed fuller knowledge. The irony in the lines is that Alexis' existence is stable, Corydon's in a state of turmoil. Corydon emphasizes, by the repetition of *silva* in lines 60 and 62, that his life must be passed in the woods, which please him above all else and have ever served as the dwelling places of the gods. The compliment to Alexis is strong: he is like a god and would add a further divinity to the pastoral pantheon. But Corydon gives away the true situation in lines 61-62: "Pallas quas condidit arces / ipsa colat." Alexis lives securely in one of those very cities which Corydon urges he leave to their founding goddess to cherish. There is slim likelihood, whatever form his pursuer may take, that Alexis would relinquish his urban life for a sylvan retreat, even though it pleased a Paris or a Corydon.[22]

Corydon proceeds to elaborate the image of line 60 and to mitigate its force. The sequence is amazing and beautiful. Beginning with the idea of violence, Corydon once more draws an analogy between himself and a hunter, this time not in the limited sense of shooting stags or capturing roebucks but in the sense of searching, both literally and spiritually, to "capture" his Alexis. This could be taken, as indeed *vestigia lustro* itself warrants, to imply reliance on brute strength, like a lion following a wolf. But the lion, whose ferocity is unimaginable within the confines of "pastoral," gives way, in the shepherd's analogies, to the wolf, the equivalent of the potential harm that untamed nature might wreak upon the pastoral world. The wolf, in turn, yields to the goat, the symbol of the

[22] The grander tension between city and country, which we find so frequently in the *Eclogues*, is here limited to the personal lives of Corydon and Alexis, but the overtones must not be dismissed.

bucolic life itself, cropping the clover with equanimity, all thoughts of violence absent.

Corydon is no lion. In fact the possibility of gentle love between himself and Alexis is renewed with the use of these images of ordinary procedure and unity: Corydon as the goat and Alexis as his clover are indispensable to each other. The goat is *lasciva* as Corydon is eager for Alexis. For the last time the latter is connected with flowers in a final, fruitless analogy with the landscape's beauty. Then, at the end of line 65, even the pursuit is blamed on Alexis. There is no violence now, only a pathetic last reference to two things so unlike as to make the whole idea of hunting and search necessary.[23]

Suddenly Corydon looks at his situation again (lines 66-73):

> aspice, aratra iugo referunt suspensa iuvenci,
> et sol crescentis decedens duplicat umbras:
> me tamen urit amor: quis enim modus adsit amori?
> a, Corydon, Corydon, quae te dementia cepit!
> semiputata tibi frondosa vitis in ulmo est:
> quin tu aliquid saltem potius, quorum indiget usus,
> viminibus mollique paras detexere iunco?
> invenies alium, si te hic fastidit, Alexim.

See, the bullocks drag home the ploughs, hanging from the yoke, and the setting sun doubles the growing shadows. But love still burns me. For what bound is set to love? O Corydon, Corydon, what madness has seized you? Your vine is half pruned on the leafy elm. Why not at least start to plait something which need demands, from twigs and pliant reed? You will find another Alexis, if this one scorns you.

[23] Virgil's model for these lines is Theocritus *Id.* 10. 30-31, but his analogies grow in intensity and are therefore more exciting.
The phrase *florentem cytisum* is used in the far more serious ending of the preceding poem (1. 78).

Time has moved on apace: far from the heat of the noonday sun, whence the laborers were escaping, we now find ourselves at sunset with the bullocks returning home from the fields. Rural life has continued with its regular order, and the preoccupied Corydon now observes that he has been no part of it. *Aspice*, he cries, marvelling at the rational existence which is really his own. Ironically, in spite of his lack of alignment with nature, he has hitherto found the symbol for his love in the heat of the sun. Though songs might hopefully provide metaphorical *umbrosa cacumina*, a certain spiritual respite, he burns (*ardebat*) in line 1 and confesses to singing *sole sub ardenti* in line 13. With the setting of the sun, therefore, and the doubling of the evening shadows, with nature herself now literally offering shade, we would expect that relief for suffering would also be doubled. The opposite still seems the case: *me tamen urit amor*. Love's fire continues even at nightfall. Corydon's association with the sun has proved false because there is no *modus* to love as there is to the sun's heat or to the processes of bucolic life. *Modus* alone can restrain that which presupposes madness and can define that type of love (to which Corydon must ultimately have recourse) which will keep the pastoral world from being destroyed or, to put it another way, prevent human beings from becoming victims of their emotions.[24] Corydon, however, still has no rationale. Man and nature, image and reality, are still at odds.

This makes the irony of his cry *quae te dementia cepit* all the stronger.[25] Alexis is *demens* because he does not follow Corydon. Corydon, on the other hand, is seized by *dementia* because love is a madness which has conquered him rather than he love. With *cepit* we may compare line 8. Even in the midday heat the flocks find shade and coolness (*pecudes*

[24] On *modus* in this sense, contrast the elegiac definition at such places as *Ecl.* 10. 28 and Propertius 2. 15. 30.

[25] For the phrase, see *Ecl.* 6. 47 and *G.* 4. 488.

umbras et frigora captant): the cattle "grasp" what they want. *Dementia cepit* reverses everything. The poet-shepherd, in spite of his role as hunter, is the one caught. And it is not his love who "seizes" him but only further *dementia*, the unreason and lack of proportion which are the lover's lot and which can destroy a shepherd unless he manages to return to pastoral harmony.

This Corydon now claims to do by turning his thoughts to vines that need pruning and to many other matters, such as the weaving of baskets, which need his attention. The metaphors, however, serve a double purpose. Take the vine and the elm, for instance: together they furnish one of the stock pastoral examples of unity. It is a union, however, which depends for its security on the constant care of the husband-man. Catullus speaks of the vine linked to the marrying elm (*ulmo coniuncta marito*), and Virgil himself mentions a soil which wreathes elms with flourishing vines (*laetis intexet vitibus ulmos*).[26] This should be an emblem of Corydon's union with "pastoral." Instead the vine is *semiputata*, half-trimmed, just as Corydon's own relationship with his world is uncared for and incomplete.

The word *semiputata* also has the secondary implication of "half considered" and seems in this sense to balance *incondita* in line 4. Corydon has been hurling his nonsense to the mountains in a vain attempt to gain a completeness which ultimately could only prove disruptive. Neither elegiac love nor *urbanitas,* in the sense ascribed to Alexis, has any place in the countryside. What really mattered in Corydon's life, pastoral practice, which is here a metaphor for poetry and its composition, lies neglected.

There is another point of balance between the poem's opening lines and its conclusion. The previously noted ambiguity of the phrase *studio inani* in line 5, when taken in con-

[26] See C. J. Fordyce (*Catullus: A Commentary* [Oxford, 1961]), on Catullus 62. 49.

junction with the word *usus*, is at least partially resolved. This is the only place in the *Eclogues* where *studium* and *usus* appear, although, as might be expected, they are quite common in a didactic treatise such as the *Georgics*. They are together, for instance, at *Georgic* 3, line 163, where Virgil speaks of cattle to be raised for the pursuits and needs of the farm: "*ad studium atque usum . . . agrestem*." The empty purpose of the opening lines—empty, that is, in terms of the shepherd's true vocation—finally leads to a realization that *usus*, country customs and pursuits, are of greater value than a destructive love. The zeal expended on fruitless song, ill-aimed and ill-conceived (*incondita*), could better be turned to higher purposes, either poetic or practical.

The ambiguity which *semiputata* raises between pastoral usage and poetic display is furthered by line 72, especially by the word *detexere*, which means, literally, to finish off by weaving (and hence contrasts with both *incondita* and *semiputata*). It can also be synonymous for "write," usually defining the completion of a work, whether prose or verse.[27] In this double sense, the weaving metaphor in *detexere* parallels the image of spinning in the phrase *carmen deductum* which Virgil uses in the sixth eclogue to compare the style of his song with the thin line of thread finely drawn from a heavy mass of wool. The equation between poetry and a shepherd's menial occupations becomes most explicit at the end of the final eclogue (lines 70-71): "haec sat erit, divae, vestrum cecinisse poetam, / dum sedet et gracili fiscellam texit hibisco" ("This will be enough for your poet to have sung, goddesses, while he sits and weaves a basket from slim hibiscus"). The "slender hibiscus" with which the poet "weaves" his song is parallel both to the literal *viridi hibisco* (*Eclogue* 2, line 30), used to round up the kids, and to the *tenui harundine*, on which the

[27] *Thesaurus Linguae Latinae* defines the metaphorical meaning as "verbis, scripto, versu exponere, pertractare." It is used in this sense by Cicero at *De. Or.* 2. 38. 158. Cf. *Ad Her.* 2. 27. 42.

poet in the sixth eclogue (line 8) plays his fine-spun lay. Both meanings are suggested by the objects with which Corydon begins to weave: *viminibus mollique iunco*. With the realization that something in his life can be woven together to completion, he begins his return to harmony with nature and embraces anew the land's simplicity.

It is bucolic poetry, not elegiac verse, that belongs to the shepherd and is compatible with his surroundings and character. For him to ponder anything else would necessarily mark the creation of the *incondita* which come from the mouth of Corydon, not the *meditata* of song truly conceived. Corydon's song has finally worked its magic—this is, after all, a poem about the power of song—not to unite him with what would prove destructive but gradually to bring him back to an understanding of where his happiness must lie.

Hence the shadows, falling as the sun sets, do prove to be calming and creative. They betoken not only the end of suffering but also a return to "pastoral" after dallying with an alien sphere that might have proven the shepherd's undoing. Unlike the conclusion of *Eclogue* 1 where the question was that of the destruction of the entire pastoral world, here the question concerns only one of that world's denizens. Nevertheless, the mere mention of *crescentis umbras* takes the reader's attention back to *maiores umbrae*, the final detail in the first eclogue. This inevitably suggests some reasons for the juxtaposition of the two poems.

Each depends closely on the challenge that hostile forces present for the pastoral myth, and one level of each poem suggests reconciliation. In each, pastoral poetry, which regularly passes as a poetry of innocence or assumed ignorance, is intellectualized by Virgil and becomes a vehicle of experience. Nature becomes a metaphor for the spiritual state of the poet. Inevitably, the continuity of "pastoral" is opposed, be it by history and its makers, as in the first eclogue, or by unhappy love and involvement with society, as here. In the one, disorder triumphs over *otium*, in the other the rationale of the shepherd's existence, demanding order and assuming permanence, is victorious. Like its predecessor, *Eclogue* 2 is also an invitation, but this time it is the enemy who is invited into the pastoral world. Alexis is no *impius miles*, but spiritually he is equally destructive. Corydon lives as part of the landscape which Tityrus offers momentarily to Meliboeus. There are no restrictions, no political overtones, no external power threatening ruin; yet he lacks the happy love which, for most of *Eclogue* 2, he considers can only come to him through Alexis. Though happy love brings order, the question remains what form this love should take.

Alexis, *formosus* though he be, is in no sense equivalent to Tityrus' *formosa Amaryllis*, a love to be sung to by a shepherd at ease under a spreading beech. His is a divisive influence: it puts Corydon's life and song out of step with the regimen of his life and the sun on which it depends, whereas "pastoral" man and his surroundings, setting and song are united. Alexis' influence makes Corydon imagine that what is actually fraught with danger brings perfection. As a result Corydon sees a split between ideal and real which should not exist in "pastoral," and he misinterprets both. The ideal becomes an urbane, sophisticated society harboring Alexis and elegiac, not pastoral, love. The true landscape is falsely envisioned as *sordida rura* while the singer becomes an emblem of *rusticitas*. All is turned upside down. Corydon, when he should be searching for beauty which would remain as timeless as the countryside, is actually in pursuit of love as temporary as it might prove fickle.

Hence "search" is a basic motif of the poem which is a study in realignment, in the reintegration of the shepherd with his surroundings. Hunting, both literal and figurative, is accordingly one of the poem's essential images. Here it is perilous and takes the shepherd out of his territory into a realm of violence and danger; it demands an unpastoral context of motion and activity, symptomatic of Corydon's own instability. When the shepherd craves the "capture" and taming of something outside his territory, he yearns for an impossible ideal. The search is for love within part of a dream world which is both attractive and true, but tensions and inconsistencies in Corydon's own sketch are evident when he attempts to envision a pastoral world which is both honest to himself and charming to Alexis. The search is also for a song that expresses this vision and hypnotizes as well. At first the answer seems Alexis and a magical reconciliation of *urbanitas* and *rusticitas* through the power of song, but it is evident from the first few lines that boorish song, *incondita* sung with empty eagerness, will not have any effect over *deliciae*. Although the search could lead Corydon away from the land and inflict upon him the same love-death suffered by one of the shepherds in the eighth eclogue, it does not. The order, permanence, and ritual stability of a life passed in harmony with nature are fortunately regained; Corydon, after a confrontation with "society," is restored from a false vision to his pastoral dream.

BEFORE TURNING to the third eclogue, one other question, much discussed but needing re-examination, must be raised: namely, the influence of Theocritus on the Corydon eclogue.[28] For his principal model, if such it can be styled, Virgil turned to the eleventh idyl of Theocritus, which mainly consists of Polyphemus' love song to the sea-nymph Galatea. The borrowings, remarkable for their change in tone from Theocritus, add another level of sophistication and wit to Virgil's poem because they attribute to a rustic shepherd, an untutored follower of Pan and practitioner of a conventionally oral art, knowledge of literary traditions which could only be encompassed by the author himself.[29] The second eclogue attains a

[28] See n. 1 above and *Intro.* n. 6.
[29] On this ironic contrast (which is really that between Corydon as the voice of a rustic shepherd and Corydon as the mask for a thor-

depth of wit unplumbed by Theocritus: Corydon is virtually allowed to parody himself. Corydon is also allowed a level of artistry quite foreign to Theocritus' Polyphemus: in addition to documenting the power of song and the trials of love, Virgil's lover's song also deals with the style, content, and declamation of poetry.

Let me offer as an example of the difference between the two poets the description of Corydon's defense of himself against the charge of being ugly (*nec sum adeo informis*, line 25). He is echoing the voice of Polyphemus, this time from *Idyl* 6, lines 34-38:

καὶ γάρ θην οὐδ᾽ εἶδος ἔχω κακὸν ὥς με λέγοντι.
ἦ γὰρ πρᾶν ἐς πόντον ἐσέβλεπον, ἦς δὲ γαλάνα,
καὶ καλὰ μὲν τὰ γένεια, καλὰ δέ μευ ἁ μία κώρα,
ὡς παρ᾽ ἐμὶν κέκριται, κατεφαίνετο, τῶν δέ τ᾽ ὀδόντων
λευκοτέραν αὐγὰν Παρίας ὑπέφαινε λίθοιο.

For truly I am not even ill-favored, as they say; for of late I looked into the sea, and there was a calm, and fair, as my judgment goes, showed my beard, and my one eye, and it reflected the gleam of my teeth whiter than Parian marble.

As Corydon summarizes it (and the words are not in Theocritus), he would surpass Daphnis himself in beauty, *si numquam fallit imago*. The "image" which Corydon sees and hopes Alexis will see is quite different from what Alexis would actually see, were he to look. It might also appear strange to Polyphemus or Galatea, since Corydon's is a world different from Alexis' on the one hand and Theocritus' on the other. Yet, with the poet's help, Corydon is playing a joke on himself. Merely by imitating Polyphemus' gesture he displays his physical kinship and conveys to the attentive reader

---

oughly cultivated poet), see Ovid's use of line 52 at *Ars Am.* 2. 267-68 (and cf. 3. 183).

the idea of a common ugliness when it is least wanted. What pampered *deliciae* is going to crave association with a rustic clod, especially one who, wittingly or not, claims intellectual and physical kinship with a gigantic, one-eyed cyclops? Yet by singing variations on Theocritean themes in the course of supposed *incondita*, Corydon is manifestly as urbane as any neoteric poet, the more so for suffering the guise of a shepherd!

Another dissimilarity is evident when one contrasts the love-song of Polyphemus in *Idyl* 11 with Corydon's lament: it is ultimately the enormous divergence in tone which strikes the reader. Superficially this is conveyed by the difference between the endings of each poem, between Theocritus' boundless *joie de vivre* and Virgil's melancholy. Even the opening of each betrays the conclusion. Polyphemus is perched on a high rock looking out to sea, talking directly to where he hopes Galatea can at least listen. Corydon stands among thick beeches and addresses his complaint to the woods and mountains, the opposite direction from where Alexis lives; the extreme geographical tension of the poem, between the city and the mountains, is partially emblematic of the turmoil confronting Corydon himself. Corydon's position implies not so much hope of success as hope of escape to wilder territory, either simply to seek relief from the passing trials of love or to search for some more enduring catharsis. Even at the start Corydon's happiness is not part of the poet's intention.

Taken as a whole, Theocritus is warm and sometimes playful whereas Virgil, even in his wit, seems to maintain a level of thought which often borders on the highly serious. By the end of *Idyl* 11 the reader has been so charmed by Polyphemus' character and verses that he knows his prayer will have a purgative effect. All through his song, the cyclops thinks of Galatea purely in pastoral terms—curds, lambs, calves, ripening grapes, all are Galatea to him. Her love would be decorative but disastrous to his world, just as Alexis' presence would ruin

Corydon. At the end of *Eclogue* 2 it is almost with a sense of relief that the reader accepts Corydon's proposition that he return to the ways of the shepherd. The suffering Corydon struggles between two *modi vivendi* which cannot meet. For the poet to suggest that they might would be to play Corydon—and the reader—false.

AT THE END of the second eclogue we have returned, with Corydon, to the bucolic life. Its problems are the chief concern of the banter between Menalcas and Damoetas with which the third eclogue opens (lines 1-29):

M. Dic mihi, Damoeta, cuium pecus? an Meliboei?

D. Non, verum Aegonis; nuper mihi tradidit Aegon.

M. Infelix o semper, oves, pecus! ipse Neaeram
    dum fovet ac ne me sibi praeferat illa veretur,
    hic alienus ovis custos bis mulget in hora,
    et sucus pecori et lac subducitur agnis.

D. Parcius ista viris tamen obicienda memento.
    novimus et qui te transversa tuentibus hircis
    et quo—sed faciles Nymphae risere—sacello.

M. Tum, credo, cum me arbustum videre Miconis
    atque mala vitis incidere falce novellas.

D. Aut hic ad veteres fagos cum Daphnidis arcum
    fregisti et calamos: quae tu, perverse Menalca,
    et cum vidisti puero donata, dolebas,
    et si non aliqua nocuisses, mortuus esses.

M. Quid domini faciant, audent cum talia fures?
    non ego te vidi Damonis, pessime, caprum
    excipere insidiis multum latrante Lycisca?
    et cum clamarem 'quo nunc se proripit ille?
    Tityre, coge pecus,' tu post carecta latebas.

D. An mihi cantando victus non redderet ille,
    quem mea carminibus meruisset fistula caprum?
    si nescis, meus ille caper fuit; et mihi Damon
    ipse fatebatur; sed reddere posse negabat.

M. Cantando tu illum? aut umquam tibi fistula cera
iuncta fuit? non tu in triviis, indocte, solebas
stridenti miserum stipula disperdere carmen?

D. Vis ergo inter nos quid possit uterque vicissim
experiamur?. . .

M. Tell me, Damoetas, whose flock is that? Is it Meliboeus'?

D. No. It's Aegon's. Aegon gave it to me the other day.

M. Poor sheep, a flock always ill-starred! While he courts
Neaera and fears lest she prefer me to him, this foreign
keeper milks the sheep twice an hour, and strength is
taken from the flock and milk from the lambs.

D. Yet be careful to hurl such insults more sparingly at
people. We know who was with you as the goats looked
aside, and in what grot (but the easy Nymphs laughed).

M. The day, I trust, when they saw me fall upon Micon's
orchard and young vines with a wicked knife.

D. Or here at the old beeches, where you, spiteful Menalcas,
broke the arrows and bow of Daphnis—you were mad
when you saw them given to the boy and would have
died if you could not do him some harm.

M. What can masters do when their knaves are so daring?
Did I not see you, scoundrel, ensnare Damon's goat,
while Lycisca barked and barked? And when I shouted
"Where's he off to now? Tityrus, pen the flock," you
lurked behind the sedge.

D. When he was beaten in a singing contest, was he not to
give me a goat which my pipe had deserved because
of its songs? If you do not know it, that goat was mine,
and Damon himself said as much to me, but he claimed
he was unable to pay.

M. You beat him in song? Did you ever own a pipe with
reeds joined by wax? Was it not you, dolt, who, at the
crossroads, used to murder a poor song on shrieking
straw?

D. Well, would you like to try, ourselves in turn, what each
can do?

This is apparently good-natured joking, patterned in some
measure upon the interchange of Theocritus' fourth and fifth
idyls. Yet behind this apparent series of superficial witticisms
is the more serious suggestion that what could be the happy
world of pastoral might be destroyed by the irrationality
of the shepherds themselves. The word *tradidit* introduces the
first example. To Damoetas, as he answers Menalcas' initial
inquiry, the word means simply "entrust" or "confide."
Menalcas' response draws a more sinister meaning to the surface: Aegon has "betrayed" his flock by putting it into the
hands of a Damoetas.

We saw at the opening of the second eclogue how the idea
of "possession" often implies the grip of a foreign sphere
upon something supposedly essential to "pastoral's" well-being.
Here possession is a concept imposed from within the inner
world. The sheep are helpless victims in the power of those
who control their destiny, in this case the shepherds themselves. The *infelix pecus*—Damoetas' flock in the eyes of
Menalcas—are a minor version of Meliboeus' *quondam felix
pecus* (*Eclogue* 1, line 74). There, to be sure, the trials extend
beyond the flocks to the shepherd himself and both symbolize that unfortunate side of the landscape which is enslaved
to ungentle reality.

There is something ominous about an *alienus custos* who
comes from another part of the rural world and carelessly
milks the sheep too often, sapping their strength and taking
milk from the lambs. Like the flocks he tends, Damoetas has a
counterpart; his is the *advena possessor* who, in the ninth
eclogue, takes the place of the *impius miles* as the deliberate
perpetrator of havoc on the land. Curiously, the verb *subducere*
is used in both contexts. In the third eclogue, the lambs' nourishment is taken (*subducitur*) from them. In *Eclogue* 9 (line 7)

the terrain itself "yields" (*subducere*) from loss of strength. This, like Meliboeus' *quondam felix pecus*, is another instance where the seemingly petty trials with which *Eclogue* 3 opens are transferred to a grander depiction of the land's demise. *Infelix*, then, may mean simply "unhappy," as the context suggests; the sheep bear the brunt of their caretakers' unconcern. That it means "ill-omened" as well only the rest of the poem will bear out. Without the reader's knowing it yet, the helpless sheep are the victims of a force which leaves the shepherds helpless too.[30]

The immediate reason, however, stems from Aegon's love for Neaera, and love is the subject of Damoetas' rejoinder. Such was Menalcas' affair that even the he-goats, most lascivious of the flock, must look askance, but this is only one of many emotions which can bring trouble. Whether from love, anger, or envy, Menalcas replies, Damoetas attacked Micon's plantations and vines, which are as helpless as the sheep. Menalcas' action as seen through Damoetas' eyes (in lines 12-15) is certainly performed out of spite.

The opening gambit, *hic ad veteres fagos*, establishes the setting for a poetic competition, and the *arcus* and *calami*, given to Daphnis instead of Menalcas, were, like the *cicuta* and *pedum* awarded at the end of the fifth eclogue, prizes for the winner. The setting hints at the change of topic introduced by *aut* in line 12. It is Damoetas' first indication of his challenge to Menalcas to have a contest for themselves. The next exchange is also concerned with a prize, this time a *caper* awarded in a contest between Damoetas and Damon. Menalcas claims that Damoetas stole the goat; Damoetas rejoins that, as victor, it was rightfully his. Damon was *cantando victus* and Damoetas' *fistula* had won the day.

At line 25 Menalcas turns the topic to song itself or, better,

[30] The word *infelix* has no counterpart in Theocritus *Id.* 4. 13 and 26, Virgil's probable model. Its full force is not discernible until the end of the poem. *Felix* is used in its religious sense at 5. 65, and *infelix* at 5. 37 has the opposite meaning of "ill-omened" (as at 3. 3).

the ability to sing. He accuses Damoetas of being untrained (*indoctus*), not having a proper pipe, singing in the wrong, unpastoral spot, and, in general, of botching every song, just as he is destroying Aegon's flock. It appears that Menalcas has to make this accusation because the previous interchanges indicate that he lost his fight with Daphnis whereas Damoetas had beaten Damon.[31] Menalcas' words are cleverly malicious. He accuses Damoetas of possessing only a shrieking piece of straw (*stridenti stipula*) instead of a pipe with joints of wax (*fistula cera / iuncta*). As we learned from the second eclogue, this is the pre-Pan stage of primitive music, before he taught the shepherds to fasten several reeds together with wax (*calamos cera coniungere pluris*). Damoetas, in Menalcas' interpretation, has only a screeching stalk which accompanies his song like the second eclogue's *raucis cicadis*, fit companions for Corydon's *incondita*. Like the *infelix pecus* over which he presides, the pitiful *carmen* becomes personified, murdered by incompetence. Hence the special point to the word *indocte*: Damoetas, who is untaught in the ways of song, uncivilized, not in the tradition of Pan, could not possibly compete.

The theme of destruction is deliberately, if unemphatically, present in these opening lines, beginning with the shepherd's inattention and injury to the flocks and extending to the attack on the trees and vines. It also reaches to the prizes of song, which are either destroyed (Daphnis' bow and arrows) or

---

[31] Menalcas, of course, indirectly implies that he is *doctus*, schooled in the ways of poetry. His "learning," strange to a rustic, will soon be apparent.

On the *trivium* as the perfect location for a bad song, see Damon, "Modes of Analogy." The *miserum carmen*—the almost-human, poor song—is the last and most important insult in the list which begins with the *infelix pecus*. The *stridenti stipula* thus becomes as important an element of "spiritual" destruction as the *mala falce* is of the actual landscape. The ambiguity is carried through in the word *disperdere* (literally, to "murder"). *Stridens* is a participle used often by Virgil for the "whizzing" noise a weapon makes as it rushes toward its goal. This is the only place where *stipula* appears in the *Eclogues*, a hint at the shepherd's further inadequacy.

fought over (the goat), and to song itself, spoiled by an in-
attentive, untutored spirit. The emotional impact, however,
is not yet meant to provoke thoughts of too serious a nature.
The power of song—the magic of poetry—is called upon
not to save the countryside, as in the ninth eclogue, but merely
to show its prowess for a small reward. Potential harm to the
landscape and song is limited to the trivial quarrels of two
shepherds with no trace of the final desolation imminent in
Eclogue 1. But even the lightness of tone cannot hide a certain
pessimism which comes to the surface in the course of the
songs themselves.

Before the singers actually commence, pledges must be
placed and the landscape described. All are ideal. Damoetas,
though he has just been chided for milking his sheep too
much, bets a heifer who comes twice (per day, one assumes)
to the milking pail and nourishes twin offspring as well. This
cannot be a failing flock if such a splendid creature is part of
it; and twins, as we saw in the first eclogue, are special signs
of productivity. Menalcas' less commonplace prize is also
quite impressive—two beech cups, the work of Alcimedon.[32]
But there are allusions in the description which go beyond
the literal (lines 35-43):

> verum, id quod multo tute ipse fatebere maius
> (insanire libet quoniam tibi), pocula ponam
> fagina, caelatum divini opus Alcimedontis,
> lenta quibus torno facili superaddita vitis
> diffusos hedera vestit pallente corymbos.
> in medio duo signa, Conon, et—quis fuit alter,
> descripsit radio totum qui gentibus orbem,
> tempora quae messor, quae curvus arator haberet?
> necdum illis labra admovi, sed condita servo.

---

[32] Beechwood is regularly used for practical objects (see, e.g., *G.* 1.
173; 3. 172), making more pronounced the contrast with the artistic,
intellectual scenes engraved on these cups. On the adjective *divinus*,
see chap. 4, p. 180.

But, since this madness pleases you, I will wager something which you yourself will grant of greater importance
—two cups of beechwood, the embossed work of divine
Alcimedon. On them a pliant vine, added by the skill of
the lathe, wraps spreading clusters with pale ivy. In the
midst are two figures, Conon and—who was the other
who marked out with his rod the whole heavens for mankind, what seasons the reaper should follow, what the
stooping ploughman? I have not yet touched them with my
lips, but I keep them stored up.

The exterior is adorned with a combination of vine (*vitis*)
and ivy (*hedera*), symbols closely associated with Bacchus
and Apollo and hence with the poet's craft.[33] They "surround" with poetry Conon and his colleague (probably
Eudoxus of Cnidus) whose works about grand astronomical
subjects have practical bearing on the georgic world.[34] Menalcas has not drunk from the cups yet but holds them *condita,*
a word as apt for describing a newly created poem as a gob-
let, fresh off the lathe.

These are strange objects for a humble shepherd to be carrying around—esoteric and highly cultivated. Whatever their
symbolic value, they reveal a level of sophistication in Menalcas that the opening banter did not imply. This is no mere
shepherd but a tutored critic who values beauty and displays
a knowledge of science outside the ken of a rustic. The revelation that we are again working on two levels at once, with
the literal world of flocks and shepherds and with the poet's
imagination and the crafting of its thoughts, is nothing new

[33] It is important to note that the vine does not appear as frame on
the cup which one of Theocritus' shepherds offers another in *Id.* 1.
29ff.

[34] On the phrase *descripsit radio . . . orbem,* see *Aen.* 6. 849-50. The
symbolism of the wagers is discussed in more detail by C. P. Segal,
"Vergil's *Caelatum Opus*: An Interpretation of the Third *Eclogue*,"
AJP 88 (1967): 279-308.

in the *Eclogues*. Damoetas is not left behind: he, too, has goblets made by Alcimedon on which Orpheus, in his role as poet-
magician, is carved with trees following him (lines 44-48):

> Et nobis idem Alcimedon duo pocula fecit,
> et molli circum est ansas amplexus acantho,
> Orpheaque in medio posuit silvasque sequentis.
> necdum illis labra admovi, sed condita servo.
> si ad vitulam spectas, nihil est quod pocula laudes.

And likewise Alcimedon made two goblets for me, and
clasped the handles with supple acanthus. In the midst he
placed Orpheus and the trees following him. I have not
yet touched them with my lips, but I keep them stored up.
If you look at the heifer, you will not praise the cups at all.

In this case the central symbol, Orpheus, is poetry itself, surrounded by the ornamental acanthus (*molli acantho*).[35] The
more practical Damoetas, however, prefers his *vitula*. Both
objects, material though they be, convey a certain idealism.
They are the goals of poetry and symbolize an extraordinary
productivity in the landscape as well as the intellectual life and
the poet's power.

After renewed challenges from both sides, Palaemon, the
judge, appears and speaks (lines 55-59):

> Dicite, quandoquidem in molli consedimus herba.
> et nunc omnis ager, nunc omnis parturit arbos,
> nunc frondent silvae, nunc formosissimus annus.
> incipe, Damoeta; tu deinde sequere, Menalca.
> alternis dicetis; amant alterna Camenae.

Commence your song, since we have taken our seat on the
soft grass. And now every field, now every tree is burgeoning. Now the woods are green and the season is at

---

[35] *Molli acantho* balances Menalcas' *lenta vitis* (line 38), as Servius
suggests. On the *acanthus* see chap. 3, p. 147 and n. 11.

its most beautiful. Begin, Damoetas; then you follow, Menalcas. You will sing in turn; the Muses love alternate songs.

The setting he describes could scarcely be more perfect; it is deliberately so, for once again the literal landscape is only the frame surrounding song. *Molli herba* is the counterpart, in the larger context of the give and take of song, of the vine and the *molli acantho* which "surround" Conon and Orpheus on the goblets. Being the inspiration for song, the setting and its every detail are noteworthy. *Consedimus*, for example, is the same word the poet will use in the opening line of the seventh eclogue to depict the position of Daphnis, also in the perfect setting for a contest:

> Forte sub arguta consederat ilice Daphnis,
> compulerantque greges Corydon et Thyrsis in unum, ...

By chance Daphnis had taken his seat under a rustling oak, and Corydon and Thyrsis had herded their flocks together.

There, though the two shepherds enter his presence together, Daphnis seems to remain aloof, the ideal arbiter of a contest which does not come to a draw, as in *Eclogue 3*, but has one clear winner. Palaemon, on the other hand, by using the form *consedimus* associates all three, umpire and contestants alike, in the beauty of the situation.

The seventh eclogue lacks the unity of tone and purpose which develops in the succeeding lines of the third. It is only Corydon whose words are continually connected with the setting. We may note, for instance, that the phrase *molli herba* recurs in his words at line 45: *muscosi fontes et somno mollior herba*. Clearer still is his announcement (in line 55) that all nature smiles (*omnia nunc rident*), and is bound to remain happy so long as the spirit of beauty, *formosus Alexis,* graces the landscape with his presence.

Returning to the third eclogue, this idealized beauty of setting, common to all, spills over into the apostrophes to Jupiter and Apollo with which the shepherds begin (lines 60-63):

D. Ab Iove principium, Musae: Iovis omnia plena;
    ille colit terras, illi mea carmina curae.
M. Et me Phoebus amat; Phoebo sua semper apud me
    munera sunt, lauri et suave rubens hyacinthus.

D. From Jupiter is my beginning, Muses. Everything is filled with Jupiter. He cherishes the land; my songs are dear to him.
M. And Apollo loves me. I always have Apollo's gifts, laurels and the sweetly blushing hyacinth, ready for him.

The Muses, and the poet, must begin with the chief of the gods. Everything, emphasized by the double use of *omnis* in line 56, is filled by his bounty. The words *mea carmina curae* take their cue from the second eclogue (line 6)—*nihil mea carmina curas*—but here not only is the earth productive but also the poet himself can sing because Jupiter cherishes him and cares for his song. Love is also what Apollo offers Menalcas who responds with appropriate *munera*.

From their happy relationship with divinity, the shepherds turn to more mundane concerns and sing the praises of their earthly loves, Galatea, Amyntas, Phyllis, Amaryllis. All seems serene, though Amyntas occasionally spurns Menalcas, and Iollas[36] apparently has the power to keep or send Phyllis to either of the shepherds. All in all, this is no competition in the negative sense but an attempt to join in depicting the perfect shepherd's life, with divine assurance and happy love.

Then, exactly halfway through the exchange, there is a sudden alteration of theme (lines 84-91):

[36] Possibly the same Iollas as at *Ecl.* 2. 57.

D. Pollio amat nostram, quamvis est rustica, Musam:
    Pierides, vitulam lectori pascite vestro.
M. Pollio et ipse facit nova carmina: pascite taurum,
    iam cornu petat et pedibus qui spargat harenam.
D. Qui te, Pollio, amat, veniat quo te quoque gaudet;
    mella fluant illi, ferat et rubus asper amomum.
M. Qui Bavium non odit, amet tua carmina, Maevi,
    atque idem iungat vulpes et mulgeat hircos.

D. Pollio loves our Muse, though she is rustic. Sisters of
    Pieria, feed a calf for your reader.
M. And Pollio himself makes new songs. Feed a bull, who
    even now butts with his horn and scatters the sand with
    his hooves.
D. May he who loves you, Pollio, come where he may re-
    joice in your presence. May honey flow for him and
    may the rough brambles bear spice.
M. May he who does not hate Bavius love your songs, Mae-
    vius, and may he also yoke foxes and milk he-goats.

The twice repeated name of Asinius Pollio, soldier, statesman,
historian and poet, has the calculated force which only the first
direct reference in the *Eclogues* to a known historical character could possess. In accordance with Virgil's intention in the
poem thus far, the appearance of the real world on the pastoral scene has nothing of the destructive potential which
Rome menaces in the first eclogue. The address to Pollio has
a special, personal cast, which admits of a series of distinctions between him and the shepherds.

As in the preceding poem, merely to imply that the shepherds' muse is *rustica* in Pollio's eyes is to place him in an urbane, sophisticated world. Besides, Pollio is a *lector* of their
songs, someone who reads what is traditionally an oral art and
is therefore all the more distinct from it. (To assume that the
songs were written down anyway is to shatter many illusions

at once.) Nevertheless the statement is clear: Pollio loves the pastoral muse, and Pollio occupies the same eminence in the shepherds' lives—and an equivalent place of honor in the poem—as Jupiter and Apollo. But the difference is twofold. First, Pollio is alive and active in numerous ways in the community at large. Secondly, he writes *carmina* himself and is an all the more valuable friend because he knows the creative mind and its necessities. He understands the "pastoral" life in its spiritual sense. In this hierarchy of values, the importance of the creator over the critic is well illustrated by the superiority of the bull, which they will feed as token for their benefactor, over the calf.

Pollio has reached a position, in some aspect of his multifarious career, at which those who love him can only rejoice. He has achieved, perhaps created, with his political courage or songs, the golden age, and Damoetas' prayer is that those who love him (i.e. Damoetas and Menalcas, as representatives of the rustic world) may accordingly gain a land where the impossible comes true, where honey flows freely and briars bear balsam. To those, on the contrary, who prefer the poetry of Bavius or Maevius, there will be no golden age but the opposite, even perversion, of it—the yoking of foxes and the milking of he-goats. It is Pollio who loves the pastoral world, no one else; Pollio who creates a golden age to which all who admire him can aspire. Bad poetry still exists and those who esteem it fail to disguise their goal as a search not for perfection but for the useless and the impossible under figures of aberration.

Nothing more need or should be said, but if there is bad poetry there is also evil in the land. Another marked change of tone suddenly comes over the poem at line 92:

> D. Qui legitis flores et humi nascentia fraga,
> frigidus, o pueri, fugite hinc, latet anguis in herba.

D. You boys who pick flowers and strawberries, springing
   from the earth, flee the spot. A chill snake hides in the
   grass.

To pick flowers and strawberries would seem to be the most
carefree of occupations. Both are products of the land often
used to represent nature's spontaneous bounty.[37] Now there is
menace, born only of nature herself, in the form of the chill
snake (*frigidus anguis*) that lurks ready to bite. Moreover
the sheep should be careful not to trust in the riverbank: it
has already caved in for the ram and is dangerous, even if it
is the source of water (lines 94-99):

M. Parcite, oves, nimium procedere: non bene ripae
   creditur; ipse aries etiam nunc vellera siccat.
D. Tityre, pascentis a flumine reice capellas:
   ipse, ubi tempus erit, omnis in fonte lavabo.
M. Cogite ovis, pueri: si lac praeceperit aestus,
   ut nuper, frustra pressabimus ubera palmis.

M. Watch out, sheep, not to venture too far. It is unwise to
   trust the bank. The ram himself is even now drying off
   his fleece.
D. Tityrus, turn back the grazing goats from the stream.
   When the time comes, I myself will wash them all in
   the spring.
M. Pen the sheep, boys. If the heat forestalls the milk, as
   recently, we will press the udders in vain with our
   palms.

There is also the danger that, even though the sheep are
herded together, the heat will cut off the milk supply again,
as it had recently. So the land poses a series of dangers: snake,
crumbling bank, treacherous stream, heat. How unlike these
vignettes are to an ideal landscape will be seen from the analysis

[37] On flowers, see, e.g., *Ecl.* 4. 23. On *fraga*, Ovid *Met.* 1. 104.

of the fourth eclogue, which contains a portrait of the true golden age. Cattle, of their own accord and without any hindrance, bring home udders filled with milk and the snake exists no more. Though Pollio may yet fulfill the promise of lines 84-89, at the present moment the shepherds' existence is in some jeopardy.

There is worse still to come (lines 100-101):

> D. Heu heu, quam pingui macer est mihi taurus in ervo!
>   idem amor exitium pecori pecorisque magistro.

> D. Alas, alas, how thin my bull is amid the rich forage!
>   The same love is the ruin of herd and herdsman.

Heu heu is a strong prelude: Corydon uses the repetition to present his realization of how ruinous Alexis actually is.[38] Damoetas claims that love is destroying herd and shepherds alike. The remark is doubly strange. It is not long since Damoetas and Menalcas spoke of the affection in which Jupiter, Apollo, and Pollio hold them. Besides, the petty tribulations, of which we heard in lines 64 through 83, can scarcely be considered of a serious nature. Now something is actually destroying flocks and their masters alike: the bull grows thin and the lambs grow scrawny (lines 102-103):

> M. Hi certe—neque amor causa est—vix ossibus haerent.
>   nescio quis teneros oculus mihi fascinat agnos.

> M. The skin of these animals scarcely clings to their bones.
>   Nor is love the reason. Some evil eye bewitches my
>   tender lambs.

Damoetas goes the easy way in claiming love as the cause. Menalcas travels one step further and takes a typically rustic refuge in superstition: not love but the evil eye is their undoing, something incapable of analysis and beyond their control.

For his purposes Virgil is understating the advent of havoc.

---

[38] *Ecl.* 2. 58.

It is, nevertheless, disquieting to recall that a delicate lamb (*tener agnus*) is what Tityrus sacrifices to his Roman god, while *teneros agnos* are the final victims of the suffering that afflicts the land here.[39] In the first eclogue Meliboeus states plainly that he will place no curse on Tityrus' happiness by an evil glance (*non equidem invideo*) but will only gaze in admiration. There is, however, nothing voluntary in *Eclogue* 3 nor is the problem caused by the shepherds themselves, as the beginning of the poem might suggest. This time the curse of the evil eye from some unknown Meliboeus works, and the gods—be they Jupiter or Apollo or Tityrus' Roman idol—no longer seem to pay heed.

In a review of the poem's changes of theme, Pollio would be considered first. He is a hero of the real world who loves "pastoral" and writes poetry himself in order to become part of, or to recreate, a golden age. There, however, is bad poetry as well, which turns the dream upside-down: the earth finds itself faced with unexpected forms of menace, first of lesser moment from the landscape, then from love, then from something beyond this which the shepherds cannot explain. And, as if to give final stress to this complete alteration of mood, the shepherds conclude their debate with two riddles which may well refer to Jupiter and Apollo (lines 104-107):

> D. Dic quibus in terris—et eris mihi magnus Apollo—
>   tris pateat caeli spatium non amplius ulnas.
> M. Dic quibus in terris inscripti nomina regum
>   nascantur flores, et Phyllida solus habeto.

D. Tell me—and you will be my great Apollo—where heaven's breadth is no wider than three ells.
M. Tell me—and have Phyllis to yourself—where flowers inscribed with the names of kings grow.

[39] In *Eclogue* 1 the sacrifice seems to work.

The names which ring out at the opening of the contest, proclaiming the affection which the gods lavish on the shepherds,
their land and their poetry, are now apparently disguised.[40]
In making a group of riddles the final challenge, Virgil may
be acknowledging a final disillusionment, as if he were saying
that those gods upon whom the pastoral life depends must
now be hidden from view. The aloof beneficence of the gods
has been carefully linked with the more imminent creative
presence of Pollio. For whatever reason the landscape is also
dependent upon him, as if he could preserve or occasion
a golden age. But things have gone wrong: Jupiter and
Apollo are veiled from sight. The reference to Pollio has already been made clear enough, and Virgil need say no more.

Palaemon ends the poem (lines 108-111):

> Non nostrum inter vos tantas componere lites.
> et vitula tu dignus et hic: et quisquis amores
> aut metuet dulcis, aut experietur amaros.
> claudite iam rivos, pueri; sat prata biberunt.

It is not possible for me to settle your mighty contest. You
are worthy of the heifer and this man, too—and whoever
shall either fear the sweetness or experience the bitterness
of love. Close off the rivulets now, boys. The meadows
have drunk their fill.

The shepherds have not really been challenging each other,
as at the poem's outset, but have presented a unity of subject
and mood at each stage of the debate. Each is therefore worthy
of the prize, as is anyone who fears for the future when love
is sweet or has already suffered love's bitternesses. The remark
is pessimistic. Palaemon's impression, as he thinks back to
the preceding songs, is that love, which is doubtless the central theme of the exchange, is open to little happiness. If it is

[40] See M.C.J. Putnam, "The Riddle of Damoetas," *Mnemosyne*, n.s.
18 (1965): 150-54.

sweet, Palaemon implies, there can only be fear of a turn for the worst. If it is bitter, there is no alternative.

From one point of view Palaemon limits the blame for the trouble, which the songs imply has come upon the land, to love alone. He acknowledges no inscrutable evil eye. Yet love takes two forms here. It appears in the relatively insignificant light banter of the early lines as the shepherds compare Amyntas, Galatea, and the rest, as well as in the shepherds' avowals of the love that Jupiter, Apollo, and Pollio bear "pastoral." If this second love were to change, the land would be in difficulty. There is no direct statement that it has. The only way the shepherds can explain a series of misfortunes is by imputing them to some unknown wrath. As at the end of the two preceding eclogues, there is an attempt to smooth over difficulties; but, unlike that of the second eclogue, the final vision of the third is scarcely a happy one. The next poem, perhaps Virgil's most famous work, taking its start from much in these lines, offers an alternative.

Sicelides Musae, paulo maiora canamus.
non omnis arbusta iuvant humilesque myricae;
si canimus silvas, silvae sint consule dignae.

Muses of Sicily, let us sing of a somewhat loftier theme.
Hedge and lowly tamarisk do not delight everyone. If we
sing of woods, let the woods be worthy of a consul.
(lines 1-3)

The first line strikes with a boldness unparalleled in the
Eclogues thus far.[1] It is Virgil's first personal address to the
Muses, and the tone is daring. The words are not a prayer
for song—a literary custom which Virgil follows elsewhere[2]
—but a proclamation that he and the Muses are going to chant
what follows together. This is no humble shepherd craving
divine influence, but an equal of the goddesses of song, a
prophet ready to sing something beyond either Theocritus or
the eclogues composed most closely under his spell.[3] This
elevation of tone and content Virgil glosses in the succeeding
lines. Humble shrubs and bushes—ordinary rustic themes—
will not satisfy everyone. As the literal *humilis casas* of Corydon's restricted world do not meet with the approval of

[1] For a bibliography of recent criticism of *Eclogue* 4 see G. E. Duckworth, "Recent Work on Vergil (1940-1956)," *CW* 51 (1957-58):
124-26; and "Recent Work on Vergil (1957-1963)," *CW* 57 (1964):
200-202.

[2] *Ecl.* 6. 13: *Pergite, Pierides*; *Ecl.* 10. 1: *Arethusa, . . . concede.*

[3] The adjective *magnus* makes constant appearances in the poem
(lines 1, 5, 12, 22, 36, 48, 49). The comparative is rarer in the *Eclogues*,
and, at 10. 72, *haec maxima* is a unique instance of the superlative. This
last, however, is the strongest of token gestures, the triumphant conclusion of the *Eclogues*.

Alexis, so too there are those who spurn reading bucolic poetry because the range of its ideas is apparently limited, its inheritance one of escape, not involvement. The challenge Virgil is now to pose himself he epitomizes in terms of symbols: he will make the "woods" of pastoral poetry worthy of a consul, performing the impossible through song.

There have been other moments in the *Eclogues* which suggested a similar tension. In *Eclogue* 1, Rome, when entering on the rural scene, is like a heaven-seeking cypress by comparison with the shepherd's bending osiers (*lenta viburna*). Tityrus, however, fails to see the defiance in his own analogies or to evaluate the distinction between himself and Meliboeus upon which the images of cypress and osier comment. Merely by doting on a muse of the woods and adopting the beauty of Amaryllis as his theme in such troubled times, he proves himself an insensitive singer, blithely ignorant of anything save constricted "sylvan" topics. Meliboeus, sensitive though he is, confines to his sorrow and does little better at paying tribute to "pastoral." The Roman soldier who brings ruin to the bucolic life in *Eclogue* 1 could be visualized as an actual example of what might happen if the Roman world of the consul were to clash with the "woods" of the sylvan life. But there both the poet's spokesmen are to some degree suppressed or inadequate voices for the value of that life. Here Virgil announces that he will offer an intellectual commentary on the same theme and defend the feasibility of a union which, after the first eclogue, might appear a misguided fantasy.

Before turning to the dream itself it is well to sketch at least a few of the dangers of Virgil's hypothetical collaboration. It is easy to state that the woods are to be made worthy of a consul and that pastoral poetry is to have its landscape confirmed by someone who might rest more easily in the pages of an epic or history, but the obstacles are many. A consul stands for two things unknown in the bucolic retreat, power and time. He is an emblem for the state and its works, the *vita activa*, the progress of civilization in peace and war. The dilemma can be restated as a double question: Can Virgil liberalize the pastoral world sufficiently to embrace such a creature as a consul within its exclusive, idealized frontiers? Can a pattern of politics and culture, subject to change and development, be evolved which could conform to a traditionally static vision?

The poem blazons a strong affirmative answer (lines 4-17):

> Ultima Cumaei venit iam carminis aetas;
> magnus ab integro saeclorum nascitur ordo.
> iam redit et virgo, redeunt Saturnia regna,
> iam nova progenies caelo demittitur alto.
> tu modo nascenti puero, quo ferrea primum
> desinet ac toto surget gens aurea mundo,
> casta fave Lucina: tuus iam regnat Apollo.
> teque adeo decus hoc aevi, te consule, inibit,
> Pollio, et incipient magni procedere menses;
> te duce, si qua manent sceleris vestigia nostri,
> irrita perpetua solvent formidine terras.
> ille deum vitam accipiet divisque videbit
> permixtos heroas et ipse videbitur illis,
> pacatumque reget patriis virtutibus orbem.

Now the last age of Cumaean song has come. The great line of the ages is born anew. Now the Virgin returns, the kingdom of Saturn returns. Now a new race is sent down from heaven above. Only do you, chaste Lucina, look benignly on the newborn boy, at whose coming the iron race shall first cease and a golden race will spring up in the whole world. Your own Apollo now reigns. In your consulship, Pollio, in yours, this glorious age will begin and the mighty months will start their course. Under your leadership, any traces of our guilt that remain will become void and release the earth from everlasting fear. He will accept the life of the gods and will see heroes consorting with gods and himself will be seen by them, and he will rule over a world made peaceful by his father's virtues.

Eclogue 4

With the first line of the poem proper we already are deep in a subject never before imagined in pastoral poetry: time. In the seventh eclogue Virgil speaks of the coming of summer to the land with the words *iam venit aestas / torrida* (lines 47-48), but this is a far cry from the poet's sudden involvement, not in the countryside's simple changes of season but in the ages of man, not in the humble *carmen* of bucolic song but in the sweeping predictions of the Sibylline seer.[4] Virgil is not the voice of the prophet but the actual singer of the oracle's truth. The world has been reborn, and time has been permitted to start again, *ab integro*, afresh, without taint or reproach. This is no simple call to agrarian order—the planting of vines in a row, say, or the birth of sheep—but to a *magnus ordo*, part of the *paulo maiora* of the first line, a renewal of time itself.

This is almost a spring song. The repetition of *iam* at the beginning of lines 6 and 7 recalls the same anaphora at the opening of Catullus' joyful hymn to the return of the Zephyr (*Carmen* 46, lines 1-3):

> Iam ver egelidos refert tepores,
> iam caeli furor aequinoctialis
> iucundis Zephyri silescit auris.

Now spring brings back warmth, lacking winter's chill; now the raging of the sky at the equinox grows silent with the soothing breezes of the Zephyr.

---

[4] On *venit iam carminis aetas*, cf. also 9. 67: *carmina tum melius, cum venerit ipse, canemus.* The return of the poet may cause the rejuvenation of song. In *Eclogue* 4 the vision expands to embrace a far grander "charm," inducing the arrival of a new schema of human existence.

On the *saeculum* as a religious rite, see L. R. Taylor, "Varro's *De Gente Populi Romani*," CP 29 (1934): 221-29; Ryberg, "Vergil's Golden Age," pp. 114-15.

On Horace's *Carmen Saeculare*, see Eduard Fraenkel, *Horace* (Oxford, 1957), pp. 364-82. Its relationship to *Eclogue* 4 deserves detailed analysis; see P. Corssen, "Die Vierte Ekloge Virgils," *Philologus* 81 (1925): 58-60.

What Catullus limits to the coming of calm after the vernal equinox Virgil expands to presage a restoration of the golden age itself.[5] Astraea, goddess of justice, who has up to now been in exile because of the ubiquity of crime, especially civil war, reappears. Her absence was very different from the un-requited love which often blights the shepherd's daily round; it indicated the present decadence of the human race as a whole.

Again Catullus offers an analogy when he observes in his marriage hymn to Peleus and Thetis that once gods and mortals had associated freely together (*Carmen* 64, lines 397-99)

> sed postquam tellus scelere est imbuta nefando
> iustitiamque omnes cupida de mente fugarunt,
> perfudere manus fraterno sanguine fratres, . . .

But after, the earth was steeped in unmentionable crime
and everyone, with grasping mind, put justice to flight.
Brothers drenched their hands with fraternal blood.

All this is past, in Virgil's optimistic vision. The kingdom of Saturn, in which men lived happily with one another in a state of nature, without the need for labor, has returned. A new race, *nova progenies*, will people the earth.

Virgil is thinking back to the moment in Book 8 of the *Iliad* when the gods ponder dragging Zeus down from heaven to earth with a golden rope, an event which the Stoics turned into an allegory of the origin of life. Specifically, however, and with a more direct purpose, Virgil is recalling lines toward the end of the second book of *De Rerum Natura* (lines 1150-60):

[5] The influence of Catullus on *Eclogue* 4 is a topic which craves more extensive treatment than it can be given here. See, e.g., Leon Herrmann, "Le poème 64 de Catulle et Virgile," *REL* 8 (1930): 211-21; E. M. Smith, "Echoes of Catullus in the Messianic Eclogue of Vergil," *CJ* 26 (1930): 141-43; Rose, *The Eclogues of Vergil*, pp. 201-3; W.F.J. Knight, *Roman Vergil* (London, 1946), 271-2; R.E.H. Westendorp Boerma, "Vergil's Debt to Catullus," *Acta Classica* 1 (1958): 51-63.

iamque adeo fracta est aetas effetaque tellus
vix animalia parva creat quae cuncta creavit
saecla deditque ferarum ingentia corpora partu.
haud, ut opinor, enim mortalia saecla superne
aurea de caelo demisit funis in arva
nec mare nec fluctus plangentes saxa crearunt,
sed genuit tellus eadem quae nunc alit ex se.
praeterea nitidas fruges vinetaque laeta
sponte sua primum mortalibus ipsa creavit,
ipsa dedit dulcis fetus et pabula laeta;
quae nunc vix nostro grandescunt aucta labore, . . .

And now its life is completely broken and the barren earth, which engendered all races and gave birth to the mighty bodies of wild animals, scarcely creates small beasts. For in my opinion, a golden rope did not let down living creatures from above into the fields, nor did the sea or the waves which lash the rocks create them, but the same earth bore them which now nourishes them of herself. Moreover she herself of her own will first created gleaming crops and happy vines for mortals, herself gave sweet fruits and happy fodder—things which now scarcely grow to maturity, though fostered by our efforts.

Though the repetition of the phrase *caelo demittere* is sufficient to intimate the influence of one passage upon the other, it is the question of tone which is of particular interest. As in the case of the quotation from Catullus' *Carmen* 64 above, Virgil has changed a pessimistic description of mankind's future into an optimistic appreciation. Catullus examines men in terms of their relationship to the gods and to each other, and their *pietas* is found wanting. The lines of Lucretius see the downfall of humanity in nature's decadence and lack of response. Both these gloomy views, which could loosely be termed either social or economic, are countered by *Eclogue* 4.

The rebirth of the ages (*nascitur ordo*) is symbolized in

the birth of a boy (*nascenti puero*) over which Diana, in her role as the goddess of childbirth, and Apollo preside. Their choice is deliberate. The absence of Apollo and his sister from the wedding of Peleus and Thetis, in Catullus' retelling, is conspicuous. How could they help solemnize a marriage whence would spring Achilles, symbol, at least to a Roman poet writing in the 50's B.C., of war's ruthless violence? This new birth is different. It is the moment when the iron race, the dwellers on the earth during the last, most decadent of Hesiod's five ages of man, will yield before a renewal of the generation of gold. Together Apollo and Diana will be called upon by Horace in the *Carmen Saeculare*, to bless the games held by Augustus in 17 B.C. on the holy occasion (lines 5-8)

> quo Sibyllini monuere versus
> virgines lectas puerosque castos
> dis quibus septem placuere colles
> dicere carmen: . . .

. . . at which the verses of the Sibyl commanded that chosen maidens and chaste youths chant the song to the gods with whom the seven hills have found favor.[6]

To make the same point some twenty-three years earlier, in the midst of times still troubled by civil war, is bold. Even while fraternal strife persists, Virgil, the seer, can prophesy that the iron race—*ferreus* is an adjective Virgil ever associates with war[7]—will collapse. In its place the golden age will be renewed, an age which a chaste goddess (the word *casta* is stressed) can bless and into which *Iustitia* can return.

The one occasion of the year 40 B.C.—the year of Pollio's consulship—which would have been particularly impressive to Virgil, a poet who is dependent on *otium* and whose horror of war the first eclogue has already fully revealed, must

---

[6] On *Eclogue* 4 and the *Carmen Saeculare*, see above, n. 4.
[7] On *ferreus* and war, see *Aen.* 10. 745; 12. 284.

have been the Pact of Brundisium. This was signed in September by Octavian and Antony, heads of the two vying factions, and sealed by the marriage of Antony to Octavian's sister, Octavia.[8] It is, however, hazardous to speculate on the reasons for a poet's rejoicing. It is equally precarious—and unnecessary—to measure the qualifications of one candidate or another to be the boy in question, if indeed a real child is meant in the first place. Virgil feels it imperative for us to know only one fact directly: this great event is to start under the consulship of Asinius Pollio, in 40 B.C.

The mention of Pollio might ordinarily come as a surprise in a pastoral poem, however broad its intellectual scope; but the reader has been prepared, from the opening words, to see a connection between Pollio and the golden age, perhaps even to imagine in him the savior of the bucolic life. He has two roles: consul and *dux*. First, as consul he is a symbol of authority and, here above all, a measure of history in time. The *magni menses* which precede the birth of this extraordinary creature, as part of the *magnus ordo* of the earth's rejuvenation and the *maiora* of the poet's *carmen*, are to begin under Pollio's tutelage. As one consul finishes his turn and leads to another, time continues on—*inibit, incipient, procedere* are verbs of motion—and the bucolic world becomes part of a universal golden age. But the poet's final prayer is for the continuity not of change but of stable perfection in a time become timeless, an age which must be dated only from its start as its conclusion will hopefully never come.

Pollio's second role as *dux* is blatantly military. A partisan for each side at one time or another during these years, Pollio—not Antony or Octavian—is to lead his people away from civil war. Under his guidance the Roman state is to be purged

---

[8] On the Peace of Brundisium and *Eclogue* 4, see D. A. Slater, "Was the Fourth Eclogue written to celebrate the Marriage of Octavia to Mark Antony?—A Literary Parallel," *CR* 26 (1912): 114-19; W. W. Tarn, "Alexander Helios and the Golden Age," *JRS* 22 (1932): 135-60.

of all traces of *scelus*. There is little doubt that Virgil means the disgrace of civil strife, to which we have seen Catullus refer so bitterly and to which Horace repeatedly returns, as in *Epode* 7 (lines 17-20):

> sic est: acerba fata Romanos agunt
>   scelusque fraternae necis,
> ut immerentis fluxit in terram Remi
>   sacer nepotibus cruor.

> Such is the case. A bitter fate and the crime of a brother's murder drive the Romans, ever since the earth flowed with the blood of innocent Remus, blood which is cursed to his descendants.

As he is a symbol of time only to make the world timeless, like the shepherd's life, so Pollio must maintain the attitude of *dux* in order that war will cease.

Again the language is that of a spring song save that not just the landscape but all mankind has been caught in the grip of fear, a less gentle grasp than ever dull winter held. *Solvitur acris hiems* Horace gladly exclaims at the breakup of the season's ice. Here the chill discontent of war, which had seemed everlasting, has been eliminated, along with traces of the crime itself, by the presence of Pollio, the *dux* who has led his people into a time of undisturbed peace.

Finally, to conclude the first part of the poem, Virgil turns again to the boy himself. This child, whose birth ushers in the new reign of Saturn, is to become immortal. He will restore that time of union between mortal and immortal which Catullus felt was lost. Speaking of the gods in generations past, he had said (*Carmen* 64, lines 384-86):

> praesentes namque ante domos invisere castas
> heroum, et sese mortali ostendere coetu,
> caelicolae nondum spreta pietate solebant.

For previously the gods were wont to visit the chaste
dwellings of heroes in person and to appear before the
mortal throng, since piety was not yet scorned.

Though the boy's role may at first appear unusual, the result
is thoroughly "pastoral": it is merely the ideal of peace expanded to touch all humanity. Nevertheless, Virgil assumes
the imminence of further war wherein *virtus*, that manly
courage which distinguishes the true warrior and raises a mortal to the level of the divine, will bring about the peaceable
reign of Apollo and the boy. Hence, as if to summarize the
broadened dialectic of bucolic song in *Eclogue* 4, Virgil has reiterated his wish that, through his magic *carmen*, woods and
consul could be reconciled.

The sword belongs to the life of the soldier and has no part
in the shepherd's life. The first eclogue illustrates the havoc it
can wreak when used by an *impius* and *barbarus miles*.
Used morally, however, exerted positively for the benefit of
mankind, it is a servant of courage. If we may follow Hesiod,
after whom later authors tend to pattern their thoughts on
this topic, there is one large distinction between this new age
and the golden era of a sylvan society living on nature's bounty
without restraint: the new golden age is to be presided over
by a hero, with human and divine links, and by Apollo, who
has connections with both the pastoral world and war. Horace,
for instance, in the *Carmen Saeculare*, must beg Apollo to lend
a sympathetic ear, *condito mitis placidusque telo*, "gentle
and benign, with spear put aside." Hence the most novel intellectual idea thus far advanced by Virgil is not so much the
rejuvenation of the ages, happy dream though that be, but the
combination of the golden and heroic eras, separated in
Hesiod's account by the periods of silver and bronze. This is
only to restate in different words that the new epoch will
reconcile "woods" and consul, pastoral *otium* and heroic
virtus, in an ideal amalgam.

The new age will come about when the boy has reached full maturity and the world has been pacified. At the moment Virgil returns to the child and imagines him newborn (lines 18-25):

> At tibi prima, puer, nullo munuscula cultu
> errantis hederas passim cum baccare tellus
> mixtaque ridenti colocasia fundet acantho.
> ipsae lacte domum referent distenta capellae
> ubera, nec magnos metuent armenta leones;
> ipsa tibi blandos fundent cunabula flores.
> occidet et serpens, et fallax herba veneni
> occidet; Assyrium vulgo nascetur amomum.

But for you, child, the earth will pour forth with no tilling, as its first gifts, ivy wandering everywhere about with foxglove, and the bean plant mingled with smiling acanthus. Of their own accord goats will bring home udders swollen with milk, and the herds will not fear mighty lions. Of itself your birthplace will pour forth harmless flowers. The snake, too, will die, and the deceitful poison herb will die. Assyrian nard will grow everywhere.

First the earth pours forth *munuscula*, small signs of its affection for the boy, which take the form of different vines.[9] What in the *Eclogues* would ordinarily be the offerings of one lover to another are expanded, in the grander design of things *paulo maiora*, to portray *tellus*, the whole earth, acknowledging the boy who has brought it new life. The vocabulary of lines 19-20 mirrors a moment in the seventh eclogue describing the arrival of spring in a landscape which is ideal due to the lover's presence (lines 54-55): "strata iacent passim sua quaeque sub arbore poma, / omnia nunc rident" ("Everywhere fruit lies strewn beneath its own tree. Now

[9] Though *munus* is common in the *Eclogues*, *munusculum* is unique.

everything smiles"). Another passage in *Eclogue* 7 also glosses
Virgil's choice of ivy and "foxglove" as the initial *munuscula*
(lines 25-28):

> Pastores, hedera crescentem ornate poetam,
> Arcades, invidia rumpantur ut ilia Codro;
> aut, si ultra placitum laudarit, baccare frontem
> cingite, ne vati noceat mala lingua futuro.

Shepherds of Arcadia, adorn your growing bard with
ivy, that Codrus' sides might burst from envy. Or, if he
praise me beyond measure, wreathe my forehead with
baccar lest he harm the future bard by his evil tongue.

To the ivy, symbol of the poet's vocation, Virgil adds in the
fourth eclogue the adjective *errantis*, with its notion of freedom. *Baccar* may well be apotropaic in the face of an evil
tongue or envious gaze. Servius notes the connection between
the two passages and observes the magic quality of *baccar,*
believing that it indicates only the beauty of the boy.[10] We
might see in the combination of ivy and foxglove a complementary accompaniment to the ideal setting, a harbinger of
poetry and prophecy, of song and magic, both of which are
prerogatives of the shepherd and his *carmen*.[11]

What is initially most noticeable in this sketch of the golden
age is the absence of labor. All agriculture is unnecessary as
the earth produces vines and herbs without cultivation, the

---

[10] *Baccar: herba est quae fascinum pellit* ("*Baccar* is a plant which
averts the evil eye"). The flower in question is more likely cyclamen
than foxglove.

[11] For acanthus as decoration, see *Ecl.* 3. 45; Propertius 3. 9. 14 (an
attribute of the art of Mys); Ovid *Met.* 13. 701. It is treated as an
evergreen at *G.* 2. 119. Usually, however, like ivy and (apparently)
baccar it was a vine, known for its flexibility: at *Aen.* 1. 649 and 711
it forms part of the border around a veil. It was also used in a crown
of triumph (Velleius Paterculus 2. 56. 2) and in a poet's wreath (Cal-
purnius *Ecl.* 4. 68). Hence acanthus here may fulfill the same role as
the ivy and *baccar*, to form a protective, yet decorative "crown," surrounding something beautiful.

goats bring home full udders of their own accord (*ipsae*), and harmless flowers spring up spontaneously in the boy's honor. All menace, whether lion, serpent, or poison plant, is absent.

Two passages elsewhere in Virgil comment on these lines. The first, which the poet himself may well be answering directly, is the couplet toward the end of *Eclogue* 3 where Damoetas warns (lines 92-93): "qui legitis flores et humi nascentia fraga, / frigidus, o pueri, fugite hinc, latet anguis in herba." *Fraga*, strawberries, are a wild plant, which turn up again in Ovid as part of nature's beneficence during the golden age.[12] The presence of flowers goes without saying, but the hidden terror of the chill snake destroys their enjoyment and ruins the perfect relationship of man with nature in the third eclogue. There Pollio seems to know of the golden age at a time when the shepherds observe their countryside being ruined. Now, because of Pollio's good offices, Virgil can imagine the possibility of a golden age restored. Secondly, we might note, with Servius, the hymn to Italy's perpetual spring in the second georgic. Here, too, amid a catalogue of nature's charms —among which is the absence of tigers, lions and snakes—the poet can state (line 152): *nec miseros fallunt aconita legentis* ("nor does aconite deceive the poor pickers").

A word on *cunabula* is in order. In the context of line 23 it cannot have its usual sense of "cradle" but must be virtually in apposition to *tellus* (with which Virgil also uses the verb *fundo*).[13] We are in the golden age when the earth itself would be expected to serve as the resting place of a new child. Lucretius clarifies the point in the course of a description of primitive man which Virgil must have known by heart (*De Rerum Natura* 5, lines 816-17):

terra cibum pueris, vestem vapor, herba cubile
praebebat multa et molli lanugine abundans.

[12] On *fraga*, see chap. 2, n. 37.
[13] Cf., however, G. E. Duckworth, "The Cradle of Flowers (*Ecl.* 4. 23)," *TAPA* 89 (1958): 1-8.

The earth furnished food for children, warm weather was their clothing, the grass, thick with an abundance of soft down, furnished a couch.[14]

In this spontaneous miracle of nature, the child is surrounded with protecting ivy and foxglove and smothered with harmless flowers which make no threat upon his life, either of themselves or from a hiding snake.

Finally we must note the universality of nature's happiness. The situation is similar to that of one lover talking to another: there is a particular intimacy about the moment which is carried by the words *munuscula* and *cunabula*. But all nature, not an individual shepherd, is the worshiper. The theme recurs again later in a variant guise.

At the moment Virgil moves to the next stage in the boy's growth (lines 26-36):

> at simul heroum laudes et facta parentis
> iam legere et quae sit poteris cognoscere virtus,
> molli paulatim flavescet campus arista,
> incultisque rubens pendebit sentibus uva,
> et durae quercus sudabunt roscida mella.
> pauca tamen suberunt priscae vestigia fraudis,
> quae temptare Thetim ratibus, quae cingere muris
> oppida, quae iubeant telluri infindere sulcos.
> alter erit tum Tiphys, et altera quae vehat Argo
> delectos heroas; erunt etiam altera bella
> atque iterum ad Troiam magnus mittetur Achilles.

But as soon as you can read the glories of heroes and the deeds of your father and comprehend the meaning of courage, little by little the field will grow yellow with soft corn and the reddening grape will hang from unculti-

[14] Cyril Bailey comments on lines 816-17 as follows: "Though these lines in general concern all animals . . . and the human race is not specifically mentioned till 822, men are included in *mortalia saecla* (805), and it is clear that in these lines Lucretius is thinking especially of the human child. *Pueris* could not refer to the young of animals and *vestem* is again a human touch."

vated bramble bushes, and hard oaks will drip dewy honey. Nevertheless a few traces of our ancient deceit will remain which order men to make trial of the sea in ships, to gird towns with walls, to cleave the ground with furrows. Then there will be another Tiphys, and another Argo to carry chosen heroes. Other wars there will be, too, and mighty Achilles will again be sent to Troy.

This is not a haphazard continuation of the substance of the previous lines. The description of the events which will accompany the child's boyhood, as he learns of the past and of his father's deeds, offers a considerable and purposeful change. By the side of decorative vines, herbs, flowers, and productive cattle we now have corn, grapes, and honey. According to Virgil's words, the first of these might seem to spring up naturally, but the other two arise only through extreme "impossibilities," wherein an object produces something completely foreign to it—in this case grapes from thorn bushes and honey from hard oak. These must be the result of magic. As any reader of the *Georgics* would be aware, labor is demanded to raise crops, grow vines, and keep a flourishing apiary; yet the golden age knows nothing of labor.

Here Virgil makes a significant transition which might be further illustrated by his address to Ceres at the opening of *Georgic* I (lines 7-8): "alma Ceres, vestro si munere tellus / Chaoniam pingui glandem mutavit arista, . . ." ("nourishing Ceres, if by your bounty the earth exchanged Chaonia's acorn for rich wheat, . . ."). The change from acorn to grain regularly betokens man's advance from primitivism to a more "cultured" existence, an advance—or decline, some say—often attributed to Jupiter's deposition of his father Saturn. For Virgil writing *Eclogue* 4, everything remains "golden": what would ordinarily come to man by the sweat of his brow is free due to nature's bounty. Nevertheless, because of the mention of grain, grapes, and honey, it is no sudden jump to the need for ploughing and sailing from which inevitably follow commerce and war.

This transition in the life of man is usually ascribed in myth to Prometheus who, by stealing fire from Jupiter, became, depending on one's point of view, either a culture hero or the originator of humanity's gradual decline from a pristine state of perfection.[15] Hence these *priscae vestigia fraudis*, which still linger on as a result of Prometheus' deceitful theft, are akin to the *sceleris vestigia nostri* (line 13), the traces of the original Roman sin which still remain to be absolved. Whatever his purpose, Prometheus' act initiated greed and ambition, and is therefore the ultimate cause of Romulus' guilt. In sum, without any incongruity we have passed—as the boy will pass—from the golden age into another heroic age in which a new group of Argonauts will set sail in search of a golden fleece and a new Achilles must storm another Troy.[16]

Virgil is elaborating ideas broached in his initial summary. The perfection of his vision, the union of pastoral stability and history, the reconciliation of the consul and the sylvan muse, cannot be achieved until the boy can comprehend the meaning of true heroism, *virtus*. At this point he can only read the praises of heroes and the deeds of his father, but the time will come, as the poet has already assured us, when, because

[15] For a summary of the varying positions of Prometheus in Greek thought, see E. A. Havelock, *The Liberal Temper in Greek Politics* (New Haven, 1957), chaps. 2-4.

For the same distinction between primal perfection and progress toward perfection in American thought, see R.W.B. Lewis, *The American Adam* (Chicago, 1955), esp. p. 5.

[16] The verbs are special. For *tempto* of attack and heroic endeavor, see *Ecl.* 1. 49 and *G.* 3. 8, among many examples. *Cingere* here means to hem in what was previously free. Elsewhere in Virgil it also means to "beleaguer" and "take by storm" (e.g., *Aen.* 1. 673). On the ship and commerce as stereotypes of opposition to the Golden Age (and the *Argo* as initiator of a new era of trouble), see commentators on Tibullus 1. 3. 37-40; Horace *Carm.* 1. 3.

of the peace his father's *virtutes* have gained, he will live the life of a hero in company with the gods. Hence, whatever the reasons for a renewal of war, it can be viewed positively by Virgil in terms of his present reasoning. This is neither escape into a never-never land nor a neo-Hesiodic, pessimistic prediction that, because we must re-experience the age of heroes, the terrible age of iron will soon be upon us again. It seeks a Virgilian dream, so rudely shattered in *Eclogue* 1, to harmonize the perfection of natural beauty—emblem of song and the poet's life—with the Roman necessity of living a practical life on the highest moral level, a life of heroic achievement through *virtus*. If there is to be another period of wars, it will effect a final purgation of the earlier *scelus*.

When the boy reaches manhood—has become a *vir* himself, ready to practise the *virtutes* he has seen in others—the world may be all-productive under his guidance (lines 37-45):

> hinc, ubi iam firmata virum te fecerit aetas,
> cedet et ipse mari vector, nec nautica pinus
> mutabit merces: omnis feret omnia tellus.
> non rastros patietur humus, non vinea falcem;
> robustus quoque iam tauris iuga solvet arator;
> nec varios discet mentiri lana colores,
> ipse sed in pratis aries iam suave rubenti
> murice, iam croceo mutabit vellera luto;
> sponte sua sandyx pascentis vestiet agnos.

After this, once time has given you the strength of manhood, the trader himself will quit the sea, and the ship of pine will not exchange wares. Every land will bear all things. Earth will not endure the harrow, nor vines the pruning-hook. Then also the sturdy ploughman will undo the yokes from his oxen; and wool will not learn the deceit of varying hues, but of his own accord the ram in the fields will change his fleece, now to sweetly blushing

crimson, now to a golden orange. Spontaneously vermilion will clothe the grazing lambs.

At last the earth will bear naturally and spontaneously all
the things which the original *fraus* of Prometheus had forced
men to produce through labor or possess through crime.
There will be no need for commerce, none for hoeing, pruning, or ploughing. And while trade and agriculture have no
part in this final ideal *otium*, nevertheless the luxuries which
mankind had previously sought through *scelus* will come
automatically.

The occupation Virgil's fancy chooses for special attention
is the dyeing of wool. In this glorious epoch ahead, there will
be no need to go in search of a unique golden fleece thereby
inaugurating a further era of commerce and war. Rather the
farmer will find in his meadows a ram who can voluntarily
change the color of his wool now to crimson, now to yellow,
and the lambs will turn vermilion as they feed. Facetious as
all this may first appear, it has a serious side: the dyeing of
wool is a frequent emblem in Roman poetry for the evils of
luxury.[17] Nature is corrupted in the pursuit of artificial charm.
The moral implications are well illustrated elsewhere by Virgil
and by Horace. In the fifth ode of his third book, the fifth of
the so-called Roman odes, Horace makes such an analogy part
of Regulus' denunciation of his fellow citizens (lines 25-30):

> auro repensus scilicet acrior
> miles redibit: flagitio additis
>   damnum. neque amissos colores
>   lana refert medicata fuco,
>
>   nec vera virtus, cum semel excidit,
>   curat reponi deterioribus; . . .

[17] On dyeing in a context of extreme decadence, see Ovid *Ars Am.* 3.
169ff. The conceit is common enough to need no elaboration, but for
a good example see Tibullus 2. 4. 27-28.

Certainly the soldier, bought by gold, will return the
bolder! You add loss to crime. Wool, tainted with dye,
does not regain its lost hues nor does true courage, when
once it has disappeared, care to be given back to the
degenerate.

The equation, of course, is between the natural hues which
the tinted wool has lost and *vera virtus*, true heroism, which
is never regained once a man has been proved a coward.
A passage at the end of the second georgic makes the same
point in more pastoral terms while giving it another negative and more realistic turn. Happy are the farmers, Virgil
exclaims (lines 459-460), "quibus ipsa procul discordibus
armis / fundit humo facilem victum iustissima tellus" ("for
whom the earth in all her justice pours forth from the ground
an easy living, far from the clash of arms"). They have no
lordly house nor inlaid doors,

> illusasque auro vestis Ephyreiaque aera,
> alba neque Assyrio fucatur lana veneno,
> nec casia liquidi corrumpitur usus olivi; . . .

nor clothes deceived with gold nor bronzes of Ephyra, nor
is their white wool stained with Assyrian poison nor is
the use of clear oil corrupted by cassia. (lines 464-66)

The mention of earth's justice to the farmer is recalled at lines
473-74: extrema per illos / Iustitia excedens terris vestigia
fecit" ("In their midst Justice planted her latest steps, as she
left the earth").[18] The phrase *tellus fundit* (which also occurs
in *Eclogue* 4, lines 19-20) and the emphasis on *Iustitia* suggests that Virgil was thinking back to the fourth eclogue.
The analogy of "dyeing" is another connection; as in the
Horatian ode, the contamination of all that is upright and

---

[18] On this particular example see Friedrich Klinger, "Über das Lob
des Landlebens in Virgils Georgica," *Hermes* 66 (1931): esp. 162-68.

sturdy is stressed—*illusas, fucatur veneno, corrumpitur.*[19] It is the deceit, the corruption of what is honest in nature, which mirrors dissension (*discordia*) among men, the occasion of civil war.

The magic ram of the fourth eclogue is a more intentionally vivid symbol than the white wool of *Georgic* 2. When the boy has grown to manhood, nature herself, as well as being munificent in every respect, will also purvey items of apparent luxury, things quite foreign to the existence of the happy, but hardy, rustic of *Georgic* 2. These new comforts will, however, lack the deceit of dyeing, which is a smaller analogue of the *fraus* and *scelus* from which discord springs. In fact, Virgil furnishes an even more specific instance of this harmless extravagance: the ram will "exchange" the colors of its fleece at will (*ipse aries mutabit vellera,* lines 43-44) making the need for commerce and barter completely unnecessary (*nec nautica pinus / mutabit merces,* lines 38-39).[20] Since the coloring of the ram is spontaneous, *virtus*—which means moral perfection, truth and honesty, as well as heroic worth—is still present: nature produces items of luxury without any false cravings on the part of mankind.

We may summarize this ladder of perfection. First, in Horace and the second georgic, dyed wool equals deceit resulting in injustice, greed, cowardice, and their consequences. The pure wool (*alba lana*) in *Georgic* 2 symbolizes the simplicity of honest nature, the farmer living a virtuous and just life of hard work. Finally, the magic ram of *Eclogue* 4, though its prowess is as impossible as brambles bearing grapes or oaks honey, is a double emblem for the new age wherein *virtus* and "civilization" can exist side by side. It denotes an ideal amalgam in nature which precludes labor and negates the causes of future war.

---

[19] The happy farmer possesses a life that is *nescia fallere*, ignorant of deceit (*G.* 2. 467).

[20] On line 43, cf. *Ecl.* 7. 11: *ipsi per prata iuvenci.*

Eclogue 4

In looking at the birth, youth, and manhood of the *puer,* we see a carefully pondered logic to the intellectual background.[21] In his youth, nature offers her *munuscula* spontaneously and profusely, though vines, flowers, and abundant milk are still far from the universal prosperity to be offered in his manhood (*omnis feret omnia tellus*). Exotic and rare as some of the vegetation might be (*acanthus* and *colocasia* are usually Egyptian, and *amomum* is labelled Assyrian), it is apparently a time when the earth needs no care, an ideal time unlike Lucretius' sketch of primitive man because there is no menace from nature.

During the next season, in which the growing boy reads about the epic deeds of his father and learns the meaning of heroism, nature is still all-fruitful, yielding grain, grapes, and honey without toil. Such instances of nature's bounty are common in portraits of paradise: only there do thorns bear grapes and hard oaks drip honey. Still, the poison of Prometheus' fraud works its harm. To those who, like Lucretius, believe that humanity was gradually civilized from a state bordering on savagery, the discovery of fire was a milestone of great importance. Not so for Virgil here. Rather, fire created the need for labor and that in turn was the source of competition in trade and war. The result of this competition was an age of heroes after whom the new Argonauts and new Achilles will be patterned.

Unlike the iron age which follows the age of heroes in Hesiod's gloomy vision of his own lifetime, the era succeeding Virgil's age of heroes is still more glorious—a golden age in which nature propagates not only the necessities of survival but also those very elements of luxury which the advances of civilization have discovered. Someone who has known the charm of richly colored garments—to elaborate Virgil's sentiment—will be loath to return to an existence of acorns and

[21] Most critics do not find a cogent order in the three parts (see, e.g., Ryberg, "Vergil's Golden Age," p. 114).

milk, however magical their engendering. In this glorious new age he may have both without the vices which ordinarily accompany their attainment.

Heroism remains as well. According to Hesiod the heroic age had two parts: the destruction of many around Thebes and Troy, and then the transplanting of the survivors to the isles of the blessed where "the bounteous earth, burgeoning three times yearly, bore them honey-sweet fruit" (*Works and Days*, lines 172-73). In Virgil's dream, the golden age is no escapist haven where men live apart but a union of mortal and immortal, of pastoral and power, achieved and maintained by *virtus* and set in an ideal landscape.

The Fates approve (lines 46-47):

> 'Talia saecla' suis dixerunt 'currite' fusis
> concordes stabili fatorum numine Parcae.

"Ages such as this, run on," the Fates cried to their spindles, agreeing on the unchanging will of destiny.

Curiously, these lines also refer directly to *Carmen* 64 by Catullus, this time to the refrain which punctuates the wedding hymn the Fates themselves sing to Peleus and Thetis (lines 326-27): "sed vos, quae fata sequuntur, / currite ducentes subtegmina, currite, fusi" ("But run on, you spindles, run on, drawing the threads which the Fates follow"). The burden of Catullus' *epithalamium*, in spite of its assurances of happiness to this marriage of mortal and divine, is the story of their hero son Achilles, whose lust for bloodshed and lack of compassion are emphasized rather than his valor. A denunciation of the immorality of modern life, the initial lines of which were quoted earlier, follows Achilles' story. For Catullus mankind and the immortals have completely lost the happy accord they once possessed. Thetis, the Argonauts, and Achilles have led only to this (lines 405-408):

omnia fanda nefanda malo permixta furore
iustificam nobis mentem avertere deorum,
quare nec talis dignantur visere coetus,
nec se contingi patiuntur lumine claro.

All things right and wrong, confused together from our
evil madness, have turned the just mind of the gods from
us. As a result they do not deign to visit such throngs or
suffer themselves to be touched by clear light.

Virgil, for a moment at least, disagrees. Catullus can cry out
early in his poem (lines 22-23): "o nimis optato saeclorum
tempore nati / heroes, salvete, deum genus!" ("O heroes, born
at the happiest moment of the ages, hail, race of gods!"). The
age of true heroism was a distinction of the past, and even then
nature made no concessions. There were moments of leisure in
life, such as the celebration of so glorious a wedding (lines
38-42):

rura colit nemo, mollescunt colla iuvencis,
non humilis curvis purgatur vinea rastris,
non glebam prono convellit vomere taurus,
non falx attenuat frondatorum arboris umbram,
squalida desertis rubigo infertur aratris.

No one tills the soil, the shoulders of the bullocks grow
soft, the humble vineyard is not weeded by the curved hoe.
The bull does not turn the clod with sloping share, the
fork of the trimmers does not thin out the tree's shade,
and darkening rust grows on the abandoned ploughs.

But they are the exception rather than the rule. Virgil claims
the opposite for both his new *saecla*, and the fates agree. It is
to be an age of peace founded upon heroism; the child, after
all, will move freely among both gods and heroes. At the same
time it is a new age of gold in the natural world.

Eclogue 4

This is the intellectual "marriage-song" which Virgil is celebrating. We have seen the importance of "union" before in the *Eclogues*. In *Eclogue* 2, for instance, one of the chief ideas is not only the happy meeting of people but the harmony of the shepherd with the cycle nature follows in the course of a day. In *Eclogue* 4 the scheme is grander. A new *ordo saeclorum* has come into being which, though associated with the boy's birth and growth, will ultimately prove stable for all mankind. The *magni menses* of this *magnus annus* which follow upon the marriage of sylvan retreat and heroic achievement, the woods of Virgilian song and the *facta* of Pollio's world of politics, are to be of lasting benefit to mankind as a whole. The newborn boy (whether or not he actually existed matters little) will become the visual symbol of this perfection.

Nature reacts with an omen which befits the grandeur of the moment (lines 48-52):

> adgredere o magnos (aderit iam tempus) honores,
> cara deum suboles, magnum Iovis incrementum!
> aspice convexo nutantem pondere mundum,
> terrasque tractusque maris caelumque profundum:
> aspice venturo laetentur ut omnia saeclo!

Enter on your mighty honors—now the time will soon be at hand—dear offspring of the gods, mighty seed of Jupiter! Behold how the earth nods with curved weight, look at the lands, the stretches of the sea, the depth of heaven. Behold how all things rejoice in the coming age!

As often in the course of this poem the words carry two shades of meaning. He is a child newborn in a rustic setting. *Suboles* means literally the shoot of a plant or the offspring of a flock; *incrementum*, its growth. *Honor* there is also, in the shepherd's world. When Silvanus, in the tenth eclogue, comes to look at the strange anomaly of a lovesick elegist among shepherds, his head is decorated with "rustic glories" (*agresti honore*). This child, however, is not a regular denizen of the countryside but an offspring of the gods. Just as he results from no ordinary pregnancy but is the product of *magni menses* bearing a *magnus saeclorum ordo*, so he will enter upon *magnos honores*, honors that would transcend ordinary public office because the future of all mankind, not just one race or generation, is dependent upon him and basks in his glory. Nor is it an ordinary child but a *magnum incrementum*, a mighty seed of Jupiter himself.

The omen of his birth, introduced by the double *aspice*, is accordingly acknowledged by the universe. The nodding of the heavens (*nutantem mundum*) is the cosmic reflection of the *fatorum numen*, the "nod" of approval the Fates bestow on the new *saecla*. The rejoicing is general: *omnia* summarizes the many ways in which mankind is affected. It reminds us that this new race will spring up in the whole world (*toto mundo*), that ivy and nard bedeck lands everywhere (*passim*, line 19; *vulgo*, line 25), and that in the future nature will produce all things. It also recalls again the poet's bold opening words. Song that devotes itself exclusively to "bushes" and humble "myrtles"—that is, to the usual pastoral topics— can scarcely expect a wide public—"non omnis arbusta iuvant humilesque myricae." The implication of the subsequent statement, "if we sing of woods, let the woods be worthy of a consul," is that the expansion of "sylvan" subjects to embrace the broader, more public values of a consul's existence will provoke a more universal appeal.

That his poetry is to be a reflection of this doubly glorious new age is the theme to which Virgil now returns (lines 53-59):

> o mihi tum longae maneat pars ultima vitae,
> spiritus et quantum sat erit tua dicere facta:
> non me carminibus vincet nec Thracius Orpheus,
> nec Linus, huic mater quamvis atque huic pater adsit,

Orphei Calliopea, Lino formosus Apollo.
Pan etiam, Arcadia mecum si iudice certet,
Pan etiam Arcadia dicat se iudice victum.

Would, then, that the last part of a long life might remain
for me and whatever breath of inspiration will be sufficient to sing your deeds. Neither Thracian Orpheus nor
Linus shall defeat me in song, though his mother give aid
to the one and his father to the other, Calliope to Orpheus,
handsome Apollo to Linus. Even Pan, were he to vie
with me and Arcadia be judge, even Pan would admit his
defeat, were Arcadia to be the judge.

The intention of the poet's prayer is clear. First, length of days
is imperative to watch the boy fulfill his promise, then the
breath (*spiritus*) to sing of his deeds. The boy himself is to
learn of *virtus*, we recall, by emulating the glories of past
heroes and the deeds of his father. Nevertheless the time of
his own heroism will come, and it must be described in a verse
form which complements its grandeur. No lyric form will do,
no slender "spirit" of the Greek muse, in Horace's phrase,
only the boldness of epic.[22] The poet, too, must become a hero.

To write epic about a contemporary who has already made
his mark is an honorable task Virgil disclaims in the prelude
to *Eclogue* 6. There he assures Varus that there will be others
who can readily sing his praises; he, on the contrary, has been
warned by Apollo to sing a fine-spun song and ponder the rustic muse on slender reed. He makes no promise of epic for the
boy in *Eclogue* 4. Were he to be granted the longevity and
the poetic strength, he might accept such a proposal. At the
moment the only way he can describe the effect of hearing
epic from the mouth of a shepherd is to visualize himself competing against the songs of Orpheus, Linus, or even Pan himself, with such a topic. No matter who might second them, be
it Calliope or Apollo, he would win, even were Arcadia,

[22] Horace *Carm.* 2. 16. 38.

Eclogue 4

the whole world of shepherd's song, to sit in judgment as
would befit such a contest.

The shepherd-poet carefully does not say that he will be
giving up pastoral song to perform this feat. He merely states
that by his words he will surpass even the founder and presiding divinity of bucolic poetry. He will raise rustic song to its
highest level of accomplishment by broadening its range to
embrace the grandeur of epic. In one sense this is only to rephrase, in terms of the rhetoric of poetry, Virgil's intellectual tour de force in *Eclogue* 4: to unite pastoral and epic
verse, to freshen the secluded, quiet waters of pastoral with
the mainstream of life at large, of history and the progress of
civilization. It is a hope as futile as the plight of Meliboeus
in the first eclogue is realistic. But this in no way negates the
achievement of the poem itself which presents (in part for the
first time) topics which were to be much discussed in the decades ahead.

From the vitality and breadth of his theme and its place in
song, Virgil concludes, as he should, by turning back to the
boy himself (lines 60-63):

> incipe, parve puer, risu cognoscere matrem
> (matri longa decem tulerunt fastidia menses)
> incipe, parve puer: qui non risere parenti,
> nec deus hunc mensa, dea nec dignata cubili est.

Begin, baby boy, to recognize your mother with a smile
(your mother endured ten long months of trial). Begin,
baby boy. Those who do not smile on their parents no god
honors with his table, no goddess with her couch.

From the *paulo maiora*, the announcement of a more exalted
programme for pastoral song, we turn to the *parvus puer*, the
tiny child central to the drama. A deliberate lightening, per-
sonalizing of the tone is distinguishable in many of the details. The intimacy which, in the earlier sketch of the baby's

162

birth, had been founded, for example, on the use of diminu-
tives (*munuscula, cunabula*) or the mention of the "smiling" acanthus, is restored by the same gesture, the smile of
child back to parents. In thinking of the boy and his future,
it is a purposeful change to turn from his ability to learn of
courage (*quae sit cognoscere virtus*), by imitation of his father's accomplishments, to the smile of recognition the baby
confers upon its mother (*risu cognoscere matrem*). Instead of
the birth pangs of the universe, the *magni menses* which precede the coming of a new age, we ponder now only the simple
pains that troubled the mother during her time of pregnancy.

The simplicity of the scene is borrowed from lines near the
end of the first *epithalamium* of Catullus (*Carmen* 61, lines
209-13):

> Torquatus volo parvulus
> matris e gremio suae
> porrigens teneras manus
> dulce rideat ad patrem
> semihiante labello.

I wish that a baby Torquatus, stretching tender hands
from his mother's bosom, might smile sweetly on his
father with lips half-opened.

It is natural that included among the prayers of a marriage
hymn should be the hope for a young son to succeed to his
father's name. Virgil's poem, too, as we have seen, celebrates a
wedding, intimate on the one hand (though no names, such
as Catullus' Iunia and Torquatus need be mentioned) yet
having general significance as well.

Virgil cannot at the end allow this double role, reflected in
the alternation of serious and playful in the poem's tone, to be
forgotten. If you do not smile on your parents, the poet intimates to the boy, you will not have a share in the life of the
gods, the prerogative of any hero. The threat has a serious

side. Virgil's imagination is responding for the last time to
the gloom which Catullus forecasts at the end of his retelling
of the story of Peleus and Thetis:

> quare nec talis dignantur visere coetus,
> nec se contingi patiuntur lumine claro.

As a result they do not deign to visit such throngs nor
suffer themselves to be touched by clear light.

The common use of *dignor* to unfold kindred material indicates this final connection between the two poets in *Eclogue* 4.
Catullus claims that the gods with reason have forgotten
man because of his crimes. Virgil, on his part, has already announced that the effects of the *scelus*, the danger of which
Catullus saw some fifteen years earlier, have been purged and
that men are once more fit companions for the gods.

Earlier in the poem, after a section on optimistic but nevertheless highly serious matters, Virgil brought things down to
earth with his playful conceit of the variegated ram. Now after
a passage on the marriage of history and poetry, he can again
afford to treat his subject wittily and imagine his magical boy,
upon whom the universe depends, as the dinner guest of a
god or lover of a goddess. The intention remains the same.
We are still dealing with a hero, someone who will restore to
mankind its aspirations toward immortality while stabilizing
a landscape of perfection. Yet this is not a philosophical treatise
but a pastoral poem, grand in conception but still the product
of a sylvan muse. The supernatural child, for all his amazing
doings, springs from a human father and mother. He will
live to have a workable relationship with divinity.

IN SPITE OF the generous optimism of its tone, the poem is
paradoxical. The dream is one-sided. In any such dialogue
between history and the essence of the pastoral world, between
process and stability, the latter must triumph or be annihilated.
The cycle of the ages will return to its starting point: the babe

will grow to manhood, but after that life must remain in an unmoved vacuum. The unalterable prayer of the Fates—*talia saecla, currite*—implies motion not as progress and change, but as permanence. Exposure to the elemental forces of reality, education at time's school, need no longer afflict mankind.

The poem is a magic *carmen*. Presenting himself as a *vates*, spokesman for the Fates and prophet of the future, the poet proposes not only to manipulate and then fix the progress of the ages but to "induce" a youthful "savior-king" who will embody the lasting values of pastoral perfection. Taken by itself the poem is a brilliant achievement, yet its very impossibility leaves lingering doubts concerning Virgil's true beliefs. In the first eclogue he surrounds Tityrus and his patron, the god-youth in Rome, with the same aura of idealism only to destroy it ruthlessly. Tityrus may exist happily in a vacuum, but he has little realization of history or of human nature. The lesson to Tityrus, the poet who can know nothing of what makes poetry because he has no knowledge of suffering, is one which Virgil is unwilling to read himself in *Eclogue* 4. Broad as the vistas and stimulating as the ideas are, the point of *Eclogue* 4 is still only a higher version of pastoral. It is an escapist, idealized world, powerful enough to presume a victory of *otium*, after a final purgation of time's processes. It is also, ultimately, a very un-Roman, unrealistic one. But Virgil acknowledges the full meaning of this distinction in his next two works. We are left only with a question: Could the new age succeed in accomplishing this unique fusion of poetry and power?

The high style and elevated discourse of *Eclogue* 4 give way as Virgil returns to a form of expression common in pastoral poetry, the dialogue between two shepherds (lines 1-7):

Me. Cur non, Mopse, boni quoniam convenimus ambo,
 tu calamos inflare levis, ego dicere versus,
 hic corylis mixtas inter consedimus ulmos?

Mo. Tu maior; tibi me est aequum parere, Menalca,
 sive sub incertas Zephyris motantibus umbras,
 sive antro potius succedimus. aspice, ut antrum
 silvestris raris sparsit labrusca racemis.

Me. Mopsus, since we who have come together are both skilled people, you at blowing through the slim reeds, I at singing verses, why do we not sit here among the elms mixed with hazels?

Mo. You are the older. It is right for me to obey you, Menalcas, whether we stay under the shadows that change with the movement of the Zephyrs or whether we enter the cave instead. Look how the wild vine has spread the cave with clusters here and there.

Gone is the lofty philosophical intent of the greatest "shepherd" of them all, prophesying his own *paulo maiora*. By contrast, the initial interplay of *Eclogue* 5, like the conversation which introduces *Eclogue* 3, appears simple and straightforward. Two shepherds are in search of a setting, a spot appropriate for their songs. Menalcas, the elder, is the more conventional. The pattern he approves is repeated at the start of *Eclogue* 7. The process of a "debate" depends on the "coming together" of singers; their song is the agreement of two ways of thinking.

Eclogue 5

Menalcas suggests a difference between them. One is especially good at playing the pipes, the other at singing. Yet, though he phrases his sentiments in part as a question, he reiterates forthwith his unity with his colleague: *convenimus* leads to *consedimus*. They are united with themselves and should be with nature. Singer and locale are each necessary for the creation of such a song as follows. The "sitting together" is as valuable—and symbolic—as the mixture of hazels and elms which Menalcas proposes as background for their performance. This distinguishes his words from previous examples of the usual setting—Tityrus at ease in the shade, Corydon among the thick beeches.

Mopsus, with deference, takes an opposite view about the right location. Shade, whether of cloud or tree, and breezes are essential attributes of bucolic song: shade to ward off the elemental heat, breezes to carry the singer's words to mountain, forest, or heaven itself. But stability and assurance are also prerequisites of the ideal retreat, and these Mopsus apparently does not find amidst rushing Zephyrs and insecure shadows. No Tityrus he. For some reason he must decline the usual setting for song and suggest instead a cave. To him it appears a marvel (*aspice* often introduces an omen) that a wild vine decks it with clusters.

Commentators on this passage usually observe a parallel with the cave of Calypso and its vine, the ἡμερὶς ἡβώωσα, described in Book 5 of the *Odyssey*. But hers is clearly a tame, cultivated arbor whereas the wild quality of Virgil's *labrusca* is underscored by the adjective *silvestris*. The vine adorning the cave which the shepherds are about to enter is pastoral, part of the scenario befitting a *silvestrem Musam*, and has nothing to do with the georgic implications of tending the grape. A cave may seem an unusual place in which to sing bucolic verses, yet it has strong symbolic associations with the composition of poetry. Here it is not ivy but the wild vine that covers the entrance, not Apollo but Bacchus whose attribute now links him with pastoral poetry and the shepherd's life.[1]

We may note, in anticipation, that it is within a cave (*antrum*) that the drunken Silenus, mentor of Bacchus, sings his *carmina* in the next eclogue. There Virgil does not challenge us with the alternative, more common *mise en scène* which Menalcas first proposes to Mopsus. Nevertheless, from the dialogue thus far we might be tempted to draw one conclusion: Mopsus is reluctant, either because of the delivery or content of his future song, to embrace the traditional location for singing. Hence we might well expect something new to pastoral song here—locale, after all, is the source of inspiration as well as a reflection of it. Mopsus' proposal involves reconciliation of vine and cave with traditional bucolic themes, elements not ordinarily mixed.

> Me. Montibus in nostris solus tibi certat Amyntas.
> Mo. Quid, si idem certet Phoebum superare canendo?
> Me. Incipe, Mopse, prior, si quos aut Phyllidis ignis
> aut Alconis habes laudes aut iurgia Codri.
> incipe: pascentis servabit Tityrus haedos.
> Mo. Immo haec, in viridi nuper quae cortice fagi
> carmina descripsi et modulans alterna notavi,
> experiar: tu deinde iubeto ut certet Amyntas.
> Me. Lenta salix quantum pallenti cedit olivae,
> puniceis humilis quantum saliunca rosetis,
> iudicio nostro tantum tibi cedit Amyntas.
> sed tu desine plura, puer: successimus antro.

Me. In our mountains Amyntas alone rivals you.
Mo. What if he should try to surpass Phoebus, too, with his songs?
Me. Begin first, Mopsus, if you have songs about your flame, Phyllis, or in praise of Alcon or to abuse Codrus. Begin. Tityrus will watch the feeding goats.

[1] On Bacchus, a cave, and the composition of poetry see Propertius 3. 1. 1ff.

Mo. Nay, rather I will try these songs which I recently wrote down on green beech-bark and noted the melody line by line. Then do you order Amyntas to vie with me.

Me. As much as the bending willow yields before the glistening olive, as much as the lowly reed to the crimson rose-trees, so much, in my opinion, does Amyntas give place to you. But say no more, lad. We have entered the cave. (lines 8-19)

Menalcas' reassurance that Mopsus has only one rival, Amyntas, inspires Mopsus' almost contemptuous rejoinder that Amyntas might as well vie with Apollo. But the reasons for Mopsus' self-confidence and the peculiarity of his request that they, or at least he, sing from a vine-shrouded cave, are still apparently lost on Menalcas. Menalcas proposes that Mopsus begin their encounter by singing of ordinary topics such as love, panegyric, or abuse.[2]

Once again Mopsus disappoints Menalcas' hopes. He disposes of stock themes as quickly as he dismissed the stock setting. His alternative is a shock to what we have come to expect of the shepherd-singer and to Menalcas' expectations as well. His song is something new, so new that it is an experiment. Moreover the themes are so exciting, strange, or novel to the bucolic mode (it cannot be a question of incompetence) that Mopsus has had to write them down on bark, a practice repugnant or at least foreign to the shepherd's oral art. He has even been impelled to note the melodic interludes as well. From the second line of the poem we could assume that Menalcas was the singer and Mopsus' virtue was playing flute accompaniments, but lines 8 and 9 acknowledge his prowess at song as well. Yet, in spite of *certet Amyntas* (line 15)

[2] Of a Phyllis we hear in *Eclogues* 3, 7, and 10. Codrus is the butt of Thyrsis' remarks at *Ecl.* 7. 26. No Alcon is mentioned in the *Eclogues* (a craftsman of that name does appear at *Culex* 67), but he may have his counterpart in the sculptor Alcimedon of *Eclogue* 3.

which echoes, only to disclaim, *certat Amyntas* (line 8),
Mopsus' language leaves the reader wondering about his song.[3]

Menalcas' words are gauged to put Mopsus—if not the
reader—at ease. *Certat Amyntas* changes to *cedit* (line 16) and
cedit Amyntas (line 18). The analogies have the same intention: they compare objects which to some degree superficially
look alike (the *saliunca*, like the rose-tree, is apparently red)
but are basically different in quality or importance. The effect
is only to strengthen our suspicion of Mopsus' divergences
from ordinary procedure. His accomplishment is anticipated
without being disclosed. Mopsus is to Amyntas as pale olive
and crimson rose-tree are to pliant osier and lowly reed. Yet
the osier and the reed—especially with the adjectives attributed to them (*lenta* and *humilis*)—are common emblems of
the bucolic way. Though this is the only place the *saliunca* is
mentioned in Virgil, the *salix* appears in *Eclogues* 1, 3 (in line
83 with the adjective *lenta* attached), and 10. Of *lentus* itself
occurrences are frequent enough that we need only recall
Tityrus *lentus in umbra* and the *lenta viburna* of *Eclogue* 1
to indicate its pastoral implications. To turn to the adjective
humilis, a like spirit accompanies Virgil's announcement in
line 2 of *Eclogue* 4 that "non omnis arbusta iuvant humilesque
myricae." Greater themes than the shepherd's ordinary concerns are sometimes required.

The last example is especially apt in connection with
Eclogue 5. Here we are not really dealing with an external
force that clashes with the spirit of the bardic shepherd's
existence—Rome against *otium*. Rather, we are concerned
with a contrast, within the bounds of song, between simple,
common themes that an Amyntas might sing (and a Menalcas at first suggest) and the grander subject that Menalcas
senses Mopsus will utter, however hesitant his introduction.
Bending osier and lowly viburnum are no match in character

---

[3] Büchner, *P. Vergilius Maro*, col. 194, observes that lines 13-15
probably refer to an experiment on the part of Mopsus.

or value for the glimmering, festive, practical olive or the brightly decorative rose.[4] Color triumphs over shape.

In other words, Menalcas' words, which are congenial to Mopsus' initial actions, tell the reader that he can once more expect themes higher than, or at least different from, the usual bucolic fare. At the opening of *Eclogue* 4 Virgil makes this a major point, speaking proudly in his own voice. Here, though Mopsus appears to retreat before his accomplishment, Menalcas has twice reassured him of his competence and of the higher value of his song. His command to begin coincides with their entrance into the cave. Mopsus has won his way with setting and song (lines 20-44):

Mo. Exstinctum Nymphae crudeli funere Daphnim
    flebant (vos coryli testes et flumina Nymphis),
    cum complexa sui corpus miserabile nati,
    atque deos atque astra vocat crudelia mater.
    non ulli pastos illis egere diebus
    frigida, Daphni, boves ad flumina; nulla neque amnem
    libavit quadripes nec graminis attigit herbam.
    Daphni, tuum Poenos etiam gemuisse leones
    interitum montesque feri silvaeque loquuntur.
    Daphnis et Armenias curru subiungere tigris
    instituit, Daphnis thiasos inducere Bacchi
    et foliis lentas intexere mollibus hastas.
    vitis ut arboribus decori est, ut vitibus uvae,
    ut gregibus tauri, segetes ut pinguibus arvis,
    tu decus omne tuis. postquam te fata tulerunt
    ipsa Pales agros atque ipse reliquit Apollo.
    grandia saepe quibus mandavimus hordea sulcis,
    infelix lolium et steriles nascuntur avenae;
    pro molli viola, pro purpureo narcisso
    carduus et spinis surgit paliurus acutis.
    spargite humum foliis, inducite fontibus umbras,

---

[4] On the olive, see *G.* 3. 21.

Eclogue 5

pastores (mandat fieri sibi talia Daphnis),
et tumulum facite, et tumulo superaddite carmen:
'Daphnis ego in silvis, hinc usque ad sidera notus,
formosi pecoris custos, formosior ipse.'

Mo. The Nymphs wept for Daphnis, killed by a cruel death
(you hazels and streams bear witness to the Nymphs),
when, embracing the pitiful corpse of her son, his
mother cried out to the gods and the stars about their
cruelty. Daphnis, in those days no one drove the pastured cattle to cool rivers. No four-footed beast tasted
the streams or touched a blade of grass. Daphnis, the
wild mountains and the woods say that even African
lions mourned your passing. Daphnis taught us to
yoke Armenian tigers to the chariot, to lead in the revelry of Bacchus and to intertwine hard spears with soft
leaves. As the vine is a source of beauty for trees, as
grapes for vines, as bulls for herds, as corn for the rich
fields, so you are a glory to mankind. After the fates
bore you off, Pales herself and even Apollo left our
fields. Often in the furrows to which we entrusted
large grains unlucky darnel and barren straw grow.
Instead of the soft violet and purple narcissus, thistles
and brambles with sharp thorns spring up. Strew the
ground with leaves, shepherds, cover the founts with
shade (such were the orders Daphnis commands to
be carried out for him) and make a tomb and on the
tomb add an epitaph: "I was Daphnis in the woods,
known hence even to the stars. Fair was the flock I
guarded, fairer I."

With his opening words we sense a reason for Mopsus'
changes. To sing of death in a sylvan setting is ominous
enough; the elegiac tone is not consonant with the pastoral
world's assumed idealism. But to mourn for the "cruel" demise
of Daphnis, bucolic hero *par excellence*, is to hint at the ruin

172

of the landscape.[5] No wonder that Mopsus does not wish
to sing his words to the hazels, the very trees who must bear
witness to nature's sorrow at Daphnis' loss! No wonder, too,
that Virgil makes his singer a bit retiring. The poet has, after
all, just sung of the happy relationship between a mother and
her son, a son who will do the impossible by subjecting progress to the notions of "pastoral." The child this mother mourns
is so important that the nymphs take up the cry of woe.

Virgil's words echo, with good reason, Meliboeus' sketch
of Amaryllis, parted from her lover (*Eclogue* 1, line 36):
"mirabar quid maesta deos, Amarylli, vocares." Tityrus seems
to her a cult figure necessary for the survival of the landscape; the pines, fountains, and shrubs which call out to him
see Tityrus the same way. But absence, though it could ultimately spell doom if Tityrus failed to return or if his mission
to Rome was a failure, is different from death within the country. This mother's bitter outbursts, hurled against the heavens
for the death of her son, betoken a deeper grief than a lover's
lamentation. Power of generation, the future, is gone and with
it the hope of continuity in nature; man must cry out against
gods rather than have divinity and the heavens bless humanity
as they do in *Eclogue* 4.

All nature is affected. This composite picture is linked to
the opening lines not only by stress on the name Daphnis,
which expectedly rings through the poem, but also by the iteration of *flumina* in lines 21 and 25. In reflecting nature's woe,
the streams are not allowed to grant their wonted sustenance.
First mentioned are the tame animals who must ordinarily
be driven to drink. Then we learn that no *quadripes* (which
elsewhere in Virgil means either a deer or a horse) tasted
water or touched grass.[6] The verbs, unique in the *Eclogues*,

[5] If we were to rely solely on the parallel with Theocritus' first *Idyl*
and on Virgil's own use of the word *crudelis* in *Eclogue* 8, the cause
would be love. *Miserabile* adds ambiguity.

[6] The word *quadripes* is applied to a deer at *Aen.* 7. 500. All other
allusions in Virgil are to horses.

convey a certain hesitancy as if these animals, distinct from the *boves*, might in any case be shy about appearing at a river bank and certainly would not be herded to water.[7] Yet they, too, feel the pull of grief. Finally—and the climax is emphasized by the word *etiam*—we are given the extreme of untamed nature: Punic lions whose suffering must be recounted by mountains, which are themselves wild (*feri*). This is the "pathetic fallacy" in an impressive form. The fiercest animals "groan" like humans and remote hills report the beasts' emotions.

These lines, from *exstinctum* to its synonym *interitum*, form a unity which thematically embraces all nature. We move from the tame pastoral of mother and nymphs, hazels, rivulets, and cattle, to more aloof forms of animal life, and finally to the wild nature of lions from distant ranges, creatures of a landscape ordinarily antagonistic to the shepherd's limited existence. Yet, whether tame or wild, human, animal, or quasidivine, near or far, all join in mourning for Daphnis, a force essential to nature but now abstracted from it. All the tensions of ordinary life are resolved in this unity, stemming from grief and betokening death.

It is an easy step from a description of nature's universal grief to a catalogue of Daphnis' accomplishments. Among them was the ability to yoke Armenian tigers, counterpart in ferocity to the wailing Punic lions.[8] Daphnis is no ordinary shepherd but a culture hero who assumes the mantle of Bacchus, one of whose chief exploits, leading to his apotheosis, was the taming of tigers. In the words of Horace (*Carmina* 3. 3. 13-15):

> hac te merentem, Bacche pater, tuae
> vexere tigres indocili iugum
> collo trahentes, . . .

[7] The verbs appear together again at *Aen.* 1. 737.
[8] Cf. Propertius 1. 9. 19.

For this reason, as you deserve, father Bacchus, your tigers draw you along, while they wear the yoke on neck untamable.

In Book 6 of the *Aeneid* Virgil makes it a hyperbolic compliment to Augustus that he surpassed the heroic accomplishments of the god of wine (lines 804-5), "qui pampineis victor iuga flectit habenis / Liber, agens celso Nysae de vertice tigris" ("Liber who victoriously guides his car with vine-covered reins, driving tigers from the lofty crest of Nysa"). Line 29 of *Eclogue* 5 makes the factual connection explicit while the swathing of the hard spears in soft leaves is a further acknowledgment of the taming of the wild through the works of civilization.[9]

The three infinitives in this list of Daphnis' accomplishments—*subiungere, inducere,* and *intexere*—have a ring about them which recalls the moment in the preceding poem (lines 32-33) where Virgil catalogues the results of Prometheus' deceit: to "make trial" (*temptare*) of the sea, fortify (*cingere*) towns, and cleave (*infindere*) furrows in the ground. The verbs which introduce each set of infinitives, *iubeant* ("order") and *instituit* ("establish") respectively, likewise parallel each other. Yet in their contrasts they set in relief the differences between these segments of two closely related poems.

In *Eclogue* 4 Virgil must admit the hardships put in mankind's path by Promethean fire because his ultimate purpose is to imagine a union between pastoral freedom and "progress," a union which, when seen in terms of the dialectic of pastoral, implies destruction of the unchanging bucolic golden age. Daphnis, unlike the destructive Prometheus, expands the scope of pastoral ideas in another direction.

Daphnis' instruction urges the land to be creative in a new

[9] At *Aen.* 7. 390 the *thyrsi* of Bacchic rites are described as *mollis. Lentus* here, of course, means "hard," not "bending," which is its usual pastoral sense.

way. He teaches the uses not of *fraus* but of energy harnessed, of wildness refined, and of wine, something which, as mentioned above, goes beyond the bucolic mode to more realistic, georgic thinking. Yet here mankind's development is limited to what easily seems natural for the rustic life, rather than pushed ambitiously into an inherently destructive quest. The taming of animals and the discovery of the vine's uses merely turn objects already available in nature to creative advantage. They do not imply a threat to the golden age but an expansion of its "practicability." At the same time these creative attributes of Daphnis imply the same search for order in human life that pervades *Eclogue* 4; here the search is viewed as the attempt to bridle unruly elements or forge neglected resources into a creative stability.

We are not surprised at the analogies which follow (lines 32-34), both specifically and generally because the georgic element predominates: bulls are the glory of herds, and crops of fertile fields. The care of cattle and the tilling of lands are occupations dependent upon labor, not *otium*. Again the poet centers his thoughts on wine, the creative relationship of vine to tree and clusters to vine. Beyond this, however, it is the idea of Daphnis as a spirit of *decus*, of beauty necessary to the land, which is stressed, something abstract in essence yet furnishing that literal charm which presides over nature as a life-giving force. When Horace speaks of his patron Maecenas as *dulce decus* or *grande decus* he means much the same thing. Maecenas' "protection," his activating presence, not only grants the poet *otium* but allows his verses their charm as well. Hence each individual thing in life should have its own *decus*, its own grace. Daphnis inspires beauty in all nature; he is its teacher and preserver. Again through the word itself (these are the only uses of *decus* in the *Eclogues*) there is a link with *Eclogue* 4, where in line 11 we learn that under Pollio's consulship the beauty of the age (*decus hoc aevi*) will commence.

The link is strengthened by the lines which follow in each

poem. *Eclogue* 4 limns the coming alive of the intellectual world through the impetus of the poet's charm. Diana officiates at this spiritual rebirth and Apollo reigns; justice returns and the Saturnian age is renewed. Mopsus' theme, in *Eclogue* 5, is exactly the opposite: instead of birth, death comes to nature. With Daphnis' demise, Pales and Apollo also depart. The appearance of *ipsa* and *ipse* in line 35 is a reversal of the frequent uses of *ipse* in *Eclogue* 4. Instead of voicing their happy concord, the fates carry off the shepherd's hero.

The result is the ruin of nature, the engendering of blight, not increase. It is ironic, but no accident, that both the verbs *nascor* and *surgo* appear in *Eclogue* 4 at lines 5, 8 and 9, and in *Eclogue* 5 at lines 37 and 39. Virgil was fond of line 37 for he repeats it, with one important change, at line 154 of the first georgic: ". . . interque nitentia culta / infelix lolium et steriles dominantur avenae" (". . . and midst the gleaming crops unlucky darnel and barren straw hold sway"). In *Eclogue* 5, as beautiful changes to ugly, waste springs from what is ordinarily productive, nondescript is born instead of colorful, and sharp instead of soft (*mollis*, in line 38, effectively recalls *foliis mollibus* at 31). Nature betrays her trust because the spirit of *decus* has departed. In *Georgic* 1, Virgil dwells on the encroachments of evil nature upon productive nature. It is a gradual thing, yet full domination by the enemy is ultimately unavoidable unless the farmer takes up the arms which Ceres has furnished him and applies them with industry. The practical aspect is not present in *Eclogue* 5, which likewise avoids mentioning the moral level which the return of *Iustitia* adds to *Eclogue* 4. Emphasis rests simply on that lack of order and creativity which the passing of beauty imposes on mourning nature.

The commands which follow, though voiced by Mopsus, are really the words of Daphnis alone, craving a return to, or continuation of, pastoral normality. The double imperatives find their parallels in the oracular young man's exhortation in

Eclogue 1—" 'pascite ut ante boves, pueri; summittite tauros.' "
—or in Meliboeus' parody of it—"insere nunc, Meliboee, piros,
pone ordine vitis." In *Eclogue* 5, however, the words have
scarcely any tinge of practicality. To scatter the ground with
leaves is merely to recreate the setting in which Tityrus dwells;
he can invite Meliboeus to spend the night upon the green
leaves, *fronde super viridi*. Covering the fountains with
shade fulfills the same purpose. The detail finds its counterpart in the *frigus opacum*, the shady coolness Meliboeus as-
cribes to Tityrus' retreat.

In this setting is to be discovered, in the future, not beauty
but a tomb. The repetition *tumulum-tumulo* is as effective,
pessimistically, as the iterations of *decori-decus*, 32-34, and *vitis-
vitibus* in 32 are, positively. As death claimed its hero, so the
pastoral world now becomes Daphnis' tomb. The initial commands, therefore, prepare not for an enhancement of the landscape's charm but for a monument to its demise. The vocabulary again demands an ironic response. *Inducite,* though it
echoes *inducere* of line 30 and thus intimates a renewal of
Daphnis' cultural efforts, is sadly disappointing. And *mandat,*
echoing *mandavimus* in line 36, where Mopsus has begun to
testify to the decline of the land, becomes only the last command possible, making a fitting symbol within the bucolic
world of its downfall.

The epitaph Daphnis orders is curious and anticipatory. As
befits Mopsus' hesitancy, which is engendered by the sadness
of his theme, the final eulogy of Daphnis is to be written, not
sung. In line 14 Mopsus is disclosed committing to bark his
carmina—words and music. Here is the last *carmen*, a written
song of death within a dying world. The shade which looms
over the tomb, instead of betokening a setting for pastoral
song,[10] suggests the *incertas umbras* (line 5), the unsure
shadows from which Mopsus has earlier escaped.

---

[10] *Requiesce sub umbra*, Daphnis himself commands Meliboeus in
Eclogue 7, when the latter has by chance stumbled upon song as well
as setting.

Eclogue 5

Once the reader has gone through the poem, he may well anticipate the subject of Menalcas' song from the words *ad sidera notus*. Daphnis' fame, while he lived, did reach the stars; but the final doublet (*formosi, formosior*), by reminding us again of Daphnis' beauty, merely stresses once more the pastoral world's loss. His beauty has not saved him from death and his passing, because it means the loss of *decus*, destroys his world. At his demise *ipsa Pales*, Pales herself, and *ipse Apollo*, Apollo himself, leave the land. Though his flocks are lovely and he himself still more handsome (*formosior ipse*), his beauty has saved neither himself nor his world. Whatever the extent of his fame, he is as subject to mortality as anyone. No wonder Mopsus retreats into a cave and writes his song rather than sings it from memory. For a shepherd to crown his verse with an apparent epitaph to his own existence is to crave his colleague's indulgence for a song nature herself cannot hear.

But the song is only a product of Mopsus' imagination. Hence Menalcas' reply (lines 45-52):

> Tale tuum carmen nobis, divine poeta,
> quale sopor fessis in gramine, quale per aestum
> dulcis aquae saliente sitim restinguere rivo.
> nec calamis solum aequiperas, sed voce magistrum:
> fortunate puer, tu nunc eris alter ab illo.
> nos tamen haec quocumque modo tibi nostra vicissim
> dicemus, Daphnimque tuum tollemus ad astra;
> Daphnim ad astra feremus: amavit nos quoque Daphnis.

To me, divine bard, your song is like sleep on the grass to the weary, like the slaking of thirst at a leaping rill of sweet water during the heat. You equal your master not only in piping but also in song. Lucky youth, now you will be next after him. Nevertheless, as best I can, I will sing these songs of mine to you in turn, and exalt your Daphnis to the stars. I will bring your Daphnis to the stars. Daphnis also loved me.

Eclogue 5

To Menalcas, the "charm" of Mopsus' verses has "recreated" nature. Whatever chaos the death of Daphnis may bring to nature is counterbalanced by song. Song becomes sleep and the slaking of thirst. It creates grass and water, the setting, as it were, to appreciate beauty. Song will renew the resting place and the fountains which are imperatives for the singer and which Daphnis' death could destroy.

Aptly, Menalcas' words imply that, before Mopsus sang, or perhaps without his song, the shepherd had been a victim of labor, to which rest and sleep bring relief, and exposed to the hot sun and to thirst not yet assuaged.[11] The parallels between lines 46-47 and Corydon's allusion at line 10 of *Eclogue* 2 to the reapers tired from the heat—*rapido fessis messoribus aestu*—are meaningful. The cattle can find coolness and shade, and the reapers gain relief, from the salad of herbs Thestylis concocts. Corydon, however, labors with unrequited love. In *Eclogue* 5 Mopsus has made us aware of the greater disaster portended for the land by the departure of its central figure. Corydon's trials are nothing when compared to the whole rustic life *in extremis*. Yet, paradoxically, merely by the power of song Mopsus can recreate life, can free the pastoral world from the terrors of his words. Still his words are, after all, song and not fact—Virgil puts Mopsus' words two removes from the direct monologue of *Eclogue* 4! The harshness of nature's violence is mollified. Sweet follows upon harsh. Man is refreshed from the same source which brought him hardship.

After verses sung away from the shade and breeze by a bard who insists upon retreating into a cave, Menalcas' words take us back outdoors, to the realm natural to pastoral song. His praises of Mopsus are significant. Instead of being prosaic and earthbound, a mirror of his actions, his words make him divine—an adjective Virgil uses in the *Eclogues* to describe the poets Linus (*Eclogue* 6, line 67) and Gallus (*Eclogue* 10,

[11] *Dulce satis umor*, sweet is water to the seedlings, says Menalcas at 3. 82.

line 17).[12] His immortality is assured. And if we had any lingering doubt that Mopsus' virtuosity rested purely on his ability to play the pipes, as suggested by line 2, they are put at rest by line 48. His verses, according to Menalcas, are the equal of his piping. They have paved the way for Daphnis' apotheosis.

Yet whatever the allusion in Mopsus' closing thoughts to Daphnis' deification and to the poet's own divine prowess at immortalizing the mundane through song, it remains for Menalcas to realize these in fact. The power of his imagination (the virtual doublet *nos, nostra* is emphatic) will raise his verses, and his hero, to the heavens.[13] No mere breezes or echoes will make his theme reverberate against the sky. The poet himself accomplishes the deed through song. Menalcas stresses by its position the most emphatic repetition, almost a litany, in the poem: *Daphnim . . . ad astra*; / *Daphnim ad astra*. It is accompanied by verbs of sheer physical power, *tollemus* and *feremus*. The effort is revolutionary, the change of tone brisk. The apotheosis of a shepherd, however great his love for those around him, is an extraordinary accomplishment. In terms of the most obvious distinctions, Menalcas changes death to life, mortality to divinity, earth to heaven, elegy to eulogy. The narrow enclosed elegiac context, tied to a dying world whose central symbol is a tomb, is changed into a sphere wide without limit.

Mopsus comments on the prospect (lines 53-55):

> An quicquam nobis tali sit munere maius?
> et puer ipse fuit cantari dignus, et ista
> iam pridem Stimichon laudavit carmina nobis.

Could any gift be greater to me than this? Not only was the boy himself a worthy subject for song, but some time ago Stimichon praised your verses to me.

---

[12] *Divinus* is also the epithet of the unknown master Alcimedon, the crafter of the prize cups in *Eclogue* 3 (line 37).
[13] Cf. *Ecl.* 9. 29, where similar phraseology depicts the power of song to deify.

Menalcas' present verses, or at least verses of his making, unlike Mopsus' own, had been heard before. They are a way of
proclaiming the durability of the pastoral life. Yet their reiteration is a *munus*, a lover's gift from poet to poet, from
Menalcas to his fellow shepherds, from Daphnis back to the
pastoral world which is transformed so as to realize its perfection (lines 56-80) :

> Candidus insuetum miratur limen Olympi
> sub pedibusque videt nubes et sidera Daphnis.
> ergo alacris silvas et cetera rura voluptas
> Panaque pastoresque tenet Dryadasque puellas.
> nec lupus insidias pecori, nec retia cervis
> ulla dolum meditantur: amat bonus otia Daphnis.
> ipsi laetitia voces ad sidera iactant
> intonsi montes; ipsae iam carmina rupes,
> ipsa sonant arbusta: 'deus, deus ille, Menalca!'
> sis bonus o felixque tuis! en quattuor aras:
> ecce duas tibi, Daphni, duas altaria Phoebo.
> pocula bina novo spumantia lacte quotannis
> craterasque duo statuam tibi pinguis olivi,
> et multo in primis hilarans convivia Baccho,
> ante focum, si frigus erit, si messis, in umbra
> vina novum fundam calathis Ariusia nectar.
> cantabunt mihi Damoetas et Lyctius Aegon;
> saltantis Satyros imitabitur Alphesiboeus.
> haec tibi semper erunt, et cum sollemnia vota
> reddemus Nymphis, et cum lustrabimus agros.
> dum iuga montis aper, fluvios dum piscis amabit,
> dumque thymo pascentur apes, dum rore cicadae,
> semper honos nomenque tuum laudesque manebunt.
> ut Baccho Cererique, tibi sic vota quotannis
> agricolae facient: damnabis tu quoque votis.

Radiant Daphnis marvels at the unfamiliar threshold of
heaven and sees beneath his feet clouds and stars. And so

lively joy seizes the woods and the rest of the countryside, Pan, shepherds, and Dryad maids. The wolf plots no treachery for the herd nor any nets a snare for the deer. Noble Daphnis loves peace. The very unshorn mountains happily hurl their shouts to the stars. The rocks themselves, the very groves resound, "a god, a very god he is, Menalcas!" Be noble and gracious to your people. Here are four altars. See, Daphnis, two are for you and two for Phoebus. Two cups, brimming with fresh milk, and two bowls of rich olive oil will I offer you year by year and, of chief importance, as we enliven the banquets with wine—before the hearth in wintertime, at harvest season in the shade—I will pour from goblets the fresh nectar of Chian wine. Damoetas and Lyctian Aegon will sing for me. Alphesiboeus will mime the dancing satyrs. These rites will ever be yours, both when we pay our due vows to the Nymphs and when we purify the fields. So long as the boar loves the mountain ridge, as the fish the rivers, so long as bees feed on thyme, cicadas on dew, so long will your honor and name and praises survive. As to Bacchus and Ceres, so farmers will also make yearly vows to you. You will bind them to their vows.

The blackness of death, never directly mentioned but implicit in the cave's retreat and the shade of the fountains and tomb, is replaced by the radiance of Daphnis, initiate into divinity. No grand spiritual adventure, no rifling of hell or journey into self-knowledge precedes this metamorphosis. The ordinary hero's craving prepares him for Olympus. Daphnis stands in amazement at the unwonted spectacle.[14] Instead of terrestial objects beneath his feet, he sees clouds and stars. The translation that Menalcas proposed to perform has been accomplished, and more. Daphnis is, as it were, beyond the stars to Olympus itself.

[14] Cf. the similar use of *miror* at *Ecl.* I. II.

Eclogue 5

The change in Daphnis posits the same change in nature. From Daphnis' epitaph, whence we learn that he is known *in silvis* yet with a reputation which extends *ad sidera*, we turn to Daphnis himself, now immortal and looking down at the stars *(sidera)*. This glance in turn effects in the woods *(silvas)* and in the rest of the countryside a reaction characterized as *alacris voluptas*. The adjective is rare in Virgil—it appears only here in the *Eclogues* and never in the *Georgics*—and the noun only slightly less so. It is *voluptas,* we recall, which "drags" Corydon along in line 65 of the second eclogue. For him *voluptas* involves the hunt which in turn suggests higher levels of search leading either to fulfillment or to destruction. His passion is the same as that of a lioness for wolf, wolf for goat, goat for clover.

Daphnis' apotheosis brings with it an opposite form of *voluptas*. Whereas Corydon speaks of the shepherd's life misled by unhappy love, Menalcas' vision is of idealism restored by the renewal of love. This is a creative, not a destructive, love. It encompasses the entire countryside, the gods (Pan), mortals (shepherds), and the semi-divine nymphs. What one would ordinarily expect to be impossible to avoid, nature's preying on her lesser brethren, will not occur; beast does not plot against beast, nor man against the animal world. *Otium,* in *Eclogue* 1, is the peaceful leisure for one shepherd to enjoy the pastoral life without the threat of annihilation. Here in *Eclogue* 5 it connotes not only that quiet which befits the shepherd-bard but also the calmness necessary for creativity, the order requisite for happiness, the subtraction of guile and deception from the world, the unification of opposites, and the harmonization of all elements of nature.

The reaction in nature is predictable. It bespeaks a return to that spontaneity crucial to the golden age. Counteracting the departure of Pales and Apollo *(ipsa . . . ipse,* line 35), the unshorn mountains themselves *(ipsi . . . intonsi montes,* lines 62-63), which before had only been able to tell of the lions' groaning at Daphnis' death, now announce their joy. The rocks themselves (*ipsae*) and the very bushes (*ipsa*) follow suit. This is not even the poet's song, so far are we now from Mopsus' lament; nature herself composes *carmina*. We may compare nature's elegy for the absent Tityrus in *Eclogue* 1, lines 38-39: "ipsae te, Tityre, pinus, / ipsi te fontes, ipsa haec arbusta vocabant." In the second part of *Eclogue* 5, the shepherd essential to the well-being of the countryside does return, and the *crudelia* which Daphnis' mother hurled against the gods and stars as well as the wailing of the earth in Mopsus' song are changed, with Daphnis' metamorphosis, into that *laetitia* which mirrors not only spiritual happiness but also rejuvenation of life in nature as well.[15] The hyperbole is particularly exciting because now it is the mountains themselves which sing (itself an *adunaton*) to the heavens. This excitement helps to further Menalcas' design to counteract Mopsus' inwardly oriented approach and the gloom of his theme by a bold reopening of the broadest vistas of pastoral which relate heaven to earth in the joy of song.

It is with a specific purpose that nature's cry to the singer —'*deus, deus ille, Menalca*'—echoes Lucretius' paean to Epicurus which opens Book 5 of *De Rerum Natura* (lines 8-10):

> ... deus ille fuit, deus, inclute Memmi,
> qui princeps vitae rationem invenit eam quae
> nunc appellatur sapientia, ...

That man was a god, a god, noble Memmius, who first discovered that way of life which is now called wisdom.

Within five more lines, Lucretius compares Ceres and Bacchus with Epicurus, to the latter's advantage. It is not surprising then to learn in *Eclogue* 5, lines 79-80, that

---

[15] There is much in common between this use of *laetitia* and Lucretius' *laetus*, an adjective constantly associated by him with productivity in nature.

Eclogue 5

Daphnis will receive yearly vows from the farmers along with Bacchus and Ceres, two of the chief divinities presiding over georgic pursuits, the one as teacher of the uses of the vine, the other as the discoverer of wheat.[16] Merely the mention of *agricolae* (a word which occurs only once elsewhere in the *Eclogues*, in 9 at line 61, where a georgic occupation is being discussed) takes us out of a pastoral existence and puts Daphnis on a par with those culture heroes whose discoveries in nature revolutionized human life and who were deified accordingly. As Epicurus refurbished man's soul, so Daphnis' apotheosis does away with evil and, in re-creating nature, sanctifies the new force which during his life he bestowed on the pastoral-georgic world.

Menalcas' prayer continues to cap motifs from Mopsus' song. The *infelix lolium* (line 37) is gone, and Daphnis himself, who had been *decus omne tuis* (line 34), will now reappear *felix tuis*. The manner in which the shepherds express their devotion is also significant. It is not just that Daphnis is to have the same number of altars as Apollo, usually assumed to be the chief god of shepherds; the offerings themselves are important.[17] There will be not only milk and oil, given freely in worship, but also much wine, whether in winter or summer. Ovid assures us that milk was among the first offerings made to the gods,[18] and Pliny the Elder, citing a *lex regia*, says "Romulum lacte, non vino, libasse indicio sunt sacra ab eo instituta quae hodie custodiunt morem" ("that Romulus made libations with milk and not wine is proved by the rites established by him, whose ritual is still preserved today").[19] Evidence is abundant that milk continued to be a

[16] On Ceres as the introducer of civilization, see Ovid *Fasti* 4. 393-416; as the introducer of civilization linked with Bacchus, see *G.* 1. 7ff. and Tibullus 2. 1. 3f.

[17] We may compare the *laudes* here (line 78) with the *laudes Alconis* (line 11) which were rejected as a poetic theme.

[18] See Franz Bömer on *Fasti* 4. 369, in his edition of P. Ovidius Naso *Die Fasten* (Heidelberg, 1958). Grass was also a primitive offering.

[19] *Naturalis Historia* 14. 88.

common offering.[20] Water, milk, and oil, not wine, were the appropriate libations to pour the Nymphs,[21] Pales, and Pan in such a ritual as lines 74-75 describe. (This ritual was perhaps the Ambarvalia, but it bears enough resemblances to other festivals connected with the land to raise doubts about Virgil's specific intention, if any.) It looks therefore as if Menalcas is adding another proof of the way Daphnis advanced civilization. After the celebration—or perhaps even as part of it—he describes the serving of wine which lends gaiety to the subsequent feast. Hence there is another, quite direct link between the institutions of Bacchus and those of Daphnis.

As we have seen, the subsequent lines (72-80) also have a pastoral context overlapped by the more realistic occasions of an agricultural regimen. *Eclogues* 2 and 3, however challenging their intellectual attitudes, are generally, though not strictly, limited to the province of the guardians of flocks. Hence to speak of Damoetas and Aegon singing (in *Eclogue* 3) and of Alphesiboeus mimicking the satyrs (in *Eclogue* 8) is to relive the atmosphere of the shepherd's world. Later when Gallus is dreaming of a pastoral life (*Eclogue* 10, line 41), he claims that Phyllis will weave garlands for him and Amyntas will do the singing (*mihi cantaret Amyntas*). Rendering vows to the nymphs is within a shepherd's province, but the announcement *et cum lustrabimus agros*, whatever the feast to which it refers, places the reader once more in a practical, georgic world to which Daphnis has allied himself as well as the poet and his poetry.[22] We are not now living off

[20] On milk as an offering see Theocritus *Id.* 1. 143; 5. 53ff.; and Tibullus 1. 1. 36 (where it is an offering to Pales).

[21] On water, etc., and not wine, as offering to the Nymphs, see Varro quoted by Servius on *Ecl.* 7. 21. On their festivals, see M. P. Nilsson, *Griechische Feste* (Leipzig, 1906), p. 442. Roman offerings to the Nymphs appear to be primarily Greek in origin.

[22] It is a fact worth mentioning that a sacred lamb (the *felix hostia*, propitious victim, mentioned at *G.* 1. 345 in close connection with both Ceres and Bacchus) is the central offering of the Ambarvalia (see K. F. Smith, editor, *The Elegies of Albius Tibullus* [New York, 1913], on Tibullus 2. 1. 15).

nature's bounty in the beneficent golden-age world of nymphs and satyrs; we are purifying the fields so that our work of taming nature will not be in vain and she will not take our efforts amiss. We will not "cut" her with furrows (*infindere sulcos*), in the terminology of *Eclogue 4,* line 33; *infindere* is a verb Virgil never uses in the *Georgics.*

Daphnis, the new god, is to have a universal effect and a lasting significance. There is no irony in the reverse "impossibilities" of lines 76-77 as there appears to be in the list at *Eclogue* 1, lines 59-63. Any person pondering the message of *Eclogue* 1 might imagine that the vision of such a god as Tityrus has seen could well slip from everybody else's imagination, if not from Tityrus' own. Daphnis is something different; elected from the country into the Olympian pantheon, he may now render eternal youth back to it. This is eternal and ubiquitous rather than lopsided influence. The basic instincts of all nature will be preserved: boars will love high hills and bees feed on thyme as long as Daphnis is worshipped. Yet, unlike Tityrus' young god who presides at Rome, Daphnis is only a dream, a divinity who can be created to continue the "pastoral life." He is not a real person who, though he has the means at hand, cannot or does not attempt to preserve its multiform idealism.

For years it was the fashion to see in the deified Daphnis a figure for the recently assassinated Julius Caesar.[23] There is, in *Eclogue* 9, line 47, a reference to the *Caesaris astrum,* the comet which appeared in the heavens in 43 B.C. as Octavian was celebrating games in honor of his adoptive father. According to Suetonius, the comet was taken to signify Julius' apotheosis. In *Eclogue* 9, Lycidas, attempting to recall Moeris' song, sings about how, at the comet's flash, the crops rejoice with wheat and grapes draw in their color. These references connect Caesar with Ceres and Bacchus—to whom Daphnis

---

[23] For a careful critique of the problem see Rose, *The Eclogues,* pp. 124ff., 130ff. On the comet, see Suetonius, *Caes.* 88.

is so closely linked in Menalcas' song—gods who are more
"advanced" than Pales and Apollo, the essentially "pastoral"
gods who figure in Mopsus' verses.

Yet one would expect that, if Virgil meant to equate Daphnis
with Caesar, he would honor him with some distinctive attribute, easily recognizable. The allegory would be important
for him, politically and personally. Yet no direct clue is forthcoming. The chief god to whom Daphnis seems to be linked,
as we have seen on several occasions in each of the shepherds'
songs, is Bacchus. But the only evidence that Julius Caesar
was connected with the rites of Liber comes from Servius'
comment on line 29 of *Eclogue* 5 in which he states that
Caesar was the first to bring the worship of Liber Pater to
Rome, a reference patently false.[24]

It is well to remember that as early as the year 41 (and perhaps before) Antony was playing the part of Dionysus in
Asia Minor and that in the propaganda of the next decade
(and beyond, of course) Octavian regularly adopts Apollo
as his patron god while Antony's protector is Bacchus.[25] But
surely we are not meant to see Antony as Daphnis, especially
if the *Eclogues* were not published until 37 B.C. or after when
the sides and issues of the final years of the civil war would
have been clearer to their author than in the middle or late 40's.
Nor can we see Octavian as Daphnis without stretching a
literal reading of the poem to the breaking point.

Questions of fact, therefore, seem to stand in the way of a
direct equation between Daphnis and Julius Caesar. Nevertheless one cannot but presume that a contemporary of Virgil would have tended at first to form such an opinion, after
reading Menalcas' lines. It is perhaps the poet's greatest

[24] See Rose, *The Eclogues*, p. 132.
[25] The evidence for Antony and Dionysus is Plutarch *Ant.* 24. See
Kenneth Scott, "Octavian's Propaganda and Antony's *De Sua Ebrie-
tate*," *CP* 24 (1929): 133-41; and "The Political Propaganda of 44-30
B.C.," *Mem. Am. Aca. Rome* 11 (1933): 46.

achievement in *Eclogue* 5 to turn the idea of a literal apotheosis to specifically intellectual purposes.

Virgil takes Theocritus' Daphnis of *Idyl* 1, victim of a *Liebestod*, and turns him into a symbol of a grand scheme of things; this Daphnis is not incomparable to the *paulo maiora* of the preceding poem and in many respects more humanely inspiriting. Out of love may come death, but from death comes a higher love. Daphnis loved the shepherds (*amavit nos quoque Daphnis*, line 52), but he also loved *otia* (line 61), that peace crucial to the shepherd's life which reconciles opposites. He is not outside, like Tityrus' Roman god, molding the land. Here there is neither the threat from the state nor the splendid, if impossible, prospect of a union of "pastoral" with progress and history. *Iustitia,* she who keeps all men just, has not abandoned the countryside finally to return. Only Pales and Apollo, mere rural divinities, were forced by death, not crime, to leave the bucolic world. Daphnis' return has brought no grandiose, formal plan of universal order but only a nobler, permanent stabilization of the increased vitality which Ceres and Bacchus once confided to the earth.

The conclusion of the poem, while reaffirming the tone of the opening lines, also looks ahead. The final repartee begins with Mopsus' response to Menalcas' song (lines 81-84):

> Quae tibi, quae tali reddam pro carmine dona?
> nam neque me tantum venientis sibilus Austri
> nec percussa iuvant fluctu tam litora, nec quae
> saxosas inter decurrunt flumina vallis.

What gifts, what gifts may I give you for such a song? For neither the rustle of the coming South wind nor the shore beaten by the surge nor streams which run down among rocky glens delight me as much.

Menalcas' reaction to Mopsus' verses was to compare them to water for the thirsty and sleep for the weary; he claimed

Mopsus' song was the purge of sorrow. Menalcas' song calls to Mopsus' mind something which gives him more delight than the whispering of wind, the crash of waves, or the roar of water rushing through rocky valleys.[26] Mopsus' analogies indicate that he has changed from someone initially wary of the outer world to a singer who revels in sound. It is a jump from seeking refuge from the shadows that change at the motion of the Zephyr to adopting the rustling of the oncoming South wind as a symbol of perfection in song. This is an external world—of noise from the sea, land, and air—with a vengeance.[27]

The comparisons underline the explicit contrasts between the two songs. Mopsus sings of loss and death in nature. Menalcas counters with a land suddenly rejuvenated through *alacris voluptas*, a love which is brisk and active, and life triumphs over mortality. It need scarcely be pointed out again how, at lines 62-64 of Menalcas' song, Virgil puts particular stress on the idea of "sound" as part of nature's renewal.[28] Even wild nature spontaneously shouts its joy. The song which the rocks and groves sing, calling back to Menalcas the implications of his words without having to echo them, is the counterpart of the verses inscribed on the tomb of Daphnis in Mopsus' elegy, inscribed because nature is moribund and dares not sing. If Mopsus' analogies now carry an occasional hint of the strength of nature's more violent side, it is only because his new theme is the direct opposite of his earlier

[26] On *saxosus*, see G. 4. 370.

[27] Elsewhere the allusions are often used as destructive elements in nature, which threaten the shepherd's safety. At 2. 58, for example, Corydon claims that his love for Alexis is the equivalent of Auster ravaging his flowers. And at 9. 43, Moeris, quoting his own lovesong to Galatea, urges her to leave the raucous ocean (*insani feriant sine litora fluctus*) and come into his quiet, shady pleasance.

[28] See Damon, "Modes of Analogy," pp. 294-95; Marie Desport, "L'écho de la nature et de la poésie dans les *Eclogues* de Virgile," *REA* 43 (1941): 270-81.

one. He admits his personal involvement in an aspect of "pastoral" which he had hitherto avoided.

The acknowledgment is enough for Menalcas to initiate his young colleague further into the mysteries of song (lines 85-87):

> Hac te nos fragili donabimus ante cicuta.
> haec nos 'formosum Corydon ardebat Alexim,'
> haec eadem docuit 'cuium pecus? an Meliboei?'

This frail reed I will give you first. This one taught me "Corydon burned for handsome Alexis," the same one "Whose flock is that? Is it Meliboeus'?"

The type of gift is common. Corydon, for instance, lists among his possessions a Pan-pipe made up of seven reeds which Damoetas gave to him. Yet this one is special on two counts: it taught the singer his verses, and the verses are Virgil's own. (The excerpts are, of course, significant quotes from the opening lines of *Eclogues* 2 and 3.) To have this pipe in his hands affords enough magic for the shepherd to be able to create. It is specifically into Virgilian bucolic poetry that Menalcas feels Mopsus has been initiated. He has proved himself a singer of pastorals, yet his response to Menalcas' song suggests not only the beauty of the quiet landscape but also something which, though part of nature, might still intrude and destroy. His horizon now embraces nature in all its variety.

Mopsus has to respond with something of equal or higher value and he gives Menalcas his sheep-hook (lines 88-90):

> At tu sume pedum, quod, me cum saepe rogaret,
> non tulit Antigenes (et erat tum dignus amari),
> formosum paribus nodis atque aere, Menalca.

But do you accept the crook which Antigenes did not get, though he often asked for it (and at that time he was worthy to be loved). Beautiful it is, Menalcas, with even knots and decorated with brass.

Eclogue 5

This particular exchange between shepherd-singers is a literary motif which goes back first to Theocritus' *Idyl* 7, where one shepherd gives another his crook as a symbol of friendship "in the Muses," but ultimately to the staff which the Muses gave to Hesiod as he shepherded his flock on Helicon.[29] That the staff was as useful to the singer as his reed we may divine from *Eclogue* 8, line 16, where Damon begins to sing leaning on his smooth olive staff as if this gave him the necessary "support" of inspiration. He is a shepherd of poets as well as sheep.

Servius makes a comment worthy of notice on the words *formosum paribus nodis atque aere*. He says: "et ab arte et a natura laudavit: 'paribus nodis' id est natura formosum; 'atque aere' hoc est pulchrum aere artificium" ("He praised it both for its craftsmanship and for its natural value: 'with equal knots,' that is, beautiful by nature; 'and decorated with brass,' that is, an object handsomely crafted with brass"). The words, which reveal in Virgil's commentator a rare symbolic vein, are also a definition of the poetic art. Its beauty depends on a combination of native wit (the word *ingenium* usually figures in this distinction) and the craft which molds a poem to form. The reed may teach song;[30] the crook also helps inspire and symbolizes to a degree the accomplishment of the poem which, like *Eclogue* 4, is another version of the union between "nature" and artifice, between static innocence and a reasoned progress. In this poem, however, progress is imagined as developing from within nature while the hero of the land, rather than an outside political force, gains the role of presiding divinity. What can be, and often are, taken as examples of the decline from Saturn's golden age to the more debased reign of Jupi-

---

[29] *Theogony*, line 30. See Gow's commentary on Theoc. *Id.* 7. 43.

[30] We may recall Cicero's praise of Lucretius (*QFr.* 2. 9. 3): "Lucreti poemata, ut scribis, ita sunt multis luminibus ingeni, multae tamen artis" ("The verses of Lucretius are just as you write—filled with flashes of genius and yet written with exceeding care").

ter—the tilling of crops, labor in the vineyard—are treated as positive values upon Daphnis' deification.

Nevertheless it is as an *ars poetica* and not so much as a vehicle for new ideas that the poem looks ahead. Mopsus has been indoctrinated into a new aspect of pastoral poetry which breaks with tradition. And Menalcas, though he has sung his themes before, becomes the mentor of Mopsus, the expositor of a bold new poetic venture which can be complemented by a tangible emblem of the imagination's art. The next poem puts the *ars poetica* in the place of primary importance. The symbol of poetry comes alive: initiation is worked on a real person. Hence the position of *Eclogue* 5 in the book as a whole proves to have been carefully chosen. It sums up the past in idealistic strains which ring harmoniously next to its predecessor. Yet it also prepares the way for the next five poems which, each in its special way, examine particular facets of poetic expression.

The fifth eclogue ends on a triumphant note, which glances back in summary on the first five poems. The opening of the sixth also looks at the past, but from another point of view (lines 1-12):

Prima Syracosio dignata est ludere versu
nostra neque erubuit silvas habitare Thalia.
cum canerem reges et proelia, Cynthius aurem
vellit et admonuit: 'pastorem, Tityre, pinguis
pascere oportet ovis, deductum dicere carmen.'
nunc ego (namque super tibi erunt qui dicere laudes,
Vare, tuas cupiant et tristia condere bella)
agrestem tenui meditabor harundine Musam.
non iniussa cano. si quis tamen haec quoque, si quis
captus amore leget, te nostrae, Vare, myricae,
te nemus omne canet; nec Phoebo gratior ulla est
quam sibi quae Vari praescripsit pagina nomen.

My muse first deigned to play in Syracusan strains and did not blush to dwell in the woods. When I would sing of kings and battles, Apollo plucked my ear and warned me: "Tityrus, it befits a shepherd to feed a fat flock but to sing a song fine-spun." And now—for there will be many eager to sing your praises, Varus, and to compose war's bitter tales—I will woo the rustic muse on slender reed. I do not sing strains unbidden. Nevertheless if anyone, if anyone charmed by love read these things, of you our tamarisks, of you the whole grove will sing, Varus. No page is more pleasing to Phoebus than one which has the name of Varus written at its head.

Eclogue 6

The words distract us, for a moment, from the "literal" shepherds' world to hear Virgil's voice, criticizing and analyzing.[1] In his preceding songs his muse had not hesitated to "dwell in the woods" and sing according to the manner of Theocritus, bard of Syracuse. As a change (imaginary or not) he decided to write epic, but Apollo thought otherwise. Though the shepherd takes delight in a fat flock, his song must be "thin," befitting pastoral style and theme, not expansive or grandiloquent.

The allusion, as has often been noted, is to the preface which Callimachus wrote, some years after its completion, to his *Aitia*, a compendium of "origins" of myths and institutions, written in the form of narrative elegy. But Callimachus was certainly no "pastoral" poet. Therefore to have the shepherds' patron god Apollo rephrase Callimachus' words and address them to Tityrus, who here represents Virgil himself, bucolic bard of the *Eclogues*, must mean one thing: part of the poem's artistic and aesthetic credo is to be a new union between Callimachus and Theocritus, between narrative poetry and customary pastoral procedure as we have grown used to it from the preceding poems. This union is abetted by the "slender" style common to each.

There is partial precedent for this union in the figure of Callimachus' literary idol, a shepherd to whom the muses "appeared," as he pastured his flock on Helicon, and inspired the *Theogony*, a didactic poem on the origin and ancestry of

---

[1] Several recent publications on *Eclogue* 6 are of particular interest: Otto Skutsch, "Zu Vergils Eklogen," *RhM* 99 (1956): 193-201; Zeph Stewart, "The Song of Silenus," *HSCP* 64 (1959): 179-205; C. G. Hardie, *Eclogue VI*, Virgil Society Lecture Summaries #50 (1960); J. P. Elder, "*Non iniussa cano*. Virgil's Sixth Eclogue," *HSCP* 65 (1961): 109-25; E. L. Brown, *Numeri Vergiliani* (Brussels, 1963), Chapter 4, "Structure and Number in the Sixth 'Eclogue'"; W. V. Clausen, "Callimachus and Latin Poetry," *Greek, Roman and Byzantine Studies* 5 (1964): 181-96.

I agree with Otis (*Virgil*, p. 127), though he seems to contradict his own statement on page 137, that *Eclogue* 6 should not be taken merely as a catalogue of "neoteric 'little epics.'"

the gods. His vocation as a shepherd, however, did not dictate any particular literary stance to Hesiod as it does to Virgil, who embarks here on an experiment as poetically daring as the fourth eclogue was intellectually stimulating. Whatever the purposes of the poem, it will broaden the prospect of "pastoral" by an amalgam of disparate poetic traditions, never before considered viable together.

These introductory words, Virgil the shepherd's version of an *ars poetica pastoralis,* are as applicable to the subsequent four eclogues as to the sixth. Each, in differing ways, scrutinizes what fits with and what disrupts the bucolic manner. Each expands "pastoral's" intellectual horizon. Apollo himself, source of inspiration and standard-maker, specifically presides over the sixth eclogue, beginning with his advice on style and concluding with the supposition that he, too, sings the very songs, summaries of which form the bulk of the poem.

Apparently Varus had asked for a long poem eulogizing his martial exploits, but Virgil's refusal to write epic is purposeful. He has already given reasons. The evaluation of the poem to follow is accordingly the more impressive: "agrestem tenui meditabor harundine Musam." The words, it has been observed, mirror Meliboeus' brief sketch of Tityrus' *otium* which opens *Eclogue* 1: "Tityre, tu patulae recubans sub tegmine fagi / silvestrem tenui musam meditaris avena." The parallel is intentional. The beginning of the second half of the book of *Eclogues* should rightly acknowledge the start of the first. But Tityrus in *Eclogue* 1 sings no songs. All we need to know is that he has the ability and freedom to do so. The first eclogue comments on the practicability of the poet's life under repressive circumstances. The sixth is a commentary on pastoral song itself—on what is possible, if unexpected, within the straitened conventions of the bucolic mode. Each poem offers a special stimulus to the pastoral manner, but the matter of the sixth, because it is concerned specifically with poetry, is introduced by the poet himself and then continued by him through an appropriate mask whom we meet in a moment.

The person who ordered the poem is kept anonymous, though a logical candidate appears before its conclusion. Meanwhile Varus is not forgotten. Should anyone, charmed by the verse, pick up the poem and read, the woods will resound with the name of Varus. There is no name which Phoebus Apollo takes more delight in seeing at the top of a page. This phraseology is interesting. It twice breaks one of the strict conventions of pastoral poetry: its stance as an oral art. In order for the groves to echo Varus' name—in order for his seduction into pastoral concerns to take place—someone must first read the poetry, someone presumably unfamiliar with such song. That it is not the song itself that delights Apollo but Varus' name on the page, no ordinary attribute of a shepherd's song, is the second indication that Virgil is patently leading his uninitiated reader into a discussion of bucolic poetry. He is breaking ordinary procedure to make his meaning clearer and the transition from one intellectual position to another more facile. Later in the poem we will find Pasiphaë's bull *herba captum viridi*, charmed by some verdant grass. Here, before we even commence, it is the reader who must be drawn under the singer's spell, into the realm of the shepherd, *captus amore*, seized by love, led by the written word. Virgil will soon begin to sing a new type of pastoral, prefaced by the sound of "Varus" but containing an initiation of greater bearing on the poet's criticism of his art.

Even now, instead of granting a song, the Muses introduce us to a singer whose relation to pastoral verse, as we have learned to conceive of it in the first five eclogues, is tenuous enough to require a detailed description of himself and his setting (lines 13-17):

> Pergite, Pierides. Chromis et Mnasyllus in antro
> Silenum pueri somno videre iacentem,

inflatum hesterno venas, ut semper, Iaccho;
serta procul tantum capiti delapsa iacebant,
et gravis attrita pendebat cantharus ansa.

Proceed, Pierian maids. The youths Chromis and Mnasyllus saw Silenus lying asleep in a cave, his veins swollen,
as always, with yesterday's wine. The garlands, just fallen
from his head, lay nearby, and his heavy tankard was
hanging by its well-rubbed handle.

Two boys, whom Servius assures us are young satyrs, come
upon the great Silenus lying drunkenly asleep in his cave. As
befits the instructor of the young Bacchus, all his attributes are
alcoholic. His veins are filled with wine, his garlands slipping
off, his tankard handle well-worn.

The youths have an ally in the attack upon their sleeping
victim (lines 18-22):

> adgressi (nam saepe senex spe carminis ambo
> luserat) iniciunt ipsis ex vincula sertis.
> addit se sociam timidisque supervenit Aegle,
> Aegle Naiadum pulcherrima, iamque videnti
> sanguineis frontem moris et tempora pingit.

Making their approach—for the old man had often deceived them both in their hope of a song—they throw
bonds made from the very same garlands about him.
Aegle, most beautiful of the Naiads, coming to the aid of
the timid pair, joins them and, his eyes now open, paints
his face and forehead with crimson elderberries.

Silenus is an "enemy" who must be approached with violence
and hurled into chains before the conquest is assured. The
reason for the attackers' temper—that Silenus had often deceived them in their hope of entertainment—reveals something more about the poet's voice. He may be a drunkard, but
he is a singer of *carmina* as well, a *vates,* a bard of charming
song.

Eclogue 6

Songs are the price of capture, with which they are associated in a special way (lines 23-26):

> ille dolum ridens 'quo vincula nectitis?' inquit.
> 'solvite me, pueri; satis est potuisse videri.
> carmina quae vultis cognoscite; carmina vobis,
> huic aliud mercedis erit.'

Smiling at their trick, he says: "Why do you weave bonds for me? Release me, lads; enough it is to seem to have the power. Hear the songs you wish. The songs are for you, for her there will be a different reward.

The language of binding and release, which *Eclogue* 8 will cause us to examine in greater detail, is magical. The witch in 8, by her incantations, "surrounds" and overpowers the object of her designs. But Chromis, Mnasyllus, and Aegle are no sorcerers. Rather, they are the ones who must imprison the maker of "charms" in order to be charmed themselves. External force must be requisitioned in order to move the spirit. Moreover, the face smeared with dye suggests more than the traditional bamboozling of a drunken, sleeping old man; it is also part of the primitive garb of a satyr, ready to "play." Mask and chains are of like importance in preparing for the performance which follows.[2]

This "refurbished" figure of Silenus moves the landscape in a visible fashion (lines 26-30):

> simul incipit ipse.
> tum vero in numerum Faunosque ferasque videres
> ludere, tum rigidas motare cacumina quercus;
> nec tantum Phoebo gaudet Parnasia rupes,
> nec tantum Rhodope miratur et Ismarus Orphea.

---

[2] The idea of deception is common enough (see commentators on Plautus *Merc.* 2. 4. 17; Martial 3. 42. 2). On the connection between anointing with dye and satyr plays, see Horace *Ars P.* 239ff. (esp. 277). The other use—the reddening of the face of a triumphant general (on which see commentators on Tibullus 2. 1. 55)—is scarcely operative here.

Eclogue 6

He begins forthwith. Then indeed you might see fauns and wild beasts dancing in rhythm, then stiff oaks wave their tops. No such delight does the rock of Parnassus take in Apollo; Rhodope and Ismarus marvel not so much at Orpheus.

In Virgilian pastoral we are used to this interrelationship between physical and metaphysical. Landscape and spirit are essentially one. What is striking here is that the qualities associated with two of the countryside's prime heroes, Apollo and Orpheus, should be reserved for Silenus, whose chief interests seem to be wine and women, rather than *carmina*. A full answer to why he should be chosen as Virgil's mouthpiece over more obvious candidates must wait for an examination of the songs themselves. At the moment, however, we might begin to take a closer look at Silenus' credentials.[3]

Servius tells us twice that Virgil's portrait of Silenus is taken from a work of the Hellenistic historian Theopompus entitled *Thaumasia* ("Marvels"), in which Silenus, drunk as usual, is caught by shepherds of King Midas at whose questioning he discourses on things natural and of old (*de rebus naturalibus et antiquis*). If we may trust this tradition, then, Silenus' chief function in *Eclogue 6* is to be a *vates*, a prophet cognizant of the past (and, as we will learn, future), who must be tamed before he is willing to impart his knowledge. He is in part Virgil's model for Proteus, singer of the story of Orpheus and Eurydice in the fourth georgic, who also suffers subjugation before playing the seer.[4] Proteus, however, changes physical shape before being apprehended and telling his tale.

[3] For more details on Silenus, see J. A. Notopoulos, "Silenus the Scientist," *CJ* 62 (1967): 308-309. For specific connections between Silenus and the creative process, see Eugène de Saint-Denis, "Le chant de Silène à la lumière d'une découverte récente," *RPh* 37 (1963): 23-40.

For the interesting thesis that Silenus is an allegorical representative of Parthenius, see E. L. Brown, *Numeri Vergiliani*, pp. 128ff.

[4] See Hardie, *Eclogue VI*, pp. 6ff.

Eclogue 6

Silenus' Protean characteristics are exhibited after his seizure, not before, and take spiritual, not visible, form in the great variety of the songs he sings. The imprisonment of Silenus in the garlands left over from the previous night's carousal suggests, like the plaiting of a basket, another metaphor for the creation of poetry. This time the tyranny is double: the imprisonment of Silenus' infinite knowledge in the mold of poetry and, more specifically, the channeling of Silenus' creative "charm" into the stream of pastoral verse.

This does not mean that Silenus' special traits are lost in the verses he sings. Again, a full exposition must rest with the songs themselves, but certain points in Virgil's understatement are already clear. Silenus is the denizen of a cave, a god of the wild (some say offspring of Pan and a nymph), whose ugly features, animal-like in most accounts, are accentuated by the elderberry dye. He is a winebibber and, according to legend, taught Bacchus the keeping of bees and the fermenting of grapes, subjects he obviously knew well. Therefore, as the intellectual father of a god who helped the world advance from a state of sylvan rusticity, he holds a didactic role in the myth of culture's development. Finally, Virgil allows to him the most explicit reference to sex in the *Eclogues*: *huic aliud mercedis erit*. Whatever his spiritual importance, Silenus' human propensities are never out of sight.

In sum, then, we have a creature of the country whose chief interests are wine and sex, but who is also a *vates*, skilled at song, and able to impart knowledge on a wide variety of topics. We might expect this knowledge to reveal the same tension we see in Silenus himself between Dionysiac revelry and Apollonian rationality, to depict life as madness put partially into order and made to conform to the rigid requirements of the poet's craft. On the one hand Silenus is a primitive creature of a time when civilization was still progressing toward a georgic era; on the other he is aware of all things from the birth of the world to contemporary life and, of equal importance, can put them into song. Ironically, though, he cannot display his skills unless he is "caught"—unless his emotional propensities are bridled by the exigencies of expression in song. Only then can he become more pastoral than Orpheus and Apollo or even surpass them by the charm and beauty of his song and animate the inanimate by the force of his personality.

With this brief sketch in mind we may turn to the songs themselves (lines 31-40):

> Namque canebat uti magnum per inane coacta
> semina terrarumque animaeque marisque fuissent
> et liquidi simul ignis; ut his exordia primis
> omnia et ipse tener mundi concreverit orbis;
> tum durare solum et discludere Nerea ponto
> coeperit et rerum paulatim sumere formas;
> iamque novum terrae stupeant lucescere solem,
> altius atque cadant summotis nubibus imbres;
> incipiant silvae cum primum surgere, cumque
> rara per ignaros errent animalia montis.

For he sang how, through the great void, the seeds of earth, and air and sea, and streaming fire as well, were driven together; how from these beginnings all things took their start and the tender globe of the earth itself grew into a mass; then how the earth began to harden and to pen Nereus in the ocean and little by little to take the shapes of things; how next the lands stood amazed at the new sun's gleam and how rains fell from above as clouds were raised aloft; of the time when first woods began to grow, and when one by one beasts wandered through unbelieving mountains.

As befits a didactic bard, knowing past and future and at the same time burdened with the Hesiodic-Callimachean poetic tradition, he begins with the genesis of the world. The description is basically scientific, with words drawn generously from Empedocles and Lucretius. There is nothing either religious or mythographical about this straight rational exposition of the origin of the visible world. Order and logic are imposed on the chaos of the great void in which, at first, all matter swirled without control. As line 36 summarizes it, nature searched for the *rerum forma*, the outline and shape to which each object must conform. The seeds of earth, air, water, and fire are driven together.[5] The land congeals (*concreverit*) out of the elements, and everything, save mankind—sun, rain, continents, seas, trees, animals—is created from this union.

It is not hard to discern the force of Silenus in the choice of themes for this opening. Literally, he sings of nature assuming order out of disorder, but, as a creative teacher, he is also giving the pattern of words to a formless series of ideas. Once "captured," the drunken, disorderly, yet all-knowing Silenus molds his ideas and gives change and commotion the stability of expression. It happens that here content and manner are the same. The satyr-bard confines the swirl of his emotions and the immensity of his wisdom to verse while the verses themselves tell of nature's search for what Frost calls "shapes against chaos," a momentary "stay against confusion" which is the necessary goal of poetry as well. Though nature must emulate the fixity of unchanging models, at the same time she battens on conflict and is pregnant with her own special power, according to Silenus' exposition. The sun gleams, to the astonishment of the lands below, rain falls, trees grow and, finally, animals wander among mountains which have never before seen such things.

There is a gradual change of emphasis, then, from nature's search for order to the "character" of nature, her powers of motion and growth. But it is even more impressive to shift from rains falling and trees growing to animals roaming. Wandering is one of the poem's motifs to which we will return below. Suffice it to observe here that with the introduction

---

[5] The verb *cogo* is used of sheep at line 87.

of live creatures by a verb which, for Virgil, regularly connotes mental aberration as well as mere roaming, the poet initiates the shift from didactic description to involvement with
the human personality. In so doing he makes the transition
from science to myth (lines 41-44):

> hinc lapides Pyrrhae iactos, Saturnia regna,
> Caucasiasque refert volucris furtumque Promethei.
> his adiungit, Hylan nautae quo fonte relictum
> clamassent, ut litus 'Hyla, Hyla' omne sonaret; . . .

Then he tells of the stones thrown by Pyrrha, Saturn's
kingdom, the birds of the Caucasus, and Prometheus'
theft. To these he adds the story of the spring where the
sailors cried out for Hylas left behind so that the whole
shore resounded "Hylas, Hylas."

Though the chronology is awry (Pyrrha was Prometheus'
daughter-in-law), the poetic scheme is carefully designed.
The change from didactic rationalism to mythology is
achieved by a brief reference to one of antiquity's time-
honored tales of creation. After creation comes the golden age
of Saturn when work was unknown and all-productive nature fulfilled men's needs. Then follows the theft of fire by
Prometheus and his punishment. Prometheus' theft was a crucial stage in man's development, but the fire brought with it
as much trouble as benefit and, according to one ancient theory
of human progress, deprived man of his former state of simple
ease (Silenus' *Saturnia regna*) and imposed upon him a whole
new technology which, in turn, seemed to necessitate a constant search to better his lot. This was progress in one sense,
but retrogression in another. It brought with it ambition and
the cares that hound the greedy man. After the discovery of
fire, the next step in cultural progress was the building of ships
and the conquering of the sea. Ambition motivated the first
great adventure across the waters, to which Virgil refers in
lines 43-44, the journey of the *Argo* to Colchis on the Black

Sea in search of the golden fleece. Thus, in just four lines we have a history, in myth, of the development of civilization beginning with a tale of creation. This history betokens society's coming of age into a world of increased technical competence balanced, some would have said, by moral decline.

Both the order of the tales and their content is paralleled partially in *Eclogue* 4. There, we recall, the golden age is restored at the birth of the boy, an age in which no menace exists and nature provides even grapes and honey without trouble. Nonetheless, Virgil continues, certain traces of our *prisca fraus* (Prometheus' theft of fire) remain which will drive men to seafaring (symbolized by the *Argo* and its helmsman, Tiphys) and war (Troy and Achilles). In *Eclogue* 4, however, the outcome of Virgil's myth of re-creation is happy. In the final act of humanity's rejuvenation, labor becomes unnecessary. Even to search for a golden fleece is inconsequential. Silenus' reference to the Argonauts serves a different purpose. Like the mention of Pyrrha, it bridges a poetic gap: it introduces through mention of Hylas and Hercules the motif of love, of human emotion, into what could have remained merely a succinct reference to mythology.

Having introduced the motif of love and emotion, Virgil then devotes the longest of his summaries of Silenus' *carmina* to the tale of the unfortunate love between Pasiphaë and the bull.[6] It is the most emotional moment in the poem (lines 45-60):

> et fortunatam, si numquam armenta fuissent,
> Pasiphaen nivei solatur amore iuvenci.
> 'a, virgo infelix, quae te dementia cepit!
> Proetides implerunt falsis mugitibus agros,
> at non tam turpis pecudum tamen ulla secuta
> concubitus, quamvis collo timuisset aratrum,

---

[6] There is an excellent discussion of this episode by Otis, *Virgil*, pp. 125ff. It seems to me arguable, however, that lines 55-60 are the words of Pasiphaë.

Eclogue 6

et saepe in levi quaesisset cornua fronte.
a, virgo infelix, tu nunc in montibus erras:
ille latus niveum molli fultus hyacintho
ilice sub nigra pallentis ruminat herbas
aut aliquam in magno sequitur grege. claudite, Nymphae,
Dictaeae Nymphae, nemorum iam claudite saltus,
si qua forte ferant oculis sese obvia nostris
errabunda bovis vestigia; forsitan illum
aut herba captum viridi aut armenta secutum
perducant aliquae stabula ad Gortynia vaccae.'

And he consoles Pasiphaë—happy, had herds not existed
—for her love of the snow-white bull. "Ah, unfortunate
maid, what madness has seized you! The daughters of
Proetus filled the fields with counterfeit lowings, yet none
of them was led by so foul a love of animals, though she
feared the plough on her neck and often looked for horns
on her smooth brow. Ah, unfortunate maid, you now wander in the mountains. He, pillowing his snowy side on
soft hyacinths, chews the pale grass beneath a black ilex
or follows another in the large herd. Close, Nymphs,
close off now the forest glades, Nymphs of Dicte, in case
the bull's wandering steps should by chance cross my line
of vision or some cows lead him to Gortyn's stables,
charmed by some green grass or following the herd."

With the use of the verb *solatur* the poet has already allowed
Silenus a deeper involvement in this theme than in those previously mentioned. Before, he had only sung (*canebat*), mentioned (*refert*) his topics, or added (*adiungit*) to them. Now,
while he sings, he consoles as well. For most of this passage, as
nowhere else, Virgil "quotes" Silenus' actual words. As a poet
must, Silenus has become subjectively enamoured of his
theme, though his desire is only an objective description of
love.

Eclogue 6

If the relationship of Hercules and Hylas was abnormal, this *concubitus* is base, beyond the bounds of the possible, a mixture of two species as unique as it is peculiar. The divergence between the two is implicit in the first two lines. She is *infelix*, unfortunate, subject to all the emotional vicissitudes of human nature, yet mated, for a while, to a bull whose chief attribute is that he is *niveus*, snow-white. She is mentally deranged by her unhappiness to the point of madness. Corydon applied the phrase *quae te dementia cepit* to his feelings about Alexis (in *Eclogue* 2, line 69). In *Eclogue* 6 the insane search to reconcile opposites has gone one stage further to suggest an impossible relationship. In comparison to the usual pastoral situation, however, things are worse still. Like the animals at the end of Silenus' cosmogony, she is now wandering among the mountains. Once she could have been happy; now, like any unhappy pastoral lover, like Corydon in the second eclogue or the shepherd in the eighth, bent on suicide, she is forced away from the center of bucolic happiness. The bull cannot be emotionally involved; she who is must suffer a reversal of life's ordinary ways.

Ironically, the perfect pastoral life is exactly what the bull himself possesses as he roams about, unresponsive, following his instincts in search of food or a female of his own kind. The setting which lines 53-54 describe is the quintessence of an idyllic landscape. Each adjective plays an important part in the picture—the whiteness of the bull, the softness of the hyacinth on which he reclines, the contrasting blackness of the overshadowing ilex, even the pale grass which he chews— they all conjure up the perfect setting.[7] This beauty belongs not to the wretched Pasiphaë but to the bull who has not only the landscape but also the love she lacks.

Silenus' delivery and Virgil's response to his emotion grow still more impassioned. In the first person Silenus calls upon the nymphs of the Cretan woodland to close off the glades

[7] On the *ilex*, for instance, we may think ahead to the rustling oak under which Daphnis reclines at the opening of the next poem.

so that they might glimpse the bull's wandering steps (*erra-bunda bovis vestigia*). The adjective serves as a deliberate re-minder of Pasiphaë's aberration and suggests a further level of meaning. Her "roaming" is, according to the pastoral con-vention, both literal and figurative. The pathless mountains mirror her spiritual anguish. The bull's search is purely ani-malistic, and he is subject to the charms of both green grass and cows.[8] There is no intimation that he either understands or cares about Pasiphaë's plight.

It is a long way in poetic theme and exposition from the creation of the world to Pasiphaë's emotional derangement, but the matter of each tale is still part of Silenus' expansion of "pastoral" in terms of his attributes and personality. Here Dionysiac passion finds expression in a perverted madness, a theme with several layers of irony when seen in a pastoral context. A realization of how different this passion is from Tityrus' love for Amaryllis is sufficient indication of the strangeness of the tale and of its divergence from a shepherd-poet's ordinary material. Not only is it ordinary love turned completely upside-down, it is a subtle inversion of the pastoral ideal as well. The bull has the perfect landscape and his choice of love—what should belong to Pasiphaë—while she is the victim of a disorienting madness which alienates her from both the landscape and the rationale of the pastoral world.

Silenus now turns to myths exemplifying love and meta-morphosis, the stories of Atalanta and the sisters of Phaëthon (lines 61-63):

> tum canit Hesperidum miratam mala puellam;
> tum Phaethontiadas musco circumdat amarae
> corticis atque solo proceras erigit alnos.

Then he sings of the girl who marvelled at the apples of the Hesperides. Then he surrounds the sisters of Phaë-

---

[8] Lines 59-60, *secutum* / . . . *aliquae* . . . *vaccae*, recall 55, *aliquam sequitur*.

thon with the moss of bitter bark and raises them up as lofty alders from the ground.

Atalanta was Milanion's bride but both, according to legend, were subsequently changed into lions who found it impossible to mate. Except that in their case true love had once been possible, it parallels Pasiphaë's misfortune, and anyone singing their story would necessarily bring in the detail of the golden apples to facilitate the transition from Pasiphaë to the sisters of Phaëthon. Because of their love for their brother they, too, suffered metamorphosis; they became alders sorrowing for his misfortune. This is a short episode, but, like the tale of Hylas with which it balances, it adds new motifs which gradually alter the reader's perspective in preparation for a longer *carmen*. One point stands out: Silenus is no longer merely "singing" his verses or even "consoling" by his words, but he is now actually creating through the power of his poetry. He "surrounds" the sisters of Phaëthon with bitter bark and "raises" them from the ground as alders. In other words, he offers further evidence of the force he exerted upon nature as he began to sing. To the initiate he demonstrates that song may seem literally to move the universe even though in reality it is only evoking an idea before our imaginations.

This demonstration makes the transition to the next episode easy (lines 64-73):

> tum canit errantem Permessi ad flumina Gallum
> Aonas in montis ut duxerit una sororum,
> utque viro Phoebi chorus adsurrexerit omnis;
> ut Linus haec illi divino carmine pastor
> floribus atque apio crinis ornatus amaro
> dixerit: 'hos tibi dant calamos, en accipe, Musae,
> Ascraeo quos ante seni, quibus ille solebat
> cantando rigidas deducere montibus ornos.
> his tibi Grynei nemoris dicatur origo,
> ne quis sit lucus quo se plus iactet Apollo.'

Then he sings how one of the sisters led Gallus, wandering by the streams of Permessus, into the Aonian mountains, and how the whole choir of Phoebus rose up for the man; how Linus, shepherd of immortal song, his hair adorned with flowers and with bitter parsley, spoke thus to him: "The Muses give these reeds to you—see, take them—which once they gave to the old man of Ascra. By them he was wont to lead down the stiff ashes from the mountains with his singing. With these do you tell the origin of the Grynaean wood lest there be any grove in which Apollo pride himself more."

It may at first seem peculiar that Gallus, friend of Virgil and living statesman and poet, should appear in such varied company. Silenus is, however, also singing of an important moment in the "myth" of Gallus, itself a spiritual metamorphosis of sorts. As such, it must be divorced from any specific reference to time and place, and considered in its context of the intellectual realm of poetry.

The sisters of Phaëthon having been changed into river alders because of love, we now find Gallus "wandering" by a stream, specified as the Permessus which flows at the base of Mt. Helicon. What may seem literal is only poetic convention. Gallus is no more actually by the banks of the Permessus than he is literally taken up by the Muses into the Aonian mountains. Silenus himself explains the symbolic meaning of the latter detail: Gallus is to become a pastoral poet in the tradition of Hesiod, bard of Ascra, and sing something to please Apollo, namely the "origin" of the legend of the Grynaean grove. But this explains only Gallus' initiation, where he will go, not whence he came.

To answer that question we must turn, with most commentators, to the tenth elegy of the second book of Propertius. There the elegist has decided it is time to take up a loftier theme than mere subjective love elegy and to give rein to his poetic steed on the plains of Haemon by dutifully singing the epic deeds of Augustus. But since he is the practitioner of a lesser genre, he has only modest gifts to offer (lines 25-26): "nondum etiam Ascraeos norunt mea carmina fontes, / sed modo Permessi flumine lavit Amor." ("Not yet have my songs known the fountains of Ascra. Love has only washed them in the streams of Permessus.") Without doubt, the stream of Permessus signifies for Propertius the source of his song, love elegy. It is a plausible hypothesis that it means the same for Gallus in *Eclogue* 6, since he was often acknowledged as the possible founder of the genre by its later practitioners. The obvious relationship between the two poems seems strong enough to suggest such a theory. Even without the help of Propertius, however, the word *errantem* in the context of *Eclogue* 6 makes the supposition reasonable. We have seen Pasiphaë "wandering" in the mountains, which is the traditional stance for an unhappy lover driven from the bucolic world. Gallus is imagined by Silenus in what was to become the conventional posture of an elegiac poet, *Permessi ad flumina*, as well as in the pose of an unhappy lover *errantem*, wandering without hope.

Gallus' "metamorphosis" is effected by one of the Muses who takes him away from this role of poet-lover up into the Aonian mountains where the Muses—Apollo's chorus—and Linus—prototype of shepherd-poets—receive him. This is Apollo's world of pastoral song, a very different experience from what Gallus' ordinary poetic practice had hitherto purveyed. The bitter bark which surrounded the sisters of Phaëthon after their metamorphosis has become the crown of bitter parsley which now adorns the locks of the newly initiated pastoral poet. His metamorphosis is, however, in no sense literal; we are dealing with fact only as the basis for legend. This is a poetic metamorphosis, experienced within the conventional apparatus of a poet's world. It takes Gallus out of the realm of love, out of Silenus' province of sex and madness, into the loftier company of Hesiod who uses a poetic form which in leading the unbending ashes down the mountainside produces the same effect on nature as does Silenus in making the stiff oaks bow. Silenus, Hesiod, and now Gallus will create nature, man, and myth by their words.

Hypothetically, then, it would appear that Virgil is suggesting, perhaps even outlining, Gallus' future career through his mouthpiece, Silenus. Whether or not Gallus followed the advice remains a mystery. In the tenth eclogue Virgil depicts his friend trifling with the idea of embracing the pastoral life, rejecting the notion, and ultimately renewing his devotion to Amor, god of elegy, and to the inspiration the waters of the Permessus might grant. Here Silenus poses a theoretical question: Can Gallus, slave of subjective poetry, so reform his intellectual inclinations as to join an imaginative sphere presided over by Hesiod and to write *origines* in the manner of Callimachus whose own chef-d'oeuvre began with chaos and continued with an elucidation of the most esoteric of legends?

There is little doubt that Callimachus' themes and poetic standards were much on Virgil's mind as he wrote the sixth eclogue. The introduction, polarized around a refusal to write in "higher" forms of poetry, and Gallus' initiation are in part modelled on the opening of Callimachus' *Aitia* as we now have it. Moreover the similarity between Hesiod's power over nature and the effect of Silenus' songs suggests a close connection between the two and Gallus' consecration as a pastoral poet and writer of *origines*. This connection fosters a logical, though unprovable, assumption that Silenus' *carmina* are, in some esoteric way, guides for Gallus to follow, even themes upon which he may pattern his future, more elevated, poetic career.

Some of these thoughts may well have been in Virgil's mind. They may even have been paramount, for his intentions are not always what they appear. Nevertheless to assume that Virgil put Gallus foremost and oriented Silenus' songs only toward him, with some secretly pragmatic goal, is to destroy the charm of the poem and make Virgil appear to have bestowed it as private property upon those happy few among the Romans of the 40's B.C. who were more interested in poetics than poetry.

Had Virgil wished to make Gallus the central figure of his poem, he would have done so, as in *Eclogue* 10. As it is, the story of Gallus' possible elevation completes an almost perfectly balanced song of songs. Silenus began with ten lines devoted to his cosmogony and now gives us the story of Gallus' poetic consecration in ten lines. The cosmogony is followed by four lines of brief sketches while Gallus' *Dichterweihe* is preceded by three lines of the same type of short vignettes. These groups balance each other and surround not the episode of Gallus but the strange history of Pasiphaë which, by a six-line margin, receives the most lengthy treatment among the *carmina*. This symmetrical structure, an Alexandrian design, redoubles the emphasis her story receives.

Intellectually, the Gallus episode concludes the *carmina* without being their culminating point; there are other songs which follow. The creation of the world, rationally analyzed in a didactic manner, leads ultimately to an equally rational exposition of a change of poetic interest, which is a "myth" in its own way, as we have seen, and a metamorphosis. For Gallus the change means the renunciation of a poetry of emotion in favor of a higher, more aloof, more descriptive sort, like that of the shepherd Hesiod, wherein the poet, though he may sing of creation and love, is above this passion himself.

The intervening *carmina* are a different sort. They introduce humanity itself and depict, through myth, its early growth. With the advent of mankind comes love, first in the Hylas story and then in the tale of Pasiphaë, the centerpiece of Silenus' songs and one of the imaginative triumphs of Virgil's *Eclogues*. Why this tale had particular appeal for the poet none can judge. It is the essence of pastoral love gone completely wrong. The setting is pastoral only because one of the protagonists is a bull, but, as we have seen, the landscape background against which this little drama is played magnifies the monstrosity.

Silenus gradually and gently mitigates the intense passion he has generated in the Pasiphaë tale, first with tales suggesting metamorphosis after unhappy love, then with purgation of a higher sort. He suggests that Gallus turn from subjective poetry to verse of a less emotional sort, that he remove himself from the adventures of life, legendary though they be, and enter into the intellectual sphere of poetic convention where love, cosmogony, and the growth of civilization are not important *per se* but for their expression in verse. Gallus, himself now a "myth," will become a creator (or recreator) of myth. This, in brief, is to renounce his proclivities as a lover and to embrace, as poet, a higher form of myth involving people merely as vehicles to express emotion in which he is not directly involved. For Gallus it is a change of literary orientation. For Silenus it is a comment on the intellectual life itself and the world of poetry and poets in Virgil's time. He has the power not only to fashion nature and renew myth but to "mold" those who themselves will do the same in their turn.

I said before that the songs of Silenus come to an end with the Gallus episode. This may not be strictly true, but the introduction to the final two tales (lines 74-81) does set them apart:

> quid loquar aut Scyllam Nisi, quam fama secuta est
> candida succinctam latrantibus inguina monstris
> Dulichias vexasse rates et gurgite in alto,
> a, timidos nautas canibus lacerasse marinis;
> aut ut mutatos Terei narraverit artus,
> quas illi Philomela dapes, quae dona pararit,
> quo cursu deserta petiverit et quibus ante
> infelix sua tecta super volitaverit alis?

Why shall I tell either of Scylla, daughter of Nisus, of whom the story goes that, her gleaming waist girt with yelping monsters, she troubled the ships of Ulysses and on the ocean's deep, alas, tore at the fearful sailors with her sea dogs? Or how he sang of the altered limbs of Tereus, what banquet, what gifts Philomela prepared for him, with what flight she sought the desert and with what wings the unfortunate creature first flew over her own home?

Quid loquar comes as a surprise. Virgil causes his reader to question why he should suddenly interrupt the catalogue of synopses from Silenus' *carmina* with a statement in the first person. The break calls attention to the fact that these two tales, of four lines apiece, are symmetrical in themselves and set apart from the previous *carmina* whose careful arrangement we have already traced. They are an appendage to what otherwise might appear complete. The autonomous symmetry of these last tales pinpoints the ambiguity about the subject of *narraverit* (line 78). Is Virgil wondering why Silenus continued on to sing of Scylla and Philomela? Or could it be that the verb is an echo of *dicitur* (line 72) and that Gallus, himself now changed into a teller of *origines*, is to sing the adventures of these ill-starred heroines?

Both questions can be answered positively. There are elements in both tales which have not appeared hitherto in Silenus' catalogue. Metamorphoses there have been, but none quite like these where, because of tragic circumstances two lovers are transformed, the one into a sea monster, the other into a nightingale. Unhappy love there also has been. But metamorphosis and unhappy love have not been combined, especially in a manner whereby the lady, luckless as a human, lives on to endure her plight in the guise of an animal. If the myth of the Grynaean grove were anything like these tales in tone and content we might propose Gallus as the subject of *narraverit* with more conviction. But it is not, at least in the legend Servius outlines, which merely consists of a contest between Calchas and Mopsus over who was the more skillful at divination. Though the ambiguity must necessarily remain, the ending of the poem gives us reason to ponder the possibilities again (lines 82-86):

> omnia, quae Phoebo quondam meditante beatus
> audiit Eurotas iussitque ediscere lauros,
> ille canit (pulsae referunt ad sidera valles),
> cogere donec ovis stabulis numerumque referre
> iussit et invito processit Vesper Olympo.

All the songs which once the happy Eurotas heard—while Phoebus played—and ordered his laurels to learn, Silenus sang (the echoing valleys bore the sound to the stars), until Vesper came forth in an unwilling sky and gave the command to fold the sheep and take their toll.

The verb *canit* is used more than any other to introduce Silenus' *carmina*, and *refert* is the prelude to his précis of the Prometheus myth (line 42). The word *omnia*, then, might well serve as summary for all the songs of Silenus. It is strange, though, that these are the songs which Phoebus Apollo "meditates" while the Eurotas "hears" them. The last time Silenus unquestionably appears in the poem is as the singer of Gallus' poetic initiation. The person who presides over that moment, however, is not Silenus but Apollo; his chorus rises to greet the new arrival and he himself is to take special pleasure in the first result of Gallus' changed poetic perspective. Hence it comes as no surprise that the songs of Silenus, and maybe even the songs of Gallus (whether real or fictitious), were, or will be, chanted by Apollo, chief deity of the pastoral pantheon. Curiously, however, the place where Apollo sings is specified as the banks of the Eurotas. This god, when he sings, does not waste his voice on the symbolic heights of Aonia but descends to a reality which more nearly reflects the spiritual situation of Gallus, *errantem Permessi ad flumina.* As Servius observes, *hunc fluvium Hyacinthi causa Apollo dicitur amasse* ("this stream Apollo is said to have loved because of Hyacinth"). So Apollo, the lofty, dispassionate priest of poetry whose Muses help consecrate Gallus, will use these songs as a sign of affection, not as an impersonal vocalization practiced in a vacuum. Is Gallus, then, merely being introduced to a higher form of love song, both "pastoral" and objective yet seeking the same results as his elegies? When Tityrus "meditates" on the pastoral muse in the first eclogue, he is only teaching the woods to echo the name of Amaryllis. Though Apollo's "meditations" here may have a more intellectual cast, the emotional result is equivalent.

The verb *meditor* in line 82 is carefully chosen from another point of view. We have seen Apollo taking up where Silenus left off, or rather we have been told that he, too, could sing the songs of Silenus. The same creative power belongs to both. The poem as a whole is a fluctuation between—and ultimately a combination of—Dionysiac emotionality and Apolline order. The representatives of both forces exchange roles to suit the poet's fancy. Now the Bacchic Silenus, though he may sing on occasion of a deranged world, brings logic to it by subduing his material to the confines of poetry. Now Apollo, aloof guardian of the Muses' heights, can descend to mortal realms and sing Silenus' songs from love.

We must not lose sight of the fact that, though the poem begins and ends with Apollo, it is Virgil himself who first uses the word *meditor* in line 8. It is Virgil who creates this special harmony out of dissonance. Here poetry is both madness and form: madness because it must tell of life, form because it raises the momentary to the stature of paradigm and imprisons it in a pattern of words. Yet Virgil has chosen to characterize not Apollo but Silenus. Apollo may command this type of song, but Silenus dictates the matter as well as the

shape. He is a god with a dash of the sub-human in his nature. Because he knows all things he is strongly involved in
life as a tension between chaos and order, violence and restraint, sex and song. These tensions which would ordinarily
be polarized around the separate figures of Silenus and Apollo
are here attributed to both. Although the case of Gallus is
different (he is being made a poet to establish a new order),
Silenus' attempts to find design in nature and in human
feelings end in chaos and pessimism, but they are now viewed
as poetry which can transform the tragedy of life's suffering
into myth. Gallus can surmount love and what to a pastoral
poet might seem a too close attachment to reality by becoming a creator of myths; he will not choose to remain, Silenus
suggests, an elegiac poet and warrior, the mere content of
myths.

Virgil, then, has a purpose in using *meditabor* at line 8.
He wishes to emphasize the oft-noted resemblances between
the initial lines of *Eclogue* 6 and the description of Tityrus
in *Eclogue* 1 in order to point out the poems' differences.
The name Tityrus, the verb *meditari*, and the verb *ludere* repeat, but the situations of the two poems are dissimilar. In
Eclogue 1 it is not what Tityrus sings—for all we know he
may have sung the songs of Silenus as well as the beauties of
Amaryllis—but the conditions under which he sings, the
"pastoral" background and the complex relationship of poetry
and society that are paramount. The sixth eclogue, on the other
hand, begins a new group of eclogues all five of which, in differing ways, contemplate the nature of poetry, specifically the
content and form of pastoral song.

But are the difficulties Virgil poses in the first five songs so
essentially different? It is no more of an imaginative accomplishment to fancy a reconciliation in a new golden age between Pollio's consular world and the shepherd's life, than to
tailor a drunken, omniscient Silenus with his poetic variety
show to fit pastoral poetry as defined by Hesiod and Callim-

achus. Though in *Eclogue* 6 we are dealing purely with poetry, it is just as hard to reconcile the extremely emotional "experience" of Silenus with the usually sheltered, illiterate life of the shepherd as it is to imagine Alexis sharing Corydon's existence.

There is little relaxation in Virgil's version of the pastoral and *Eclogue* 6 is hardly an exception. It is an experiment. New subject matter and a new manner of presentation combine to engender an excitement rare even in the *Eclogues*. Questions to which commentators have offered only tentative answers abound. The introduction reveals much about the poetic tradition by which Virgil is expanding the contents of pastoral poetry; but, though the framework of presentation is partially Callimachean, the sudden appearance of Silenus is unique. By the end of the poem the reader understands that only a primitive creature of the untamed earth, such as a satyr—part brute, part god, teacher of Bacchus and knowledgeable about man and the universe—could unify such dissonant elements and give the logic of poetic form to a world essentially contradictory and sometimes ugly. Born before yet seeing beyond most mortals, he seems above what he sings, a participant in what Yeats calls, in *Sailing to Byzantium*, the "artifice of eternity." Yeats, however, imagines himself "out of nature," ready to take a shape of gold or enamel

> Or set upon a golden bough to sing
> To lords and ladies of Byzantium
> Of what is past, or passing, or to come.

Silenus is more than an impersonal mind, a poet divorced from his mortal frame. The flesh is very much with him and his warmest expressions, as *vates*, are elicited in empathy not abstraction. If he rewards Chromis and Mnasyllus with the "charm" of his songs and gives pleasure to mesmerized nature, he also promises something even more matter-of-fact to the nymph Aegle. Thus the metaphysical and the physical, the

Eclogue 6

form of song and the vitality of myth, the knowledge to sing
of all things, whether they be primitive or sophisticated,
and the wit to express them magnetically all merge in one
character, the perfect vehicle for Virgil's expansion of the
horizons of his song.

M. Forte sub arguta consederat ilice Daphnis,
    compulerantque greges Corydon et Thyrsis in unum,
    Thyrsis ovis, Corydon distentas lacte capellas,
    ambo florentes aetatibus, Arcades ambo,
    et cantare pares et respondere parati.

By chance Daphnis had taken his seat under a rustling
oak, and Corydon and Thyrsis had herded their flocks
together, Thyrsis his sheep, Corydon goats whose udders
were swollen with milk. Both were in the prime of life,
both Arcadians, equally ready to sing and to answer.
(lines 1-5)

Meliboeus' detached description of the scene into which
he stumbles might mislead us into believing that there was little connection between the seated Daphnis and the two
shepherds, Corydon and Thyrsis.[1] Everything depends on
accident (*forte*). First there is Daphnis and his setting, then
the coming together of the two shepherds in his presence, and
finally the fortuitous advent of Meliboeus who reports the
whole thing from memory (because the Muses delight in recalling alternate songs, and apparently he does too). The poem
is the chance but necessary union of all three parts and could
not exist with any one lacking.[2]

[1] On the seventh eclogue see, most recently, Pöschl, *Die Hirtendichtung Virgils*, pp. 93-154, with the modifications and reservations of
Hellfried Dahlmann, "Zu Vergils siebentem Hirtengedicht," *Hermes*
94 (1966): 218-32.
[2] *Eclogue* 7 is often linked with *Eclogue* 3 because of the amoebean
style common to each. But the superficial differences—*Eclogue* 7,
unlike 3, is quoted by an onlooker and at its conclusion a prize is
awarded—point up the crucial distinction. *Eclogue* 7 is specifically
about song and its composition.

Eclogue 7

Each detail in the introduction of Daphnis is significant. With *consederat* (as well as *compulerant* in the next line) we have compared the opening lines of the fifth eclogue:

> Cur non, Mopse, boni quoniam convenimus ambo,
> tu calamos inflare levis, ego dicere versus,
> hic corylis mixtas inter consedimus ulmos?

That Mopsus insists on going into a cave to sing does not detract from the beauty which Menalcas sees in a stance amid hazels and elms. We may also recall the brief description of the model locale for the competition in the third eclogue (lines 55-57):

> Dicite, quandoquidem in molli consedimus herba,
> et nunc omnis ager, nunc omnis parturit arbos,
> nunc frondent silvae, nunc formosissimus annus.

Yet in the seventh eclogue Daphnis is neither contestant in the song nor judge of its merits. (We need no one to tell us the outcome by the end of the poem.) Even so his presence under the ilex tree is crucial. The poet tells us so very early in the poem as if to forewarn the uninitiated reader: the ideal shepherd must be at hand to preside over this coming together *in unum*.

What seems to typify the two shepherds is union amid diversity. They are both in the flower of their youth, both Arcadians (that is, shepherds gifted in song), both prepared for the give and take of amoebean verse. They will prove to be as different as the two flocks they drive. Yet, if we look beyond the literal to the suggested metaphor behind it, the poem which follows, though apparently consisting of challenging and diverse segments, will ultimately develop all the component parts of a pastoral song. The presence of Daphnis, exemplar of poet-shepherds, is essential to the search for perfect song in a perfect setting.

Daphnis also has something in common with the Tityrus of

the first eclogue. His is a very similar idyllic retreat. There is in each case a shepherd named Meliboeus who looks in on this happy world with cares of his own which prevent his being part of it, save for a moment. In the first eclogue his trials are universal; in the seventh they are restricted to a shepherd's ordinary rustic cares. Such similarities only put the distinction into relief. In 1, the ideal existence is one man's good fortune. It is vaguely suggested to the reader of 7 that the *seria* (line 17) of Meliboeus could be a smaller version of the suffering which will drive the Meliboeus of 1 into exile.

In *Eclogue* 7 there is no question of man intervening to save or demolish the myth. The presence of Daphnis is magical. There is no hint of outside menace, only stress on Meliboeus' luck at finding himself at a source of bucolic verse. The distinction may be observed in the change from *patulae sub tegmine fagi* to *sub arguta ilice*. Each tree purveys the requisite shade, although the ilex has none of the symbolic overtones of Tityrus' shielding beech. It is merely *arguta*, but this in itself tells us something about Daphnis and about the poem. To call a tree "clear-voiced" within the conventions of bucolic poetry is not merely to refer to the wind rushing through its branches.[3] In *Eclogue* 8 (line 22), the lovesick shepherd refers to the rustling grove and talking pines (*argutumque nemus pinusque loquentis*) of Maenalus, which hear his love songs and return the consolation which no mortal can convey. *Arguta ilex* reveals that, unlike the first eclogue, this is to be a song specifically about poetry and, in particular, about the contest as a means for searching out the ideal.

The remainder of the introduction elaborates these suggestions (lines 6-13):

> huc mihi, dum teneras defendo a frigore myrtos,
> vir gregis ipse caper deerraverat; atque ego Daphnim
> aspicio. ille ubi me contra videt, 'ocius,' inquit,

---

[3] See Pöschl, *Die Hirtendichtung Virgils*, p. 54.

Eclogue 7

'huc ades, o Meliboee; caper tibi salvus et haedi;
et, si quid cessare potes, requiesce sub umbra.
huc ipsi potum venient per prata iuvenci;
hic viridis tenera praetexit harundine ripas
Mincius, eque sacra resonant examina quercu.'

Hither, while I was warding off the cold from the tender
myrtles, my he-goat, the lord of the flock himself, wandered off. And I behold Daphnis. When he sees me in
turn, he says "Come over here quickly, Meliboeus; your
ram is safe and your kids; and, if you can relax awhile,
rest in the shade. Hither the bullocks of their own accord will come through the meadows to drink; here the
Mincius interweaves its green banks with tender reed and
the swarms buzz in the sacred oak.

By means of the summarizing *huc*, Virgil announces a further
disparity between the lives of Daphnis and Meliboeus. Meliboeus must work to shield the defenseless myrtles against the
hardships of nature. Daphnis is completely at leisure. There
is no cold to bother him: his invitation to Meliboeus to join
him *sub umbra* suggests the usual pastoral escape from the
sun's rays into some cool spot, rather than the menacing
frigus.

It is the straying of the *caper* that causes Meliboeus literally
to make the transition from one realm to the other. The word
ipse looks two ways. In terms of the unfortunate shepherd,
who has lost his he-goat and herd, *ipse* means "even he." The
same word takes on the idea of "spontaneously," if seen in
terms of the magical spot into which the he-goat strays. It
anticipates the use of *ipsi* in line 11 where the cattle come of
their own accord to drink. We are thus suddenly drawn, along
with Meliboeus and his flock, into an ideal landscape where
nature grants willing benefits to the fortunate without any
balancing effort on their part: we are drawn into the world of
Eclogue 4, where goats readily bring home full udders (*ipsae,*

line 21), where the earth spontaneously pours forth flowers (*ipsa,* line 23), and the ram automatically (*ipse,* line 43) changes the colors of his fleece.

Deerraverat is a word which helps us visualize the transition. It is the goat's *error,* his wandering course, which leads Meliboeus to see Daphnis. The word transmits Meliboeus' alarm upon noticing his flock missing, but the browsing of cattle where they will, unattended, is also an aspect of the bucolic retreat. It is the complement in the natural world of Tityrus' freedom to sing. The automatic wandering of the he-goat into Daphnis' presence is part of the "charm" this special god bestows on his setting, that perfect background in nature necessary to the spontaneous creation of song.

At the end of the little drama comes the simple but very effective phrase: *atque ego Daphnim / aspicio.* The verb itself, if we may judge from other usages in the *Eclogues,* suggests surprise at a phenomenon so strange, under the circumstances, as to take on the character of an omen.[4] The narrator, humble Meliboeus, has found himself face to face with Daphnis, hero of shepherds. In the space from *defendo* to *aspicio,* Meliboeus' life has changed completely. Just how fantastic this landscape must be to the newcomer, Daphnis' words make clear. They are an invitation out of the ordinary into the sublime.

The initial command, *ocius . . . / huc ades, o Meliboee,* may be designed to put the shepherd's mind at rest, but the phrase *huc ades* has a particular force. It recalls, through anaphora, the *huc* in line 6 and anticipates the *huc* and *hic* with which lines 11 and 12, which contain further details of the landscape's beauty, begin. Virgil is fond of this mode of address when one character, usually a lover, is trying to draw someone else into the country from a milieu foreign or antagonistic to it. We have observed it, for instance, in the second eclogue (lines 45-46) as Corydon outlines the charms of his rustic life for the urbane Alexis: "huc ades, o formose puer: tibi lilia plenis /

---

[4] See e.g., *Ecl.* 2. 66; 9. 58.

ecce ferunt Nymphae calathis." We will see *huc ades* again
in the first line (39) of Moeris' prayer to Galatea in *Eclogue* 9.
There the contrast between the mad flood in which Galatea
lives and Moeris' flourishing spring is, in some degree, parallel to the disparity between Meliboeus' working life and the
ease of Daphnis.

With Daphnis all is "safe" whereas Meliboeus must "defend" his myrtles against a harshness of nature that does not
penetrate Daphnis' sacred spot. Daphnis himself distinguishes
between their two lives at line 10 when he grants that Meliboeus will find rest in the shade, but only if he will give up his
cares for a moment. In this respect, too, the little episode seems
a minor version of the universal cataclysm which has stricken
the rural world in the first eclogue. There, of course, we gain
the impression that Meliboeus is merely gazing into Tityrus'
happy idyll from a vantage point of his own. Here, two spheres
of lesser contrast are juxtaposed, *contra* (line 8).

Eclogue 1, we recall, also ends in an invitation: "hic tamen
hanc mecum poteras requiescere noctem / fronde super
viridi." If the losses to which each Meliboeus must submit are
scarcely comparable, we may also note the difference in the
reasons given for their invitations. Rest in the shade is a temptation in either case. In *Eclogue* 1, however, Tityrus offers only
apples, chestnuts, and cheese, the usual *munera*. Daphnis is
a more sophisticated divinity, a reflection of the perfection of
the landscape and of a golden age where nature cherishes men
who need not toil. Above all Daphnis invites Meliboeus into a
world he can enter, a world of the imagination, to attend a
contest in search of poetry worthy of such a landscape. We
are to hear a poem specifically about verse and its composition,
with no menacing historical overtones to bother the shepherds
as they sing.

Perhaps the most significant detail in this landscape is di-
vulged only in Daphnis' final words. This is no ordinary
stream, its green banks shaded by tender reed, but Virgil's
Mincius. The spell is deepened rather than broken by this in-

trusion of reality upon the idyllic scene. The reader is asked to ponder the actual existence of Daphnis' realm within the confines of Mantua. Mantua contains two worlds, the one inside the other. It provides countryside for the regular needs of a rural community, and within this it shelters—at least in the poet's mind—a retreat for the imagination. Nature herself, in the form of the Mincius, "interweaves" (*praetexit*) this scene by the river bank with the tender reed (*tenera harundine*), the humble source of the poet's slender song (*tenui harundine* in *Eclogue* 6, line 8).[5] The river bank is another of nature's emblems (parallel to the *arguta ilex*) for the art of poetry; it is an attribute of the poet's spiritual life, upon which he depends for the recognition and description of the beautiful.

The river Mincius makes several other dramatic entrances into Virgil's poetry, but none more significant for *Eclogue* 7 than the passage at the beginning of the third georgic (lines 12-16) anticipating his own achievement:

> primus Idumaeas referam tibi, Mantua, palmas,
> et viridi in campo templum de marmore ponam
> propter aquam, tardis ingens ubi flexibus errat
> Mincius et tenera praetexit harundine ripas.
> in medio mihi Caesar erit templumque tenebit. . . .

First I will bring back to you, Mantua, the palm of Idumaea and on a green field I will set up a marble temple beside the water, where great Mincius wanders through its slow windings and interweaves its green bank with tender reed. In the midst of this will be Caesar, and the temple will be his.

Further details of the poet's prowess follow; his skill as a chariot driver in honor of Caesar and the beauty of the temple itself, the scenes of Roman victory on its doors and the statues

---

[5] *Texo*, at 10. 71, is used metaphorically for the "weaving" of poetry. The Mincius here parallels the ivy and the vine which surround the work of Alcimedon on the cups of *Eclogue* 3, or the ivy and *baccar* which decorate the birthplace of the child in 4.

of ancestral heroes which adorn its interior, are described. This is no literal edifice but the figurative fabric of an epic Virgil contemplates singing after the completion of the *Georgics*. The landscape, however, is both factual and symbolic at the same time. Literally, the temple is to be in Mantua on the banks of the Mincius, but like the "temple" itself, the setting is only the formalized landscape of the mind. The river Mincius, like the ivy which trails around the goatherd's cup in Theocritus' first idyl, is a symbol for that poetry which frames and enhances the deeds of Caesar and which instills with imaginative vigor what the temple can pretend is still mere fact.

The verbal parallels between these passages from *Eclogue 7* and *Georgic 3* suggest that even in *Eclogue 7* Virgil is writing with similar symbolic overtones. In the passage from *Georgic 3* there is the intimation that Virgil's imaginative world—for which the pastoral setting is only a metaphor—can somehow be reconciled with those individual, heroic exploits which represent the progress of history to the extent that it embraces them within its limits. In *Eclogue 7* there is no such grand and expansive scheme. The vision does not extend beyond the confines of the countryside. Daphnis is no Caesar, nor are Corydon and Thyrsis Olympic competitors, victors over the Nile and Parthia, or heroic descendants of Assaracus; their contest is of little universal importance. Nevertheless there is at least a possibility that Virgil, the self-announced future writer of epic, is already visible in the lowly Meliboeus who stumbles upon Daphnis and the two shepherds and recreates, in words, both their ideal setting and the song they sing. This setting, like that in *Georgic 3*, represents the realm of the imagination, here deliberately restricted to pastoral song. We are to be privileged onlookers at the creation of poetry.

Daphnis adds one last detail to conclude his account of the setting: *eque sacra resonant examina quercu.* We have already learned that the landscape offers an unreal blend of safety, relaxation, spontaneity, and protection. To conclude, Daphnis observes the sound of the bees buzzing in Jupiter's oak. We need only recall Tityrus' retreat in the first eclogue, alive with a variety of music, or Daphnis' *arguta ilex* to realize the importance of the humming swarms. They complement a model setting.

Meliboeus' response is to think yet again of his problems: he cannot leave his flocks at home and escape into this dream world because he has no Alcippe or Phyllis to pen the lambs for him. On the other hand, he wants to be a listener at this contest. Line 17 stresses the difference for the last time: "posthabui tamen illorum mea seria ludo" ("Nevertheless I put their 'play' ahead of my own work"). The tension in Meliboeus' life, between the *ludus* of poetry and the *seria* of practical concerns, is resolved in favor of Daphnis.

Corydon begins the contest and Thyrsis responds (lines 21-28):

C. Nymphae, noster amor, Libethrides, aut mihi carmen,
    quale meo Codro, concedite (proxima Phoebi
    versibus ille facit) aut, si non possumus omnes,
    hic arguta sacra pendebit fistula pinu.

T. Pastores, hedera crescentem ornate poetam,
    Arcades, invidia rumpantur ut ilia Codro;
    aut, si ultra placitum laudarit, baccare frontem
    cingite, ne vati noceat mala lingua futuro.

C. Nymphs of Libethra, my love, either grant me such a
    song as you gave my Codrus (he makes verses the closest
    to those of Phoebus) or, if we are not all capable of this,
    here my sounding pipe will hang on the sacred pine.

T. Shepherds of Arcadia, adorn your growing bard with
    ivy, that Codrus' sides might burst from envy. Or, if he
    praise me beyond measure, wreathe my forehead with
    baccar lest his evil tongue harm the future bard.

Corydon, learned shepherd, addresses the Muses as guardian Nymphs of the fountain of Libethra on Helicon. They are to be the inspiration for his poetry because of his love for their mistress and hers for him. Should they not grant him such a song as they have to Codrus, most Apolline of poets, he will hang up his pipe once and for all on the sacred pine as an offering to Pan.

The poet emphasizes this introductory petition with subtle care. He associates Corydon with the Muses not only in general—we have just learned from line 19 that they take delight in recalling amoebean contests—but specifically in their role as pastoral nymphs. *Quis caneret nymphas?* Who will sing for the nymphs, Lycidas asks in *Eclogue* 9, line 19, now that Menalcas is gone. There is a necessary, almost personal, bond of affection between the singer and his inspiration. Without love, inspiration means nothing. We need only remember how often each shepherd in the third eclogue, where the contest ends in a draw, makes the same point. There Damoetas begins with an appeal to Jupiter, *illi mea carmina curae* (line 61); Menalcas counters with *et me Phoebus amat* (line 62); and both later speak of the affection they bear for Pollio and he for them, *Pollio amat nostram Musam* (line 84).

Virgil specifically relates Corydon to the setting of Daphnis. *Hic* (line 12) associates him with the beautiful river bank, and the adjectives Corydon applies to his pipe and the nearby pine on which he might hang it, *arguta* and *sacra*, recall *arguta ilice* (line 1) and *sacra quercu* (13) to reaffirm the connection. Save for the alternative Corydon proposes, his petition bears a marked verbal likeness to Virgil's appeal to the nymph Arethusa for his final pastoral song (*Eclogue* 10, lines 1-3):

> Extremum hunc, Arethusa, mihi concede laborem:
> pauca meo Gallo, sed quae legat ipsa Lycoris,
>   carmina sunt dicenda: neget quis carmina Gallo?

> Grant me this, my last task, Arethusa. A few verses must be sung for my Gallus, yet such that Lycoris herself might read them. Who would deny verses to Gallus?

Corydon, in other words, announces his dependence on the Muses to activate the power of song and prays for their help. Thyrsis, by contrast, already assumes for himself the titles of *poeta* and *vates*. He need not turn to the Muses for aid, but feels it essential only to address his fellow shepherds and demand the ivy crown as recognition of proven abilities. Virgil conveys his distaste first in the clear personal contrast between humble, affectionate Corydon, who speaks of his love for the Muses and calls Codrus *meus* though he is a potential rival, and proud Thyrsis who wants Codrus to burst from envy. There are more subtle tonal discrepancies as well. Thyrsis thinks of himself not as a singer of pastoral songs but as the statuesque image of a poet. Codrus is to burst from envy not because of what he hears but because of what he sees. (There is a pun on the word *invidia* almost as if Thyrsis is visualizing Codrus' inability to give him the evil eye!) In sum, Thyrsis' verses are only a literal reminder to his fellow shepherds that he is a budding poet. They are scarcely comparable to Corydon's gentle appeal.

Aside from general questions of manner and tone, some of the verbal details of Thyrsis' reply are ill-chosen. In his use of the symbols for poetry, he reveals the level on which his verses are to be interpreted. As a *poeta* he is to have the traditional ivy crown so as to arouse the envy of Codrus. As *vates* he will wear the apotropaic *baccar* to ward off the effects of Codrus' *mala lingua*. In *Eclogue* 4 (line 19) both *hedera* and *baccar* are put forth by the ground to lend grace and protection to the baby boy who is to initiate the new golden age. Thyrsis superstitiously assumes these emblems and makes his art dependent solely on himself, not on any *carmen* which the Muses might bestow as a token of their love. In his view, he must possess not inspiration (which he assumes) but only that superficial fabric of magic, which serves negatively to undermine his competitor, or the ivy crown itself, external assurance of achievement.

Worse still—to dwell on the implications of the words for a moment—is the suggestiveness of *crescentem. Hedera* and *invidia* have the same position in adjacent verses, but one cannot very well crown something that is "growing." Perhaps the crown will break. Perhaps the poet himself will continue expanding. Yet, whatever the explosive implications for Thyrsis, suddenly the metaphor is attached to Codrus who will himself split from envy. And, to add the insult of sound to the injury of an ill-chosen figure of speech, the poet makes Thyrsis repeat the vowels of *invidia* in the word *ilia*, the sides which are to do the bursting.

We may visualize more distinctly the difference between Corydon and Thyrsis here if we appeal to the words with which Lycidas prefaces his refusal to sing in the ninth eclogue (lines 32-34):

> et me fecere poetam
> Pierides, sunt et mihi carmina, me quoque dicunt
> vatem pastores; sed non ego credulus illis.

> The maidens of Pieria made even me a poet. Songs, too, I have. The shepherds also call me a bard, but I put no trust in them.

The Muses fashion a poet because they bestow the impulse to write *carmina*. The shepherds merely grant the title *vates* to someone they see is inspired. They can recognize and acknowledge power, not purvey it. Thus Corydon, in the fashion of a proper poet, begins a true song by announcing his debt to the Muses. Thyrsis, already grandly appropriating the title of *poeta*, though at the same time calling himself only *crescens*, urges his fellow shepherds to crown him poet, a role reserved by tradition for the goddess nymphs of Pieria or Helicon. Corydon is creating a song, Thyrsis an editorial.

As we turn from Corydon's invocation of the Muses and its virtual parody by Thyrsis to their appeals to Diana and

Priapus, the same contrasts in taste and good judgment become further apparent (lines 29-36) :

C. Saetosi caput hoc apri tibi, Delia, parvus
et ramosa Micon vivacis cornua cervi.
si proprium hoc fuerit, levi de marmore tota
puniceo stabis suras evincta coturno.

T. Sinum lactis et haec te liba, Priape, quotannis
exspectare sat est: custos es pauperis horti.
nunc te marmoreum pro tempore fecimus; at tu,
si fetura gregem suppleverit, aureus esto.

C. To you, Delian goddess, tiny Micon offers this head of a shaggy boar and the branching antlers of a long-lived stag. Should this fortune remain, you will stand completely of smooth marble, with your ankles bound by a crimson buskin.

T. It is enough, Priapus, for you to expect a bowl of milk and these cakes each year. You watch over a poor garden. Now for the time being we have made you of marble, but be you of gold, if births fill up the flock.

Through Corydon, first reading Micon's inscription and then probably speaking his words, the presence of Diana is welcomed into this scene of ilexes, oaks, and pines. The boar and the stag are fitting symbols of the goddess of the wild. Hunting itself, though sometimes a necessity for the shepherd, is never part of his usual life. We need only remember the roebucks, discovered in a dangerous valley, which Corydon offers Alexis in the second eclogue. By making the head and the antlers a dedicatory offering and by promising Diana her own statue, Corydon makes the goddess and the gifts to her part of the stability of the pastoral world. There could be no such statues in the wild realm of boars and stags, yet they would fit well under the oaks by the Mincius' bank. The humble appropriateness of the gift becomes all the more apparent

234

from the giver's name, Micon, the small one, dedicator of a shaggy boar's head and a set of branching antlers.

Equally effective is the language itself: it has balance and power. There is only one word, *et*, which does not have a close grammatical connection with some other. To add to the interest and excitement of the passage there is the favorite Roman color contrast between the white marble of the stone and the red buskin which the proposed statue is to wear.[6] Again the adjectives *levi* and *puniceo* fit handsomely with their nouns, the marble smooth because its figure is graceful and nimble, the buskin crimson because it belongs to a huntress. Moreover *hoc proprium*, balancing *caput hoc*, is sung not as a threat to demand productivity—this is no farmer or gardener speaking —but simply as a prayer that the head be an acceptable offering to the patroness of the hunt. May she be happy with her gifts and reward Micon accordingly.

By contrast the bumpkin Thyrsis turns to the Priapus in his garden (as far as he is concerned we could no longer be in Daphnis' secluded spot) and flippantly dictates to him what he considers ample for him to receive as an offering. This is no prayer. For a god, it is bad enough to receive only a bowl of milk and some cakes once a year, yet it is even worse to be told by a mortal that such a trifle is sufficient. And then to be told, what he already knows well because he is in the midst of it, that he watches over a poor garden, is salt in the wound. The offering is scanty, the garden unproductive, and the god does not seem to be doing his job very well. Therefore he should not expect more. This is an ultimatum which is still more boorish by contrast with Micon's offering. Micon craves only that his preliminary gift be fitting to the goddess in order that he may add something more beautiful. Thyrsis lays down a condition for the god to fulfill before he will get anything further. Majesty has given place to rudeness.

[6] See Fordyce on Catullus 61. 9f.

Some of this difference in tone stems from the subject matter itself: a handsome Diana and an ugly Priapus. Nevertheless there is one blatant instance of inconcinnity within Thyrsis' lines. It is both comic and strange, though not impossible, for a statue of Priapus to be made of either marble or gold.[7] We expect a statue of Diana to be executed in marble, but Priapus' figures were usually wooden. It is even more unsuitable that the god be made of such patently rich material when he presides over a garden which is poor and is himself allowed by its owner only the smallest of offerings each year. The consequent tension, missing from Corydon's harmonious words, is fantastic and unreal.

The divergence between the extreme poverty of the garden and the glaring richness Thyrsis demands is further underscored by the arrogance of Thyrsis' address to the god. The prosaic *fecimus*, for instance, means that in Thyrsis' eyes Priapus, god though he is, should be well aware that he is the creation of the human hand and should be indebted to Thyrsis accordingly. At line 36 we would expect an honorable expression of good will to balance Corydon's *stabis*. Instead we find a virtual command to the god to become gold. We have come a long way from Corydon's self-effacing prayer, acknowledging complete dependence on the goddess, to Thyrsis' reminder to Priapus that the god is fully dependent on him. This further sets off the ludicrous contrast between unproductive garden and overdecorated garden god. The attempt to do Corydon one better stresses the disharmony. Here, as before, Thyrsis turns Corydon's preceding utterance into something extreme, negative, and unseemly.

In the next theme and variation, the two shepherds vie at composing invitations for Galatea to come visit them (lines 37-44):

[7] On the material for Priapus statues, see Hans Herter, *P.-W.* 44, cols. 1922-23.

C. Nerine Galatea, thymo mihi dulcior Hyblae,
   candidior cycnis, hedera formosior alba,
   cum primum pasti repetent praesepia tauri,
   si qua tui Corydonis habet te cura, venito.

T. Immo ego Sardoniis videar tibi amarior herbis,
   horridior rusco, proiecta vilior alga,
   si mihi non haec lux toto iam longior anno est.
   ite domum pasti, si quis pudor, ite iuvenci.

C. Galatea, offspring of Nereus, sweeter to me than the
   thyme of Hybla, whiter than swans, lovelier than pale
   ivy, as soon as the bulls seek the stalls from pasture,
   come to me, if any yearning for your Corydon grips
   you.

T. Nay, may I seem to you more bitter than Sardinian
   grass, rougher than broom plant, cheaper than seaweed
   cast up on the shore, if this day does not even now seem
   longer than a whole year. Go homeward, well-fed
   bullocks, go home, if you have any modesty.

The ugly images which Thyrsis uses to express his hyperbolic
devotion to Galatea destroy Corydon's subtle equation of her
with natural beauty.[8] The initial comparison is between *thymo
mihi dulcior Hyblae* and *Sardoniis amarior herbis*. The conceit in the first instance is beautifully worked out. Corydon,
lover of Galatea, imagines himself as a bee tasting love which
is sweeter than the most delicious thyme. This image recalls
Tityrus' Hyblaean bees and the hedge they feed upon
(*depasta*).[9] Corydon hopes that, after the cattle have had their
fill (*pasti*), love will come to satisfy the shepherd in turn.

---

[8] I cannot believe (with Rose, Dahlmann, and others) that Thyrsis'
words are meant to be Galatea's reply. The orientation is thoroughly
wrong.

[9] See Gow's commentary on Theocritus *Id.* 1. 146 and 7. 82 for
further associations of poets, poetry and honey.

Eclogue 7

It is only a step from thyme to the sweet honey which, according to most ancient authorities, came from the flower itself. The nurturing of the true poet on honey is an idea which Virgil would have found in Theocritus. At line 146 of Theocritus' first idyl the goatherd prays for Thyrsis: "Filled may your lovely mouth be with honey, and the honeycomb." Honey is a metaphor for the beauty of his words. The story of Daphnis in the seventh idyl, like that of Comatas, contains an even more elaborate description of the same phenomenon (*Idyl* 7, lines 78-85):

ᾀσεῖ δ' ὥς ποκ' ἔδεκτο τὸν αἰπόλον εὐρέα λάρναξ
ζωὸν ἐόντα κακαῖσιν ἀτασθαλίαισιν ἄνακτος,
ὥς τέ νιν αἱ σιμαὶ λειμωνόθε φέρβον ἰοῖσαι
κέδρον ἐς ἁδεῖαν μαλακοῖς ἄνθεσσι μέλισσαι,
οὕνεκά οἱ γλυκὺ Μοῖσα κατὰ στόματος χέε νέκταρ.
ὦ μακαριστὲ Κομᾶτα, τύ θην τάδε τερπνὰ πεπόνθεις·
καὶ τὺ κατεκλάσθης ἐς λάρνακα, καὶ τὺ μελισσᾶν
κηρία φερβόμενος ἔτος ὥριον ἐξεπόνασας.

And he shall sing how once a wide coffer received the goatherd alive by the impious presumption of a king; and how the blunt-faced bees came from the meadows to the fragrant chest of cedar and fed him on tender flowers because the Muse had poured sweet nectar on his lips. Ah, blessed Comatas, thine is this sweet lot; thou too wast closed within the coffer; thou too, on honeycomb fed, didst endure with toil the springtime of the year.

To return to the compliment Corydon is paying Galatea: she is not only sweeter than honey to him (*dulcior* is an amatory word) but also raised to the level of a symbol for the source of the poet's inspiration for beautiful song.

Thyrsis' reply is consistently unfortunate. He imagines himself in a hopefully unattainable place: surrounded by that foliage which is the most repellent to bees, which here symbolize Galatea. This is the reverse of Corydon's beautiful picture. In Thyrsis' words, if Galatea does not take care, she will be the one to feed on bitter grasses. We need refer only to Lycidas' prayer for Moeris' good fortune in *Eclogue* 9, line 30—"sic tua Cyrneas fugiant examina taxos . . ." ("as you would have your swarms flee the yews of Corsica . . .")—to realize how unhappy the comparison is, even if Thyrsis means the opposite. Thyrsis has not thought about the full nature of the comparative adjectives he is using. Those intent on looking at his words for their misconceptions might say that he will only become more bitter than Sardinian grasses if Galatea does not come to him. The implication is that he already is quite as bitter. Corydon's adjectives are simple compliments to Galatea, not insults to himself.

The rest of the comparisons follow this pattern. For Corydon, Galatea remains the essence of poetic beauty and love, whiter than swans and lovelier than pale ivy.[10] Swans and ivy, emblems of Venus and Bacchus, are the perfect complements of the lover-poet's world. We have seen the ivy so used earlier in the poem. And, though it is its attribute of whiteness that receives special emphasis here, the swan is a part of the poet's world of music. There are references, for instance, to the song of the swan in both the succeeding eclogues: in 8, line 55, competition between owl and swan is considered an impossibility, and in 9, line 29, the poet promises that singing swans will bear the name of Varus to the stars, if Mantua is saved. Yet, as a source of inspiration for the bard—as well as the honeyed herb on which he might feed, the white swan to complement his love, and the ivy to acknowledge his supremacy in song—Galatea surpasses all in beauty.

We have seen how closely Corydon's initial address to the Muses parallels the introduction to the tenth eclogue. Here there is a close connection with the fifth eclogue. The adjec-

[10] On the idea of whiteness see Pöschl, *Die Hirtendichtung Virgils*, pp. 120-21.

tives *dulcis, candidus*, and *formosus* all appear there within the compass of thirteen lines. At the end of Mopsus' song, the shepherd sings Daphnis' epitaph, concluding with Daphnis' description of himself (line 46): "formosi pecoris custos, formosior ipse." In reply Menalcas terms Daphnis *candidus* (line 56), radiant on the threshold of Olympus. And finally Menalcas, in thanking Mopsus for his song, compares it to the slaking of thirst with sweet water (*dulcis aquae*, line 47). The songs are about something beautiful and bright and are sweet accordingly. Here, too, the song and its object are inseparable. In the case of Galatea it is her special beauty which is the center of the poet's thoughts. Her loveliness inspires the poetry which is, in turn, the poet's song of love for her. Perfect beauty and song are one.

Thyrsis, by contrast, continues with jarring comparisons. Instead of the color and beauty of *candidior* and *formosior* we have the ugly and valueless, *horridior* and *vilior*; instead of swans and ivy, broom plant and seaweed. Some details are particularly ill-chosen. We have spoken of *Sardoniis herbis* above. The adjective *amarus* is inept not only in a negative contrast with its counterpart, *dulcis*, but also because—in spite of its direct association here with Sardinian herbs—it is a word which Virgil himself applies to Doris, goddess of the salt sea, in *Eclogue* 10 (line 5). There the sea is bitter and brackish in the eyes of the shepherd-poet appealing for inspiration from the pure spring of Arethusa. It is scarcely a compliment to the Nereid Galatea to have her lover apply something from her realm to himself in a pejorative tone.[11] The same is true of *horridus*, one of the common Latin words to describe the swollen, roughened sea.[12]

The phrase *proiecta vilior alga* further affronts good taste. Though the comparison is proverbial, Thyrsis is again apply-

[11] For seaweed in such comparisons, cf. Horace *Sat.* 2. 5. 8; *Carm.* 3. 17. 10. On *ruscus*, see *G.* 2. 413-14; Columella 10. 374-75.

[12] E.g. Horace, *Carm.* 3. 24. 40.

ing directly to himself something ugly from Galatea's world. In none of his comparisons is there any attempt to establish the happy equation which Corydon handsomely creates. *Amarus, horridus*, and *vilis* are scarcely the positive words necessary to entice one lover to another. When the comparisons which accompany them are equally mistaken, then their effect cannot help being the opposite of the shepherd's desire and turning his hopefully false self-deprecation into something palpably real.

Looking at verbal construction, Corydon's song is unified in itself, beginning with the vocative *Nerine Galatea* and ending with the prayer of the last word, *venito*. Thyrsis lets his audience wait in vain for an explanation of *tibi* in line 41. It is a rude shock to find Corydon's vocative and imperative applied in the end not to Galatea, in the hope that she might come, but to the cattle to go homeward out of shame. Once more we are forced to note how everything that Thyrsis sings is centered upon himself. Unlike Corydon, he assumes that Galatea is ready to come. He is merely spending a long day waiting. The difference between Corydon's prayerful hope that Galatea will have regard for him (*cura*, line 40) and Thyrsis' command that the cattle flee the spot whither Galatea is bound to come is great. By the mere beauty of his verses, Corydon goes far toward seducing Galatea out of her marine world into his. As in the Diana stanza, Corydon's words bring what might ordinarily be considered foreign to pastoral into contact with it, thereby increasing its prestige and beauty.

From the invitations we pass to descriptions of the setting (lines 45-52):

C. Muscosi fontes et somno mollior herba,
    et quae vos rara viridis tegit arbutus umbra,
    solstitium pecori defendite: iam venit aestas
    torrida, iam lento turgent in palmite gemmae.

T. Hic focus et taedae pingues, hic plurimus ignis
  semper, et adsidua postes fuligine nigri;
  hic tantum Boreae curamus frigora, quantum
  aut numerum lupus aut torrentia flumina ripas.

C. Mossy springs and grass, softer than sleep, and green
  arbute, protecting you with its scant shade, ward off the
  solstice from the flock. Now sweltering summer comes,
  now the buds swell on the bending shoots.

T. Here is a hearth and oily brands, here is ever a great fire
  and doorposts black with constant soot. Here we care as
  much for the chill of Boreas as a wolf does for the number of sheep or raging streams for their banks.

Corydon directs his attention to the beauty of a rural scene, as
spring turns toward summer. His description shows much in
common with Daphnis' idyllic spot: *umbra*, line 46, recalls
umbra, line 10, and *viridis praetexit ripas*, line 12, anticipates
viridis tegit arbutus, line 46. These details recurred to Virgil
in the *Georgics*, first when thinking of the landscape to which
pregnant cattle should retire (*Georgic* 3, lines 143-45)—

> saltibus in vacuis pascunt et plena secundum
> flumina, muscus ubi et viridissima gramine ripa,
> speluncaeque tegant et saxea procubet umbra.

They feed them in open glades and along full streams,
where there is moss and the bank is greenest with grass,
where grottoes protect them and the shade of a rock
stretches afar.—

and then when contemplating the type of place most favorable
to bees (*Georgic* 4, lines 18-20)—

> at liquidi fontes et stagna virentia musco
> adsint et tenuis fugiens per gramina rivus,
> palmaque vestibulum aut ingens oleaster inumbret, . . .

But let clear springs be near and pools green with moss
and a slender rivulet stealing through grass; and let a
palm or a spreading wild-olive overshadow the entrance.

In discussing this *locus amoenus*, it is important to note that
Corydon visualizes himself within it, already surrounded by
fountains and grass and protected by the shade of the arbutus. *Defendo* back in line 6 refers to the ordinary labors of
Meliboeus before he enters into Daphnis' haven of the imagination. *Defendite* here is a prayer that this beauty and security
will be preserved from the elements in nature that menace
it.

The resemblance Corydon's description bears to many passages in Lucretius and Horace is remarkable. From the latter
we note, from the first ode of book one, the setting in which
he places his man of leisure (lines 21-22): ". . . nunc viridi
membra sub arbuto / stratus, nunc ad aquae lene caput sacrae"
(". . . now with his limbs stretched under a green arbute,
now at the gentle source of a holy fountain"). There is also
the famous address to the *fons Bandusiae* which grants its coolness to the flocks and inspiration to the poet in Horace's
Carmina 3. 13. Servius, in his comment on line 47 of the seventh eclogue, rightly refers to *Odes* 1. 17, a poem of particular
importance here because Horace directly associates an idealized
natural setting, which the grace of Faunus shields from external trials, with the poet's existence away from the harshness of reality, free for love and poetry.[13]

It was observed above how verbal parallels link the setting
Corydon describes and the perfect world of poetry in which
Daphnis sits. Only once in the *Eclogues* does Virgil make
a direct metaphorical connection between setting and song,
and in that one instance the words are close to those Corydon
uses here. At the end of Menalcas' verses on the death of

[13] On *Carm.* 1. 17 and *Carm.* 3. 13, see above, Chapter 1, pp. 47-48.
On the phrase *muscosi fontes*, see the context of Hor. *Ep.* 1. 10. 7.

Daphnis, Mopsus praises his song, we recall, in the following terms (*Eclogue* 5, lines 45-47):

> Tale tuum carmen nobis, divine poeta,
> quale sopor fessis in gramine, quale per aestum
> dulcis aquae saliente sitim restinguere rivo.

For a moment song is sleep and the coolness of water during the summer heat. Paradoxically, pastoral poetry both creates and is created by its setting. The real blends indistinguishably with the spiritual in this private, imagined paradise.[14] In the preceding strophe, Corydon visualizes Galatea as his essential source of love and poetry. Here the setting becomes first a requisite for singing and then part of the beauty of the song itself.

Thyrsis' reply to Corydon is at variance. From a rustic retreat on a summer's day, with all nature flourishing, we pass to the soot-blackened interior of a house warmed against the winter's cold. Thyrsis' words are not only a point by point denial of the charm of Corydon's evocation, they are almost a parody of the ideal bucolic setting. The threefold *hic* recalls the *huc* and *hic* of the introduction and the perfection they conjure up, only to emphasize the difference. Daphnis extends an invitation to leave the workaday life of a shepherd and enter a land of song. Thyrsis proposes a setting so un-pastoral as to make song impossible. The *rara umbra* of Corydon's verses contrasts with the oppressively thick blackness which Thyrsis suggests. Escape from the *solstitium* into coolness is challenged by an interior which is all heat—*focus, taedae, plurimus ignis*.

Most words in Thyrsis' song have a bucolic cast. *Pinguis* appears frequently in the *Georgics* as an attribute of soil and

---

[14] The spondees of line 45 are impressive and suggestive of sleep.

On the comparison of 7. 47ff. with 4. 4f., see above p. 139. The verb *turgeo* appears elsewhere in Virgil only at *G.* 1. 315. On the swelling of the grapes see Pöschl, *Die Hirtendichtung Virgils*, p. 135, n. 36. These lines may have been the inspiration of a particularly beautiful moment in the *Pervigilium Veneris* (ed. Clementi, lines 22ff.).

cattle; *plurimus* can suggest plentiful rainfall, as in line 60 below; *adsiduus* is applied to spring itself, in *Georgic* 2. 149. But here, instead, each is turned to opposite purposes. The analogies Thyrsis uses in lines 51-52 are especially ill-conceived. Within a pastoral poem, he all but equates himself with anti-pastoral symbols: the wolf, who eats all the sheep he can get his jaws on, and the raging stream which gnaws away at the river bank. The wolf needs no comment. For the beauty of a setting near calm water, one need only refer to line 12 of the introduction.

The imperatives for the setting in which a shepherd's poetry can be created are absent from Thyrsis' words. First of all it is winter and nature is far from bursting with the creativity which is her response to the poet's song. One detail can illustrate the gap between the two shepherds here. Corydon's *aestas torrida* is mimicked by Thyrsis with *torrentia flumina*, but Corydon's verses are a prayer to keep *aestas torrida* away from his lovely spot. Even were *torrida* to imply a destructive side to nature, Corydon immediately sets the suggestion aside with his lovely line about the swollen buds, ready to burst forth. Thyrsis, on the contrary, virtually equates himself with what might well ruin the landscape. There is no song in his wintry world.

Finally, the tone of Corydon's words follows a noticeable pattern once more. The word *defendite*, addressed to elements essential to this setting, looks back to *concedite* in line 22 where the shepherd appeals for inspiration, to *venito* in line 40 where he pleads with Galatea, and to the implied imperatives of Micon's dedication. Corydon's words are again an appeal to preserve that on which the myth depends. Thyrsis assumes what he has, and boasts of it in anti-pastoral terms.

The next interchange continues the discussion of the setting but adds the detail of the influence a lover's presence or absence has on nature (lines 53-60):

C. Stant et iuniperi et castaneae hirsutae:
   strata iacent passim sua quaeque sub arbore poma;
   omnia nunc rident: at si formosus Alexis
   montibus his abeat, videas et flumina sicca.

T. Aret ager; vitio moriens sitit aeris herba;
   Liber pampineas invidit collibus umbras:
   Phyllidis adventu nostrae nemus omne virebit,
   Iuppiter et laeto descendet plurimus imbri.

C. Here are junipers and shaggy chestnuts. Everywhere
fruit lies strewn beneath its own tree. Now everything
smiles. But if beautiful Alexis were to leave these hills,
you would see the streams go dry.

T. The field is dried up. The thirsty grass is dying from the
air's blight. Liber begrudges the shade of the vines to the
hills. At the coming of our Phyllis, the whole wood will
grow green. Jupiter will descend with the bounty of
plentiful rain.

The theme of Corydon's lines is that love is necessary to complete the beauty of the bucolic landscape. When Corydon sings
to Alexis in the second eclogue (*o formose puer*, lines 17 and
45), it is with the intent of restoring the shepherd's personal
happiness by bringing love into the countryside. Here the idea
is expanded to the point of the pathetic fallacy. All nature depends on the beauty of Alexis. Were he to leave, love would
depart with him and with love, beauty, which in turn presages
the ruin of the setting and poetry. We are dealing with a
place for love and song combined, as we may infer by appealing once more to *Eclogue* 3, lines 56-57, and Palaemon's
words of encouragement to the competing shepherds: "et nunc
omnis ager, nunc omnis parturit arbos, / nunc frondent silvae,
nunc formosissimus annus." Beyond that, the chestnuts and
fruits seem to have particular bearing as examples of the gifts
one rustic lover offers another.[15] These are among the *munera*

---

[15] With the phrase *sub arbore poma* (line 54), cf. *Ecl.* 1. 37: *in arbore*

Corydon extends to Alexis in *Eclogue* 2, lines 51-52. Neither *omnia* nor *passim* are words used lightly. The latter appears elsewhere in the *Eclogues* only in 4, line 19, where the poet is describing the *munuscula* which the earth spontaneously brings forth. While Alexis is a part of the land, all is productive, just as, when the boy of the fourth eclogue grows to manhood, every place will bear all things (*omnis feret omnia tellus*).

Corydon's verses, then, are the hope of the second eclogue become actual fact. (The repetition of names may not be coincidence.) We may recall, for contrast, the effect of Amaryllis' sorrow during the absence of Tityrus (*Eclogue* 1, lines 36-39). Nature's joyous reaction to the presence of Alexis, the spirit of love, is that trees liberally strew their produce beneath them.

Corydon, while possessing the ideal, lets it be known that he realizes the fragility of his dream. He relies on nature's willingness to provide succor and escape from her destructive side.

Thyrsis' verses are again a pessimistic reversal of Corydon's theme. Though hope for the future is possible, at the moment love is absent and nature is dying. Thyrsis' words look back to Corydon's while denying their present validity. The reflection of *herba* and *umbra* at the end of lines 45 and 46 in the endings of lines 57 and 58 is undeniable.[16] If we limit our attention strictly to setting, everything is prosperous and fresh in Corydon's world whereas it withers from blight in Thyrsis' picture.[17] For Corydon the shade of the arbutus pro-

---

poma. In *Eclogue* 1 the implication is that the fruit remains on the tree until it is gathered. This function Amaryllis forgets to perform while her lover is absent. In *Eclogue* 7 the situation is reversed. Love is present and the trees drop their fruit automatically.

[16] The same two words end *Ecl.* 8. 14-15.

[17] The contrast is furthered by the opposition between the very spondaic line 45 and the rushing dactyls of 57, each illustrating its theme.

tects; for Thyrsis, Bacchus begrudges cover for the hills. Thyrsis' reason for the blight in nature is the absence of love. Phyllis' return, he suggests, will bring green. (With *adventu* and *virebit* we might compare *venit* in 47 and *viridis* in 48.) But his suggestion is a wish for the future, not a description of present bliss. Hence we review the horror of Corydon's picture of absent love in *Eclogue* 2, with the added twist that nature herself reflects the lover's suffering by dying. *Moriens* recalls Corydon's *mori me denique cogis?* in *Eclogue* 2, line 7. No mossy fountains here, and certainly not the *umidum solstitium* for which Virgil orders the farmer to pray in *Georgic* 1, line 100, and against which Corydon craves protection in lines 45-48.[18]

With Phyllis' advent everything will change and the whole grove will grow green. (*Omne* echoes Corydon's *omnia nunc rident,* line 55.) But the undeniable beauty of line 59 is immediately undercut by the phraseology of 60. From a completely dried-up land—*aret, moriens,* and *sitit* make the point as explicit as need be—where there is no shade, we are suddenly transported to a land which is drenched with a good downpour of rain. In terms of sound, the jingle of the change from *umbras* to *imbri,* at the ends of lines 58 and 60, is not happy, and the phrase *Iuppiter plurimus* has an unfortunate similarity to Thyrsis' *plurimus ignis,* at the end of line 49.[19]

Water and shade are crucial to the shepherd's landscape, but the coming of rain, important as it is for georgic pursuits, portends the dampening of any shepherd-singer's spirits. Rain is always the assumed replenishment of the countryside's springs, rarely a stated necessity. As in his picture of the interior of a home in winter, Thyrsis again betrays a certain practicality in his word choice which has little to do with the beauty of the pastoral myth. Phyllis' coming may bring the requisite rain, but it will also involve her in a workaday world, different from

---

[18] We recall Daphnis' command (line 10): *requiesce sub umbra.*
[19] The phrase *Iuppiter plurimus* is even a bad pun.

the smiling land of juniper, chestnuts, and love in purely
bucolic terms, the land where Alexis already resides.

There is one final interchange (lines 61-68):

C. Populus Alcidae gratissima, vitis Iaccho,
   formosae myrtus Veneri, sua laurea Phoebo;
   Phyllis amat corylos; illas dum Phyllis amabit,
   nec myrtus vincet corylos, nec laurea Phoebi.
T. Fraxinus in silvis pulcherrima, pinus in hortis,
   populus in fluviis, abies in montibus altis;
   saepius at si me, Lycida formose, revisas,
   fraxinus in silvis cedat tibi, pinus in hortis.

C. The poplar is most dear to Hercules, the vine to Bacchus,
   the myrtle to lovely Venus, his laurels to Phoebus. Phyllis
   loves the hazels. As long as Phyllis loves them, neither
   the myrtle nor laurel of Phoebus will surpass the hazels.
T. The ash is most beautiful in the woods, the pine in gardens, the poplar by streams, the fir on lofty mountains.
   But, handsome Lycidas, should you visit me quite often,
   the ash in the woods, the pine in the gardens would yield
   place to you.

Corydon's conceit is beautifully worked out. Phyllis, though
only a shepherd's love, is equated with a goddess, ranked with
Hercules or Bacchus, Venus or Apollo. Each of these divinities has a favorite tree or plant, but Phyllis loves the hazels
and, through her affection, they are raised from neglect to
love and admiration, even surpassing Venus' myrtle and Apollo's laurel. The hazel, because Phyllis loves it and the poet her,
becomes nature's symbol for love and poetry.

This is a variation on a motif which runs throughout Corydon's strophes. In the first stanza, because the Muses are his
love he has inspiration to write and to hope for success like that
of Codrus, whose verses are nearest to Apollo's. In the third
stanza his love is Galatea, who is associated with honey, swans

and ivy—symbols of the poet's craft and achievement as well as of loveliness in nature. Poetry and love form an essential unity. The next two strophes deal specifically with the beauty of the setting and the necessity of love and beauty for nature's happiness and productivity. Nature responds to beauty as much as the poet to love.

The key line, 63, of this final variation on the motif states only three things: Phyllis, love, hazels. (The line is a combination of straightforward and chiastic order. Both the name Phyllis and the verb *amo* are repeated. The word *corylos* is balanced grammatically and melodically by the immediately following *illas*. Only *dum* stands alone.) Here, as elsewhere only in the Galatea strophe, the shepherd's mistress is specifically connected with the symbols of love and poetry, myrtle and laurel, and directly equated with Venus and Apollo.[20] Yet in her special way Phyllis supersedes even these divinities because of her beauty. Her affection for the hazel raises it to the stature of an emblem of song and beauty beyond even the laurel and the myrtle, and she surpasses Galatea because she already lives in the countryside. The worlds of inspiration and divine presence in the first two strophes, and of love and natural beauty in the subsequent three, are here combined in a graceful union which equates Phyllis with love and nature and offers her as the final example of their irrevocable connection with song and the art of poetry.

Although Thyrsis' contrasting comparison at first seems apt, the result is only that Lycidas is equated with a tree and the speaker is allied to the woods, gardens, streams, or mountains amid which the tree is placed. This double infelicity tempers the mood established by Corydon.

As in his previous songs, Corydon's verses here are a veiled prayer to maintain the *status quo* of ideal pastoral. Like the

[20] On the laurels and poetry, see Pöschl (*Die Hirtendichtung Virgils*, p. 145) who points out the connection between the mention of Phoebus and the opening strophe.

last exchange, Thyrsis' response seems a comment not only on Corydon's immediately preceding verses but also on the penultimate group as well. Here *Lycida formose* suggests a link with Corydon's *formosus Alexis* in line 55, and the parallel *at si* openings abet the equation. A comparison with either group of lines, whether devoted to the presence of Alexis or Phyllis' love for the hazels, puts into relief the sadness of Thyrsis' words. For Thyrsis nature's beauty rests on Lycidas' presence, the dubiety of which he underlines by his use not only of the conditional but also of a verb of coming and going (*revisas*) which implies fluctuation in Lycidas' emotions. His potential for happiness or suffering is dependent on the personal whim of someone outside the land. Phyllis' place in the landscape will keep it flourishing. Thyrsis implies that Lycidas' beauty will surpass that of the poplar or the pine only if he returns more often. Something wrong, either in tone, time, or setting, always creeps into Thyrsis' lines to break the spell of loveliness created by Corydon.

The main force of the competition stems from a comparison of each set of strophes, to see in what sense—idea, diction, tone, or whatever—Corydon is superior to his rival. Looked at in uninterrupted sequence Corydon's songs form a composite picture of pastoral beauty. His vignettes, though they deal with varying elements in the bucolic world, offer in essence different views of a single theme. Each time, by contrast, Thyrsis runs awry due to lack of taste or propriety. Unfortunate choice of subject matter and ineptness of presentation combine to prove his downfall. By introducing intrinsically antagonistic elements into a setting which craves harmony and aptness of tone and expression, he repeatedly breaks the impetus Corydon has started toward a verbal re-creation of that charm which the presiding genius of Daphnis demands.

This is not to maintain that there is nothing charming or important in Thyrsis' words. The presence of a more realistic countryman, whose utterances are occasionally almost comic, intentionally undercuts Corydon's constant lyricism. Thyrsis is a singer whose words betray a strongly practical bent in competition with one who, in his search for the perfect in nature, can make of sporadic verses an harmonious whole. There is nothing negative about Thyrsis; his prodding is creative.[21]

As the introduction suggests, the poem is more than a study in decorum. It is a meditation, in dialogue form, on the idealism of pastoral song and what is appropriate to it. From the very beginning when the shepherds herd their flocks together, the poet tells us there are differences between the protagonists. While Thyrsis' herd is of sheep, Corydon's is of goats, distinguished because their udders are *distentas lacte*. Assuming that he falls into the pattern Apollo suggests to Virgil at the opening of *Eclogue* 6, Corydon's song, as a result, will be appropriately "fine-spun."

The difference is developed in the course of the contest. The poet's use of the word *contendere* twice in this poem (lines 18 and 69), and only here in the *Eclogues*, stresses the idea of competition. As the two shepherds vie with each other, Daphnis, Meliboeus, and ultimately the reader, as unprejudiced listeners, are meant to make a comparison between them and see which is worthy of his setting and theme. Corydon constantly wins by these rules. Just as, on a literal level, nothing extraneous or unwonted can come into this setting unless it deserves access, so, figuratively, the setting is a symbol of that perfect poetry which results from its inspiration. Nothing discordant can be uttered without shattering the spell and proving the worthlessness of the utterance. The poem is a search for the ideal within the ideal, for a hymn to pastoral love and poetry which harmonizes with the perfect landscape.

Hence in spite of their differences, both the cave of Silenus

---

[21] "Thyrsis," in Greek, means "goad"; "Corydon," "lark" (a point made by E. E. Beyers, "Vergil's Eclogue 7—A Theory of Poetry," *Acta Classica* 5 [1962]: 43, n. 18).

in *Eclogue* 6 and the tree under which Daphnis sits serve as settings for the type of poetry which in each instance follows. In 6, Silenus sings of many themes and many types of song; variety is an essential point. He knows all things and can change poetry into infinite shapes. Daphnis remains the ideal shepherd, at leisure in a perfect locale, presiding over a competition which by trial and error defines what the pastoral can contain and what it must reject. Meliboeus' role in this process should not be neglected because he is the ideal spectator whose *seria* make us aware that he, the ordinary shepherd (and we, the common reader) have entered a world that exists only in the imagination, the world in which song is created.

As an invitation into the rural poet's world, *Eclogue* 7 bears comparison with the lyric which Robert Frost used as a dedicatory poem for several of his volumes, entitled "The Pasture":[22]

> I'm going out to clean the pasture spring;
> I'll only stop to rake the leaves away
> (And wait to watch the water clear, I may):
> I sha'n't be gone long. — You come too.
>
> I'm going out to fetch the little calf
> That's standing by the mother. It's so young
> It totters when she licks it with her tongue.
> I sha'n't be gone long. — You come too.

The processes of poetry are as the cleaning of the spring and the fetching of the calf, licked into shape by its mother's tongue. The poem draws inspiration from the clearness of the pond and youth of the newborn calf. The poet rakes the leaves and fetches the calf. These are the two activities particularly stressed through the lack of parallel rhyme between "spring"

[22] From *Complete Poems of Robert Frost*. Copyright 1939, © 1967 by Holt, Rinehart and Winston, Inc. Reprinted by permission of Holt, Rinehart and Winston, Inc., and Jonathan Cape, Ltd.

and "calf." The next two lines in each stanza do rhyme, as for a moment the reader is drawn lovingly into the poet-farmer's special activities. Then the last lines in both verses are the same, a refrain. The repetition is not only a further hypnotic extension of the invitation but also a proposal—as the change from lack of rhyme to rhyme to refrain already suggests—that the several aspects of the poet's world, beautiful in themselves, are absorbed into a general vision of poetry. The details, which are but examples of clarity and love, are essential in any world of poetry. One feels that Frost could continue adding to this litany of beauty and the ways of the creative mind but stops, instead, with the right proportion of incitement to allow the reader to make the transition from his own thoughts into the processes of Frost's imagination and thence into his book.[23]

The seventh eclogue fulfills the same double vision. First it invites the reader, through the eyes and ears of Meliboeus, into Daphnis' spiritual world of poetry, away from the cares of reality. Meliboeus is swept by chance into what at first seems only a particularly utopian landscape but soon becomes the realm of the imagination at work, challenging, crafting, resolving. The reader is asked to watch, for a brief moment, the actual "cleaning" and "fetching" and "licking" of which Frost speaks. We learn, with Meliboeus, not only the "where" but the "how" of pastoral poetry.

[23] With the Frost poem we may compare one of Rilke's earliest lyrics, "Weisst du, ich will mich schleichen" from *Advent* (Frankfurt, 1927). Reprinted through the kind permission of Insel-Verlag.

> Weisst du, ich will mich schleichen
> leise aus lautem Kreis,
> wenn ich erst die bleichen
> Sterne über den Eichen
> blühen weiss.
>
> Wege will ich erkiesen,
> die selten wer betritt
> in blassen Abendwiesen—
> und keinen Traum, als diesen:
> Du gehst mit.

As with the seventh, the introductory verses of the eighth eclogue reveal much about the poem as a whole. In this instance, the prelude consists of three parts: a description of the effect of the songs to be sung, a dedication (probably to Pollio), and a brief sketch of the setting.

The first part, like the opening of *Eclogue* 1, is a cycle of five lines:

> Pastorum Musam Damonis et Alphesiboei,
> immemor herbarum quos est mirata iuvenca
> certantis, quorum stupefactae carmine lynces,
> et mutata suos requierunt flumina cursus,
> Damonis Musam dicemus et Alphesiboei.

The Muse of the shepherds Damon and Alphesiboeus— at whose competition the heifer stood mesmerized, forgetful of the grass, at whose song lynxes were charmed and rivers stood still, their courses changed—let us sing to the Muse of Damon and Alphesiboeus.

The implication is that Damon and Alphesiboeus have the Orphic powers attributed to Silenus and Hesiod in *Eclogue* 6, the ability to move physical nature through the spiritual force of their songs. The examples illustrating this magical effect are apt. So powerful are their songs that they can reverse the innate processes of nature to make the impossible happen. The heifer stands in wonder, forgetful of her pasture; lynxes are mesmerized; streams alter their courses and grow still. Quiet descends on nature as the magic of poetry changes the unchangeable.

Here the verb *miror* means not only "admire" but also "be

enchanted by" sound and spectacle. Virgil uses *miror* in a similar sense to represent the reaction of Mt. Rhodope to the music of Orpheus, which seems second to that of Silenus in the context of *Eclogue* 6 (line 30).[1] But the effects of song are not limited to tame nature. Lynxes, creatures of the wild, are also moved. In fact, *stupefactae* is stronger than *mirata*. Virgil employs the cognate *stupeo* to depict the charm exerted by the voice of Orpheus on the underworld (*Georgic* 4, lines 481-82): "quin ipsae stupuere domus atque intima Leti / Tartara" ("Even the houses themselves and the inmost realms of Death were spellbound"). And Horace combines *stupeo* with *carmen* in his description of Cerberus, entranced by the verses of Sappho and Alcaeus (*Carmina* 2. 13, lines 33-35):[2]

> quid mirum, ubi illis carminibus stupens
> demittit atras belua centiceps
> auris. . . .

What wonder, when the hundred-headed beast, mesmerized by the songs, lowered his dark ears.

As for the verb *requiesco*, its two other appearances in the *Eclogues* suggest an almost magical relaxation from great tension. We have seen its use at 1. 79, in Tityrus' invitation to Meliboeus to rest for a night in the ideal pastoral setting. Here it is aptly conjoined with Meliboeus' uses of *miror*, as if he could be enchanted by seeing the landscape with the clear vision of one who must now give it up! From the seventh eclogue, we remember Daphnis' command to a less troubled Meliboeus (line 10): "et, si quid cessare potes, requiesce sub umbra." He, too, is to be mesmerized out of his regular pur-

---

[1] *Miror* is also used at Horace *Carm.* 2. 13. 30 in the sense of "be mesmerized."

[2] On the meaning of *carmen* see Otto Seel, "Carmen, Eignung und Eigenart des Lateinischen als Dichtersprache," *Gymnasium* 71 (1964): 250-67, esp. 252f. On these lines as a whole see Desport, *L'Incantation Virgilienne*, pp. 17-18.

suits into the realm of poetry. If *requierunt* implies respite from ordinary action or greater trials, *mutata* suggests, in stronger language, the physical effect of song. The verb reappears later in the poem as the lovesick Amaryllis alludes to the force of Circe's incantations over the companions of Ulysses (line 69): "carminibus Circe socios mutavit Ulixi" ("By songs Circe changed the companions of Ulysses").

In sum, these opening lines offer examples of the hypnotic force of song to draw attention to itself and, as a result, to bend the world to its will and compel nature to forget her wonted ways. We are being introduced to bucolic verses specifically concerned with the magic of poetry, where the effects are not simply seen in hyperbolic asides, as in *Eclogue* 6, but are caused by the words themselves. While pondering the Orphic qualities of pastoral song, we will watch poetry at work before our eyes.

Only with lines 6-13 do we have the dedication:

> Tu mihi seu magni superas iam saxa Timavi,
> sive oram Illyrici legis aequoris,—en erit umquam
> ille dies, mihi cum liceat tua dicere facta?
> en erit ut liceat totum mihi ferre per orbem
> sola Sophocleo tua carmina digna coturno?
> a te principium, tibi desinam: accipe iussis
> carmina coepta tuis, atque hanc sine tempora circum
> inter victricis hederam tibi serpere lauros.

Whether you are now passing the rocks of mighty Timavus or skirting the shore of the Illyrian sea, O will that day ever dawn when I myself will be allowed to tell of your deeds? O will it ever be my opportunity to bear through the whole world your songs, which alone are worthy of the buskin of Sophocles? With you is my beginning; for you I will sing my last. Receive the songs begun by your orders, and allow this ivy to creep around your forehead amid the laurels of victory.

No name is mentioned, but Pollio is presumably the dedica-tee.[3] The lines describe the course of his journey home from a campaign against the Parthini to a place where he can receive in person the poet's homage.

The lines are nicely balanced: the two interrogative sen-tences, both beginning with *en erit*, are preceded and followed by a look at Pollio's present situation. The first *en erit* clause, while not a *recusatio*, a refusal to sing of Pollio's exploits in epic form (like the complete denial at the opening of the sixth eclogue), does postpone such an adventure until some vague future moment. This implies the publication of Pollio's *carmina* (probably plays) to a more universal audi-ence than they now possess. But any sense of expansion—in subject, genre, or even acclaim—gives way to the quiet im-plied in the command *accipe*. Pollio's present goal is home and rest after the performance of heroic *facta*. There is to be a rec-onciliation between Pollio's world and the poet's, as the pas-toral ivy and heroic laurel join in Pollio's triumphal wreath. Both these motifs, of return and of binding, will recur throughout the poem.

We come then to the spot in which the poet sketches the place where the two shepherds, Damon and Alphesiboeus, sing (lines 14-16):

> Frigida vix caelo noctis decesserat umbra,
> cum ros in tenera pecori gratissimus herba:
> incumbens tereti Damon sic coepit olivae.

Scarcely had the cool shade of night left the heavens—that time when dew on the tender grass is most appetizing to the flocks—when Damon, leaning on his smooth olive staff, begins thus.

Time and place are of equal importance.[4] The time is dawn, the moment between night and day when the dew makes grass

[3] But see now Peter Levi, "The Dedication to Pollio in Virgil's Eighth Eclogue," *Hermes* 94 (1966): 73-79.

[4] The phraseology deserves comparison with *Ecl.* 7. 45-46.

particularly tasty to the sheep (and poetry especially lovely
to the hearer?). Virgil seems to have been fond of line 15
for he uses it again in the third georgic as part of an idyllic
glimpse of flocks at pasture early on a spring morning
(lines 322-26):

> at vero Zephyris cum laeta vocantibus aestas
> in saltus utrumque gregem atque in pascua mittet,
> Luciferi primo cum sidere frigida rura
> carpamus, dum mane novum, dum gramina canent,
> et ros in tenera pecori gratissimus herba.

But when, at the Zephyrs' call, joyful summer sends
either flock to the glades and meadows, let us hurry to the
cool fields at the first light of Lucifer, when the morning
is young, while the sward is hoary and the dew on the
tender grass is most appetizing to the flock.

And, with masterly ease, Virgil moves from the scene in
which Damon sings to that in which the protagonist of his
song finds himself. I will assume at the start, to save confusion later, that the name of Damon's shepherd is Tityrus. We
are not actually given it until line 55, near the end of
Damon's song. Though no direct attribution is made even
there, the context urges it as a strong possibility.

The setting is the same. The morning star rises, anticipating
a day which is *almum*, which nourishes as dew the grass and
grass the flocks (lines 17-20):

> nascere, praeque diem veniens age, Lucifer, almum
> coniugis indigno Nysae deceptus amore
> dum queror, et divos, quamquam nil testibus illis
> profeci, extrema moriens tamen adloquor hora.

Come, arise, Lucifer, preceding genial day while I make
lament, deceived by the unfaithful love of Nysa, my be-
trothed, and in my final hour before death yet call upon
the gods, though their witness has helped me not at all.

Eclogue 8

One of the lessons the second eclogue teaches is that a shepherd's happiness depends on the way he merges his life with the rural daily round. Anything which tends to destroy this union should be eschewed. Happiness comes from stable love and from the ability of the shepherd to live within the terms the land prescribes. If such a life is not possible, the whole framework collapses. For this reason we become suddenly aware of the great gulf which separates Damon from the hero of his song.

Far from being at one with his world, exactly the opposite is the poor shepherd's plight. His life is the reversal of nature's way. While nature is coming alive (*nascere*), he is dying (*moriens*); while nature is starting afresh in the early hours of the day, Tityrus finds himself already in his last moments (*extrema hora*). The day star cherishes the land while he is ruined by unrequited love. The process of dissolution seems complete. So far is he at odds with nature that death seems his only recourse. The position of the shepherd is clarified by a closer examination of the phrase *indigno deceptus amore*. Virgil describes Gallus in the tenth eclogue as perishing from unworthy love (*indigno amore peribat* in line 10) There the word *indigno* means "unrequited," but here it also suggests "shocking" because unexpected.[5] Nysa has reversed the shepherd's normal existence. Far from being a *coniunx*, she is a force for disruption.

Looking specifically at the words *deceptus amore*, we recall how the possible reader of Virgil's poetry, at line 10 of *Eclogue* 6, could be *captus amore*, charmed by its beauty. But *deceptus* also has a more sinister ring: it can, of course, mean "misled," as the shepherd was cajoled into believing that the false was true. Yet it has overtones of magic, too. We read, for instance, in lines 37-38 of Horace's *Carmina* 2. 13 (also quoted above) how, at the sound of Sappho and Alcaeus singing "quin et Prometheus et Pelopis parens / dulci laborum

---

[5] See Fordyce's commentary on Catullus 101. 6.

decipitur sono" ("even Prometheus and the father of Pelops were beguiled of their trials by the sweet sound"). So beautiful and effective is the magic of their voices that Prometheus and Tantalus are made to forget their sufferings. In the case of *Eclogue* 8, however, the magic has been put to use for evil purposes: our poor shepherd has been led astray by love to the point of turning his life upside-down.[6]

The only way to console himself now is to voice his complaints to the gods, though they have been of no help in the past. The special enigma of this remark will be examined later. The general point is elucidated by the refrain, which now appears for the first of nine times, and by the shepherd's subsequent, more detailed description of his surroundings (lines 21-24):

> incipe Maenalios mecum, mea tibia, versus.
> Maenalus argutumque nemus pinusque loquentis
> semper habet, semper pastorum ille audit amores
> Panaque, qui primus calamos non passus inertis.

> Begin with me, my flute, a song of Maenalus. Mt. Maenalus always has rustling grove and talking pines, and always gives ear to the loves of shepherds and Pan, who was the first not to allow the reeds to remain idle.

The complaining lover complements his setting: he plays a *tibia*. This is the only mention of the *tibia* in the *Eclogues* and has no part in the refrain of Theocritus' first *Idyl*, on which this line is in small part modeled.[7] A *tibia* is not simply synonymous with an ordinary shepherd's reed but is deliberately chosen as the most appropriate instrument to accompany a lament.

Lucretius twice associates the *tibia* with a particular locale, and his line is the same in each case. In the first (*De Rerum*

[6] We may compare the position of Corydon at *Ecl.* 2. 70ff.
[7] See Theocritus *Id.* 1. 64ff. and its variations beginning at 94 and 127. On the *tibia*, see Gow's commentary on *Id.* 20. 29.

Natura 4, line 585), Lucretius is discussing the invention of such creatures as satyrs, nymphs, fauns, and Pan, by the imaginations of those in wild and deserted landscapes who do not want to consider themselves alone, especially without any gods (though in fact, at least to Lucretius, they are). It is in empty spots (*per loca sola*, line 573), midst shadowy mountains (*montis inter opacos*, line 575), in places deserted by the gods (*loca deserta ab divis*), that the countryfolk say one hears strange sounds (lines 584-85):

> chordarumque sonos fieri dulcisque querellas
> tibia quas fundit digitis pulsata canentum.

And the sounds of chords are heard and sweet complaints which the flute pours forth, touched by the fingers of the singers.

Such is the remote region where the *tibia* plays laments which are sweet because associated with love.

Lucretius' second mention of the *tibia* comes in Book 5, line 1385. Speaking of the gradual development of man's knowledge of sound and its reproduction, he first discusses the imitation of birds, then the discovery of hemlock stalks (lines 1384-85):

> inde minutatim dulcis dedicere querellas
> tibia quas fundit digitis pulsata canentum, . . .

Thence little by little they learned the sweet complaints which the flute pours forth, touched by the fingers of the singers.

Again it is lovers' complaints which are sung to the *tibia* in a remote, deserted place. Here its sounds pour forth "avia per nemora ac silvas saltusque reperta / per loca pastorum deserta atque otia dia" ("through pathless groves, woods and glades, through the remote haunts of shepherds and their pleasances under the skies"). In accepting this imaginative world of lonely hills which Lucretius must dismiss, Virgil has adopted not only the use of the *tibia* and the location but also the quasi-elegiac tone of lament for unhappy love. He has, moreover, as if to challenge his predecessor, made the setting specifically in the shadow of the Arcadian Mt. Maenalus, the mountain at which Pan was wont to sing of his *amores*.

In thinking of the setting, we must remember that it is bucolic only in the sense that shepherds come there to sing of unrequited love. Such, in general terms, is the position of Corydon in *Eclogue* 2, *solus*, singing to the mountains and woods. It is also, to anticipate for a moment, even more specifically the landscape in which Virgil places the lovesick Gallus (*Eclogue* 10, lines 13-15):

> illum etiam lauri, etiam flevere myricae,
> pinifer illum etiam sola sub rupe iacentem
> Maenalus, et gelidi fleverunt saxa Lycaei.

Even the laurels, even the tamarisks wept for him, even pine-bearing Maenalus and the crags of chill Lycaeus wept for him as he lay under a lonely rock.

Tityrus finds himself alone, beneath Mt. Maenalus, in a rugged spot far from his wonted paradise, as far from perfection as his love is lacking in idealism. Both Corydon and Gallus, in their laments, conjure up a perfect realm, completed by love's presence. In *Eclogue* 2, Corydon prays that Alexis might consent to inhabit the country with him (*mecum*, line 28) or join him to imitate Pan in the woods (*mecum*, line 31). In 10, Gallus speaks of his love lying with him (*mecum*, line 40) under a supple vine—the ideal location and a very different place from the actual setting in which he finds himself, *sola sub rupe*. He suggests to Lycoris: *hic ipso tecum consumerer aevo* ("here with you I will be eaten away [by love] for my whole life").[8]

---

[8] Ultimately, however, there is a difference between the suicidal cry *vivite silvae* (8. 58) of Damon's protagonist and Gallus' *concedite silvae* (10. 63), the announcement of his re-entrance into reality.

Hence the bitter sadness that Tityrus must address a wood
that is *argutum* and pines which are *loquentis*. In his loneliness, it is inanimate nature that will give slight comfort by
echoing his song.[9] Instead of enjoying responsive love, he has
only the mountain and his *tibia* to keep him company in his
sorrow: *mecum, mea*. But so important is even this small consolation of their presence that, in the last line of his song, prior
to complete withdrawal in suicide, real or imagined, it is these
two words which he omits in a pitiful, final variation of the
refrain.

More directly than in the second eclogue, the landscape
proves that the shepherd's usual way of life has been upset.
The reader is already prepared for his description of the circumstances which brought on this unhappiness (lines 26-30):

> Mopso Nysa datur: quid non speremus amantes?
> iungentur iam grypes equis, aevoque sequenti
> cum canibus timidi venient ad pocula dammae.
> Mopse, novas incide faces: tibi ducitur uxor;
> sparge, marite, nuces; tibi deserit Hesperus Oetam.

Nysa is given to Mopsus. What may we lovers not expect?
Now griffins will be mated with horses, and in the coming
age shy does will come to drink with hounds. Mopsus, cut
new torches. A bride is being brought to you. Scatter the
nuts, bridegroom. For you Hesperus leaves Oeta.

The impossible has happened to Damon's poor shepherd.
Nysa, who had been his, belongs to Mopsus. It is like griffins mating with horses or does coming to drink with hounds.
These two specific *adunata* have a special purpose in this
context. They are examples of the union of things so opposite as to be beyond belief, of the reconciliation of elements

---

[9] This is the particular sadness of the shepherd's *allocutio*—the only
consolation comes from nature, not man. (On the *allocutio*, see commentators on Catullus 38.)

ordinarily at war. *Iungentur* echoes *coniugis* (line 18) and anticipates *coniuncta* (line 32). The real union has been broken and a false one (in his eyes) has taken its place, so false that in the next generation the deer and the dog that pursues it will live in peace. The time will be nature's golden age. The lives of the happy pair, therefore, will progress toward perfection. Tityrus' life tends away from "pastoral" toward death.

Then, as if to parody his situation, he refers to the epithalamium to be sung for Mopsus and his bride, the cutting of the torches, the bridal procession, the throwing of nuts, and the traditional reference to the appearance of Vesper over Oeta.[10] For the latter, commentators note how the chorus of maidens in Catullus' second epithalamium, *carmen* 62, announces (line 7): *nimirum Oetaeos ostendit Noctifer ignes* ("Certainly Noctifer (the Evening star) shows his Oetaean fires"). There is a double irony in the symbolic appearance of Hesperus for Mopsus. In the rural world the rising of the evening star means the cessation of all activity. At the end of the sixth eclogue, Vesper stops the song and forces attention back to the more prosaic tasks a countrydweller faces before nightfall.[11] For our lovesick shepherd, however, the appearance of Hesperus would serve not as a symbolic reminder of commitments but as an emblem of the epithalamium, of the arrival of the star which to all lovers means marriage.

In the phrase *tibi deserit Hesperus Oetam* the first word receives special stress, as in the statement which ends the preceding line (*tibi ducitur uxor*). It is only for Mopsus that Nysa is brought and Hesperus rises. From what our shepherd tells us, he may never have seen its rising at all. His song opens during the nighttime (the night after the wedding?),

[10] See also, e.g., Sappho frag. 104 in Edgar Lobel and D. L. Page, eds., *Poetarum Lesbiorum Fragmenta* (Oxford, 1955); Catullus 64. 329.
[11] *Ecl.* 6. 84, and cf. *Ecl.* 10. 77; *G.* 4. 186, 434.
There is also irony in the use of *desero* at line 30 (one of its two appearances in the *Eclogues*). Hesperus' desertion of Oeta is a different symbol for Mopsus than Nysa's departure from the shepherd.

but with an ironic appeal to the morning star, Lucifer, to appear. Again, reversal is the motif which predominates. It is not his fate to experience the happiness of watching Hesperus on his wedding night. Even worse, though he may yearn for the rising of Lucifer, his prayer is that the coming of day will put an end to his suffering, not offer a renewal of his association with the landscape and the star that brings the happy dew and nourishing day, as we might at first hope or expect.

A possible pattern begins to suggest itself for his song: it is partially an inversion of an epithalamium, in pastoral terms. One shepherd is forced out of his natural role to look at the rising of Lucifer; symbolically, at the same time (the singer uses only the imperative or the present tense in lines 29-30), the bride is led toward the house of Mopsus as, for him at least, Vesper rises over Oeta.

The next stanza elaborates the shepherd's cause for sorrow by describing Nysa's reasoning ironically (lines 32-35):

> o digno coniuncta viro, dum despicis omnis,
> dumque tibi est odio mea fistula, dumque capellae
> hirsutumque supercilium promissaque barba,
> nec curare deum credis mortalia quemquam.

O you are married to a worthy man, while you despise everyone, and while my pipes, while my goats, my shaggy brow and flowing beard are loathed by you. You do not believe that any of the gods cares for mortal affairs.

She might consider herself joined to a deserving husband (*digno coniuncta viro*) if only because the shepherd is so superficially ugly. From Tityrus' shepherd's point of view he has suffered from the unworthy love (*indigno amore*) of someone who had been his *coniunx*. But the final bitterness lies not so much in the fact that she is to be united to someone else but in her reasons for rejecting him.

266

Eclogue 8

In the second eclogue, Corydon attempts to draw Alexis into his life by describing as lovely what might seem repellent to urbane eyes. Damon's shepherd, instead of enticing someone into the shepherds' world, is rejected because of a union in which he has no part. Love has come, but not for him. The qualities with which Corydon tries to seduce Alexis have been reversed and thrown in the face of Damon's shepherd. He neither pipes well nor is he particularly handsome—he is the one expelled.[12]

The orientation is different in the case of Corydon: since his suffering comes from outside, he can always fall back on the countryside and become part of its humble regimen again. For Tityrus the essence of his life—the love and song which is the product of a happy communion of man with man, and man with nature—has been lost. His only recourse is complete withdrawal which, for a shepherd who insists on his integrity, may mean suicide.

His world has been destroyed from within. Things had not always been so (lines 37-41):

> saepibus in nostris parvam te roscida mala
> (dux ego vester eram) vidi cum matre legentem.
> alter ab undecimo tum me iam acceperat annus;
> iam fragilis poteram a terra contingere ramos:
> ut vidi, ut perii, ut me malus abstulit error.

Within our orchard I saw you as a small child picking dewy apples with your mother—I was your guide. I had just then begun the year that follows on eleven. I could now touch the frail branches from the ground. When I saw you, how I died! How wretched a frenzy swept me away!

Suddenly we are back in the center of the ideal and in a time remote from the present. The passage is modeled partially

---

[12] See Otis, *Virgil*, pp. 111-13, for a discussion of the parallels these lines have in Theocritus.

on Polyphemus' description of his first meeting with
Galatea, in the eleventh idyl of Theocritus (lines 25-29):

ἠράσθην μὲν ἔγωγε τεοῦς, κόρα, ἀνίκα πρᾶτον
ἦνθες ἐμᾷ σὺν ματρὶ θέλοισ' ὑακίνθινα φύλλα
ἐξ ὄρεος δρέψασθαι, ἐγὼ δ' ὁδὸν ἀγεμόνευον.
παύσασθαι δ' ἐσιδών τυ καὶ ὕστερον οὐδ' ἔτι πᾳ νῦν
ἐκ τήνω δύναμαι· τὶν δ' οὐ μέλει, οὐ μὰ Δί' οὐδέν.

I fell in love with thee, maiden, when first thou camest
with my mother to gather hyacinth-flowers on the hill, and
I showed the way. And having seen thee, from that day
forth even until now I cannot cease; but naught thou
carest, nay, naught at all.

The setting of the encounter, which Theocritus leaves vaguely
as "on the hill," Virgil specifies as within the shepherd's "en-
closures," *saepibus in nostris*. The phrase is noteworthy first
for the possessive—she was then part of something that belonged to him—and then for the location itself. Virgil's only
other use of the word *saepes* in the *Eclogues* is in *Eclogue* 1,
line 53, where Meliboeus describes the hedge which encloses
the happy Tityrus. Such a place is the sequestered spot in
which Damon's shepherd first saw Nysa, a spot which contrasts with his present position, lonely under Maenalus and contemplating suicide. The contrast is in time-scheme as well
as locale. The shepherd is talking of some distant past, when
both he and she were young and their love new. *Malus error*
is merely a comment on the past from his present vantage. The
whole milieu suggests a happiness now distant.

Into one moment Virgil has concentrated many of the metaphors which are ordinarily associated with young love and
marriage. As the young shepherd watched Nysa picking dewy
apples, his was the joy that the sheep find now in Damon's
world, cropping the tender, dew-covered grass. We may think
of Sappho's charming comparison of a bride to an apple red-

dening on a high branch which the pickers cannot quite reach,
or of many such comparisons in Catullus—of a bride to a sprig
of myrtle which the Hamadryades nourish with dewdrops, to
a hyacinth in the garden of a rich lord, or to a flower, *in saep-
tis hortis* ("in a garden hedged off"), which remains lovely
while still untouched.[13]

Virgil takes these similes and makes them real for an instant in the lives of the young boy and girl. She has reached
an age when she can pick apples and he, too, can touch the
tender branches. But these gestures become, through Virgil's
artistry, both literal and symbolic at the same time. They are
the awakening of love. The suggestiveness inherent in what
for Sappho and Catullus are only comparisons comes alive in
fact as well. The setting is pastoral love.[14]

At the center of his lament, then, the shepherd returns in
space, back to the perfect landscape, and in time, to the first
love of youth, when the bucolic metaphors common to an
epithalamium could be a reality. In spite of the fact that the
translation appears quite direct, there is an overtone in the
Latin *dux ego vester eram* which does not come through in
the Greek ἐγὼ δ' ὁδὸν ἁγεμόνευον. This is partially because
the possessive adjective is prominent here, as in the preceding line. The word *dux* looks ironically back to the phrase
tibi ducitur uxor (line 29). Time was when the shepherd was
the *dux* and was almost in the position of leading the bride
home in marriage. (Again, as in the rest of the description,
the hint is latent in the metaphor, not specific.) We can also
see why Virgil has diverged from his model by making the
mother not the shepherd's, as in Theocritus (line 26), but
Nysa's. The change seems less whimsical when we reflect that
in the preparations for and festivities during a wedding, as
described for example in Catullus' wedding hymns, it is nat-

[13] Catullus 61. 21-25; 61. 87-89; 62. 39ff.
[14] For the expression of lines 37-38 cf. *Ecl.* 2. 51-2. On the apple as
symbol, see Gow's commentary on Theocritus *Id.* 5. 88.

urally always the bride's mother, not the groom's, who is sad because her child is being torn from her.[15]

The idyllic picture does not last long; it is, in fact, destroyed in the making. Line 41 serves as a transition from this internal security of time past to the unhappy present. The word *vidi* recalls the center of the vision at line 38, but is immediately undercut with *perii*, no elegiac lover's idle cry but the harbinger of suicide. The lover has recalled the past only to see again how violent a revolution love caused in his life. The first part of the line is an imitation of two passages in Theocritus: *Idyl* 2, line 82, where Simaetha declares her passion for Delphis ("I saw, and madness seized me") and *Idyl* 3, line 42, where the shepherd sings of Atalanta's love for Hippomenes ("Atalanta saw, and frenzy seized her"). But the second part of the line —*ut me malus abstulit error*—is completely Virgil's own. Its importance rises accordingly. It would be inadequate simply to define *error* as a type of tragic *amor*. Emotional and literal description are one. The landscape again serves as subjective symbol as well as objective reality. The *error* is love, but a type of love which has symbolically torn him away (*abstulit*) from the perfection of youthful dalliance, and literally drawn him out of his usual landscape into the solitude of the mountains.

This tale is but another version of Pasiphaë's lot (*Eclogue* 6), except that in her tragic case there was never any possibility of true love. The poet rather stresses the abnormal madness which leads directly to Pasiphaë's present sorrow—*tu nunc in montibus erras*. Whatever the difference in detail between the two stories, a similarly jarring *nunc* brings Virgil's shepherd back from the brief joys of the past to present horror. Though central to his lament and effective for the contrasts and tensions it poses and elaborates, the episode in the orchard is but an interlude set between moments of despair (lines 43-50):

[15] Catullus 62. 21ff.; 64. 379.

nunc scio, quid sit amor: duris in cotibus illum
aut Tmaros aut Rhodope aut extremi Garamantes
nec generis nostri puerum nec sanguinis edunt.
   incipe Maenalios mecum, mea tibia, versus.
saevus amor docuit natorum sanguine matrem
commaculare manus; crudelis tu quoque, mater:
crudelis mater magis, an puer improbus ille?
improbus ille puer; crudelis tu quoque, mater.

Now I know what love is. On flinty rocks either Tmaros
or Rhodope or the farthest Garamantes bore him, a child
not of our race or blood. Begin with me, my flute, a song
of Maenalus. Harsh love taught a mother to stain her
hands with the blood of her children. You were cruel too,
o mother. Was the mother more cruel or the boy more
wicked? That boy was wicked. You were cruel, too, o
mother.

We have been shown a picture of *dignus amor*, such as
Nysa and Mopsus will have in their union. The shepherd now
turns to *indignus amor* and personifies him as one who might
have been born on the slopes of Tmaros or Rhodope. A shepherd would not have chosen these mountains for their hyperbolic remoteness—after all we find Orpheus singing to
Rhodope and Ismarus in *Eclogue* 6, line 30, as if they regularly listened to his song. Rather the references serve to unite
Tityrus' present location, singing to Mt. Maenalus, with such
a spot as could give birth to bitter love. If the phrase *duris in
cotibus* is antithetical to *saepibus in nostris*, it is because the
change of time and place serves to underline the difference between love once requited and present trials beneath the rocks
of Maenalus. The reference to the *extremi Garamantes* also
serves a specific purpose: it alludes, in geographical terms, to
the extremes to which despair can drive a man. Whether we
think back to the shepherd's statement that this is his *extrema hora* (line 20) or anticipate his announcement that

the poem is his *extremum munus* (line 60) as he prepares to leap into the sea, the hint is the same.

Virgil uses the expression *duris cotibus* in a later context which sheds some light on these lines. At *Aeneid* 4, line 365, Dido rebukes Aeneas:

> "nec tibi diva parens, generis nec Dardanus auctor,
> perfide, sed duris genuit te cotibus horrens
> Caucasus, Hyrcanaeque admorunt ubera tigres."

"Faithless one, no goddess was your mother, nor was Dardanus begetter of your race, but rugged Caucasus bore you on his flinty rocks, and Hyrcanian tigers suckled you."

She has called him *crudelis* before (line 311) and will again (line 661). As the speech quoted comes to a climax she prophesies her imminent suicide and then cries for revenge: *dabis, improbe, poenas* ("Shameless one, you will pay the penalty"). (The poet himself had already addressed an aside to *improbe Amor*, line 412.) [16] In turning to the hated figure of her deserting lover, Dido thus combines characteristics which Virgil, in *Eclogue* 8, has his lovelorn shepherd divide between Amor and his minion, Medea. One of these is *improbus* because he provides the occasion and the means, the other *crudelis* because she actually carries out the deed. In the context of *Eclogue* 8 Medea becomes simply an emblem for Nysa, Amor's slave, who would go beyond the use of magic to murder even her children. The "murder" here is the shepherd's suicide. He is the innocent and helpless victim of forces which neither know nor care for what is honest in human emotions, which might think it natural for Medea to steep her hands in the blood of her offspring.

Virgil seems to have in mind another passage from one of the epithalamia of Catullus (*Carmen* 62, lines 20-23):

[16] On *improbus*, see R. G. Austin's commentary on *Aen.* 4. 386 in *Aeneid: Book 4* (Oxford, 1955).

Eclogue 8

Hespere, quis caelo fertur crudelior ignis?
qui natam possis complexu avellere matris,
complexu matris retinentem avellere natam,
et iuveni ardenti castam donare puellam.

Hesperus, what crueler fire courses through the heavens?
You who can tear a daughter from the embrace of her
mother, from her mother's embrace tear the clinging
daughter, and give the chaste maid to a burning youth.

The parallels are too numerous to be fortuitous. There is the
same stress on the word *crudelis*, the same mother-daughter
situation, the same use of chiastic order strengthened by direct
verbal repetition. But the results in each case are different.
In the one, at the rising of Hesperus, the child is torn from
her mother (*virgines* are speaking!) to become a bride. For
Virgil's unhappy shepherd, the mother has now become the
murderer of her children, urged on by *saevus Amor*. As in
the case of the earlier symbolic tension between Lucifer and
Hesperus, the tone of an epithalamium has been recreated
only to be reversed. Such reversal is the keynote of the remainder of the shepherd's song (lines 52-61):

nunc et ovis ultro fugiat lupus, aurea durae
mala ferant quercus, narcisso floreat alnus,
pinguia corticibus sudent electra myricae,
certent et cycnis ululae, sit Tityrus Orpheus,
Orpheus in silvis, inter delphinas Arion—
incipe Maenalios mecum, mea tibia, versus—
omnia vel medium fiat mare. vivite silvae:
praeceps aerii specula de montis in undas
deferar; extremum hoc munus morientis habeto.
desine Maenalios, iam desine, tibia, versus.

Now let the wolf of his own accord flee even sheep, let
hard oak bear golden apples, the alder bloom with narcissus, let tamarisks drip rich amber from their bark, let

owls vie even with swans, let Tityrus be Orpheus, Orpheus in the woods, Arion among the dolphins—begin with me, my flute, a song of Maenalus—nay, let all become the ocean's midst. Farewell, woods. Headlong I shall be borne from the peak of the lofty mountain into the waves. Receive this as the last gift of the dying. Cease, my flute, cease now verses of Maenalus.

If the set of *adunata* in lines 27-28 was devoted to the union of opposites, this group, longer and climactic, centers on reversal of the usual order in life. The first five examples are all drawn from nature. The ordinarily frightening wolf is to flee before the sheep, hard oaks will bear golden apples, and so on. The fifth instance, "let owls vie with swans," gives the reader pause. Though it, too, is taken from the natural world and borrowed partially from Theocritus,[17] it has metaphorical associations with poetry and poets other than Theocritus. For example, in the ninth eclogue[18] the modest Lycidas claims that for him to challenge either Varius or Cinna would be like a goose contesting the beauty of a swan's song.

The hint in the example of the swan and the owl is applied to men in the next line. Let Tityrus (the probable name of this unfortunate soul who is obviously not an ordinary shepherd) sing like Orpheus. Let Tityrus, whose *fistula* has been despised by his girl, suddenly move nature with his song or soothe the powers of darkness. Better still, as he prepares to plunge from his bucolic world into the destructive ocean, let him become an Arion, able to charm the creatures of the sea and maybe save his life.

Up until the last item, the list seems an anticipation of the golden age which the shepherd is losing and which he assumes, with some irony, will come about through the marriage of Mopsus and Nysa. His words are a valedictory to perfection. Yet there is the lingering hope that, even in the act

[17] Theocritus *Id.* 1. 136.   [18] *Ecl.* 9. 35-36.

of suicide, the impossible magic of the new era—or his song—will reach him and effect a transformation from lamenting shepherd to triumphant Arion.

The end comes swiftly as the implications of the change in milieu from Orpheus to Arion are realized. The sea begins to triumph over sylvan pastoral. With *deferar,* the shepherd announces that the withdrawal begun at line 41 (*abstulit*) is about to be completed. And line 60, in which the poet-shepherd offers his song as a last *munus* to his woods, finishes the cycle (*extrema moriens hora* leads directly to *extremum munus morientis*) and line 61 apparently ends life and song at once.[19]

Taken as a whole, Tityrus' song is, both temporally and spatially, a movement out of the center of the idyllic landscape toward death. The change from happy to unhappy love causes a complete alteration in the shepherd's spiritual state which drives him, literally, first to the lonely mountain, to sing of his despair, and then into the sea. His words stress the idea of union, necessary in the bucolic life, and illustrate how disharmony cannot be reconciled with the ideal but forces departure from it—and death—on the shepherd. In terms of structure, the poem is a wedding hymn gone awry; it leads not toward marriage and happy love but away from it, not toward deeper satisfaction within the pastoral framework but toward a shattering of the myth.

It must be remembered that this song is not only a lament but also a direct appeal to the gods: *quamquam nil testibus illis / profeci,* the shepherd cries sorrowfully. Though he has previously called them to witness something to no avail, he nevertheless makes one last appeal. But witness what? For what purpose does he want their assistance? His remark is

---

[19] On the power of such a prophetic curse as *munus habeto,* see A. S. Pease (ed.) on Cicero *De Divinatione* (Urbana, Illinois, 1920), 1. 63, and on Virgil *Publi Vergili Maronis Aeneidos Liber Quartus* (Cambridge, Mass., 1935), line 612.

clarified somewhat by one of the accusations he hurls at Nysa (line 36): *nec curare deum credis mortalia quemquam*. The gods had been called upon to testify to some transaction between Tityrus and Nysa (he does, after all, designate her his *coniunx* at line 18). Though she apparently scorns such witness, he would hope through his appeal to prove her wrong. We are again reminded of Dido (*Aeneid* 4, lines 519-21):

> testatur moritura deos et conscia fati
> sidera; tum, si quod non aequo foedere amantis
> curae numen habet iustumque memorque, precatur.

About to die, she calls on the gods and the stars who perceive her fate. Then she prays to whatever just and mindful divinity cares for lovers inequitably united.

Dido implements her prayer with the use of magic and with a prediction of Aeneas' future which, as her madness increases and she nears death, grows to the fullness of a curse. We might expect Tityrus to curse Nysa and pray that her good fortune now be reversed, but he does not. Nor is there any direct use of magic, unless we consider the whole song as a type of unbinding magic which releases the victim from the clutches of a passion which has been too strong or, in his case, from the deceitful charms of Nysa.[20]

There is a prayer, however. We have treated the sets of *adunata* in the poem as deliberate impossibilities, uttered by the shepherd to complement his upset existence. One group (lines 26-27) is put in the future, as if these things might actually occur because Nysa and Mopsus have come together. But the other set is presented in the subjunctive: now that he knows what his love really is, let the wolf flee the sheep, and so on. The prayer also involves the shepherd: line 55 asks that Tityrus become like Orpheus in the woods, possessing

[20] Both alternatives are operative in the case of Dido. But her prayers for release from love end only in Iris' "unbinding" of her imprisoned limbs. See below pp. 283-84 and n. 25.

the power to move the physical world of nature with his song. Line 56 requests that if he must leave the pastoral life for the foreign and destructive, let him become, like Arion, capable of salvation by the charm his song exerts over the dolphins. In other words, Tityrus prays not negatively against Nysa (as Dido curses Aeneas) but positively for himself—for the power to have *adunata* become real through the quasi-magical force of his song.

If we believe in the power of poetry to move the unmovable, then we cannot help but think that in the end song may triumph over suicide and poetry restore the happiness which now seems irretrievably lost. We are thus back in the atmosphere of the poem's opening lines as the processes of nature are halted or reversed because of the captivating fascination exerted by the verses of Damon and Alphesiboeus. Damon relates Tityrus' final prayer to be gifted with such charm, although we never learn whether the prayer succeeds.

JUST TWO LINES intervene before Alphesiboeus begins (lines 62-63):

> Haec Damon: vos, quae responderit Alphesiboeus,
> dicite, Pierides; non omnia possumus omnes.

Thus Damon. Do you, maids of Pieria, sing what Alphesiboeus answered. We are not all capable of all things.

The poet for a moment speaks in his own *persona*. He had sung the words put into Damon's mouth, but to sing the song of Alphesiboeus he is unable. The Muses themselves must do this: *dicite, Pierides*. Line 63 has a proverbial ring (similar phrases are used in *Eclogue* 6 at line 13, and 7, at line 23) and could well be left simply as an acknowledgment that the poet has not memorized more than one song. But *possumus* is a strong word which reminds us that this poem is in part about the power of song. A similar force is given to the verb *possum* in *Eclogue* 3, lines 28-29, as the two contestants prepare to begin: "vis ergo inter nos quid possit uterque vicissim / experiamur?" The Muses themselves are needed to sing the verses of Alphesiboeus, without even the poet as intermediary. Perhaps the poet's magic was not strong enough to save Tityrus after all.

He, or better they, begin forthwith (lines 64-68):

Effer aquam, et molli cinge haec altaria vitta,
verbenasque adole pinguis et mascula tura,
coniugis ut magicis sanos avertere sacris
experiar sensus; nihil hic nisi carmina desunt:
ducite ab urbe domum, mea carmina, ducite Daphnim.

Bring forth water, and gird these altars with a soft fillet, and burn rich verbena and strong frankincense, that I may attempt with magic rites to reverse my lover's chill response. Here nothing is lacking save songs. Lead home from the city, my songs, lead home Daphnis.

The setting is unlike that of the preceding song. Instead of the expansive scope of Tityrus' purview, we find ourselves within a house, spectators at a ritual so personal and private, so careful in its most minute detail, that the listener (or reader) who views the scene seems almost an intruder. This time the protagonist is a woman: lines 101 and 106 (where the witch claims to have been dilatory in carrying out the command of 101) suggest that she is called Amaryllis.[21] She is alone, perhaps, as is the lovelorn shepherd of the first part. But we need only compare the two opening lines of each song—

[21] That the name belongs to her maid is also arguable (but Medea— e.g., in Ovid *Met.* 7. 185—performs magic alone). The indoor setting is proven from *fer foras* (101) and from the barking of the dog *in limine* (107) which makes no sense if the witch is outdoors. The *altaria* (64, 74, 105) were probably in the house's *atrium* and the initial command *effer aquam* probably refers to the bringing of lustral water from a side chamber to the *impluvium*, not outdoors (as, e.g., Plautus *Mil.* 1332).

Eclogue 8

Tityrus' addressed to the morning star, commanding it to rise, hers centered upon herself and concerned with two tiny details of her magic rite—to realize the distinction between them.

The first parallel only enlarges the difference: this, too, is a song about a *coniunx*, presumably unfaithful. The protagonist in each case has been left forlorn, but there the resemblance stops. Tityrus is fleeing his ordinary life and ready to commit suicide, while his love remains happy with someone else. In the case of Alphesiboeus' heroine, it is her lover who has left the country for the city. The city and the sea are equally antipastoral and extreme, the latter implying destruction by nature, the former menace of a sociological character. It is the orientation which is dissimilar. Though our new "singer" remains unhappy, nevertheless she lives in her own private, magic, rustic retreat. All she needs is the return of her *coniunx*. For this she resorts to magic and, in particular, to the use of *carmina*.

We may visualize something of this changed perspective more clearly by turning for a moment to the second idyl of Theocritus, the plot of which is concerned with Simaetha, a deserted woman who has recourse to magic to bring back her lover. That Virgil knew the poem well goes without saying. It is the changes he makes which, as usual, help reveal his poetic purpose. We may start with a comparison of the intercalary refrains which the two poets put into the mouths of their characters. The words Alphesiboeus has his heroine sing have been quoted above. Here is Simaetha's cry: Ἶυγξ, ἕλκε τὺ τῆνον ἐμὸν ποτὶ δῶμα τὸν ἄνδρα ("My magic wheel, draw to my house the man I love").

Though in each refrain the protagonist wants to bring her lover home, Virgil's *ab urbe* is unique. His is a pastoral poem in a way Theocritus' is not: the second idyl is set in the city. Simaetha speaks of dogs howling in the town, of the neighbors next door, of the *palaestra* and *gymnasium* where her lover goes. The plot takes place amid the coming and going, gossiping, and *symposia* of an urban existence. In Virgil, on the contrary, unhappy love is complemented by its background of conflict between city and country, and motion between the two. Whereas Tityrus was drawn out of the country, Alphesiboeus' heroine remains alone in the country and must bring her lover back from the hostile city. We may note, too, that, wherever Simaetha sings, the *mise en scène* is the open air. She calls on the moon not only during each repetition of her second refrain but at the beginning and end of her song as well. In *Eclogue* 8 there is little suggested save the inner darkness of a house, a confined and private world within a rural setting.

There are other differences between the two refrains. Simaetha mentions the name of Delphis with due frequency in her verses, but Virgil's heroine draws attention to the fact that her lover is none other than Daphnis by putting his name in the refrain and thus making it a necessary part of the incantation. Daphnis, unlike Delphis, is the chief pastoral hero whose presence is as necessary for the bucolic world in general as it is for his girl in particular. The refrain reinforces this need.

Finally there is the difference between Simaetha's use of the *iynx* wheel as her primary magical instrument and the *carmina* in the refrain of *Eclogue* 8. Both form explicit parts of the ritual, but *carmina* have a special role (lines 69-71) :

> carmina vel caelo possunt deducere lunam,
> carminibus Circe socios mutavit Ulixi,
> frigidus in pratis cantando rumpitur anguis.

Songs are even able to draw down the moon from heaven. By songs Circe changed the companions of Ulysses. The chill snake in the meadows is burst by singing.

These uses of magical incantations are proverbial.[22] But our rural witch has a purpose in the analogies. The bringing of the moon down from the heavens (*deducere*) parallels her command to the songs to charm Daphnis back from the city (*ducite ab urbe*). Charms can make physical changes too (*mutavit*), when put into the hands of a Circe. The verb is chosen to refer the reader back to line 4, where the final effect of Damon and Alphesiboeus' songs on the world of nature is described: *et mutata suos requierunt flumina cursus.*

The private context of our rustic Circe's songs is expanded for a moment to remind us again that, whatever the personal goals of her incantations, the whole poem—both its constituent parts—is a hymn to that power in song capable of molding nature, animate and inanimate, to its will. The two songs are individual variations on this theme. Tityrus prays to become Orpheus to perform the impossible. Alphesiboeus' sorceress boldly states what song can do. (*Possunt* is a strong word, recalling *possumus*, line 63.) The correct charms are all she is missing. As we listen to her begin and sense her assurance, we scarcely need the further association with the opening lines to know that she will be successful where Tityrus may well have failed.[23] The outcome of the incantation rests not only on its potent details but on her determined realization of the power of poetry to inspire and charm.

We need not look at all the parts—it is, after all, the litany itself which matters most—but some are salient. Her first gestures, for instance, are as follows (lines 73-78):

> terna tibi haec primum triplici diversa colore
> licia circumdo, terque haec altaria circum
> effigiem duco; numero deus impare gaudet.

[22] On the bursting of the snake see Friedrich Marx on Lucilius frag. 575.
[23] Cf. line 75 with lines 19-20, and 35.

ducite ab urbe domum, mea carmina, ducite Daphnim.
necte tribus nodis ternos, Amarylli, colores;
necte, Amarylli, modo et 'Veneris' dic 'vincula necto.'

First I surround you with these three strings of threefold
hue. Three times I draw the image around these shrines.
The god rejoices in uneven numbers. Lead home from the
city, my songs, lead home Daphnis. Weave three colors,
Amaryllis, in three knots. Hurry and weave them,
Amaryllis, and say "I weave the bonds of Venus."

Theocritus has Simaetha use the number three and "binding"
is important in her ritual,[24] but neither motif, especially the
latter, has the prominence given them in *Eclogue* 8. Beginning
with *cinge* in line 64, we pass to *circumdo* and *circumduco*,
and then to the threefold use of *necto* in lines 77-78. Virgil
gives particular emphasis to this last line by making it completely different from its Theocritean counterpart (*Idyl* 2, line
21). Simaetha commands her maid to strew barley grains on
the fire: πάσσ' ἅμα καὶ λέγε ταῦτα· 'τὰ Δέλφιδος ὀστία
πάσσω' ("Strew them on, and say the while, 'I strew the
bones of Delphis'"). In *Eclogue* 8, scattering is turned to its
opposite, binding, and the bones of Delphis are metamor-
phosized into the chains of Venus with which the sorceress
hopes to enthrall her absent lover. These are not idle alterations
but important segments of a ritual of forced return which
begins with the notion of "leading," "surrounding," and then
"binding." The charms, which are both literal and figurative,
are expected to have both a physical and a mental effect.
Though the chains are only of love, they will, she prays, first
tie her lover up, then bring him home. The ultimate result is

[24] On the number three, see *Id.* 2. 43; on "binding," *Id.* 2. 3, 10 and
159. For discussions of three in magic, see Hermann Usener, "Drei-
heit," *RhM* 58 (1903): 1-47, 161-208, 321-62; Eugene Tavenner, "Three
as a magic number in Latin Literature," *TAPA* 47 (1916): 117-43.

a restriction of his world of escape in the city to the narrow
confines of the country and her house and love.

Virgil is fond of the idea of "binding" as an attribute of
power and sometimes magic.[25] The clearest example in the
Eclogues is the manner in which Chromis and Mnasyllus surprise Silenus in *Eclogue* 6. First they approach him (*adgressi,*
line 18, a verb our witch uses at line 103); then they put him
into bonds (*iniciunt ipsis ex vincula sertis*). His response, we
recall, is an amused fulfillment of their wishes (lines 23-24):
"ille dolum ridens 'quo vincula nectitis?' inquit. / 'solvite
me, pueri; satis est potuisse videri. . . .' " In magic, the appearance of power is paramount and is often equivalent to the
power itself. In the case of Silenus, the literal binding would
seem imperative before he could, or at least would, reveal the
magic of his songs.

Another result of magic, this time purely spiritual, can be
seen in the case of Dido. So much has she been enchanted
by the force of her passion for Aeneas that only at the moment of her death does Virgil show Iris releasing her bound
limbs: *luctantem animam nexosque resolveret artus* (*Aeneid*
4, line 695). We are prepared for the expression by Dido's
announcement to her sister, in line 479, that she has found
a way *quae mihi reddat eum vel eo me solvat amantem*
(". . . which might return him to me or release me from my
love for him"). Her statement, pretense or not, does not take
account of the more tragic alternative which ultimately is
forced on her: to lose her lover and yet remain so bound by
the charm of her love for him that suicide is the only outcome.
Death, not unbinding magic, is her release. The Massylian
priestess will give her potent charms (lines 487-89):

> haec se carminibus promittit solvere mentes
> quas velit, ast aliis duras immittere curas,
> sistere aquam fluviis et vertere sidera retro, . . .

[25] See above n. 20 and Pease's commentary on *Aen.* 4. 487.

Eclogue 8

With her incantations she promises to release the minds of those she wishes, or to send harsh love-pangs to others, to halt the flow of streams and turn the course of stars backward.

But she is the bound, not the binder, and cannot even relax in sleep (lines 529-30): "at non infelix animi Phoenissa neque umquam / solvitur in somnos" ("But the mind of the Phoenician queen is never released into slumber"). Her final cry begins (lines 651-52): "'dulces exuviae, dum fata deusque sinebat, / accipite hanc animam meque his exsolvite curis'" ("'Sweet relics, while the fates and god allowed, receive my life and release me from these pangs'"). Yet so enchained is she that not even suicide fully releases her limbs. It remains for Iris to do that. *'Te isto corpore solvo'* ("I release you from this body") she can announce at last (line 703), granting Dido freedom from life and love.

Servius is correct when he notes that the etymological connection between the name Daphnis and *laurus* gives a special symbolic effect to burning the laurel in hopes of charming Daphnis. At line 85, however, the poet adds a simile particularly effective and wholly of his inspiration (lines 85-89):

> talis amor Daphnim qualis cum fessa iuvencum
> per nemora atque altos quaerendo bucula lucos
> propter aquae rivum viridi procumbit in ulva
> perdita, nec serae meminit decedere nocti,
> talis amor teneat, nec sit mihi cura mederi.

May such love seize Daphnis as when a heifer, tired from searching for her mate through woods and deep groves, collapses in despair in the green sedge by a stream of water, and does not remember to withdraw until late in the night—may such love seize him, and may I not give a thought to its cure.

284

These lines balance 37-41, in their structural placement within the song and in their artistic change of mood. Tityrus' words look at a past which contrasts with present suffering —the essence of happiness which can never be re-established. This analogy, the stronger for being from animal rather than human life, effects an equivalent change in its context. Alphesiboeus' sorceress couches her wish in a form that might seem an "impossibility" now but one that is partly realized by the end of the poem. She prays that Daphnis' love for her may become like that of a *bucula* for her *iuvencus*, a young cow for her bullock. In other words, she wishes that her present mental condition would become his, that he would be seized by the yearning which now possesses her (there is no implication yet of change on her part) and take the role of the heifer, tired out from her wandering search. If Daphnis falls into the clutches of love even to a small degree, it will show that the magic is working. Were his desire to become as strong as hers and as hard to bear, the present situation would be completely reversed.

This reversal can be visualized from another point of view. The sorceress wishes Daphnis will become the *bucula* who places the center of her existence in the quiet of home. Her role of sorrowful searcher among woods and steep groves is strange to her because, like Pasiphaë, her wandering quest takes her away from home into the mountains. On the other hand, Virgil's witch imagines herself, if only for the supposed anguish it might cause for Daphnis, in the place of the *iuvencus*, careless of hearth and love. She is to become, for an imagined moment, like Pasiphaë's *iuvencus*, wandering away in search of other *amours* and feeding places. In short, the orientation has been reversed from what it should be. If we take the analogy of pastoral landscape (representing Alphesiboeus' sorceress, home, and fidelity) versus city (symbolizing Daphnis and infidelity) and apply it to the lives of this *bucula* and *iuvencus*, the heifer is in the unpastoral setting, in the woods of wandering and unhappiness instead of the static quiet of home and love.

The setting of the heifer's final collapse could be rather pleasant.[26] *Ulva* was much used in antiquity as fodder for sheep and cattle, and the water of the river and the green sedge should offer an appetizing spectacle. It is, however, an easy step for the poet to slip from mere analogy into a symbolic equation of animal and man, and this heifer is moved by an emotion which takes her beyond the ordinary concerns and instincts of an animal. She is *perdita*, mesmerized and destroyed by love. She remembers nothing, not even to return home in the evening, the strongest of habits for cattle.[27] Like the heifer at the beginning of the poem, she is *immemor herbarum*, so beguiled by song as to forget to browse. And like Corydon in the second eclogue (he is also *perditus*), the *bucula* is enchanted by unhappy love out of the regular pattern of pastoral life (which in both instances is also a metaphor for emotional stability). So is Daphnis, sylvan hero lost in the city, to be charmed by her incantations (which are, in turn, part of the magic which the Muses inspire Alphesiboeus to sing).

The distinction between the songs of Damon and Alphesiboeus is outlined more clearly by a comparison of these two focal episodes: the orchard scene and the *bucula* simile. The one suggests present dissolution of a former ideal, an abstraction which can lead only to suicide. The simile, on the contrary, reverses nature. He who had been unfaithful before will find himself gripped by a passion so strong that he will become the one who searches. The love which drew him away

[26] We may compare *Ecl.* 7. 11-12 and, out of many other instances, Lucretius *De Re. Nat.* 2. 29 and 5. 1392; *G.* 3. 464ff. On the specific meanings of *ulva*, see Eugène de Saint-Denis, "Des vocabulaires techniques en Latin," *Festschrift* Marouzeau (Paris, 1943): 59. On *harundo* as fodder, see also *Aen.* 10. 709f.

[27] Not to speak of late at night!

will now ensure his return to her. The ominous city will not prove so destructive as the sea. Unhappy love creates two different results. Tityrus is forced from the land because the only love that could make him happy has gone elsewhere (within pastoral). Amaryllis, though alone in the country, is ready through her charms to bring back into the landscape the one who belongs to her (and it).

Hence, as she reverts to her *carmina*, the general notion of return is put in a specifically bucolic manner. For example, we may note lines 91-93:

> has olim exuvias mihi perfidus ille reliquit,
> pignora cara sui: quae nunc ego limine in ipso,
> terra, tibi mando; debent haec pignora Daphnim.

These relics that treacherous one left me, his dear pledges. These now, on the very threshold, I entrust to you, o earth. These pledges owe Daphnis.

At one point in her ritual, Theocritus' Simaetha burns a fringe of the cloak of Delphis as an emblem of himself. The parallel ends with the keepsakes. What Amaryllis does with the *exuviae* of Daphnis is quite another thing. She buries them in the earth, at the threshold of her house (*limine in ipso*) with a prayer to *terra*. There is some intrinsic force in nature itself which is of special value in bringing Daphnis back. The threshold is important, too. It is not long hereafter that Hylax, barking *in limine* (line 107), will give notice that her lover has actually returned.

Even less Theocritean is the next set of ingredients (lines 95-99):

> has herbas atque haec Ponto mihi lecta venena
> ipse dedit Moeris (nascuntur plurima Ponto);
> his ego saepe lupum fieri et se condere silvis
> Moerim, saepe animas imis excire sepulcris,
> atque satas alio vidi traducere messis.

These herbs and these poisons, picked in Pontus, Moeris himself gave to me (they grow abundantly in Pontus). With these I have often seen Moeris become a wolf and hide in the forests, often conjure spirits from the depths of tombs and lead sown crops from one field to another.

In *Idyl* 2, line 161, Simaetha speaks of the evil drugs she keeps in a box at her disposal, lest the present rites prove unsuccessful, but there any resemblance ends. Virgil dwells at length on tangible charms for a reason quite different from that of Theocritus. The *adunata* are coming closer and closer to the possible. Amaryllis is making use of *herbae* and *venena* with which she herself has seen Moeris effect the unbelievable.

In a sense these lines balance the two sets of *adunata* in Tityrus' song, but there is a growing distinction. In his song the gulf between fact and fiction expands to the point where prayer alone can achieve Tityrus' wish. In the witch's case, the gap is gradually narrowing. Earlier she was confident that incantations could move the physical. Here she shows still more assurance. She has seen what Moeris could do with the objects he has given her. By using poisons culled from Pontus, even though they are second-hand, she becomes the counterpart of Medea—not the child-murderer, whose victim Tityrus remains, but another Circe, personification of the magician, trying to use her arts positively for recovery rather than for destruction. The powers which she has seen Moeris possess, to change himself into something else and to summon objects from one sphere into another, are important to her. The first makes him a pastoral Circe and gives her visible evidence that such mutations are within her grasp. Though these *carmina* are physical, her desire is only a spiritual one, as she states it in lines 66-67. She merely wants *coniugis sanos avertere/sensus*, to reverse her lover's chill response. She states negatively the positive results she wishes for her magic. She wants *avertere* to become *advertere*, and he who is now *sanus* toward her to become *insanus* so that he will return to her. *Excire* and above all *traducere* (which has the same verbal relationship to *ducite* in the refrain as does *deducere* of line 69) are important as examples of magic, growing more and more literal and positive.

Though the poem is drawing to a climax, Amaryllis' next piece of magic ends with a cry of near despair (line 103): "nihil ille deos, nil carmina curat" ("He cares nothing for the gods, nothing for songs"). This resembles Tityrus' accusation against Nysa: "nec curare deum credis mortalia quemquam." It is, however, still closer to the opening of Corydon's lament for Alexis (*Eclogue* 2, lines 6-7): "o crudelis Alexi, nihil mea carmina curas? / nil nostri miserere? mori me denique cogis?" Is death a necessity for the sorceress as it is for Tityrus and appears at first to be for Corydon? Though we are left in doubt for a moment, the tenor of her song has led us to believe otherwise and the ending is not disappointing (lines 105-109):

> aspice: corripuit tremulis altaria flammis
> sponte sua, dum ferre moror, cinis ipse. bonum sit!
> nescio quid certe est, et Hylax in limine latrat.
> credimus? an, qui amant, ipsi sibi somnia fingunt?
> parcite, ab urbe venit, iam parcite, carmina, Daphnis.

Look, the ash itself, while I delay bringing it out, has of its own accord caught the altars with trembling flame. May it be a propitious omen! Something it is, for certain, and Hylax is barking on the threshold. Are we to believe it? Or do lovers fashion their own dreams? Leave off, leave off now, my songs. Daphnis comes from the city.

The ending takes nothing essential from Theocritus. *Aspice,* as usual, introduces an omen; here its use is particularly impressive because we expect some magical sign that the ritual has worked or failed. The spontaneity of the reaction suggests a positive outcome.²⁸ But it is the way the omen makes its appearance that is of symbolic importance. Amaryllis has mentioned the altar twice before, at lines 64 and 74. It is the center of her home, the place where her rites take place. This she "surrounds," almost as if it were Daphnis himself, first girding it with a fillet and then leading the image of Daphnis around it three times. To have this seized by flames which she has already equated with her love, in line 81, can only be an omen for the good. Even after the reassurance of Hylax' barking she still has doubts. Is the spontaneity of the omen (*ipse*) only a figment of a lover's imagination (*ipsi*)? For the first time she does what no good witch should do: she debates the efficacy of her magic and casts doubts on the whole procedure. Yet, in spite of her misgivings, the *carmina* do work. Indifference gives place to love as the power of song succeeds in drawing Daphnis back home from the city. Like the Amaryllis of the first eclogue, she has regained her lover and pastoral can be whole again.

It is only by thinking of the two songs together that we can analyze something of the poet's success in the eighth eclogue. Like *Eclogues* 6 and 7 it is a poem about the possibilities of bucolic verse, as form and as idea. Each of the tales the shepherds sing is a tiny drama wherein the emotion of a "ritual" presentation seems at odds with the static assumptions of a rustic setting. The intercalary lines in each serve both to break the onward push of the plot toward its predictable conclusion and to heighten the tension through insistent litany. Though both tales are concerned with *amor*, one is a tragedy while the other builds toward a happy ending.

For the first shepherd, the journey out of pastoral toward the mountains of loneliness and the sea of death is the reversal

²⁸ One need only refer to *Ecl.* 4. 43-45 for similar uses of *ipse* and *sponte sua* applied to the variegated sheep who serve as omens of the new age. There is also the double use of *aspice* at 4. 50 and 52.

of an epithalamium which has been sung for someone else. He sings to the music of his *tibia* in the shadow of Maenalus an ironic parody of the song that will be sung to Hymen at the wedding of Mopsus and Nysa. This is also an internal journey of self-realization, a journey out of a happy landscape to a bleak terrain which complements the shepherd's spiritual suffering. The ending of Damon's song suggests that the ordinary poet-shepherd could, given extraordinary circumstances, be gifted with the powers of Orpheus to alter mortal things with his purely spiritual powers. But this is only a hint, for the burden of the piece lies in the emotions which one man's tragic insight into the realities of his life can arouse in the reader.

The balancing song is, by comparison, in every sense positive. Rather than the dissolution of one individual being, we are presented with a union of two people which represents the reconciliation, not the shattering, of worlds. We may think of the contrast, first, quite literally, in terms of action. Though Tityrus is singing in one spot, the reader thinks of his song, broadcast to the heavens, as a studied movement away from pastoral toward a climax defined totally in terms of motion. The song must cease only because the singer is about to leap from the mountain into the sea. In the second song, chanted within the witch's house, even the pastoral figure remains static, as it should, while a sense of action is forced on the figure outside. The climax, which now betokens life instead of death, is also static, rather than emotive. Alphesiboeus' witch can order her magic to stop because Daphnis has returned.

To summarize the difference briefly: The first song is essentially a tragic vision, looking to the end of the pastoral dream. The second offers a renewal of happiness after a time of uncertainty and trial. The one is concerned with one man's inner crisis over unhappy love and the resolution to die. The other depends for effect on external power but is of no less spiritual importance: song re-creates pastoral bliss.

Eclogue 8

Nevertheless, dramatic as the individual songs are, the whole is set in such a way as to offer a contrast between the stability of the frame—Damon and Alphesiboeus singing at dawn to their flocks—and the constant movement in what they sing. The totality is once more a meditation on bucolic poetry, this time specifically concerned with how love can either destroy or re-create the pastoral myth. But beyond that, the poem is a hymn to the magic power of song. Virgil has succeeded in conforming to an essentially static form dramatic songs depending on ritual and magic and leading toward either the failure or the success of the pastoral dream.

Eight: *Eclogue* 9

L.　Quo te, Moeri, pedes? an, quo via ducit, in urbem?
M.　O Lycida, vivi pervenimus, advena nostri,
　　(quod numquam veriti sumus), ut possessor agelli
　　diceret: 'haec mea sunt; veteres migrate coloni.'
　　nunc victi, tristes, quoniam fors omnia versat,
　　hos illi (quod nec vertat bene) mittimus haedos.

L.　Where are you making your way, Moeris? Is it where
　　the road leads, to the city?
M.　O Lycidas, we have lived to see the time—something we
　　never feared—when a foreigner, owner of our little plot,
　　could say: "These are mine; move elsewhere, you old
　　tenants." Now overcome, bitter, since chance turns all
　　things, we send these goats to him—and may it turn out
　　badly. (lines 1-6)

Whoever turns to the ninth eclogue after reading the eighth,
as the poet intended, will be struck by two details in the opening line. The first is the presence of Moeris, the name given
to the shepherd-magician of lines 96-99 in 8, who can turn
himself into a wolf, call spirits from the tomb, and move har-
vests about. He, we have just been told, had given Amaryllis
herbs and poisons culled in Medea's Pontus, which had aided
in charming Daphnis home from the city. Is Moeris in *Eclogue*
9 to be a magician, or is the identity of name coincidental, as
often in the *Eclogues*?

The second resemblance between the opening line of
Eclogue 9 and the preceding poem is verbal, and its effect is
less open to debate than the repetition of names. Virgil has
taken a segment of the refrain Amaryllis used—"ducite ab urbe
domum, mea carmina, ducite Daphnim"—and turned it to a

different purpose. Lycidas asks Moeris where he is going: "an, quo via ducit, in urbem?" To speak of a walk in pastoral poetry is unusual. The pastoral is, in general, a static form whose melodies are sung by shepherds at leisure in a setting of beauty. Yet here not only the repeated *quo*, but also *pedes*, *via*, and even *ducit* imply that Moeris' and Lycidas' world is in a state of unrest.

The phrase *via ducit* itself is strange. It stresses—what is already apparent from the ellipsis of the verb in the opening question—that Moeris is undertaking this journey unwillingly.[1] His feet are taking him, not his desire. The way leads him on, not the mind. He is an involuntary, passive actor, being drawn out of the country.

There is a tone of astonishment in Lycidas' inquiry. *Quo* means almost "why," as well as "whither." How is it, asks Lycidas, that his feet can bear Moeris along, especially toward the city? The reference to the city, coming emphatically at the end of the line, adds a further ominous note. Urban civilization plays an important role in the *Eclogues* as foil to rural concerns, and in the first eclogue Tityrus does describe, from an idealized vantage, the results of his Roman journey. But Lycidas finds Moeris in the act of walking toward the city. His journey is in progress, and it is far from happy. Whereas in the first eclogue, Tityrus goes to Rome and returns with his bucolic life assured him; in the ninth, there is nothing to be gained from the city. It is toward the antithesis of the shepherd's life that Moeris and Lycidas now proceed.

Hence the verbal connection with *Eclogue* 8 intimates a contrast between the two poems. Amaryllis' refrain attracts Daphnis out of the city back to where he belongs: poetic magic restores the love which had been shattered by departure. The opposite is apparently happening here.

[1] See the commentary on line 1 in Conington. This journey has a very different character from that mentioned at *Ecl.* 1. 20-21, though the practical purpose appears the same.

Eclogue 9

Lycidas' questions imply retreat from the land and dissolution rather than unity. Moeris' response heightens these impressions. Before giving us the real answer four lines later— he is bringing goats to the city—Moeris elaborates the suggestion of Lycidas' words. His indirection demands that the reader seek a reason for it beyond the strictly factual. The passion in Moeris' cry—*O Lycida*—brings to the surface all the tensions which the opening queries prompt. We may pause on the first words after the apostrophe, *vivi pervenimus*. So serious are the implications of the walk that it is a matter of life and death, and so far-reaching its importance that Moeris intimates they have already reached some dread destination.

Vivi implies that the event which they have experienced has been so violent (no mere literal journey this!) that it is a wonder they are alive to tell of it. Time and its passage, power and its purposes, have entered into the ordinarily timeless bucolic quietude. The country, to its imminent harm, has become part of history. To balance this journey, literally to the city but symbolic of life's tragedy, there is an arrival in the country. *Pervenimus* anticipates its neighbor *advena*, the newcomer who has brought the horror about. He is, in Moeris' words, *nostri possessor agelli*, and he has come to take possession of the shepherds' lands.

The word *possessor* strikes an ominous note which is reinforced by the first phrase Moeris puts into the mouth of the new owner: *haec mea sunt*. Once the idea of ownership and possession is introduced into a bucolic context, the dream is broken. Moeris has now been made to see what was once his, a realization that would have been strange while his life remained ideal. The foreigner forces upon the land not only his presence but concepts which are ruinous to pastoralism. Strange to the shepherds and ignorant of their purposes, he owns that over which, in their eyes at least, he has no rights. The impersonal menace of this usurper Virgil conveys by juxtaposing *advena* to *nostri*, *possessor* to *agelli*. Possessiveness is

295

his attribute.[2] Moeris' words, on the other hand, especially the affectionate diminutive *agellus*, convey his love for the land. We are reminded, as we will be often, of *Eclogue* 1 and Meliboeus' devotion to the acres he must lose.

When Moeris describes the situation as something "which we never feared" (*quod numquam veriti sumus*), he offers another illustration of how peculiar such an event is to the countryside, from which all fear and menace should be absent. The pastoral stance retains a certain deliberate naïveté which isolation engenders and fosters. Here the imminence of the real world brings not only fear but a reversal of all norms. The journey to the city is only the beginning. The new owner has commanded: *veteres migrate coloni*. The threat and then the actuality of expulsion have come upon the bucolic retreat.

The new owner's words are those of a victor over his defeated foe. They provoke the vision of a whole people forced to leave their land. He thinks of the old inhabitants in his terms, which are essentially political and economic. To him they are slavish dwellers on the soil (*coloni*), shepherds and farmers working another man's property. That this could have been the actual situation makes no difference. To reveal the matter so directly, and as part of an order into exile, is to give the myth a double blow. The idyll is ruined both literally and conceptually at once.

Other aspects of the intruder's words are also disquieting. That he changes the loving *agellus* into the neuter *haec* is perhaps of little moment. *Mea*, however, cannot be as easily dismissed, nor can the contrast it offers with *nostri* be put aside. This contrast is the same distinction which runs through the opening lines of the first eclogue between *tu*, meaning Tityrus,

[2] On possession as ruinous to the idyll, see Poggioli, "Naboth's Vineyard," p. 21. On the legal formula *meum est*, see the commentary on *Ecl.* 1. 47, in *P. Vergili Maronis Bucolicon Liber*, ed. C. G. Heyne, 4th ed. edited by G.P.E. Wagner (Leipzig, 1830).

and *nos*, Meliboeus and his fellow sufferers. In 9 the effect is no less strong. Apparently without knowing what he has gained, the *advena possessor* owns by himself (according to all the poet wants his readers to know) the fields which were the heart of the landscape. For a moment he is the brutal, ignorant counterpart of Tityrus in 1. There though a soldier might come and dispossess Meliboeus, *otium*, at least, remains for Tityrus. The vision is not utterly destroyed. In 9, as *nostri* yields to *mea*, there is no compensation whatsoever.[3] The poem marks the beginning of ruin for the countryside and flight for its inhabitants, this time without exception.

There is another link between the command and the first eclogue. This is a similarity with the language in which the oracular young god tells Tityrus to continue his life as usual (line 45): "'pascite ut ante boves, pueri; submittite tauros.'" The reader who has felt the force of *Eclogue* 1 as a whole, however, might be tempted to see in the intruder's words a more realistic reversal of the god's improbable utterance. In Moeris' eyes the intruder's mandate is the fulfillment of the wishes of that fickle goddess, Chance. To the superstitious shepherd he is only fortune's minion and the kids conveyed to the city are an offering to an unkindly deity. Moeris prays that the presentation may be a bad omen and that the sacrifice of the *haedi*, if such be their role, may not turn out to be propitious at all. But the fact that they must even be offered is troubling. To anticipate for a moment, it is only a step to the understanding that the shepherd's curse is as ineffective in a negative way as his poetry will prove to be positively. The new owner's and the old tenant's spheres are so divergent that neither the imprecation nor the charm of the latter could presume to have power over the former's evil physical presence.

Vertat and *versat* are to be taken closely together. The curse

---

[3] The same contrast may possibly be felt between *hos haedos* and *illi*, at the opening of line 6. The shepherds are, like the goats, going toward the city, only to be "sacrifices" of a higher sort.

will hopefully have the effect of reversing the present state of things and restoring the independence of the shepherd's world. The language is deliberately archaic and is the first hint that Moeris may, at least partially, be a pathetic counterpart of the wonder-working magician in the eighth eclogue.[4] He is a believer in the traditional spells which a shepherd might be expected to practise and cannot realize that against the pressure of military might and history's progress the inheritance of primitive religion can have little strength. This theme is familiar from *Eclogue* 1: as the land is destroyed, its values and customs die with it. Fortunes may change, as Moeris prays they will, but the breaking in of history on the pastoral trance, because it makes importunate demands incapable of control, puts a mark on the land as unchangeable as it is disastrous.

To put it another way, the *possessor*, as Virgil sees him, is the instrument of *fors* which upsets the present state of things, turning an "owner" into one dispossessed. While to the shepherds there is a possible cycle of chance and change, the poet himself notes a higher law: the inevitability of death. Hinted at in the words *vivi* and *veteres*, it is reaffirmed in the phrase *nunc victi*.[5] The emphasis on life and death is more startling in a region unused to any vicissitudes of time and place. The conquering foe and the menace of mortality make this journey sinister both for the shepherds themselves and for the land from which they have been driven.

Death seems imminent not only for the men but for the beasts they carry with them. *Mittimus* parallels *pervenimus*. The goal of both men and goats is the terrible habitat of the new owner. But *mittimus* means more than "send": they are not "sending" the goats but taking them along with them as

---

[4] On the language itself, see T. E. Page, ed., P. Vergili Maronis *Bucolica et Georgica* (London, 1937), on line 6.

[5] The sound of these four lines is crafted with particularly splendid effect.

they go. As part of Moeris' challenge they are to be "hurled" at the enemy. From being the conquered ones, the shepherds are to become the victors, and the kids, now spoils of the present victor, will be the instrument of revenge in the reversal of roles —all this, to be sure, only if the curse works! These ideas arise in the mind of one shepherd as the result of two brief questions put to him by his colleague. The interplay, though in the form of a competition, actually presents a united picture which is maintained for the course of the poem.

The difference between this introduction and those to the preceding three poems provokes a question essential to an understanding of Virgil's art: What is the relationship of *Eclogue* 9 to *Eclogues* 6 through 8? Why place it here in the collection? The opening of the sixth, as we have seen, offers a division half way through the ten poems. It begins with the poet himself renouncing epic in favor of the products of a slender reed. Yet for the remainder of the poem we hear not the poet's voice but summaries of *carmina*, sung by a silen to young devotees of his art. It is a poem about poetry, about the poet's own feelings for his art, about the content and meaning of pastoral song.

The amoebean contest of 7 has often been compared with the third eclogue which is also a "debate" between two shepherds. But there is one difference between them which establishes 7's closer allegiance to 6 than to 3. The whole contest in 7 is a quotation.[6] The reader does not partake in the interchange directly but views it through the eyes of a recreator, the shepherd Meliboeus. The cave of Silenus is described in some detail in the preceding poem and in *Eclogue* 7 the perfect location of Daphnis' *otium* is of parallel significance. Only there can Corydon and Thyrsis vie with each other in search of the beautiful. This, too, is a song about poetry, viewed from afar by a spectator.

The eighth eclogue, like the sixth, has a double introduction

[6] See chap. 6, n. 2.

(here Pollio replaces Varus as the dedicatee). But the place of honor is given to the first five lines which precede the dedication and which forewarn us that we are to have a poem about the magic of song. Again Virgil is commenting on his art, this time on the charm it can exert to perform the impossible, given the proper circumstances. What, then, of the sudden introduction to 9 where, unlike any of the three preceding poems, we plunge directly into life itself? Is this change merely meant as a contrast or is this also a poem concerned with pastoral song?

Lycidas' reply to Moeris' tale of woe is one of surprise (lines 7-10):

> Certe equidem audieram, qua se subducere colles
> incipiunt mollique iugum demittere clivo,
> usque ad aquam et veteres, iam fracta cacumina, fagos,
> omnia carminibus vestrum servasse Menalcan.

> Yet certainly I had heard that, from where the hills begin to slip away and lower their ridge in gentle incline all the way to the water and the aged beeches, their tops now broken, your Menalcas had saved everything by his songs.

Lycidas looks to the past, to a time when things could be understood with assurance (*certe*), when Menalcas was said to have preserved the land. *Vestrum Menalcan*, Lycidas calls him, as if he stood as symbol and spokesman for many. He had apparently pitted his *carmina* against the powers outside, but could he play Orpheus to tame the violence of those who bring ruin and exile as well as to move the trees? If chance overturns all things (*omnia*, line 5), will the poet's song have the ability to reverse the workings of fortune and save everything (*omnia*, line 10)? Can poetry, intimate and crucial part of bucolic life that it is, preserve it from destruction?

Lycidas looks at the landscape in a special way: he measures it off from the distant hills down to the plain and the beeches at the water's edge. All of this is at stake. The metaphors could be applied to elements in a landscape alone, yet each has its special power beneath the surface. *Se subducere* apparently means that the hills slope gently off into the distance. But the reflexive tends to personify the mountains, making them not only recede but withdraw. We may compare the pessimistic aura Lucretius gives the word when he speaks of the earth suddenly stealing away from under our feet (*terra se pedibus raptim subducat*)[7] or old age taking things away from our sight (*ex oculis vetustatem subducere nostris*).[8] Here the compound *subducere* is deliberately placed near the powerful *ducit* of line 1. The landscape along with those who had peopled it, the poet hints, is beginning to retreat, like a defeated army.

There is an alternative to death or exile. The next infinitive phrase, *iugum demittere*, though literally applied to the mountains' slope, also suggests the bowing of the neck under the yoke of slavery. It is not fortuitous that the verb *mitto* should recur in a compound so shortly after its use in line 6. The shepherds, as slaves to their new owner, must send the baby goats as offerings; the passive landscape must resign itself to a gentler submission. The adjective *mollis* is an effective attribute of humble nature, yielding and defenseless, its hills levelled. The retreat or enslavement of the land is only another symbol of the end of freedom.

The phrase *veteres iam fracta cacumina fagos* is disquieting. There is a close resemblance between Lycidas' description and one aspect of the place where Corydon sings in the second eclogue (line 3)—among the thick beeches with their shady tops (*inter densas, umbrosa cacumina, fagos*). In the poet's eyes, as he writes Lycidas' words, the trees in the land have now become old and the tops, which once offered that shade so necessary for the singer, are broken. The omen of the

[7] *De Re. Nat.* 1. 1106.   [8] *De Re. Nat.* 2. 70.

stricken oaks (*tactas quercus*) in the first eclogue finds its counterpart in the *fracta cacumina* here.

Whether or not the absent poet brings salvation, he is attempting to preserve a landscape whose beeches are old, like the expelled *coloni* themselves (*veteres,* lines 4 and 9), and whose broken crests (*iam fracta*) are the landscape's reflection of the defeat of the shepherds who had sung beneath them (*nunc victi*). Shepherd and land are indivisible and song is a product of the union. One cannot exist without the other and each suffers from the other's misfortunes. If the shepherds are beaten, the landscape, too, is subdued.

The trials of shepherd and land sketched in Lycidas' words are approached from another point of view in Moeris' reply (lines 11-16):

> Audieras, et fama fuit; sed carmina tantum
> nostra valent, Lycida, tela inter Martia quantum
> Chaonias dicunt aquila veniente columbas.
> quod nisi me quacumque novas incidere lites
> ante sinistra cava monuisset ab ilice cornix,
> nec tuus hic Moeris nec viveret ipse Menalcas.

You had heard, and that was the rumor; but, Lycidas, our songs have as much strength amid the weapons of Mars as, they say, the doves of Chaonia at the onslaught of the eagle. And, had not a crow on the left warned me beforehand from a hollow ilex to cut short the new strife somehow or other, neither your Moeris here nor Menalcas himself would still be alive.

Audieras, Moeris says, pointing up Lycidas' use of the word at line 7 (*audieram*).[9] Rumor is one thing, truth another. Those who should have heard the poet's song and been moved

---

[9] See also line 45 (*audieram*). Hearing in this poem is almost as important as singing. Verbal repetition is constant and striking in these lines. (*Nostri* and *nostra,* for another example, appear in lines 2 and 12.)

by it have turned a deaf ear—and not only on Menalcas. *Carmina nostra*, while referring back to *carminibus* in the preceding line, brings the songs of Moeris and perhaps even of Lycidas, the spectator apparently surprised by the disaster, into the picture. The *carmina* of the shepherds, spiritual products of a spiritual world, have as much effect against the weapons of Mars as doves against an eagle's onslaught.

The comparison is a commonplace, but it has a special purpose in this context. The reader has been prepared for mention of *tela Martia* by the metaphors in much of the preceding language, especially *victi* and *fracta*. The simile of the dove and the eagle extends the negative implications. In speaking of songs versus spears, we seem to be dealing with totally antagonistic objects, having no possible relation to each other. Can the metaphysical aspects of poetry offer any challenge to, or even be defended against, the brutal force of Mars' weapons?

The epithet *Chaonias* is not otiose. It refers specifically to Dodona, joint shrine of Jupiter and his consort-daughter, Dione-Aphrodite. Expressed in mythological terms, the eagle-dove analogy is seen in passing as the tension between the warrior god Mars and the love goddess Venus. But the "doves" of Chaonia were also the sacred priestesses of Dione and the prophets of Jupiter's famous oracle.[10] Hence Virgil is pointing not only to the poet's vulnerability but also to his oracular powers as a *vates*, predictor of the future. Within the framework of *Eclogue* 9, this analogy is disturbing. To have an eagle's violence yield before the meek dove is an impossibility. The seduction of Mars by Venus, in its most famous occurrence in ancient literature, the opening of *De Rerum Natura*, is a dream to which the underlying pessimism and constant

[10] On the cult and oracle at Dodona, see A. B. Cook, *Zeus* (Cambridge, 1914), I, 443; II, 350ff.; Sophocles *Trachiniae* ed. R. C. Jebb, (Oxford, Eng., 1892) pp. 200-206; L. R. Farnell, *The Cults of the Greek States* (Oxford, 1896), I, 38ff.

tension in the remainder of the poem give the lie. Here the poets and their scene are doves caught in circumstances against which they have no power.

To a Roman the *aquila* would also suggest the standard of a legion. This meaning lends a special power to the verb *venio*. It refers the reader back to the *advena*, the new owner whose claims to the land are backed by Roman might. The irony can be more fully appreciated by comparing the use of *valent* with *possunt* in *Eclogue* 8, line 69, where Amaryllis discloses the possible strength of her *carmina*. Against the hard facts of present conditions, songs avail but little (at least according to Virgil facing the difficulties in Mantua). It is not just a question of peace and war; the whole imaginative world is at stake. The pastoral doves, symbols of poetry and love, are preyed on by the eagle of Roman might. The physical harm done to shepherds and their land is symptomatic of a more subtle loss of spiritual values.

Though his *carmina* fail him, the poet-shepherd still retains one of the negative aspects of a *vates*, the ability to predict oncoming doom. It is not a question of saving the land but only of the survival of Moeris and Menalcas. The *sinistra cornix* is a direct omen. The crow had apparently uttered a warning to stop new strife and the shepherds had interpreted its message properly. But the *cornix* was more often negative than positive, a prophet of gloom and foreteller of rain.[11] Moreover, the oak inside of which it sits is hollow. Perhaps the tree is dead and the bird croaks from within to escape from what it foreordains.[12] The whole phrase *cava ilice* is especially

[11] On the crow as harbinger of rain, see commentators on Hesiod *W. and D.* 747; Aratus *Phaen.* 950ff.; *G.* 1. 388f.; Horace *Carm.* 3. 17. 12-13 and 3. 27. 10.

[12] Servius comments: "ilex enim glandifera arbor est, quae quoniam vitiosa est, vitium possessionis ostendit fore per milites, clamore gaudentes et litibus" ("for the holm oak is acorn-bearing, which, because it is subject to decay, shows that the decadence of ownership comes about in terms of the soldiers, who rejoice in shouting and strife").

pessimistic when compared to other descriptions of the ilex tree in the *Eclogues*: in 6, line 54, the bull lies at ease *ilice sub nigra*, and in 7, line 1, Daphnis sits under its rustling leaves (*sub arguta ilice*). There are no connotations of lush foliage or the happy buzzing of a hive here in 9, only the hint of impending death. The Chaonian doves have yielded to a sinister crow giving a negative warning from a hollow oak. Finally, the word *viveret* implies that Menalcas, the saving bard, is in the same position as the two shepherds in line 2: *vivi*, alive in a doomed land. But the struggle has turned from a battle over the land into something of greater value, a fight for poets and poetry.

Lycidas' reply shows that he has come to realize the full implication of Moeris' words (lines 17-20):

> Heu, cadit in quemquam tantum scelus? heu, tua nobis
> paene simul tecum solacia rapta, Menalca?
> quis caneret Nymphas? quis humum florentibus herbis
> spargeret, aut viridi fontis induceret umbra?

> Alas, could such a crime occur to anyone? Alas, Menalcas, was your solace nearly torn away from us along with yourself? Who would sing the Nymphs? Who would strew the ground with flowery grasses or cover the fountains with green shade?

The force of war can do many things but the crime of killing a poet is unbelievable to a shepherd because it means killing that beauty upon which the countryside depends. (*Rapta* in this regard balances both *victi* and *fracta*.) When the word *scelus* appears at *Eclogue* 4, line 13, it seems to apply to the original Roman sin of Romulus killing Remus, the cause and paradigm of future civil wars. That the poet-shepherd Menalcas, one of the "doves" of pastoral, should fall victim to the violence of a feud in which he is not involved elicits a double *heu* from Lycidas. Not only do the innocent suffer with the guilty but the life of the imagination can be ruined by a world of power because it happens to live by fields and flocks which are exposed and helpless.

The presence of the poet and his songs is crucial to the landscape, but in this case his voice was special because it provided *solacia*, distraction from trial. To sing of the nymphs we might expect to be within any poet's competence. To strew the ground with flowers and cover fountains with shade goes beyond the charm of words alone to the magic, Orphic power of poetry to create anything—in this case the ideal setting for song. But this is still within the special, privileged context of the pastoral imagination.

Lines 19-20 are closely related to line 40 of *Eclogue* 5 where the dying Daphnis demands of his shepherds: "spargite humum foliis, inducite fontibus umbras." In *Eclogue* 9 the literal has become figurative. The tangible honors due the dead Daphnis are changed to the ability of the absent poet to simulate the loveliness of nature, to recreate it, so to speak, in the mind's eye, perhaps even to bring it into being. Menalcas is the Daphnis of *Eclogue* 9, the savior-poet who can create the necessities of the ideal landscape, flowers for the ground and shaded fountains. He can make that *frigus opacum*, the darkened coolness which forms such an exquisite part of Tityrus' retreat in *Eclogue* 1. *Spargeret* and *induceret* prove him the possessor of the same power as Silenus. He, we recall, not only sings, as does Menalcas here (*caneret*),[13] but also consoles when his theme demands (*solatur*, line 46), offering the same *solacia* as are taken from the shepherd's world with Menalcas. Silenus appears literally to create with words, just as Menalcas "scatters" flowers and "draws" shade over the fountains.

Spargeret and *induceret* have special importance in *Eclogue* 9. *Spargo* is one of the verbs regularly associated, for instance, with the casting of weapons. *Et nos tela spargimus*, Turnus says to Latinus in *Aeneid* 12.[14] The *advena* who inflicts him-

---

[13] *Ecl.* 6. 31, 61, 64, 84.
[14] "We, too, hurl spears" (*Aen.* 12. 50-51).

self on the land might well hurl literal *tela Martia*. The "weapons" of Menalcas are only *carmina* through which he can scatter not spears but flowers. He has the charm to shelter fountains from the sun's glare, but can he repel a force which knows nothing of nature? *Induco* implies the same double force. Confined to pastoral ideas it means only to "cover over," but seen in terms of the poem's larger concerns it suggests seduction, the drawing of something from one sphere into another. In this intricate pattern of verbal interrelationships it contrasts with *subducere*—the defeated hills leading themselves off—and the initial *via ducit*—the shepherds being drawn away toward the city. With Menalcas gone, can the process be reversed? According to Moeris, his talents have hitherto been of no avail.

At line 21 Lycidas, in the role of eavesdropper, keeps Menalcas directly before our eyes and makes the vision clearer by recreating an actual instance of his song (lines 21-25):

> vel quae sublegi tacitus tibi carmina nuper,
> cum te ad delicias ferres Amaryllida nostras?
> 'Tityre, dum redeo (brevis est via) pasce capellas,
> et potum pastas age, Tityre, et inter agendum
> occursare capro (cornu ferit ille) caveto.'

Or [who would sing] the songs of yours which I recently overheard on the sly, when you were making your way to our love, Amaryllis: "Tityrus, feed the goats until I return (the trip is short), and when they have eaten, Tityrus, drive them to water and in driving beware of running up against the he-goat. He butts with his horn."

Though the word *tacitus* has ominous overtones to be more fully revealed later, the sense of the passage is positive and strong. There is a distinction between the songs which Menalcas recently sang and the condition in which the shepherds now find themselves, especially with their spokesman absent. The setting of the verses attracts attention because it is purely bucolic, without any note of menace. Menalcas is not on his way unwillingly to the city but only to his girl Amaryllis; the difference is stressed through the change of subject, from the impersonal *te pedes* of line 1 to the *te ferres* of 22.

The song and the lines which precede it are Theocritean and in large measure a quotation from the first five verses of the third idyl where another shepherd prepares to depart and serenade another Amaryllis:

> Κωμάσδω ποτὶ τὰν Ἀμαρυλλίδα, ταὶ δέ μοι αἶγες
> βόσκονται κατ' ὄρος, καὶ ὁ Τίτυρος αὐτὰς ἐλαύνει.
> Τίτυρ', ἐμὶν τὸ καλὸν πεφιλημένε, βόσκε τὰς αἶγας,
> καὶ ποτὶ τὰν κράναν ἄγε, Τίτυρε· καὶ τὸν ἐνόρχαν,
> τὸν Λιβυκὸν κνάκωνα, φυλάσσεο μή τυ κορύψῃ.

I go to serenade Amaryllis, and my goats graze on the hill, and Tityrus herds them. Tityrus, sweet friend, graze the goats and take them to the spring; and mind the he-goat, the tawny Libyan, lest he butt thee.

Lycidas, in other words, still thinks of Menalcas in Theocritean terms, as if nothing could break the spell. One of the significant changes that Virgil has made from his model is to stress the idea of journey. He is faring to his love, but he will return and the way is not long (*brevis est via*). There is no comparison here with the *via* on which Moeris has set out. The landscape has not been affronted by reality. Menalcas' road leads to his girl and the threat to this carefree rustic life —a possible clash with the butting he-goat—is slight and comes from within the land. Tityrus need assume the duties of his friend only briefly: there is no question about his quick return.

Moeris replies with something far different (lines 26-29):

> Immo haec, quae Varo necdum perfecta canebat:
> 'Vare, tuum nomen, superet modo Mantua nobis,
> Mantua vae miserae nimium vicina Cremonae,
> cantantes sublime ferent ad sidera cycni.'

Nay, these verses which he sang to Varus, though not yet
finished: "Varus, provided Mantua be spared us—Mantua, alas, too near unfortunate Cremona—singing swans
will bear your name aloft to the stars."

The initial words *immo haec* appear together in only one other
place in the *Eclogues*: in *Eclogue* 5, line 13, where Mopsus
protests that he will not sing any of the stock themes which
Menalcas expects but will try songs so new that he has had
to write them down. The distinction between Menalcas'
songs and present situation is also partially operative here,
but its implications are more crucial to the countryside. With
the mention of the name Varus, balancing the pastoral
Tityre of line 23, we are suddenly in an alien world of real
people and Rome, a challenge to the bucolic life. No wonder
the verses are *necdum perfecta*: they cannot be completed at
all in present circumstances. Menalcas has almost been killed,
and the pastoral life, the poet bitterly admits, can depend on
the creative presence of a shepherd-bard. "Pastoral" is fighting
for survival—in historical terms because Mantua was too near
the lands confiscated at neighboring Cremona. Until Varus
restores Mantua to its rightful owners—the importance of the
factual reference is stressed by the repetition—song is impossible. This time a challenge has come to the shepherds from
without. The world of the imagination is lost until both land
and singer are redeemed and independence renewed.[15]

How important the specific reference to Mantua is to Virgil
may be seen from *Georgic* 2, lines 198-99, where, as part of a
catalogue of soil types, he notes: "et qualem infelix amisit
Mantua campum / pascentem niveos herboso flumine cycnos"
("... and such a field as ill-starred Mantua lost, feeding white
swans by a grassy stream"). The passage which follows por-

[15] The use of *vae* is unique in Virgil. It recalls the repetition of *heu*
in line 17 and further underlines the poem's sadness. It is perhaps too
fanciful to hear in it a reflection of the vocative *Vare*, who could, but
might not, save.

trays the ideal landscape in terms of Mantua itself. The swans mirror and symbolize this beauty. By the time the second georgic was written, Virgil could look back and see Mantua as *infelix*, having finally suffered the fate of *misera* Cremona. But Menalcas' words in *Eclogue* 9 imply that this doom can still be averted and the poet-swans still sing, if Varus takes the right steps.

Swans are the birds of Venus and hence, like the doves of line 13, part of that fragile side of the pastoral myth which suffers easily from encroachment. They are also the singers of heroic epic, "birds of Maeonian [Homeric] song" in Horace's words.[16] Menalcas, therefore, in promising that the name of Varus will be raised to heaven by singing swans, is hinting that he may write an epic in praise of Varus and retract the refusal with which *Eclogue* 6 opens.[17] There, in line 12, the *Vari nomen*, described as pleasing to Apollo, stands at the head of a bucolic poem which has nothing to do with Varus himself—all the compliment Virgil feels he can pay. Menalcas, with his apostrophe *Vare, tuum nomen*, pledges something further. Native swans of Mantua will become singers of epic, if their land survives.

So striking are Moeris' words, perhaps because they contrast with the dream of the previous excerpt from Menalcas' verse, that Lycidas replies with an invitation (lines 30-32):

> Sic tua Cyrneas fugiant examina taxos,
> sic cytiso pastae distendant ubera vaccae,
> incipe, si quid habes. . . .

As you would have your swarms flee the yews of Corsica,
as you would have your heifers swell their udders from
feeding on clover, begin, if you have something to sing.

[16] Horace *Carm.* 1. 6. 2. Cf. also *Carm.* 2. 20. 9; 4. 2. 25.

[17] Assuming, arbitrarily, that the reference in each poem is to the same Varus, probably Alfenus Varus. See now L. P. Wilkinson, "Virgil and the Evictions," *Hermes* 94 (1966): 320-24.

So happy is he with what Moeris has sung (or with the fact that he has sung at all) that Lycidas' reply is an appeal for more. It is not unlike Virgil's own prayer to Arethusa, at the beginning of *Eclogue* 10, to grant inspiration for his final pastoral poem. It follows more specifically, however, the pattern of Damoetas' request to Menalcas at line 52 of *Eclogue* 3 (*quin age, si quid habes*) and Menalcas' to Mopsus at lines 10-12 of *Eclogue* 5 (*incipe si habes incipe*).[18]

If, says Lycidas, Moeris wishes to have his swarms of bees shun what is bad and his heifers nourished by good fodder, if, in a word, he would have nature flourish and the world become ideal again, he must sing. Not only must he try to re-create through his verses the spirit of the first excerpt (*pastae vaccae* recalls the use of *pasce* and *pastas* at 23 and 24), but he must also try, especially by composing new and original verses, to replace Menalcas and become, for a moment at least, the Daphnis-figure upon whom the shepherds depend.

Yet it is strange that after the poem has already run almost half its course one protagonist should turn to the other and beg for a song. Moreover, though he sang one of the previous excerpts, Lycidas denies any attribution of talent to himself (lines 32-34):

> et me fecere poetam
> Pierides, sunt et mihi carmina, me quoque dicunt
> vatem pastores; sed non ego credulus illis.

The maidens of Pieria made even me a poet. Songs, too, I have. The shepherds also call me a bard, but I put no trust in them.

It is as if the first two excerpts from Menalcas' songs had been a species of competition at the end of which the young Lycidas, somewhat like Mopsus at the opening of 5, protests that, when compared with Moeris, he is neither a *poeta* in the eyes

---

[18] We have had a thoroughly different use of *incipio* at line 7. Each, in its own way, is the beginning of the end.

of the Muses nor a *vates* to the shepherds. He claims he is
not one who can both sing and understand the ways of nature, the double role of the Chaonian "doves." *Carmina* here
are of twofold value: they are the beautiful songs which the
Muses of Pieria inspire, but they are also incantations which,
though not necessarily formal poetry, have a physical effect.
Because his poems fit into the second category, Lycidas says
that the shepherds designated him a *vates*—bard, soothsayer,
expounder of eternal things to untutored minds.[19] By juxtaposing the words *fecere* and *poeta*, Virgil's shepherd puns on
the origin of *poeta* from the Greek ποιητής, which is itself
derived from the verb ποιεῖν. Lycidas should be a "doer,"
his *carmina* should have the strength, if not to rival Menalcas and attempt to save the land, at least to challenge those
of Moeris and sing against great odds. But he does not trust
the attribution of such powers to himself. This has been no
match. The shepherds' sole purpose was to attempt to recall
someone else's songs to relieve their yearning and perhaps even
to strive through recollection to re-establish the past. It is almost as if the master poet, in whose hands their safety rests,
were present.

Lycidas adds one other comment (lines 35-36):

> nam neque adhuc Vario videor nec dicere Cinna
> digna, sed argutos inter strepere anser olores.

For I still seem to sing nothing worthy of a Varius or a
Cinna but to cackle like a goose among singing swans.

We can only guess at the allusion. If the poem hitherto has
presented the challenge of history to the bucolic world, we are
now introduced to aspects of poetry beyond the possibilities of
the pastoral. Cinna, the neoteric poet and friend of Catullus,
wrote at some point in his career a *propempticon* for Pollio

[19] Specifically on *vates*, see Hellfried Dahlmann, "Vates," *Philologus*
97 (1948): 337-53; and Hermann Rupprecht, "Über Wortstellung als
Hilfe zur Wortdeutung in der bukolischen Dichtung Vergils," *Gymnasium* 70 (1963): 21-22.

and was therefore quite likely a friend of those upon whom
Virgil and his countrymen depended at this time.[20] About the
poet Varius we may be more certain. By the time Horace's
first book of satires was published (probably in 35 B.C.),
Varius had already established a firm reputation as a writer of
epic, a reputation he maintained in later years in spite of his
achievements as a dramatist.[21] Perhaps, then, by comparing
Varius and Cinna to swans, Virgil puts into Lycidas' mouth
a further *recusatio*. Were he to depart from his calling as shepherd (and singer of idyls) and try his hand at a narrative poem
in celebration of his contemporaries, he would sound like a
goose among swans when compared to Varius and Cinna.
His is not the strange role, envisioned by Menalcas in lines
27-29, writing the saving epic.

If Lycidas expected Moeris to take on this role, his reply and
the song which accompanies it must have been disappointing.
Not only is it not epic, it is not even creative but rather something of his own past work, itself scarcely remembered (lines
37-43):

> Id quidem ago et tacitus, Lycida, mecum ipse voluto,
> si valeam meminisse; neque est ignobile carmen.
> 'huc ades, o Galatea; quis est nam ludus in undis?
> hic ver purpureum, varios hic flumina circum
> fundit humus flores, hic candida populus antro
> imminet et lentae texunt umbracula vites.
> huc ades; insani feriant sine litora fluctus.'

[20] Whether or not he was the Cinna mistakenly killed at Caesar's
funeral is a moot question. Since *Eclogue* 9 seems likely to refer to
events which took place after 42, either it is a different poet named
Cinna or the legend is a concoction. Reason commends the latter
alternative.

[21] See *Sat.* 1. 10. 43ff. There is probably a deliberate contrast between
the phrases *forte epos* and *acer Varius* and Horace's famous judgment
on the *Eclogues* as *molle atque facetum* which occurs in the next line.
Varius and Virgil are linked as epic poets in *Ep.* 2. 1. 245-50. According to Servius (on line 36) *anser* is an allusion to a poetaster Anser,
friend of Antony.

That is what I am doing, Lycidas, and silently pondering it to myself, if I have the strength to remember. It is
not a trifling song. "Come hither, Galatea; for what
sport is there in the waves? Here is purple spring, here
the earth pours forth varied flowers along the streams, here
a white poplar leans over the cave and bending vines
weave shadows. Come hither; let the mad waves strike
against the shore."

Ago reminds the reader of line 24 where the verb is used twice
to describe the herding of goats. But, even though Moeris still
seems to possess the ability to recall his own works, the hesitant
tone of the introductory lines conveys more strongly than before the shepherd's sense of inadequacy. Lycidas called himself
tacitus in line 21. There we tend to let the epithet pass as a reference to his shyness in the presence of the chief bard. To have
the word reappear in line 38 (these are the only uses of *taceo*
in the *Eclogues*) is of greater, more ominous, significance. The
pastoral is a form which depends on sound, on the joy of
song and the echoing response of woods and hills.

If this word is foreboding, the phrase *si valeam meminisse*
is more so. *Valeam* itself recalls the desperate *carmina nostra
valent* (lines 11-12), where song was pitted in unequal combat against the weapons of war. There it is poetry which has
endured the loss of power and vitality, but here it is the poet
himself, the magician of the bucolic life, who suffers. Moeris
warns that the ability not only to create new things (the necessary and continuous rejuvenation of nature) but even to
recall his past work threatens to leave him.

One need not stress again the importance of memory in
bucolic poetry, which is regularly stylized as an oral form. The
whole of the seventh eclogue is sung from memory and within
it the poet takes two occasions to remind us that the Muses delight in recalling beautiful song. Meliboeus ends that song
with the important *haec memini* (line 69). To mention only

Eclogue 9

two other passages, the Eurotas orders its laurels to learn
Apollo's songs by heart, at the end of *Eclogue* 6 (line 83),
and in talking of song at the opening of the last eclogue, Virgil
varies the proverb: "non canimus surdis, respondent omnia
silvae" ("We do not sing to deaf ears. The woods echo everything.").

Moeris' quoted song does, however, restore the mood of lines
23-25. It recreates the essence of bucolic love. The first passage,
quoted from Menalcas, concerns love: the road, we recall,
leads to Amaryllis. Moeris' song is dedicated to one of the
erotic-pastoral themes Virgil inherited from Theocritus, the
passion of the cyclops Polyphemus for the sea nymph Galatea.
Specifically Virgil has in mind Theocritus' *Idyl* 11, lines
42-49:

> ἀλλ᾽ ἀφίκευσο ποθ᾽ ἁμέ, καὶ ἑξεῖς οὐδὲν ἔλασσον,
> τὰν γλαυκὰν δὲ θάλασσαν ἔα ποτὶ χέρσον ὀρεχθεῖν·
> ἅδιον ἐν τὠντρῳ παρ᾽ ἐμὶν τὰν νύκτα διαξεῖς.
> ἐντὶ δάφναι τηνεί, ἐντὶ ῥαδιναὶ κυπάρισσοι,
> ἔστι μέλας κισσός, ἔστ᾽ ἄμπελος ἁ γλυκύκαρπος,
> ἔστι ψυχρὸν ὕδωρ, τό μοι ἁ πολυδένδρεος Αἴτνα
> λευκᾶς ἐκ χιόνος ποτὸν ἀμβρόσιον προΐητι.
> τίς κα τῶνδε θάλασσαν ἔχειν καὶ κύμαθ᾽ ἕλοιτο;

Nay, come to me, and thou shalt fare well enough. Leave
the green sea to pulse upon the shore; thou wilt pass the
night more pleasantly in the cave with me. There are bays
and slender cypresses; there is dark ivy, and the sweet-
fruited vine, and water cold, which wooded Etna puts
forth for me from her white snowfields, a draught divine.
Who would rather choose the sea and its waves than these?

Virgil makes several changes which, if anything could, add to
the idealism of the passage. The repetition of *huc* and the
threefold use of *hic*, as we have often seen, are recurrent in the
Eclogues at moments of happy invitation into some special
retreat.

The setting here is even more perfect than in the first quotation. The slight menace inherent in the land—there it was the he-goat who strikes with his horns (*ferit*), here it is the mad waves beating against the shore (*feriant*)—is now relegated to the outside. The sea borders the pastoral world but is completely foreign to it, and the contrast between the two realms increases the sense of ideal beauty in Galatea's entering and bringing love to the shepherd's land.

The whole is an ironic foil to the situation into which the shepherds are presently being swept. The landscape preserves its grace by the presence of love, and love comes, Moeris prays, by Galatea's making her way out of the violent sea into the bucolic paradise. There is a tragic difference between this sketch, a fruitless product of wishful thinking, and the real journey of Moeris away from fields which no longer belong to him. Now even the imagination, which could temporarily stave off the horrors of real life, scarcely works. In the quotation, the landscape remains a flourishing, springtime oasis of perfection filled with shady coolness. The pliant vines themselves weave small shadows (the diminutive is particularly effective), and the season is purple with flowers. But this is the song of a dreamer. The reader's thoughts inevitably turn back to the *fracta cacumina* which are now the shepherds' lot.

Certain details here which are not in Theocritus would seem to be especially Virgilian. The word *ludus*, for instance, has no counterpart in *Idyl* 11. It implies here, as it does in the distinction Meliboeus draws in *Eclogue* 7 between his *seria* and the *ludus* of the two shepherds, that the inner realm purveys both love and poetry (a regular ambiguity of *ludus*). But the main alteration from Theocritus, the setting as it appears in lines 40-42, seems expressly to recall lines 19-20. The details of a land covered with flowers and protected by shade are the same. Hence, in noting the gemlike charm of this perfect spot, we reflect with dismay that not only the lines themselves, as poetry, but the picture they create are dependent

on the poet and his presence. In him alone rests the ability
to create the words with their magical power which is vital
not so much for bringing Galatea home from the sea as for
evoking in the reader's mind what may not exist at all.

We have moved from the suggestion that Menalcas might
create the world of which he sings to a final realization that
such a creation is impossible and memory useless, when the
landscape is destroyed and its guiding spirit removed. Virgil is
not engaged in singing a light and charming song. He is
meditating on something much more crucial: the creative role
of the artist and the need for the right setting in order to create. Both are now lost. Sadder still, the perfection of the past
is no longer something which could have been real (as in
lines 23-25) but only myth. As the unreality of the quotations
grows, the desperation caused by the background against
which they are sung keeps pace.

Lycidas answers with a second quotation from Moeris' work
(lines 44-50):

> Quid, quae te pura solum sub nocte canentem
> audieram? numeros memini, si verba tenerem:
> 'Daphni, quid antiquos signorum suspicis ortus?
> ecce Dionaei processit Caesaris astrum,
> astrum quo segetes gauderent frugibus et quo
> duceret apricis in collibus uva colorem.
> insere, Daphni, piros: carpent tua poma nepotes.'

What of the verses I heard you singing alone under the
clear night sky? I remember the rhythm, if I could but
recall the words: "Daphnis, why are you looking up at
the time-worn risings of the stars? Look, the star of
Caesar, offspring of Dione, has come forth, the star at
which the wheat grows glad with grain, at which the
grape draws in its color on the sun-drenched hills. Graft
your pears, Daphnis. Your descendants will pick the
fruit."

The occasion is night, and the sky must be clear for him to sing at all. But it is not so much on Lycidas' inability to create a song as on his near failure even to remember a quotation that the reader's attention is riveted.

Turning to the excerpt itself, we find ourselves again in a strange world as Moeris, in Lycidas' recollection, addresses Daphnis and calls his attention away from the old stars, which formerly would have guided the shepherd's seasonal course, to observe the new *Dionaei Caesaris astrum*, the comet of the deified Julius Caesar appearing in the clear night sky. In other words, Moeris has come upon Daphnis, relying on the usual risings and settings of the constellations to foresee the prospects of agriculture. This system of observation is one of the few stable things upon which the countrydweller can rely, as Virgil states directly in *Georgic* 1. 257: "nec frustra signorum obitus speculamur et ortus" ("Nor do we look in vain at the risings and fallings of the stars"). It parallels the shepherd's scrutiny of the oaks in *Eclogue* 1, and the crow earlier in 9 for signs of the pleasure and displeasure of gods now quite remote.

The reference to the star of Caesar is another allusion to a world of fact outside "pastoral," a world now working upon the land for better or worse. It implies that the dispensation of a Caesar can agree with the countryside and exert a benign influence on its crops and vines. The epithet *Dionaei* is significant. Were we to equate Dione with her daughter Venus, we might be tempted to see in the word an attribution to Caesar of the love and beauty associated with Venus which are so necessary for the land to survive. But Dione herself, as previously noted, was worshipped with particular veneration at Dodona, so the adjective may be a specific reference back to the mention of Chaonian doves in line 13.

The epithet serves as a further ascription of oracular power to the shepherd-poets in their role as *vates*. It is only within such a framework that it becomes clear why Caesar is labelled

Eclogue 9

Dionaeus. He is appealed to as someone who might protect and cherish the singers' domain and the doves and swans who sing and reflect its charms. In other words, within the context of Lycidas' quotation, the warlike qualities associated with someone like Caesar can be reconciled, through his link to Venus, with the idea of creativity. The dove can now live with the eagle and the *carmina* of the poet triumph over the *tela Martia*. The vision of a Caesar become a sign for pastoral is ideal, like that of the young Roman god bestowing his blessing on Tityrus' retreat. But can the weapons of Mars be put aside for a fruitful union between myth and reality, history and the eternal idyll?

There are already verbal overtones that partially negate the reassurance of the dream. The mention of *colles*, for instance, underscores the fact that the hills, as described in line 7, are in reality being subjugated and destroyed rather than cultivated. Moreover, here the word *duco* is connected with the fertility of nature, though in line 1 it describes the shepherds' departure from a dying world. And there is something still more frightening.

Most critics are rightly struck by the resemblance between the last line of the excerpt and the command which the newly exiled Meliboeus ironically gives himself in *Eclogue* 1, lines 73-74 ("insere nunc, Meliboee, piros, pone ordine vitis. / ite meae, quondam felix pecus, ite capellae"), when mimicking the order given the more fortunate Tityrus by his oracular Roman god in line 45 ("'pascite ut ante boves, pueri; submittite tauros'"). The likelihood is slim that such imperatives will be of any use to Meliboeus as he prepares to depart from his land. It is only the *ite . . . ite* to the goats that makes any sense in his life. They may go on grazing, even though they be as accursed as he. Nevertheless a common view of the command given Daphnis in *Eclogue* 9 sees it as a genuine wish for the future. Moeris and Daphnis may still find a way to bring about the miracle of reconciliation between Caesar's world and their own. Such a view is doubtless valid in terms of the quotation itself: within its context the command is meant to be highly optimistic and to look toward the future with eager hope. In a broader perspective it is parallel to *pasce capellas* in line 23. But we must not forget that this, too, is a quotation and as such deserves to be treated with as much suspicion as the oracle in 1 and Meliboeus' burlesque of it.

We have seen from the preceding excerpt that Moeris' verses can re-create an ideal landscape. But when those verses are compared to lines 19-20 it became clear that such perfection depended wholly on the poet and his presence. If he and his milieu are left unchallenged, then idealism can be preserved. But if, when the poet is forced against the world of power, he is nearly killed, then the whole bucolic existence escapes death just as narrowly. These words of Moeris by themselves may be seen as a hope for the blessing of Caesar upon rural life. When viewed in relation to the poem as a whole, when the *tela Martia* threaten to destroy the land, we can anticipate nothing but despair. Since it is now virtually impossible to plant trees, there is little chance that Daphnis' posterity will be able to gather their fruit. All continuity is destroyed along with the landscape.

In both the first and ninth eclogues, the rural world depends ultimately on the whim of Rome. In thinking back to *Eclogue* 1 with Moeris' present words in mind, the exile of Meliboeus lingers in the mind longer than the happiness of Tityrus, even though he seemed to have the blessing of those in power. An idealistic dream of survival is, in both cases, a fantasy.

Each of these four quotations is handsomely unified in itself, but taken as a whole they alternate between Theocritean and Roman themes in a culminative pattern. The first and third songs are clearly Theocritean in reminiscence and effect, offering the reader a vision of undisturbed *otium* and the poet a chance to sing traditional themes and ponder traditional values. The second excerpt breaks into this happy sequence by announcing, with bold directness, the dependence of Mantua on Varus and his colleagues. The effect of such an acknowledgment of life's starker necessities is stressed by a return, in the third quotation, to Theocritean make-believe. The external world cannot be so easily dismissed, and in the final quotation reality takes perfected shape as the beautiful star of Caesar.

Viewed by themselves or as a culminating sequence, the songs claim that a happy union between the pastoral life and Rome is possible. Looked at in relation to the poem as a whole, the impression they convey is ironic. Poetry itself, especially song only remembered, has little chance to cope with the actual situation.

A further acknowledgment of this fact appears in Moeris' reply (lines 51-55):

> Omnia fert aetas, animum quoque; saepe ego longos
> cantando puerum memini me condere soles:
> nunc oblita mihi tot carmina, vox quoque Moerim
> iam fugit ipsa: lupi Moerim videre priores.
> sed tamen ista satis referet tibi saepe Menalcas.

Time takes away all things, even memory. I recall that often as a boy I put to set the long sun's day as I sang. Now I have forgotten so many songs. Voice itself has now also fled Moeris. Wolves saw Moeris first. Nevertheless Menalcas will often repeat your songs to you as much as you like.

Something of the tone of line 51 can be sensed as early as the last line of the song about Daphnis. However ideal in itself, Daphnis' world contains an element of sorrow: his admission that time passes even within paradise is applied to the present by Moeris. Were we to read the phrase *omnia fert aetas* by itself, as the preceding and subsequent pauses urge, we might be tempted to see a relationship between it and *Eclogue* 4, line 39—*omnis feret omnia tellus*—where the poet is describing the all-bountiful earth in the season when the miraculous boy has grown to manhood. But the next two words, *animum quoque*, quickly dispel any optimistic illusions. Time is taking away, not bringing, and the saddest of the losses is the poet-shepherd's forgetfulness of his songs.

This is stronger language than Moeris' earlier opinion (line 5) that chance turns all things (*fors omnia versat*). There the hope of change is still possible. Fortune's wiles may yet bring about a negation of sorrow and a renewal of past happiness. Moeris now holds out little expectation of this, at least for himself. Rather *omnia* is close to its use in line 11. Menalcas might have saved everything, but actually little or nothing has been salvaged, not even the ability to think. By laying stress on the word *aetas*, Moeris introduces again the concept of time's passage, a concept strongly at variance, as we have noted, with the static qualities of *otium*. It is not so much the aphorism itself that matters as the application Moeris makes of it to himself: his mind and above all his memory and his ability to sing have been lost.

The word *memini* recalls *meminisse* in line 38 and *memini* in 45. In both these instances there was a certain hesitancy which bordered on failure, but Moeris' use of the word is especially pathetic. He remembers not songs to sing at this crucial time but only the fact that, when all was happy, he once spent long days singing. The change from the time when Moeris was a boy to the present is underlined by *nunc* and *iam* in lines 53 and 54. These were also, we remember, two of the key words with which Virgil unifies the poem's opening lines: *nunc victi* of line 5 leads to *iam fracta* in 9. The desolation of the spirit and the destruction of the land come to the same thing.

Each phrase gains further significance from contrast with the past. In the first eclogue, the Roman god claims to direct

his command to *pueri*, youths who will continue the bucolic
tradition. In reality, however, for all the reader knows, the
command is only given to one *senex*, Tityrus, emblem of a
sheltered but, perhaps even for him, dying tradition. Moeris,
though he is Tityrus' partial counterpart, lacks even a dream
of perfection, to say nothing of the possibility of actually
realizing it again.

Oblita is another in the long series of participles by which
the poet contrasts past and present. It is decisive because it admits that memory, the perquisite of bucolic poetry, has at last
yielded to forgetfulness. The spirit has been conquered. The
only hope (and here *refert* is an optimistic counterpart of the
gloomy *fert* with which Moeris had begun)[22] is that Menalcas
will return and bring back with him the power of song, but
this hope Moeris limits, with *tibi*, to Lycidas alone. Even Menalcas could not restore Moeris' former ability.

The ruin of the land is reflected in the progressive degenera-
tion of Moeris from creative singer, to mere repeater of his and
others' songs, to one whose voice has fled. *Fugit* is a strong
word. We recall its use by Meliboeus in *Eclogue* 1, line 4:
fugimus. The flight of Moeris' voice and Meliboeus' exile are
comparable. Virgil has rephrased the saying about the man
who fails to see the wolf before the animal sees him. The wolf
is also the proverbial predatory enemy of the flock. The
sentiment brings to a climax the series of images which began
with the literal *possessor advena* and continued with *tela
Martia*, the *aquila*, and *aetas*. The wolves are another emblem
of ruin come upon the land and those who people it; they
are the last instruments of the ravages of time and Rome.[23]

Lycidas' long response raises more doubts than it dispels
(lines 56-65):

[22] The balance between lines 51 and 55 is strengthened by the
repetition of *saepe* in each.
[23] See G. Cipolla, "Political Audacity and Esotericism in the Ninth
Eclogue," *Acta Classica* 5 (1962): 57.

Eclogue 9

Causando nostros in longum ducis amores.
et nunc omne tibi stratum silet aequor, et omnes,
aspice, ventosi ceciderunt murmuris aurae.
hinc adeo media est nobis via; namque sepulcrum
incipit apparere Bianoris. hic, ubi densas
agricolae stringunt frondes, hic, Moeri, canamus;
hic haedos depone, tamen veniemus in urbem.
aut si nox pluviam ne colligat ante veremur,
cantantes licet usque (minus via laedit) eamus;
cantantes ut eamus, ego hoc te fasce levabo.

By your conversation you put my yearning at a distance.
And now the whole level plain lies silent for you and,
look, the breezes of the roaring wind have died down.
Just near here is the middle of our journey; for the tomb
of Bianor begins to appear. Here, where the farmers are
stripping the thick leaves, here, Moeris, let us sing; here
put down the kids. At all events we will reach the city.
Or, if we feel that night may gather rain before this, we
may yet make our way onward singing (the journey is
less troublesome). That we may journey singing, I will
relieve you of this burden.

Causando, a relatively prosaic word more frequently used
by the orators than the poets, balances *cantando* in line 52,
and is almost a final denial of Moeris' ability to sing. It not
only has its usual sense of "plea" or "excuse" but also means
something like "pretend," or "distract from reality," in this
case by conversation. Lycidas realizes that their vain attempts
at song have been a sham, that real song cannot be sung until Menalcas returns, and that quotation and excuse will serve
only so long as an escape. Moeris' last words have merely post-
poned their *amores*, their yearning for the absent Menalcas.
In longum is both temporal and geographical, and *ducis* seems
to imply a road away from reality into the faraway land of
contemplated song. The subterfuge of attempting to conjure

up Menalcas and his songs takes both shepherds for a while
into a world of solace and happiness which is no longer their
own. Yet we now begin to feel that even were Menalcas to return there is little hope of safety, if songs have no power
against spears. Even his role of giving *solacia* will be useless
if the shepherds lose their land.

In longum ducis suggests more than escapism: it serves as
an ominous reminder of the poem's initial journey, *quo via
ducit,* toward the city. Hence we are prepared for the contrasting *nunc* of the present when it reappears in line 57 ac-
companying the description of a natural phenomenon which
is patently symbolic. The word *aspice* is regularly used in the
Eclogues to call attention to some occurrence strange enough
to be a *monstrum*.[24] The sign here is the sudden and complete
silence of the plain, with the fall of every breeze.[25] Perhaps the
event seems good to Lycidas for *canamus* (line 61) intimates
his willingness to attempt another song.

Viewed in the perspective of bucolic poetry as a whole, however, it is less happy. A shepherd's song cannot survive without sound.[26] The utter quiet of the plain means that nature
can no longer take part in the singing, and nature's response
is a necessity from the smallest details—the "rustling" oaks
under which Daphnis sits at the opening of *Eclogue* 7, for
instance—to the grandest—such as the woods and mountains
which hear Corydon's song in 2 or the poet's own in 10. In particular, breezes are of special moment for they absorb and re-
iterate the shepherd's song.

The general need for sound to complete the shepherd's
idyllic setting is best illustrated in the first eclogue, where
Meliboeus describes Tityrus' haven. Meliboeus sees beauty
in many details, but it is the need for sound that he stresses

---

[24] For other examples see *Ecl.* 7, line 8, and chap. 6, n. 4.
[25] It seems hard to reconcile an interpretation of *aequor* as "sea"
with a setting in Mantua, though the majority of critics take it as such.
[26] See Damon, "Modes of Analogy," *passim.*

most: the buzzing of the bees, the singing of the vine-dresser, the cooing of the pigeons and the wood-doves. When he later summarizes the disaster of his exile in the phrase *carmina nulla canam* (line 77), he could well be thinking back to the inspiration for song that will always be near Tityrus but never again near himself. In 9, there is no possibility of relief. Like the use of *omnia* in line 10, *omne aequor* and *omnes aurae* allow no escape. The absence of sound is not the only foreboding feature of this description. The levelling process in the landscape, which the metaphors *subducere* and *demittere* suggested in lines 7 and 8, has been completed. This plain on which all is now still has no relieving features, no rises to break the monotony, above all no hills or rocks to echo their voices.

Stratum and *ceciderunt* are aptly chosen. The first describes a piece of land which lies flat, "stretched" before the viewer. It is also the last in the series of past participles which runs through the poem. Partly for this reason the reader's attention turns back especially to the phrase *nunc victi* in line 5. *Stratum* contains the same ambiguity. More often than not in Virgil it refers to a fallen enemy, overthrown or slain.[27] Just as we learned at the opening of the poem that the shepherds were like a people who had suffered defeat at the hands of a stronger power and that the land was submitting to the same tyranny, now the poet reveals through metaphor that the ruin is complete. The land is flattened and overwhelmed —silent as death. *Ceciderunt* has the same effect. We speak of the "fall" of a breeze (and Virgil uses the verb in the same meteorological sense elsewhere),[28] but we might well ponder its constant appearance in the *Aeneid*, as one foe falls before a mightier opponent. With the levelling of the land and the collapse of the breezes, the landscape also yields tragically to something more demanding.

[27] See, e.g., *Aen.* 3. 247 (of cattle); 10. 326.
[28] E.g., *G.* 1. 354.

It may be that Lycidas means his next words to be com-
forting. They are, after all, half way on their journey and it
seems a good place to stop and sing. Moreover, the use of *hinc*
and the threefold *hic* should mean that Virgil is introducing a
description of the ideal landscape. The poet adopts such an
outline in the first quotation from Moeris' songs, the invitation to Galatea. No wonder Lycidas suggests that this is a place
for song—*canamus*. And the phrase *media via* could be interpreted positively to suggest further escape. The shepherds
now find themselves somewhat away from their fallen land
and not yet in the city whence the disaster emanates.

But such reassurance grows dim upon closer examination.
The repetition of *via* in lines 59 and 64 reminds the reader
that the journey on which they find themselves is leading
steadily out of the countryside, and the adjective *medius* more
truly portends that they are deeply in the trouble which *via* implies. Even from Lycidas' point of view the announcement
that the road will do less harm if they sing (*minus via laedit*)
suggests that the way possesses only evil, which can be miti-
gated, not dispelled.

Like nightfall at the end of *Eclogue* 1, the road could betoken a retreat from reality. They might sing, though they
have not tried. Yet Lycidas' naïve proposal, like Tityrus'
invitation to Meliboeus, further underlines the impending horror which the observant onlooker would already have perceived in every detail of the landscape. At the end of the ninth
eclogue both shepherds are like Meliboeus without even a vision of Tityrus' dream world. Menalcas has left the land and,
for all the reader knows, has not saved it even for himself.

There are still two more specific points by which Lycidas
characterizes this dead land: the appearance of the tomb of
Bianor (according to Servius one of the mythical founders of
Mantua) and the stripping of the boughs by the farmers.

We will have occasion below to examine Theocritus' seventh
idyl which, to some degree, served as Virgil's model in writing

Eclogue 9. It is necessary to mention here that in the seventh idyl the tomb of a certain Brasilas is used as a sign which will apparently show the speaker and his companion, Eucritus, when they have come half way on their journey. It is a landmark and nothing more. In the context which Virgil supplies to the appearance of Bianor's tomb, the effect is sinister, as if the poet were saying, with one grand gesture, not only that death has its place in Arcadia but also that, at least for this particular moment in its history, death is at the core of the pastoral world. The founder of Mantua is worshipped not as a Daphnis, whose tomb in the fifth eclogue becomes the center of the land, but as a symbol of mortality. Mantua finds its emblem in death, not life. The tomb of its founder becomes the focal point in a journey away from poetry.[29]

Apparere, like *aspice*, is a word which often presages an omen. Here the poet does not leave his thoughts to vague ambiguities of metaphor but states his purpose with the finality of a symbol which epitomizes the dying world surrounding the shepherds. No mere signpost this, and scarcely an indication of a good place for song. *Ecce*, which in line 47 introduces the appearance of the star of Caesar in the make-believe of Moeris' last song, becomes *aspice* and *apparere*, which announce omens of the situation ruling the shepherds' existence. This is no saving divinity or harbinger of prosperity, come into their ken, but death itself, steadfast and firm, toward which they are forced to make their way. Any idealized vision is reversed and negated.

The stripping of the leaves must be viewed in much the same way. That it is an essentially georgic, unpastoral occupation matters little;[30] that it anticipates the coming of winter,

---

[29] On the idea of death in the pastoral landscape, see the influential article by Erwin Panofsky, "Et in Arcadia Ego," reprinted in *Meaning in the Visual Arts* (New York, 1955), pp. 295-326. I cannot agree with him, however, that Virgil's version of Arcadia is in any sense an idealized Utopia (see 298ff.).

[30] See *G.* 1. 305.

when all happy rural pursuits come to a halt, makes us pause, given the context. The action of the farmers, in tearing off the thick foliage (*densas frondes*), destroys one of the imperatives of bucolic song: shade. Instances of the importance of shade are numerous—the *umbracula* which the bending vines will make for Galatea in Moeris' first song (line 42), the *densas, umbrosa cacumina, fagos* under which Corydon sings (*Eclogue* 2, line 3), or even the *frigus opacum* which Tityrus will forever possess (*Eclogue* 1, line 52). The loss of shade and the disappearance of the breezes combine to eliminate any chance of a revival of song.

Hence the introduction of *hinc* and *hic* is misleading. The poet is almost parodying his idealistic utterances elsewhere. There is to be no relief for the burdened shepherds, no *solacium* through song, only a constant visual reminder that the landscape is being annihilated and that they are making their way out of the countryside to its destroyer. As they depart, the last signs of beauty go with them.

The phrase *tamen veniemus in urbem* is ironic on the lips of Lycidas. He himself has now become part of the journey about which he questions Moeris at the start of the poem. (*In urbem* comes in the same emphatic position in each line.) Yet Lycidas does not seem to realize its implications. In spite of his command, they cannot put down the goats which, like the songs they sing, are victims of a higher power. The *aquila veniens* of line 13 forces them to make their journey. Lycidas fails to understand that the completion of their walk, away from their rural haven through the fallen landscape, will mean the end of poetry.

What follows is still less reassuring. There is an almost hypnotic reiteration of the need for cheering song; *canamus*, the anaphora of *cantantes* in lines 64-65, is followed by *carmina* and then *canemus*, all in the space of seven lines. Night is pressing upon them, not the *pura nox* in which Moeris could sing of Daphnis and Caesar's benign star (line 44), but a dark night which threatens rain and eliminates any faint hope of inspiration. As in line 3, Virgil underscores the presence of fear in the lives of the shepherds. When the day is done they have no steading toward which to retire, no green leaves, such as those on which Tityrus invites Meliboeus to spend his last night in the country, only the darkening rainy road toward the city.

The final phrases of Lycidas' words offer the culminating irony. To sing while walking is a contradiction in pastoral terms, where the quiet of a shady rest is a necessity for song. Moreover, for Lycidas to take the *haedi* from Moeris is merely to transfer the burden, not do away with the imposition of carrying it in the first place. Finally the implication of the word *fasce* is unpromising. The meaning Virgil usually gives it is "burden," that which is heavier to bear than one's just lot. The marching Roman soldier is so described in the third georgic (lines 346-47): "non secus ac patriis acer Romanus in armis / iniusto sub fasce viam cum carpit, . . ." ("just as when the brave Roman in the armor of his fatherland hurries on his way bearing an unjust burden"). It is considered a glory of the bees when they take on more than their due share of a load (*Georgic* 4, lines 203-204): "saepe etiam duris errando in cotibus alas / attrivere, ultroque animam sub fasce dedere" ("Often, too, as they wander amid the flinty rocks, they wear away their wings, and yield their life willingly under their burden").

But the real *fasces* which threaten Moeris and Lycidas are impossible to control. This is the last exemplar of that world of power, the world of the foreign owner and *aquilae*, to which the shepherds are subject. If the "eagle" symbolizes the capability of war to overturn the land, the *fascis* serves as a warning that it is the might of politics, the influence wielded by a Varus or a Caesar, which is also helping bring ruin when it could be used to save. If the burden is thought of only as kids, it can be made more bearable, not eliminated. If the larger perspective of governmental control is brought into the picture, the shepherds become mere pawns, victims of a doom quite inescapable.

Moeris' reply is more realistic. Although Lycidas apparently thinks that the way can be made less tedious and the burden lighter by song, Moeris, with two commands, swiftly dispels the dream (lines 66-67):

> Desine plura, puer, et quod nunc instat agamus;
> carmina tum melius, cum venerit ipse, canemus

> Say no more, lad, and let us be about what now hangs over us. We will sing songs better then, when he himself has returned.

This is the last appearance of *nunc*, the final summary of present gloom. *Instat* suggests not so much the impending downfall of nature as the outside forces of violence, the eagle and the spears of Mars, which turn the carrying of goats into a *fascis* imposed on slaves. The tone of physical menace the word conveys can be seen in a phrase such as Horace's *voltus instantis tyranni*,[31] describing the tyrant whose threatening face does not frighten the just man.

Agamus, too, has an unpastoral, sinister ring. As mentioned previously, the vocabulary Virgil uses to describe the omen of the fallen breezes and the tomb of Bianor (*aspice incipit apparere*) turns our attention back to Moeris' words as he visualizes the sudden appearance of Caesar's star (*ecce processit*). We tend to compare the dream world of Moeris' imagined union between pastoral and politics with the reality of the destroyed landscape in which the shepherds are walking. *Agamus* has much the same effect—prosaic, clear-cut, and devastating. We recall the use of *age* and *agendum* in the first, very bucolic, excerpt from Menalcas' songs and make the same contrast between idyllic *otium*, with its negligible trials, and the necessities of the present.

[31] *Carm.* 3. 3. 3.

Eclogue 9

In fact the only reassuring note in the whole poem is the last line which hints that song may be possible again, if and when Menalcas himself, the poet-savior, returns successful.[32] *Venerit* is remarkable. Linguistically it is an echo from lines 2, 13, and 62 which deal with the advent of the disruptive new owner and with the shepherds' dark journey. Moeris hints that there may be a journey of a different sort if Menalcas restores song. It is the one ray of hope.

TAKEN AS A WHOLE, the poem has a balanced unity which depends on two contrasting emotions: optimism and defeat. There is in the excerpts from Menalcas' and Moeris' songs an ascending order of optimism. It is as if, in their dreams prior to their enforced departures, the two worlds symbolized by purple spring and by Caesar could live at peace, as if the static unchanging order necessary to the myth could be maintained. But the fantasy, once imagined by Menalcas and Moeris and now quoted back, is first damaged by the protestations of impotence with which the shepherds intersperse their singing and then effectively destroyed by the framework of reality with which they are surrounded.

With the vivid directness of fact and symbol, Virgil shows the depredation which armed might can wreak on a helpless enemy whose strength is only spiritual. Taking full advantage of metaphor and ambiguity, he conjures up the fallen land through the shepherds' eyes. Whatever the passing optimism of the quotations, it is cancelled with all the devices at a poet's command. Once the impulse of arms has forced its way into the pastoral world, all its beauty is broken.

What was previously subject only to the unchanging laws of nature now becomes the victim of an authority whose existence ought never to be acknowledged. What is conventionally depicted as immortal and untouched by the ravages of time, now feels its existence perishing as inspiration departs from

[32] *Ipse* (67) echoes *ipse Menalcas* (16).

the land. Song is replaced by the oppressive hand of a restrictive society which appropriates all the freedom which the creative mind holds expedient. Freedom now depends on the Orphic figure of Menalcas who attempts a seemingly impossible task of reconciliation and healing. He can create and, through creation, save, but the chances of his success are scant.

There is one phrase—*desine plura, puer*—in Moeris' final words which may help explain more clearly the poet's intent. We saw earlier how Virgil recalls the introduction to the fifth eclogue at two important moments: the phrase *immo haec* used by Moeris at line 26 and Lycidas' command *incipe, si quid habes* at line 32 both echo the interchange of Menalcas and Mopsus in *Eclogue* 5 at lines 10-15, as they discuss a subject for the latter's song. In the same passage Menalcas uses the phrase *desine plura, puer,* as they enter the cave just before Mopsus actually begins to sing: "sed tu desine plura, puer: successimus antro." Menalcas' meaning is that he will countenance no further apologies on the boy's part; nothing should prevent Mopsus from beginning his song then and there.

If previous comparison with the fifth eclogue suggests some inadequacy—when Moeris' *immo haec* prefaces only a quotation from Menalcas and Lycidas' urgent *incipe* is answered with an excerpt from Moeris' past songs—the bitterest irony is this final parallel. What should come near the poem's beginning (as it does in 5) now appears at the end of a poem in which song was discovered to be impossible. The use of *desine* here should be like Menalcas' appeal to Mopsus, to stop the introductory banter and get on with his song. Instead it parallels in tone and meaning the final, suddenly altered, appearance of the refrain of Damon's sad song in the preceding poem: "desine Maenalios, iam desine, tibia, versus." There, though unhappy love has apparently driven a shepherd to commit suicide, nevertheless the song itself is only the imagined effort of Damon at his ease. *Desine* at the end of *Eclogue* 9 is different. It indicates neither the prelude nor the conclusion of a sad song imagined in a happy setting but the end of poetry itself. We have been plunged into a situation where setting and song, landscape and inspiration, are together lost.

We may now face more squarely a question posed earlier: How close is the relationship between the ninth eclogue and the three poems which immediately precede it, and what is this relationship? The brief summary earlier in the chapter indicates the importance in two of them of the dedication and the setting as a revelation of the content and meaning of the subsequent songs. Gone is the mythical cave of Silenus, who knows all things and can change poetry into infinite shapes; gone is the perfect landscape of Daphnis and the charmed world of Damon and Alphesiboeus. Gone, too, is the series of removes between the poet and his reader illustrating how the songs were sung, which reaches the point in *Eclogue* 8 where Virgil is narrating how the Muses inspired Alphesiboeus to quote the words of the lovesick Amaryllis! In their place is something provocative: a dialogue between two real shepherds about the present trials of life and the problems of song. Like its predecessors, it is a poem concerned with poetry, but one in which songs are barely remembered and creativity totally absent.

This is a meditation on the significance of context. Seen as a whole, *Eclogue* 9 describes the search for a setting which the opening lines tell will be futile under present circumstances. Now, because the landscape has been ruined, the poem becomes a compelling social document as well. The pathetic quotation of former songs may offer momentary solace by recalling a dream world in which the imagination was allowed to ramble at will. Memory even dangles the hope that Varus can save Mantua or that the farmer will find Caesar blessing his acres. But in the perspective of the whole, remembrance serves as passing comfort in an atmosphere gone wrong.

In the seventh eclogue the ideal setting for poetry can still be found on the banks of the real Mincius, whither the shepherd Meliboeus stumbles by chance and remains at Daphnis' request. In 9, on the contrary, we have two shepherds already in what was once an ideal setting, forced to flee. Not only is the land destroyed by an enemy encroaching from outside, but the poet-shepherds themselves have been driven out. In brief, the ninth eclogue is one large introduction before a song which does not, indeed cannot, materialize. As such, it is the culmination of the sequence which began with the sixth eclogue and is the more effective for denying that pastoral song, whatever form it take, is still possible.

We are now in a better position to understand something of the relationship between the charming seventh idyl of Theocritus and *Eclogue* 9. To summarize briefly the plot of Theocritus' poem: Simichidas, who narrates the whole story in the first person, is walking from the city, accompanied by Eucritus and Amyntas, to a harvest festival in honor of Deo to be held on the property of Phrasidamus and Antigenes. They fall in with a goatherd, Lycidas, who questions Simichidas about his destination. Simichidas replies with a challenge that he is equal to Lycidas as a singer. He requests that they give over the day and the walk to song, even though he himself scarcely feels he deserves the reputation he possesses. Lycidas, after complimenting him, sings the tale of young Ageanax, whom he wishes to respond to his love, now voyaging over the seas to Mitylene. If Ageanax returns in safety, Lycidas vows, he will hold a feast at which Tityrus will sing of the dying Daphnis and of the captive goatherd and singer Comatas, fed on honey by bees. Simichidas replies with verses about the love of Aratus, scorned by Philinus. "May Pan chasten him," the poet prays. Even so, Philinus is like a too-ripe pear, soon to fall, and Aratus should turn his attention elsewhere.

Neither singer comments on the other, but Lycidas gives Simichidas his staff as a token of friendship and takes leave by a road on the left. Simichidas and his companions continue on to the farm. There they feast in a setting of rural splendor. They recline on rushes and fresh leaves, among poplars and elms, near water pouring from a cave sacred to the nymphs. Here are the lines devoted to the sounds of nature they hear (lines 138-42):

τοὶ δὲ ποτὶ σκιαραῖς ὀροδαμνίσιν αἰθαλίωνες
τέττιγες λαλαγεῦντες ἔχον πόνον· ἁ δ᾽ ὀλολυγών
τηλόθεν ἐν πυκιναῖσι βάτων τρύζεσκεν ἀκάνθαις·
ἄειδον κόρυδοι καὶ ἀκανθίδες, ἔστενε τρυγών,
πωτῶντο ξουθαὶ περὶ πίδακας ἀμφὶ μέλισσαι.

On the shady boughs the dusky cicadas were busy with their chatter, and the tree-frog far off cried in the dense thornbrake. Larks and finches sang, the dove made moan, and bees flitted humming about the springs.

There are pears and sloes in abundance and wine like that served by Chiron to Heracles.

Such a bald summary, though it does no justice to the richness of Theocritus, may at least demonstrate that this, too, is a poem about poetry, a duel in song. But a juxtaposition of the two poems, in general or in detail, ends with the realization that at every turn Virgil evokes the memory of Theocritus only to suggest something else. The idyl has in common with the ninth eclogue the fact that it is one of the most firmly localized of Theocritus' pastoral poems. Several references can be traced to the island of Cos. Likewise, *Eclogue* 9 makes sense only if visualized as taking place in Mantua at a time when new tenants could come into the land and demand the exile of the older farmers. This is all we learn from the poem and all we need to know to understand its background.

Just this summary is enough to indicate the difference between the two poems. Starting with the revelations of the opening lines, Simichidas and friends are journeying from the city into the country to seek relaxation at a harvest festival.

This orientation toward urban life makes it plain that to
Theocritus the pastoral form which some of his idyls take is
in many respects a sophisticated diversion from the involve-
ments of city life; tiny dramas of rustic love and debates in
song can be played against a charming, fictional backdrop.
Such a scenario occasionally blends references to actual people
and places into the spiritual landscape of art, as in the seventh
idyl. Nevertheless there is usually sufficient barrier between
the poet's imagined world and the realities of human life to
assure that the emotions drawn from the reader are tenuous
and pleasant and do not demand concentration on more pro-
voking problems.

Virgil's poem, on the other hand, is centered on the shepherd's world and views all external forces as fraught with potential destruction. A journey out of the country toward the
city, instead of vice versa, is symptomatic of more far-reaching
intellectual discrepancies between Virgil and Theocritus. For
example, Lycidas' protestation that in comparison with the
singing of Varius and Cinna his is like a goose among swans, is
modelled on *Idyl* 7, lines 37 and following. Simichidas, too,
admits that he is a voice of the Muses and that everyone calls
him the best of singers although he is unwilling to believe
them (lines 39-42):

> ‘οὐ γάρ πω κατ᾽ ἐμὸν νόον οὔτε τὸν ἐσθλόν
> Σικελίδαν νίκημι τὸν ἐκ Σάμω οὔτε Φιλίταν
> ἀείδων, βάτραχος δὲ ποτ᾽ ἀκρίδας ὥς τις ἐρίσδω.’
> ὡς ἐφάμαν ἐπίταδες·

'For in my own esteem I am as yet no match in song
either for the great Sicelidas from Samos or for Philetas,
but vie with them like a frog against grasshoppers.' So,
with a purpose, did I say....

We should expect the alteration of names, and Virgil's change
from the frog-grasshopper comparison to the goose-swan

Eclogue 9

analogy is for a purpose, as we have seen. The most important variation can best be illustrated by noting the word ἐπίταδες ("on purpose"). In spite of his apparent modesty, Simichidas' words have a hidden design: to induce Lycidas to sing first so that he can later cap him in song. The spirit of Virgil's Lycidas is different. His shyness is real. He literally cannot sing and in his eyes the comparison of his voice to a goose's cackle is justified. He may, of course, be trying to prod Moeris to sing (*incipe*, he urged a few lines before), but there is no hint whatever that their verses will be directly compared. Unfortunately Moeris replies not with a new song, as does Lycidas in *Idyl* 7, but with a further excerpt from old verses which he hardly remembers.

Idyl 7 is a poem about joy in song, about the beauty and variety of poetry, set in the context of a journey to a haven of particular beauty. The ninth eclogue is opposite in tone and meaning. Virgil's road leads not toward the glorious retreat of a harvest festival but out of the country in the direction of the city, through a landscape wherein song is impossible.

To Virgil, the challenge posed by what is foreign to the land becomes an issue of vital importance. The tension resulting from this challenge, analyzed in its many guises, is one of the fundamental elements of originality in the *Eclogues* and is typical of their essential pessimism. Virgil's pastoral world is no longer the quasi-literal sphere of withdrawal and escape which Theocritus imagines as relief from the complexities of urban life. Rather "pastoral" is in essence a whole mode of being, the summation in one varied, multifaceted metaphor, of the poet's spiritual state. It is all too easy to challenge such a fragile creation. Even the necessary cares which nature imposes upon the shepherds often form a contrast with the ideal setting. Only in his imagination can Virgil conceive a vision in which woods and consul are conjoined, and "pastoral" (that is, poetic freedom) is reconciled with war, politics, and history's advance.

Eclogue 9

Sometimes, as we have observed, the challenge to inner security arises from love which expels the shepherd from his happy state of oneness with the orderly, unchanging laws of nature to review his situation from a distance. Love can lead in either of two directions, to suicide, which means that the violence of emotion has made the shepherd break completely with his world, or to harmony with the schedule of rustic life. The forces antagonistic to the land, however, are not always so simple or so directly related to the connection of the individual to his environment. There are poems in which these external powers have grown to the point of such menace that the shepherds' realm as a whole must cower. This tension, as we have seen, is critical to an understanding not only of the ninth eclogue but also of the first, to which we must turn again briefly for the further light its comparison sheds on the meaning of the ninth.

In both poems Virgil is grappling with a problem which confronted all the Augustan poets, the relationship of individual freedom to arbitrary rule. In these eclogues, liberty means the *otium* of the pastoral myth which allows the poet-shepherd-magician, subject to no compulsion, to tend as well as to "create" his flocks.

There are some superficial distinctions between the two poems. In the first eclogue the dream world is preserved for Tityrus, courtesy of the new young divinity in Rome. In the ninth, there is not even this mitigating vision, shallow as it is. Although both shepherds, in the first, have been singers, Tityrus alone can continue to create. Yet the loss of poetry is only one part of the general malaise from which Meliboeus suffers due to the victory of slavery over liberty. In the ninth the failure of poetry is the specific theme rather than just one of many sorrows connected with the destruction of the land, as in the first. Nevertheless the loss of Mantua and the loss of poetry only prove again that once politics and war impose on the imagination, all integrity will vanish.

Eclogue 9

For some reason both Virgil and Horace, the two greatest poets of the Augustan age, felt compelled to conceive a dream world which served not only for spiritual escape but as a touchstone against which reality could be judged. This is natural in a time of revolution, when standards of all types are in flux. But to destroy the poet's vision is to grant that there is little possibility for the creative mind to play an important role at such a period. We may wonder at the use of bucolic poetry as a vehicle for these ideas. The delicate pastoral myth is easily shattered when confronted with the problems of society. The ideal landscape, as Virgil fancies it, cannot be receptive to the concerns of mankind as a whole and survive, nor can those whose life is devoted to the state be expected to possess total sympathy with the poet's "escape." If the poet be allowed to imagine this visionary world and preserve it (especially if this dream is partially formed from the reality of a Mantua or, in Horace's case, a Sabine farm), then there is hope that life, as a poet would see it, can survive even when pitted against the needs of a growing empire.

The first eclogue shows what happens when the power to free or enslave is left in the hands of an autocracy; the ninth comments specifically on the place of poetry amid the results of civil war. The fourth, on the other hand, maintains that a union between the bucolic "landscape" and society can be achieved by a return of the Golden Age which the poet sees ahead. It would be oversimple to state that Virgil preserved the same balance between optimism and pessimism in his subsequent poetry. His admiration for the accomplishments of Rome is constantly tempered by a stronger, more negative awareness that they are not achieved without loss. The vision of the *Aeneid* may appear less demanding, perhaps even clearer and more realistic than that of the *Eclogues*, because the polarities are less violent. There we do not, after all, have two thoroughly opposed spheres of existence as we do in the first and ninth eclogues, but only two societies fighting each other, one of which seems to present better credentials and set its sights on higher ideals than the other.

Whatever Virgil's fluctuations of mood as he wrote his epic, the end of the *Aeneid* is not the compromise suggested by *Eclogue* 4 visualized in epic terms, but rather his final restatement of the trials of the shepherds in the first and ninth eclogues, which say with equal finality that there is no reconciliation between individual freedom and the uses of empire. As for the *Aeneid*, whatever we may think of the character of Turnus, his suffering and death have much in common with the exile of Meliboeus or of Lycidas and Moeris, as they make their dark and rainy way toward the city.

Extremum hunc, Arethusa, mihi concede laborem:
pauca meo Gallo, sed quae legat ipsa Lycoris,
carmina sunt dicenda: neget quis carmina Gallo?
sic tibi, cum fluctus subterlabere Sicanos,
Doris amara suam non intermisceat undam,
incipe; sollicitos Galli dicamus amores,
dum tenera attondent simae virgulta capellae.
non canimus surdis, respondent omnia silvae.

Grant me this, my last task, Arethusa. A few verses must be sung for my Gallus, yet such that Lycoris herself might read them. Who would deny verses to Gallus? Hence, if you would not have bitter Doris blend her stream with yours as you glide under the Sicilian wave, begin! Let us sing the troubled loves of Gallus, while the snub-nosed goats crop the tender shrubs. We do not sing to deaf ears. The woods echo everything. (lines 1-8)

The phraseology of this appeal to the fountain Arethusa is striking. We have been schooled by earlier *Eclogues* to believe that the life of the shepherd-poet is one of remarkable *otium*, offering complete freedom from care in a landscape complementary to the creation of poetry which is play (*lusus*). If Virgil on occasion treats serious matters in a more elevated tone than appears suitable for "rustic" topics, never (elsewhere in these poems) does he speak of the act of writing as a *labor,* something to be struggled over, especially something which is *extremus*, the last of its line, with ominous intimations of mortality.[1] We have come a long way from Tityrus' easeful life to a prayer that Arethusa grant one final poetic toil.

[1] For *extremus,* see also *Ecl.* 8. 20.

A partial reason for this "labor" we are told forthwith: Gallus has asked for songs and Virgil feels the necessity of fulfilling the request of his poet-friend. But this could not have been any ordinary commission, such as a Pollio or a Varus might arrange. As we have learned from the sixth eclogue, Gallus and his poetry are close to Virgil, who would be expected to pay attention to his listener's intellectual concerns. For Gallus, who understands the traditions of the myth, Virgil might perhaps have written a purely "pastoral" song. These *carmina* are special, however. They are verses *quae legat ipsa Lycoris.* For Gallus' mistress Virgil must do what an ordinary bucolic poet cannot seem to do—he must write something to be read. In the fourth eclogue Virgil speaks of the boy being able, after a time, to read the praises of heroes and the deeds of his father.[2] But this is to speak of history, whether prose or verse. In the introduction to the sixth, he ventures the hope that someone charmed by love might read his verses. Yet the immediate result is to include his hypothetical reader in nature's world of sound and joy: "te nostrae, Vare, myricae, / te nemus omne canet." Lycoris is another matter. For her Virgil must blend customary elements of pastoral poetry with enough of the elegiac material she is used to receiving from her poet-lover to make the present effort understandable, even palatable.

This problem is part of the reason for the poet's *labor,* but it raises other problems which the poem itself will gradually resolve. Once more we are dealing with a poem concerned with the content and meaning of the pastoral world and, specifically, with the type of song that expresses it in words. We have previously seen Virgil make use of other *genera* of poetry for special purposes. Elements of an epithalamium, for instance, are intentionally used in *Eclogues* 4 and 8. But the essence of a marriage hymn, with its search for unity, reconciliation of tensions, and generally happy tone is not foreign to pastoral

[2] *Ecl.* 4. 26.

343

otium. Elegy is a different matter. Gallus is an elegiac poet, and Lycoris his mistress. Their poetic world depends on an urbane and sophisticated view of love's trials and delights. None of this is compatible with the "rustic" life. The poet's "trial" is rightly, therefore, *in extremis*. He seems bound to fail. But how he attempts to resolve the tensions he has created or, more portentous, what form the inevitable failure takes will be important.[3]

Virgil follows his ominous announcement with a prayer to Arethusa which is also a curse. To reverse the poet's words, he cries: "If you do not begin (to grant me the inspiration I need for song), then as you travel your magic way from Greece to Sicily, may the bitterness of sea water mingle with the fresh sweetness of your stream and spoil the charm of your fountain." Though the mention of the Syracusan Arethusa as a specifically pastoral fountain is nothing new (we are rightly meant to think of Theocritean and Sicilian traditions of shepherds' songs),[4] an address to the nymph of the fountain as a source of inspiration is an innovation. It is the manner and matter of the appeal that are unusual, however. This is no simple water sprite, but a devotee of Artemis deliberately represented by the poet in the act of escaping from the arms of the river-god Alpheus and making a magically untainted course

[3] On *labor* and elegiac love, see commentators on line 64 below; on Propertius 1. 1. 9; and on Tibullus 1. 4. 47. Other instances are given in Pichon, *De sermone amatorio*, p. 180. Servius (on line 1) raises another interesting point, observing that the *labor* is not difficult for the poet but that Virgil, in addressing Arethusa, is saying "rem tibi laboriosam, scilicet ut nympha, virginitate gaudens, praestes de amoribus cantilenam" ("that the matter is hard for you, namely that you a nymph, priding yourself on your maidenhood, should bestow a song about love"). Pastoral is a "virginal" form of poetry. For Arethusa—or Virgil, the shepherd—to sing *amores* is as unusual as the discovery of Gallus under Maenalus.

On the merging of pastoral and elegiac elements in *Eclogue* 10, see Robert Coleman, "Gallus, the Bucolics, and the Ending of the Fourth Georgic," *AJP* 83 (1962): 55-71.

[4] E.g., Theoc. *Id.* 1. 117; Moschus 3. 77.

under the sea to become a spring, inspiration for shepherds' verses.[5]

This spring is, we must suppose, Virgil's emblem for all bucolic poetry as he begins to write his final eclogue. The pastoral is a form of song which ideally should maintain a course free from the "stain" of foreign elements and remain the offspring of a remote world, delicate and aloof from the violence of conscious suffering. But the presence of love's madness within the shepherd's retreat suggests the mingling of bitter with sweet against which the poet prays.[6] There is a hint that the pursuit of the passionate Alpheus may yet bring about the destruction of the chaste Arethusa as she flies toward Syracuse. As always in the *Eclogues*, if these two antagonistic realms do clash, it can only result in the collapse of the pastoral myth.

For Virgil to hint that this doom may be love's triumph is to preach a symbolic homily directly to Gallus, and less obviously to himself. For the moment he is only the singer of Gallus' woes. The subject matter of the shepherd's song, even if it is love, is of little importance so long as the shepherd himself is not the victim of the trials he imputes to others. If he is, he must either return to "pastoral," as does Corydon in the second eclogue, or withdraw, the course chosen by Da-

---

[5] Devotion of Arethusa to Artemis is a common theme. See, for instance, Arethusa as huntress in *G*. 4. 344; and *Aen*. 3. 694f. Also Servius on line 1 (quoted above, note 3); Ovid *Met*. 5. 572ff.; Statius *Sil*. 1. 2. 203, etc.

[6] The adjective *amarus* denotes that "bitterness" which is ruinous to nature (see *Ecl*. 7. 41). The waters of "pastoral," especially pastoral love, are sweet and fresh. See *Ecl*. 5. 47 and, for love, 3. 110, where the contrast between happy and unhappy love is seen in terms of *dulcis* versus *amarus*. No such union could or should be possible in a pastoral context. For *amarus* in elegy see Pichon, *De sermone amatorio*, p. 83, and H. E. Butler and E. A. Barber, eds., *Propertius* (Oxford, 1933) on Propertius 1. 1. 33. Lucretius (4. 1133-34) speaks of the *amari aliquid* which can well up even within the fountain of delight (*de fonte leporum*) and choke off love.

mon's shepherd in *Eclogue* 8, although there the singer himself has no part in the action. Here the shepherd-poet is apparently like his flocks, as aloof from the emotional aspects of his song as the snub-nosed goats innocently cropping the sprouts.[7] The variation of the proverb in line 8 seems to express only the poet's joy in the resounding echo from the woods which greets his song, not any personal concern for, or involvement in, what he sings.

We have learned only the topic of this song, requested by Gallus—the story of the latter's *sollicitos amores*. Carefree "pastoral" rarely sees such a thing: the elegiac, unpastoral word *sollicitus* appears only here in the *Eclogues*. Rustic love involves dalliance with a Phyllis or an Amaryllis, not infatuation. At line 9 we begin to hear of the setting of Gallus' troubled love:

> Quae nemora aut qui vos saltus habuere, puellae
> Naides, indigno cum Gallus amore peribat?
> nam neque Parnasi vobis iuga, nam neque Pindi
> ulla moram fecere, neque Aonie Aganippe.

What woods or what glades held you, maiden Naiads, when Gallus was dying of an unworthy love? For neither the ridge of Parnassus nor of Pindus, nor Aonian Aganippe detained you.

Indigno amore peribat is a close description of his suffering. We have seen it once before in the tale of Damon's unhappy shepherd who also suffers from unrequited love (*indigno*

---

[7] The lines contain several words not used elsewhere in the *Eclogues*: *attondent, simae, virgulta* and *surdus*. With *simae capellae* most critics compare Theocritus *Id.* 8. 50: σιμαὶ ἔριφοι. One might note also *Id.* 3. 8, where the shepherd calls himself σιμός, offering this as a reason why Amaryllis rejects him. The goats are *simae* here because they are ugly and have nothing to do with the strange world of passionate love. Gallus is unused to nature's instinctive order. The reason for the practical overtones in the vocabulary will be clearer at the poem's conclusion.

amore—*Eclogue* 8, line 18) and who is forced to cry *ut vidi,
ut perii* even after the first glimpse of his girl (line 41). These
expressions are elegiac and strange to pastoral; they occur
only at these two moments in the *Eclogues*. So foreign is their
concomitant emotion that Damon's shepherd, as we have seen,
is driven to his death. What then of Gallus? How can he be
allowed into the country, apparently dying of an "unworthy"
love?[8]

The lines which surround the suggestion of unworthy love
clarify the questions somewhat, only to raise further doubts.
They are modelled, as any literate Roman would have recognized, on the lines with which Thyrsis opens his pastoral
elegy on the death of Daphnis in the first idyl of Theocritus
(lines 66-69):

πᾷ ποκ᾽ ἄρ᾽ ἦσθ᾽, ὅκα Δάφνις ἐτάκετο, πᾷ ποκα, Νύμφαι;
ἦ κατὰ Πηνειῶ καλὰ τέμπεα, ἦ κατὰ Πίνδω;
οὐ γὰρ δὴ ποταμοῖο μέγαν ῥόον εἶχετ᾽ Ἀνάπω,
οὐδ᾽ Αἴτνας σκοπιάν, οὐδ᾽ Ἄκιδος ἱερὸν ὕδωρ.

Where were ye, Nymphs, where were ye, when Daphnis
was wasting? In the fair vales of Peneius or of Pindus? for
surely ye kept not the mighty stream of Anapus, nor the
peak of Etna, nor the sacred rill of Acis.

Yet in spite of the similarity of question and explanation, these
lines are at variance with Virgil's. Theocritus' Thyrsis wonders
where the nymphs were as Daphnis lay dying. Though they
might have been by the Peneius or on Pindus, they certainly

[8] The parallels with *Eclogue* 8—the flock cropping grass, and a
shepherd singing of someone else's suffering (which in 10 takes on a
new twist)—are clear. The difference may be recorded in vocabulary
at the start: *indigno deceptus amore* is changed to *indigno amore
peribat*. As for the distinguishing words, the first (*deceptus*) has overtones of magic suitable to *Eclogue* 8, the second (*peribat*) is essentially elegiac. The history of each love varies accordingly. The phrase
indigno amore is an important addition by Virgil to his Theocritean
source.

were not with him under Etna, by the streams of Anapus
and Acis. By their presence, in rivulets nearby, they might
have consoled him or even lent more tangible aid. Virgil
makes a different point, of special importance to an understanding of *Eclogue* 10.

Where were the pastoral Muses when Gallus needed help,
is the question Virgil asks. They were neither on Parnassus
nor Pindus nor by the fountain of Aganippe. It is not, however, their presence at the apparent deathbed of the youth
that matters at all but their attendance at the traditional sources
of poetic inspiration, here specifically of bucolic song.[9] In
some way, yet undisclosed to the reader, the inspiration of
bucolic song to Gallus is going to be a crucial element in the
attempt to save him from the love-death that *peribat* implies.

This raises another contrast between the two poems. Gallus,
we soon learn, has little clear connection with the landscape
in which he is placed. Daphnis, on the other hand, belongs
under Etna's shadow. He is in the actual setting which, for
Virgil, is the source of song. At line 117 of the first idyl Daphnis bids farewell to Arethusa (Virgil's pastoral Muse) and

[9] Servius seems therefore only partially correct when he comments:
"videtur hoc dicere, quia, si cum ipso fuissent musae, id est si dedisset
operam scribendis carminibus, non incidisset in tantas amoris angustias"
("he seems to say this because, if the muses had been present with him,
that is, if they had given him the task of writing songs, he would not
have fallen into such amatory difficulties").

Parnassus, Pindus, and Aganippe are mentioned only here in the
Eclogues. On Pindus, see Horace *Carm.* 1. 12. 6 (with the accompany-
ing note in *Q. Horatius Flaccus*, ed. Adolf Kiessling; 8th ed., ed.
Richard Heinze [Berlin 1955]). On Aganippe, the spring-nymph as
source of inspiration, see commentators on Callimachus frag. 696
(*Opera I: Fragmenta*, ed. Rudolf Pfeiffer [Oxford, 1949]) and Catullus
61. 28-30. She corresponds to Arethusa, but in less specifically pastoral
terms.

On the difference with Theocritus, see Gow's commentary on *Id.* 1.
66, which misses the point of Virgil's changes. The same motif of the
presence or absence of divinity at a crucial moment is used by Callimachus (frag. 75 in Pfeiffer) where the presence of Artemis is stressed.

at line 140 he goes to a river (possibly even Arethusa again, or a neighboring stream) which closes over him. In the seventh idyl we learn that the "hill" was troubled for the lovesick Daphnis and that the oaks which grew by the bank of the river Himeras sang in mourning. Daphnis is one with the landscape and it grants him immediate sympathy.[10]

Further on in *Idyl* 7 (lines 76-77) we should note that the oaks sang Daphnis' dirge: εὖτε χιὼν ὥς τις κατετάκετο μακρὸν ὑφ᾽ Αἷμον / ἢ Ἄθω ἢ Ῥοδόπαν ἢ Καύκασον ἐσχατόωντα ("when he was wasting like any snow under high Haemus or Athos or Rhodope or remotest Caucasus"). Though he is actually not there at all, the effect of unhappy love is to seem to remove him from his rural quiet and place him under remote hills, melting like snow. It is an imaginative master stroke on Virgil's part to take a simile in Theocritus and expand it into the landscape where the suffering Gallus is placed. Neither literally nor metaphysically is he near Arethusa. Rather he is to be found beneath Lycaeus and Maenalus, the mountain from which Pan must be summoned in *Idyl* 1 to bring comfort to Daphnis.[11] There is nothing in Theocritus to suggest that the real hills of Arcadia could grant Daphnis peace. There is little in Virgil. On the contrary, the hardship provoked by the trials of love is transferred from the calming oaks by the river's edge to a lonely landscape of chill rocks which reflects the soul's state. Whatever the prospects for the future, there is little immediate solace for Gallus in this complementary union of setting and spirit, and little inkling of what form any possible connection with the pastoral world will take.[12]

If a comparison with the first *Idyl* reveals that Virgil is again

---

[10] *Id.* 7. 74-75.   [11] *Id.* 1. 123-26.

[12] The attempt by Friedrich Leo (*Hermes* 37 [1902]: 14ff.) and H. J. Rose (*The Eclogues of Vergil*, pp. 108ff.) to find actual reasons to put the historical figure Cornelius Gallus in Arcadia at this time is forlorn.

dealing specifically with poetry, it also forces the reader to analyze the relationship between Gallus and Theocritus' Daphnis. The Daphnis of *Idyl* 1 is the ideal shepherd, beloved by
all nature, who vowed to give love a fall and not yield to
the maiden who wanders about, searching for him.[13] As a result he wastes away, a victim of Aphrodite's wrath. Though
love is a theme common to each poem, Virgil's sketch of Gallus, at least hitherto, is the antithesis of Theocritus' Daphnis.
Here is the poet of elegy *par excellence*, suffering the elegist's
stock malady of unhappiness brought on by his love for Lycoris
which, at the moment, she chooses not to return. Why has an
elegist suddenly appeared in a pastoral preserve, in a context
which forces a comparison with nature's prime hero?

The next lines continue with further direct acknowledgment
of *Idyl* 1 (lines 13-15):

> illum etiam lauri, etiam flevere myricae,
> pinifer illum etiam sola sub rupe iacentem
> Maenalus, et gelidi fleverunt saxa Lycaei.

Even the laurels, even the tamarisks wept for him, even
pinebearing Maenalus and the crags of chill Lycaeus
wept for him as he lay under a lonely rock.

Here Virgil follows lines 71-75 of *Idyl* 1 wherein we are told
how animals, wild and tame, mourn the dying Daphnis. But
this is no Sicilian riverbank on which we find ourselves in
Eclogue 10. Virgil places the lovesick Gallus among the rocks
and crags of Arcadia whence Daphnis calls Pan in *Idyl* 1
(lines 123-26):

> ὦ Πὰν Πάν, εἴτ᾽ ἐσσὶ κατ᾽ ὤρεα μακρὰ Λυκαίω,
> εἴτε τύγ᾽ ἀμφιπολεῖς μέγα Μαίναλον, ἔνθ᾽ ἐπὶ νᾶσον
> τὰν Σικελάν, Ἑλίκας δὲ λίπε ῥίον αἰπύ τε σᾶμα
> τῆνο Λυκαονίδαο, τὸ καὶ μακάρεσσιν ἀγητόν.

[13] *Id.* 1. 82-83, 85.

O Pan, Pan, whether thou art on the high hills of
Lycaeus, or rangest mighty Maenalus, come to the Sicilian
isle and leave the mountain peak of Helice and the
high tomb of Lycaon's son wherein even the Blessed
Ones delight.

It is natural enough to expect that the unhappy poet should
find himself beneath Pan's mountain, as does Damon's shepherd in *Eclogue* 8, seeking comfort in the echo of his song.
But the details are novel. Though the *mise en scène* is literally in Arcadia, it can in no sense be considered bucolic. Cold
rocks and lonely crags have little to do with the shepherd's
inner pleasance. Rather they offer as much contrast to it on
one side (we might call it "nature") as urban society does
on the other. The shepherd in *Eclogue* 8 finds himself under
Maenalus only when forced from his rustic happiness into
an extreme state, bordering on despair. A comparison with
Tityrus, *patulae sub tegmine fagi*, or Daphnis in *Eclogue* 7,
sub arguta ilice, indicates the impossibility of finding comfort
in such a spot.[14]

If this is one difference between Virgil's and Theocritus'
poems, there is another still clearer. The only parts of nature
which actually mourn for Gallus are inanimate: laurels,
myrtles, and the chill cliffs.[15] For Daphnis, on the other hand,

[14] Compare Virgil's description of the landscape in which Orpheus
wanders after the loss of Eurydice in *Georgic* 4 (lines 508ff.; 517ff.).
    The idealistic notions that have often clouded analysis of Virgil's
depiction of Arcadia (as, for instance, in Bruno Snell, "Arcadia: The
Discovery of a Spiritual Landscape" in *The Discovery of the Mind*
[Oxford, 1953], pp. 281-309) have now been sufficiently counteracted.
See, for instance, Gunther Jachmann, "L'Arcadia come paesaggio
bucolico," *Maia* 5 (1952): 161-74.

[15] The threefold use of *etiam* gives particular emphasis to its appearance in line 14. Within the limits of the "pathetic fallacy," the mourning of chill mountains is quite a different thing from the echoed cry
of laurels and myrtles. That the mountain offers an emotional response
is all the more hyperbolic given the fact that in ancient literature the
chill hardness of remote hills is almost universally symbolic of lack
of love.

all animals from the gentlest kine to the fiercest lions bewail his suffering. He is part of their existence and his death is their great loss. For Gallus it is not the creatures of nature who mourn but only the setting. The reason for this is perhaps not far to seek. The cattle cannot weep for him as they can for Daphnis in *Idyl* 1 (or *Eclogue* 5, for that matter) because they do not know him as part of their world. The inanimate landscape, on the other hand, can comfort anyone with its echo. Tamarisks and laurels can sing, but only as a reaction to words and music given them by others. They reflect Gallus' lament. The actual inhabitants of "pastoral," from the animal world to its human and divine denizens, can only stand amazed at this creature whose whole existence must seem strange to them. They, too, sense that he should be singing of love in a different context and in a different way.

It is reasonable to ask another question which the remainder of the poem alone can answer: Could this place, so filled with potential destruction for the bucolic ideal (as *Eclogue* 8 has shown), have any legitimate connection with elegy? Or has Virgil merely imagined Gallus in a natural setting to facilitate the transition into the shepherd's world? As in the case of any possible link between Gallus and Daphnis, Virgil hints at a poetic distinction, visualized thus far as a tension between ways of life which are mutually exclusive. For the world of elegy, suffice it to quote here the simile with which Propertius adorns his first poem.

The unhappy poet finds no success in his love for Cynthia and lives with passion unabated and gods adverse. He tells of some, however, who have better luck (lines 9-16):

> Milanion nullos fugiendo, Tulle, labores
>   saevitiam durae contudit Iasidos.
> nam modo Partheniis amens errabat in antris,
>   ibat et hirsutas ille videre feras;

ille etiam Hylaei percussus vulnere rami
saucius Arcadiis rupibus ingemuit.
ergo velocem potuit domuisse puellam:
tantum in amore preces et benefacta valent.

Milanion by avoiding no trials, Tullus, overcame the
harshness of cold-hearted Atalanta. For now he wandered distraught in the caves of Parthenius, and went to
face shaggy beasts. Moreover, stricken by a blow from the
club of Hylaeus, he groaned from his wound by the crags
of Arcadia. Therefore he was able to overcome the swift-
footed maid. Such an effect have prayers and good deeds
in love.

To suggest a definite parallel between Gallus, *sola sub rupe*
under the mountains of Arcady, and Milanion, *saucius Arcadiis rupibus* undergoing the *labores* that finally won him his
girl, is to go beyond what Virgil has already told his reader.
We will return to Propertius later, but the parallel in setting
raises points worthy of consideration. Virgil has placed his
friend at a crucial imaginative and spiritual juncture, of
which setting is the external reflection. Is he, the lovesick elegist, underdoing the necessary trials to win his mistress or seeking escape into nature's wildness? Or is this wildness but a
stepping stone into the realm of pastoral which likewise offers
a retreat contrasting with the traditional rigors of the elegist's
life?

With these questions in mind we must return to the setting
(lines 16-18):

stant et oves circum (nostri nec paenitet illas,
nec te paeniteat pecoris, divine poeta;
et formosus ovis ad flumina pavit Adonis)

The sheep, too, stand around. (We do not trouble them;
do not be troubled by the flock, divine poet. Even beautiful Adonis fed sheep by the streams.)

This is the only example Virgil gives of the animal world's reaction to the plight of this poet, so strange to them. The sheep merely stand around. So unused are they to him (and, we assume, he to them), that Virgil must make excuses for their presence or, put more positively, urge Gallus not to take an immediate dislike to them. After imagining him into this setting, Virgil then envisions his first reaction to it. Sheep are a prime symbol of the pastoral world and its poetry, and Virgil senses the possibility of immediate hate on the part of sophisticated elegist and sheep alike. But how can Gallus move from Maenalus into a true pastoral landscape if he develops an initial dislike of something so essential?

This problem notwithstanding, the words are an invitation into pastoral. We may compare the doubling *paenitet-paeniteat* with the only other use of the word in the *Eclogues*, in 2 at line 34.[16] Corydon is telling Alexis how he can imitate the song of Pan: "nec te paeniteat calamo trivisse labellum: / haec eadem ut sciret, quid non faciebat Amyntas?" The situations are similar. Corydon, like Virgil in 10, is trying to persuade the urbane Alexis to enter his world. Though he fails in his purpose (as Virgil, too, ultimately will) he outlines some of the potential joys of a shepherd's life, among them singing and playing on the pipe. But there is a stress to Virgil's words in the tenth eclogue which gives them a level of intention different from Corydon's plea in 2. Virgil is talking to someone who is already a *divinus poeta*, who has made his mark on a contrasting branch of poetry. Gallus is not only a friend of Virgil and a man of the world, but he is also probably the first writer of subjective love elegies in the form later refined by Tibullus, Propertius, and Ovid.

The analogy of Gallus to Adonis is, therefore, carefully chosen to suit this particular moment in the plan of *Eclogue*

---

[16] On the many parallels between *Eclogues* 2 and 10 see Büchner, *P. Vergilius Maro*, col. 169; Luigi Alfonsi, "Dalla II alla X Ecloga," *Aevum* 35 (1961): 193-98.

10.[17] Gallus is not so much a necessary spirit of beauty as was Alexis in *Eclogues* 2 and 7. As yet he knows nothing of the bucolic life and the only hint we have had of any affection for him from within the pastoral world comes from the poet-shepherd himself. Rather Gallus is compared to the beautiful Adonis, one of Venus' special favorites (suitable comparison for the lover of Lycoris and the writer of love poetry) who could, in spite of his divine paramour, still feed sheep by the river. But Virgil is begging the final question which he raises with the emphatic address, *divine poeta.* Love and the feeding of sheep may not be irreconcilable elements (though the example of Daphnis, the ideal shepherd, is kept before us), but what of their respective representations in poetry? To rephrase an earlier question: Can the writer of subjective love elegies also embrace a "rustic" world and write pastoral poetry?

The question remains as Virgil continues his exposure of Gallus to things rural in the form of those who come to gaze upon, and offer advice to, the stricken poet (lines 19-30):

venit et opilio, tardi venere subulci,
uvidus hiberna venit de glande Menalcas.
omnes 'unde amor iste' rogant 'tibi?' venit Apollo,
'Galle, quid insanis?' inquit 'tua cura Lycoris
perque nives alium perque horrida castra secuta est.'
venit et agresti capitis Silvanus honore,
florentis ferulas et grandia lilia quassans.
Pan deus Arcadiae venit, quem vidimus ipsi
sanguineis ebuli bacis minioque rubentem.
'ecquis erit modus?' inquit 'Amor non talia curat,
nec lacrimis crudelis Amor nec gramina rivis
nec cytiso saturantur apes nec fronde capellae.'

[17] On Adonis as shepherd and at the same time lover of Aphrodite, see Theoc. *Id.* 1. 109; 3. 47. Of Gallus' connections with "Aphrodite" we have little doubt. But he is no Adonis unless he likes sheep, here apparently a matter of some question.

The shepherd came, too, the slow swineherds came, Menalcas came, wet from the winter's acorns. All ask: "Whence arose this love of yours?" Apollo came. "Gallus, why this madness?" he says. "Your beloved Lycoris has followed another through snows and rough camps." Silvanus came, his forehead wreathed with rustic crown, waving fennel flowers and tall lilies. Pan, god of Arcadia, came, whom we ourselves saw, reddened with the crimson berries of the elder and with vermilion. "Will there be an end?" he says. "Love does not care for such things. Cruel love is not sated with tears, nor the grass with streams, nor bees with clover nor goats with leaves."

First comes the shepherd (his flock has preceded him), then the swineherds. They are followed by Menalcas, who with good reason is the first visitor named directly. He makes us think back not only to the protagonist of *Eclogue* 3 but also to that Menalcas of the preceding eclogue, the shepherd-poet whose absence spells the momentary or final doom of the pastoral existence. He is like Meliboeus in 7, for he too comes from utilitarian affairs into a situation concerned specifically with poetry. He stands for something in between the life of the humble shepherd or swineherd and the divinities who appear next. He is that special being who is involved in the practicalities of the bucolic existence and yet is able to raise it to a superhuman level with his poetry. Were we to think of him in the terms which *Eclogue* 9 suggests, we might well grace him with the epithet Virgil applies to Linus in the sixth eclogue: *divino carmine pastor*. Then comes Apollo, one of the countryside's essential divinities, to make the coverage complete and serve as a transition to his colleagues Silvanus and Pan, the last to appear and the most important.

Looking simply at the figures who form this catalogue we are struck by the difference between it and the list of those who watch Daphnis suffer, according to Theocritus, in *Idyl*

1—first Hermes, then neatherds, shepherds, and goatherds, then Priapus, and finally Aphrodite herself.[18] Save for the common presence of those whom one would expect to find in any countryside, the figures are dissimilar. Hermes and Priapus have possible kinship with Daphnis and each has some partial connection with the landscape, though the garden-god Priapus is more georgic than pastoral. The presence of Aphrodite would ordinarily spell disaster for the rustic life.[19] Hence the culmination of Virgil's catalogue is carefully chosen to point out the purpose in his alteration. Aphrodite entered into Daphnis' life and destroyed him because he remained faithful to a vow of Artemis-like purity. In contrast Gallus comes from a sphere which already belongs to Venus and finds himself in a setting where he can be visited by all the rural world, even by three of its most famous divinities.

Yet Gallus' world is as strange to the shepherds as Daphnis' is to Aphrodite in *Idyl* 1. The verbs ἦνθε and ἦνθον, which Theocritus uses five times in his catalogue of Daphnis' visitors, are paralleled by the sixfold appearance of *venio* in these lines from *Eclogue* 10. Each group, arriving to look at the victim, knows the cause of his ailment and their inquiries offer a degree of comfort. But Daphnis, already dear to the nymphs, is in his proper setting and in the end is absorbed into the waters of his spring Arethusa, next to which he sings his final complaint. Gallus must appear unusual to Pan and his colleagues first for the peculiarly strong emotion to which he is subject, then for the landscape in which he is placed, which they must leave their special province to visit.

[18] *Id.* 1. 77-95. On the list of divinities present and the differences between *Ecl.* 10 and *Id.* 1, see Coleman, "Gallus, the Bucolics, and the Ending of the Fourth Georgic," esp. p. 60.

[19] So strongly is *Amor* considered an anti-pastoral divinity that it is the conceit of his inclusion in pastoral that is a major point of Tibullus 2. 3. That Tibullus was thinking of *Eclogue* 10 as he wrote is clear from the several parallels (e.g. Tib. 2. 3. 11 and *Ecl.* 10. 18). In Tib. 2. 1 Cupid is visualized as a god whose return to the countryside (where he was born) could only spell disaster.

The first question they put to Gallus is not like Hermes' initial inquiry in *Idyl* 1 (lines 77-78): "Who torments thee, Daphnis? Of whom, friend, art thou so enamoured?" Virgil's shepherds are not initially concerned with the person involved but with the strange power of the emotion he suffers. This power is stressed by the use of *tibi* but is already inherent in the emphatic *iste* ("that love of yours"). Then Apollo makes his revelation. Daphnis' death, we recall, is caused by Aphrodite because of a maid who is in love with him and wanders about searching. Gallus' girl is the real Lycoris who not only has nothing to do with rural life but, to make matters worse, is unfaithful to him and goes off with someone else.

Apollo, the seer, appears to know a good deal about Gallus' life and about the conventions of elegy as well. *Quid insanis?* is an elegiac expression. The answer Apollo supplies must seem naïve in the eyes of the elegist, though the detail must be supplied to the reader. The fact that Lycoris has run off with a soldier, through snow and dreadful campsites, is the reason for Gallus' unhappiness, which to Apollo borders on madness. What is striking about Apollo's words, however, is not their artlessness; they introduce a new world into the poem and draw the reader's attention away from the parading specimens of rusticity to the other claims upon Gallus—Lycoris and the elegy. And in viewing Gallus as an elegist, we must look specifically from the vantage point of Rome. *Conscia Roma* is the center of the elegist's existence. It is from Rome that Lycoris would depart with her soldier friend for faraway snows. Apollo's words sound a note which is elegiac, yet practical and Roman. In each respect they are discordant with the gentler voices of a sylvan muse.

Apollo raises the question of Gallus' frenzy and apparently settles it to his own satisfaction. There is no need for passion now since his girl has left him, and that is that. Then come Silvanus and Pan, each of whom is separately sketched by Virgil. The epiphany of Pan (*quem vidimus ipsi*), painted with the vermilion with which triumphant Roman heroes were colored, puts into relief the importance of the occasion.[20] In the opening lines of *Georgic* 1, in the list of divinities called upon by the poet to lend aid as he undertakes his new task, Pan and Silvanus have the place of honor, yielding only to Augustus who had become the poet's special divinity. Pan holds the position of Augustus here. That the role of Silvanus and Pan in *Eclogue* 10 is also of a poetic nature is a point which will be discussed later. At the moment we should note how Pan takes up where Apollo left off, but with more understanding of the manner in which Gallus suffers. '*Ecquis erit modus?*' he asks. Is there no limit to Gallus' love?

The meaning of Pan's question, and its elegiac cast, is elucidated by line 30 from Propertius 2. 15: "verus amor nullum novit habere modum" ("True love knows no limit"). This is an elegist speaking, of course, but Pan wonders whether or not the same sentiment should be applied to Gallus (as Gallus would certainly assume and maybe want). The word *modus* seems originally to have been used of a piece of land with fixed bounds. In *Georgic* 2, line 20, Virgil uses *modi* for the individual types of growth nature has given plant life. This, too, has the sense of physical confinement. The best commentary on the passage, however, is gained from a comparison with *Eclogue* 2, line 68, where the lovesick Corydon cries: "me tamen urit amor: quis enim modus adsit amori?"

In each of these instances the word has several overtones. If in a physical sense it defines something fixed in time or space, something limited by laws of growth and stability, metaphysically *modus* means the containment of emotion by subjection to any of the rules which hold sway over the universe. It is not misleading to think of its companion virtue as *moderatio*, reason in the face of irrationality. Thus Corydon,

[20] For the color, see commentators on *Ecl.* 6. 22 (as well as above, chap. 5, n. 2) and Tibullus 2. 1. 55, etc. On *video* and the epiphany of a divinity, cf. *Ecl.* 1. 42.

for example, looks at his emotional state and judges its abnormality against the standards of regularity to which the physical realities surrounding him conform. The sun's heavenly course maintains an exacting discipline and the shepherd's life follows a stipulated order dependent on the sun's *modi*. But emotion, when seen in terms of Propertius' elegiac definition, is without bounds; it transcends any confining norms which might serve as models of human behavior, especially if one happens to be a poet-shepherd.

Lack of *modus* is anti-pastoral because it destroys that order and fixity which are necessary to regulate nature, especially emotion. Pan compares Love's craving for tears with the desire bees have for clover, goats for foliage, and pastureland for water. But these are imperatives on the level of animal instinct, necessary for survival and for the preservation of beauty. Love's yearning for tears is beyond this. By defining its cruelty in these terms, Virgil proposes reasons why elegiac love is essentially antagonistic to "pastoral" and is indeed quite uncreative when seen from the shepherd's viewpoint. *Amor* himself, like Gallus, is a lover and he yearns especially for tears. But Virgil leaves vague the frame of reference which surrounds *talia* in line 25. Does it mean Gallus' tears specifically (and we recall how the landscape echoes his cries) or some more general situation of which they are but a part? Gallus' words, which follow, give a further explanation. We need only mention here what the reader might well already expect, that Gallus, the elegist, of necessity yields to the disorder which Apollo and Pan see in his life, while Corydon, the poet-shepherd, whose love is outside the ordinary rustic existence, reasonably accepts the pastoral life again.

Gallus begins his reply (lines 31-34):

> tristis at ille 'tamen cantabitis, Arcades' inquit
> 'montibus haec vestris, soli cantare periti
> Arcades. o mihi tum quam molliter ossa quiescant,
> vestra meos olim si fistula dicat amores!'

But sadly he replies: "Nevertheless, Arcadians, you will sing these things to your mountains. Arcadians alone are skilled at singing. O how gently my bones then would rest if one day your pipe would sing of my loves!"

He first observes what for him probably would have been a paradox, that the shepherds can happily and unceasingly sing of love as long as it is not their own.[21] *Haec* picks up *talia* in line 28. If the shepherds were to sing after his death of the trials that led to it and of his loves in general, then his bones would lie at peace. Gallus begins again where *peribat* (line 10) left off, with a further announcement that his love-death is imminent. But the notion that he, poet of elegiac love, will be buried in the land of shepherds is itself ingenuous. Once more, Virgil, with careful irony which in the end he turns back on himself, gives us Gallus' mistaken idea of "pastoral." Gallus would undoubtedly enjoy being considered a figure like Daphnis, the handsome hero who dies of love and whose tomb (as we learn from *Eclogue* 5) would be a focal point for the sylvan world. But if we may judge from Daphnis' reaction in the first idyl, to be reminded of his unhappy experience with love is the last kind of comfort which he needs, either while dying or after death. Gallus' thinking is diametrically opposed to this. He wants the quiet of what he considers to be a rural tomb and yet demands the elegiac comfort of hearing *amores* sung after his death.

The paradox is reflected in his choice of words. *Ossa quiescant* is a common enough phrase. Virgil uses a variation of it, for instance, at *Aeneid* 6, lines 327-28:

[21] It is interesting that when Gallus begins his tale of woe he addresses his plaint to the shepherds (*Arcades*, lines 31 and 33). One of the two additional times the word is used in the *Eclogues* (the other is 7. 4) is at 7. 26, where the proud Thyrsis calls upon his confreres, *pastores Arcades*, instead of the Muses, assuming already the possession of their inspiration. Gallus, on the other hand, because the Muses are away from their traditional seats, can only seek aid from the shepherds. The higher level of poetic madness, which can grant comfort and create a new spiritual milieu, is missing.

nec ripas datur horrendas et rauca fluenta
transportare prius quam sedibus ossa quierunt.

Nor is Charon allowed to carry them across the dread
banks and roaring floods until their bones lie in a quiet
resting place.

Gallus' request has nothing to do with the underworld except
that without a quiet burial no admittance is granted to the
realm beyond the Styx. At *Aeneid* 6, line 371, Palinurus asks
Aeneas to take him across the waves "sedibus ut saltem placidis
in morte quiescam" ("that at least in death I may have a quiet
resting place"). The Sibyl unfortunately reminds him that
this is impossible because he is *inhumatus*. He does not have
the proper *sedes* of a tomb in the world above.

Still, there is something beyond the mere *quies* of a proper
burial that Gallus seeks. *Quam molliter*: "How softly my bones
would rest in their tomb," he cries, "if your pipes sang of my
loves!" *Molliter* is an elegiac word (this is the only place it
appears in Virgil's major works) and adds a special touch to
Gallus' request. We may watch, for example, the uses of *mollis, molliter*, and *quies* in Propertius' third elegy of his first
book. At line 7 the poet speaks of the *mollem quietem*, the soft
quiet which his mistress breathes as he steals silently in upon
her. At line 12 he attempts to approach her couch *molliter*, but
ends not daring to disturb her sleep (*quies*, line 17). Finally, at
line 34 we find her leaning with her elbow on a soft couch
(*in molli toro*) as she begins to lecture her returning lover on
his supposed infidelity.[22] Even presupposing a death and burial
in Arcady, Gallus cannot do without that elegiac flourish
which reveals something more essential to him than a rustic
tomb. When, a moment later, he describes for Lycoris the

[22] See below, pp. 383-85. That bones in the tomb will have a happy
rest if a lover is faithful is also an elegiac conceit. See Propertius 1. 19.
18 and cf. Cynthia's final words to her poet at 4. 7. 94: "'. . . mecum
eris, et mixtis ossibus ossa teram'" ("'you will be with me, and I will
rub bone against mingled bone'").

beauties of the scene, *mollia prata* are among the ingredients of perfection. For Lycoris the adjective would add amatory connotations to suit Gallus' passing purpose.[23]

Before looking further at Gallus' speech, it is well to bear in mind another contrast which runs through the poetry of Propertius and which is of some interest here: that between this *mollis quies*, associated with the elegiac conception of love, and the *dura quies* of the elegiac love-death. We will examine later an imposing instance of this contrast in the eighteenth poem of his first book of elegies, where a pastoral landscape, in which the poet seeks escape, turns into one so un-elegiac as to threaten imminent harm. The phrase *dura quies* is taken over by Virgil in the *Aeneid* to describe a harsh death, and that certainly is implied by Propertius.[24] But we are dealing with the ambiguities of elegiac verbal custom as well as the obvious implications. In the landscape of Propertius 1. 18 the only *quies* possible is *dura,* which implies not only death but specifically that type of death which lacks love. Gallus' demise, on the other hand, will be *mollis* because, pastoral as the context in which he finds himself is, the shepherds will remind him of his elegiac past as they continue to sing of his loves.

Thoughts of death do not long remain with him (lines 35-43):

> atque utinam ex vobis unus vestrisque fuissem
> aut custos gregis aut maturae vinitor uvae!
> certe sive mihi Phyllis sive esset Amyntas,
> seu quicumque furor (quid tum, si fuscus Amyntas?

---

[23] The adjective *mollis* appears approximately forty times in Propertius alone. In the *Eclogues* the word is only used to describe inanimate objects, usually the soft and gentle aspects of the landscape. On *mollia prata,* see *G.* 2. 384 and 3. 521. Propertius (3. 3. 18) puts the phrase into Apollo's mouth to describe the locale over which Propertius' little wheels should roll, after he has given up the mighty chariot of epic!

[24] *Aen.* 10. 745; 12. 309.

et nigrae violae sunt et vaccinia nigra),
mecum inter salices lenta sub vite iaceret;
serta mihi Phyllis legeret, cantaret Amyntas.
hic gelidi fontes, hic mollia prata, Lycori,
hic nemus; hic ipso tecum consumerer aevo.

And would that I had been one of you, either a guardian
of your flock or trimmer of the ripening grape. Certainly
whoever my love was, whether it was Phyllis or Amyntas
(what then if Amyntas is swarthy? Violets are dark and
dark are hyacinths, too), would lie with me amidst willows under a pliant vine. Phyllis would pluck garlands for
me, Amyntas would sing. Here are cool springs, Lycoris,
here soft meadows, here a grove; here with you I would
be eaten away (by love) for my whole life.

In fact, he begins to turn from thoughts of death to contemplation of what it might have been like had he been part of the
pastoral world—*ex vobis unus.* Thus far there has been a contrast between their mountains (*montibus vestris*) and his
bones (*mihi ossa*), their pipe (*vestra fistula*) and his loves
(*meos amores*). Could these have been ultimately united, he
ponders.

The first thing involvement with the shepherd's calling
brings to Gallus' mind is the role of guardian of a flock or
dresser of the ripening grapes. Immediately thereafter he
thinks, as we would expect, of love. First it is love such as he
might consider *à la mode* in pastoral. The figures are typical.
A Phyllis appears in *Eclogues* 3 and 7, and in 5 (at line 10)
Menalcas proposes the *Phyllidis ignes* as a topic for Mopsus'
song. We also come upon an Amyntas in the second, third,
and fifth eclogues. (In the third, at line 66, he is characterized
by Menalcas as *meus ignis.*) With the names changed to
Amaryllis and Menalcas, these lines of Gallus' are akin to
Corydon's outburst in *Eclogue* 2, lines 14-16:

nonne fuit satius tristis Amaryllidis iras
atque superba pati fastidia? nonne Menalcan,
quamvis ille niger, quamvis tu candidus esses?

Was it not better to endure the bitter wrath and proud
disdain of Amaryllis? Better to endure Menalcas, though
he is swarthy, though you fair?

The repetition of *niger* seems deliberately to reflect one context in the other. Corydon, Amaryllis, and Menalcas exemplify
love Gallus has known within "pastoral," difficult, perhaps,
but tame in comparison to the feelings that the unpastoral
Alexis arouses. Even here, as Gallus begins to imagine the
possibility of bucolic love, he calls his rustic *amour*—someone comparable to Phyllis or Amyntas—*quicumque furor,*
again an elegiac concept. The word *furor* is used only once
elsewhere in the *Eclogues* and that later in this poem (line 60).
Yet so much a part of the pastoral world does he already
imagine himself that he feels impelled to take up one of its
stock motifs, to anticipate objections that his love is *fuscus* and
answer them with the equally stock comparison to flowers!

The scenery begins to alter as Virgil allows us to watch Gallus imagining a rural life. We know from line 14 that he is literally *sola sub rupe iacentem*, beneath pine-bearing Maenalus.
With the thought of Phyllis making his garlands and Amyntas singing to him, Gallus fancies that his love would lie with
him among willows under the pliant vine—"mecum inter
salices lenta sub vite iaceret." This is a large change. For *sola*
we now have *mecum*, and in place of the rocky mountain
slopes Gallus finds himself beneath an arbor! For a moment,
but again only in thought, we have put aside the suffering
lover's lonely stance among empty hills, for the happy center
of ideal pastoral, the *otium* of love, leisure, and song.

The vision grows brighter still. Though Phyllis and
Amyntas be true denizens of the landscape, Gallus' particular

ideal cannot be completed without the presence of his love,
Lycoris. The hierarchy of emotional progression follows an almost geographical pattern. First there is the appeal to the shepherds at line 31, as if Gallus had no special part in their world
and they were to sing his sufferings to the mountains, taking
the same pose he would, were he a lovesick shepherd. Then
we pass within the magic circle, first to a mention of rustic
loves and then, finally, to the possibility of Lycoris herself coming into the countryside, to unite the elegiac and pastoral
worlds and give final shape to Gallus' momentary dream of
perfection.

So much does Gallus now assume himself part of the bucolic
world that he can pretend to play the shepherd-lover and
offer an invitation to Lycoris in phraseology we have frequently seen Virgil use elsewhere.[25] A major point of the second eclogue is Corydon's summons to Alexis—*huc ades, o
formose puer*—and the enumeration of the beauties he will
find there. But the essential idea of the poem is the completion
of perfection through love (*mecum*, lines 28 and 31). Were
Gallus really in the position of Corydon (as he imagines himself for an instant), he might be confronted with similar
difficulties; but in reality his situation is different. We might
also recall Moeris' quotation of his own song to Galatea in the
preceding poem. The song is the perfect picture of love coming into the countryside from outside and is little distant from
the cool fountain, soft fields, and grove which Gallus imagines
are his to offer Lycoris.

Even here, however, the elegiac element is not entirely
absent. At the culmination of the invitation Gallus cannot suppress a yearning for his particular kind of love—*hic ipso tecum
consumerer aevo*. The phrase is particularly hard to interpret.
It certainly has something of the meaning assigned to it by

[25] See 1. 51-56 (*hic . . . hic . . . hinc*), especially 1. 51-52 for details
(*inter flumina nota / et fontis sacros*). *Mecum* (1. 79) anticipates
mecum (10. 40) and *tecum* (10. 43).

critics, for instance by Conington ("Here we grow old together, decaying by mere lapse of time") and by Fairclough ("Here, with thee, time alone would wear me away"). Though the phrase *consumere aevum* is Lucretian, the verb *consumo,* which does not appear elsewhere in the *Eclogues,* conveys the special elegiac meaning of "to pass" or "spend" in love.[26] To see this we need only refer to Cynthia's rebuke to her lover Propertius: "namque ubi longa meae consumpsti tempora noctis?" ("For where have you used up the long nighttime that belonged to me?"). Her addition of *meae noctis* underscores the importance of Gallus' *tecum* in an elegiac as well as a pastoral sense. Hence we may venture a further periphrasis: "I would pass the time of this whole age with you," that is, for an elegist, "I would be consumed with love for you for this whole age." The only other unpastoral note is the reference to the passage of time; this shatters the bucolic spell and, along with the ambiguity of *consumo,* suggests momentarily the theme of death of which the elegists were so fond. Nevertheless, the totality is Gallus' present ideal, a quasi-elegiac love in a setting of rural serenity.

But the idea of a happy Lycoris in such a locale is as ridiculous to an elegiac poet as it might be pleasing to a writer of idylls. Thus from the imagined world of what might have been we plunge with challenging briskness into the present (lines 44-49):

> nunc insanus amor duri me Martis in armis
> tela inter media atque adversos detinet hostis.
> tu procul a patria (nec sit mihi credere tantum)
> Alpinas a, dura, nives et frigora Rheni
> me sine sola vides. a, te ne frigora laedant!
> a, tibi ne teneras glacies secet aspera plantas!

[26] For *consumere aevum*, see Lucretius *De Re. Nat.* 5. 1431. For elegiac uses of *consumo*, see Propertius 1. 3. 37 and Tibullus 1. 9. 62-63.

Now a mad love of hard Mars holds me in arms, in the midst of weapons and hostile foes. You, far from your native land (would that it were not for me to believe such a thing), ah, hard-hearted creature, you look at Alpine snows and the chill of the Rhine alone, without me. Ah, may the chill not harm you! Ah, may the sharp ice not cut your tender feet!

Virgil is fond of this contrasting use of *nunc*. In *Eclogue* 8, lines 43 and 52, for instance, it marks the difference between youthful, idyllic love and the shepherd's present woes. Each of the four uses of *nunc* in the ninth eclogue demands a juxtaposition of the former happy world and the present ruin which confronts the city-bound shepherds. Here in *Eclogue* 10 Virgil gives us a contrast which is unexpected.

There is nothing startling up to the phrase *insanus amor*. Love has been the theme of the poem,[27] and we remember Apollo's question: *"Galle, quid insanis?"* But Gallus' thoughts suddenly turn away from his passion for Lycoris to another aspect of his life, his career as a soldier and politician which he characterizes as an insane love for harsh Mars. The imaginative jump leaves the reader disoriented, but the revelation is of significance. Instead of *inter salices* and underneath a pliant vine, we are now *tela inter media atque adversos hostis*. For soft meadows we have in exchange the arms of the hard god of war. The verbal contrasts, for which *nunc* prepares the way, emphasize that this type of *amor* is equally insane, when visualized in bucolic terms. We need refer only to Moeris' statement in *Eclogue* 9, lines 11-13—that poetry has as much effect in confrontation with the weapons

[27] The word appears in lines 6, 10, 21, 28, 29, 34, 44, 53, 69, and 73. Curiously there are only two other uses of *insanio* and *insanus* in the *Eclogues*: *insanire*, at 3. 36, where the shepherds are about to indulge in the "madness" of song, and *insani* applied to the waves of Galatea's maddened, unpastoral province, at 9. 43.

stability of pastoral endurance. Chalcidian verses will be exchanged for what Virgil styles, at the beginning of *Eclogue* 6, *Syracosio versu*, the verse of Theocritus, which involves living in *silvae* and possessing a *silvestrem Musam*. The lines are reminiscent of the way in which Virgil describes his achievement in those words which may have opened the *Aeneid*: "ille ego, qui quondam gracili modulatus avena / carmen" ("I am he who once sang his song on the slender reed").

There is no implication that the contents of the *carmina* are to be changed. In fact Gallus explicitly says the opposite. Whether he will clothe them in an elegiac or a pastoral garb, his songs will still be concerned with love. But, though the topic remains the same, the change of style denotes a change in the tenor of emotion as well. The sylvan loves of "pastoral," proclaimed to the accompaniment of the Sicilian shepherd's pipe, are of a different emotional order from the subjective strains of elegy. Here *pati* is the key word. It is the shepherd-poet's lot to endure the trials of love without the complaint which is a stock in trade of the elegist. To quote an example outside of *Eclogue* 10, one need only recall Corydon's outburst against Alexis in *Eclogue* 2 (lines 14-15): "nonne fuit satius tristis Amaryllidis iras / atque superba pati fastidia?" ("Was it not better to endure the bitter wrath and proud disdain of Amaryllis?"). He, too, is comparing the suffering he has experienced from ordinary love with the more excruciating torture to which unpastoral Alexis is subjecting him. For Gallus, the role of Alexis is first assumed specifically by Lycoris and then expanded to embrace the whole antagonistic elegiac world.

He will express his loves by writing them on trees and as the trees grow, claims Gallus, so will his loves. The idea is beautiful yet disquieting. The custom of writing the name of one's beloved on a wall or carving it on a tree dates from time immemorial. It seems to come into classical literature with

of Mars (*tela inter Martia*) as doves do against eagles—to realize the resulting antagonism.

These lines must be taken in close conjunction with those which follow. From the *me* of line 44, Gallus as the soldier and slave of Mars, we change to the emphatic *tu* meaning Lycoris, at 46. Nor is this a Lycoris imagined into a happy landscape, but a more realistic Lycoris about whose peregrinations we have been forewarned by Apollo's description at line 23: "perque nives alium perque horrida castra secuta est." This vision as well as that of Gallus the soldier offers a challenge to the previous dream. The snow, cold, and ice are opposite to the cool fountains and smooth fields of the shepherd's life. (Perhaps the poet wants us to think of Lycoris' tender feet finding a more appropriate setting amid soft meadows than on Alpine slopes.) Gallus' dream postulated union (*tecum*); reality purveys dissolution and infidelity (*me sine*). Lycoris is *sola* only from Gallus' point of view, because she is not with him. Actually he is alone (*sola sub rupe*) while she keeps company with someone else.

The stance, one need scarcely observe, is again elegiac. Commenting on line 46 Servius announces cryptically "hi autem omnes versus Galli sunt, de ipsius translati carminibus" ("But all these verses are Gallus', taken over from his poems"). What he means by *omnes* is a moot question. It is only from line 46 to line 49 that Gallus places himself in one of the stock situations of the elegiac lover, deserted by his girl. We may quote as an interesting parallel (the verbal similarities are striking)[28] lines near the beginning of Propertius' eighth elegy

[28] See especially Jean Hubaux, *Festschrift* Deonna (Brussels, 1957): 269-77 (=*Properziana*, 31-38). The resemblance had already been noted by P. J. Enk (ed., *Propertius, Elegiarum Liber 1: Monobiblos* [Leiden, 1946]) in his commentary on 1. 8. 9, and Alfred Ernout ("Note sur Properce, I, 8, 9-16," *Mélanges* Grat [Paris, 1946]: 22, n. 2). On this and other echoes of the *Eclogues* in Propertius and Tibullus see, among others, Franz Skutsch, *Aus Vergils Frühzeit* (Leipzig, 1901), pp. 12-14; Jean Hubaux, *Les thèmes bucoliques dans la poésie latine* (Brussels, 1930), pp. 91ff.

in his first book where he also has apparently been deserted by Cynthia for someone who is going to take her to chill Illyria (*gelida Illyria*) (lines 5-8):

> tune audire potes vesani murmura ponti
> fortis, et in dura nave iacere potes?
> tu pedibus teneris positas fulcire pruinas,
> tu potes insolitas, Cynthia, ferre nives?

Do you have the steadfast courage to hear the roaring of the maddened sea, and have a hard boat for your bed? Or press the fallen frosts with tender feet? Or endure, Cynthia, unaccustomed snows?

The setting in which Lycoris now finds herself has an ironic connection with Gallus' present plight. Her infidelity has drawn her into a context reminiscent of that into which her hard-heartedness has driven Gallus. And her new lover is a soldier, the career which Gallus himself pursues. Nevertheless, facing up to his military duties also involves acceptance of Lycoris' infidelity.

Taken as a whole, these six lines reflect the two sides of Gallus, his two loves, one for *durus Mars* and the other for *dura Lycoris*.[29] Each is a hard taskmaster but essential in Gallus' life. The realistic note of each—the arms of Mars, the Alpine snows, and the cold of the Rhine—jars strongly with any rustic idyl, indistinct in time and place.[30] Gallus acknowledges that true "pastoral," which he has so comprehensively conceived and summarized, is challenged by the realities of his double

---

[29] The three other uses of *durus* in the *Eclogues* are at 4. 30; 8. 43 (*duris in cotibus*, where love dwells); and 8. 52 (*durae quercus*, which can lose their wonted nature and bear honey or apples only as an *adunaton*). Ovid (*Am.* 1. 9, esp. 11-16) offers an example of how the landscape of a lover's trials and the setting for military exercises can be combined.

[30] On *patria*, see *Ecl.* 1. 3-4 (all told the only uses of the substantive in the *Eclogues*).

---

life, his mad love for Lycoris (and its expression in e[legiac] verse) and his passion for Mars and the affairs of war.

Gallus has shown his listeners what might have been [and] what now is. Then, virtually half way through his la[ment,] with a suddenness to which we have now become accusto[med,] he switches to the future (lines 50-54):

> ibo et Chalcidico quae sunt mihi condita versu
> carmina pastoris Siculi modulabor avena.
> certum est in silvis inter spelaea ferarum
> malle pati tenerisque meos incidere amores
> arboribus: crescent illae, crescetis, amores.

I will go and the songs which I composed in Chalcid[ic] verse I will sing on the pipe of the Sicilian shephe[rd.] Surely it is better to suffer in the woods among the lairs [of] beasts and to carve my loves on tender trees. They w[ill] grow, you will grow, my loves.

The previous lines intimated a challenge between two [kinds] of landscape which, in turn, implied contrary ways of life[. We] now have a direct statement of what we have long sensed. [But] this controversy is concerned directly with problems of p[oetry] as well. On the creative level it is a conflict between pas[toral] and elegy, and is only given physical form in the actua[lity] of the surrounding landscape.

Though certainty is impossible, Probus assures us [that] *Chalcidico versu* refers to elegies written by Euphorio[n of] Chalcis, the "color" of whose works Gallus followed in [his] verse.[31] Gallus would then be saying (what seems a l[ogical] addendum to his previous thoughts) that he will give u[p the] elegiac coloring to his poetry in favor of a more pastoral [tone.] The elegiac pattern of unhappiness will be replaced by [a]

---

[31] See "Probus" on 10. 50 (in *Appendix Serviana*, ed. Herr[mann] Hagen [Hildesheim, 1961]).

Aristophanes, and there are examples of it in Theocritus and Callimachus (Acontius inscribing the name of Cydippe). Propertius gives a new twist to the theme in the eighteenth elegy of his first book (lines 19-22).[32] Gallus' version—that love grows with the tree—is also apparently new. But, as in the case of the verb *consumo*, he gives an elegiac turn to what might otherwise have remained essentially a pastoral conceit. It is strange even to think of the elegiac Lycoris involved with the countryside. It is almost an anomaly to think of Gallus, within "pastoral," celebrating his love for her by writing on trees. But the thought that love can grow, whether from presence or absence, is basically an elegiac *topos*. Again we may illustrate with a *sententia* from Propertius, this time from the twenty-first elegy in Book 3, lines 3-4:

> crescit enim assidue spectando cura puellae:
> ipse alimenta sibi maxima praebet amor.

Indeed yearning for my mistress grows with gazing on her unceasingly. Love himself provides his greatest nourishment.

The image of potentiality in *cresco* can only be disastrous. "Pastoral" confines and orders all things, especially emotion. Though much about elegiac poetry is highly stylized, it still cannot accept the presence of idealism, especially in a setting which limits emotional expression. Elegiac love neither seeks nor remains subject to any such limits as "pastoral" demands for its survival.

One other point is troublesome. In the bucolic world, which relies on memory for its song, the idea of writing is suspect. When Moeris states at the outset of the fifth eclogue that he is about to sing "in viridi nuper quae cortice fagi / carmina descripsi et modulans alterna notavi," the reader takes special notice. We have also seen the strategic value of *legat* in line

[32] For the *topos* see Pfeiffer on Callimachus frag. 73; Enk on Propertius 1. 18. 22. (See p. 383 for Propertius 1. 18. 19-22.)

2 of *Eclogue* 10 as a signpost that the subsequent verses will be to a degree elegiac.

There is still another difficulty: although the writing of the name of one's beloved on a tree is a regular topic of amatory literature, one wonders whether *tenerisque meos incidere amores / arboribus*—the carving of names or even verses (*amores* is rightly ambiguous)—is the proper occupation for someone who has just espoused the attitudes of a pastoral poet. Virgil stated that *sollicitos Galli amores* would be the subject of his song and Gallus himself has recently announced that his bones would rest quietly *vestra meos olim si fistula dicat amores*. It should now be Gallus' role to sing of his loves, to do what he had previously claimed was impossible and take over Virgil's position at the poem's outset. This he does not seem prepared to do.

At line 55 Gallus makes another sudden alteration in imaginative perspective (lines 55-60):

> interea mixtis lustrabo Maenala Nymphis,
> aut acris venabor apros. non me ulla vetabunt
> frigora Parthenios canibus circumdare saltus.
> iam mihi per rupes videor lucosque sonantis
> ire; libet Partho torquere Cydonia cornu
> spicula. . . .

Meanwhile I will explore Maenalus in company with the nymphs or I will hunt wild boars. No frosts will prevent my surrounding the glades of Parthenius with hounds. Even now I seem to make my way among rocks and sounding groves. It is a joy to shoot Cydonian arrows from a Parthian bow.

We have visualized, with Gallus, the bucolic life in relation to his present trials and future plans as a possible pastoral poet. *Interea* heralds an intervening stage between his double life of elegiac poet and soldier and his imagined future existence

374

as pastoral poet and rational lover. We are back in the setting
of the poem itself, on the wild slopes of Maenalus, where Gallus has been singing all this time.[33] Yet this is no longer a
dread refuge, scene of negative yearning for a love-death, but
the same landscape turned to a different purpose. It is as unpastoral in its way as the world of elegy and Rome. Though
hunting can be accepted as a necessity for shepherds (we
think of the several references to it in *Eclogue* 3, for instance),
as an actual occupation, or especially as a metaphor for search
and pursuit, it is at variance with that peace and unity which
the bucolic life assumes. The "hunting" metaphor which runs
through *Eclogue* 2 is a reflection of Corydon's insecurity.

Mixtis nymphis is gratuitous and enlightening, indicating
that even here the elegist does not completely suppress himself. But in general the setting now means something different from what the poem's opening might have led us to expect. For this brief dream[34] Gallus is neither lovesick shepherd nor elegist but someone apart, a stranger to love of either
the pastoral or the elegiac variety. One of the many tongue-
in-cheek suggestions Ovid offers the distraught lover in the
Remedia Amoris, to rid himself of the *otia* he declares to be
the greatest cause of unhappiness, is to take up hunting as part
of a general pattern of escape, literally from Rome but symbolically from practical or spiritual problems.[35] This is what

---

[33] *Gelidi* (in line 15) anticipates *frigora* (57); *rupe* (14) leads to
rupes (58).

[34] *Videor* is particularly suggestive of a dream. The expression
seems to be imitated by Horace at *Carm.* 3. 4. 5-7, as he thinks of a
setting which inspires him to play the role of *vates*. It is possible that
Gallus, too, is imagining himself in a context which he hopes might
inspire him to the composition of poetry in the manner of the Sicilian
shepherd. For an elegist this is the height of fancy as well as folly.

[35] See Ovid *Rem. Am.* 222. On the *topos* of change of scene as illustrated in therapeutic literature and adopted by Cicero in *Tusc. Disp.*
4 and by the elegiac poets, see K. Prinz, "Untersuchungen zu Ovids
Remedia Amoris," *WS* 36 (1914): 64ff.; and L. P. Wilkinson, *Ovid
Recalled* (Cambridge, 1955), p. 136. Horace's ode to Lalage (*Carm.*

Eclogue 10

Gallus now proposes to do by surveying Maenalus for boars, enduring the Arcadian cold, surrounding Parthenian glades with hunting dogs, and twisting Cydonian arrows against his prey.

We may summarize the ideas Gallus has thus far presented. At the start of his lament Gallus thinks of himself purely as an elegist, accepting the anomalous posture of someone dying an elegiac love-death in wild country on the verge of the bucolic world. He then ponders what it might have been like to be a part of rural life, which he describes vividly to Lycoris. This is a feat of the imagination for he is still among the lonely rocks and chill crags of Lycaeus, a far cry from *gelidi fontes* and *mollia prata*. Nevertheless his words are virtually an invitation to Lycoris—and to himself—to enter the pastoral idyl. As he reaches the climax of his invitation, he suddenly announces *hic ipso tecum consumerer aevo*. At the most important place in a catalogue of bucolic symbols we find the poet once more acknowledging his reliance on an elegiac liaison. For him the pastoral myth could only be viable if it included within its precincts the hostile force of elegiac love.

We might expect Gallus to realize straightaway the impossibility of such a union. Though he does come to this conclusion in lines yet to come, he turns first to reasons why his present life cannot afford even the opportunity to contemplate such a vision. With *consumerer* we are in the realm of what might have been. With *nunc* (line 44) the fancied dream vanishes, and we plunge back into Gallus' real life of double *amor,* for Mars and Lycoris, each *durus* or *dura*, hard and unbending and hence contrasting with *molliter* and *mollia prata*. The truth is that his existence is impossible in the bucolic world. Instead of being cured by his imagined sojourn, he becomes further assured of the necessity of his double insanity.

---

1. 22) is thus a witty reversal of the usual approach, that love will be forgotten if the lover places himself in some superficial extreme (see Steele Commager, *The Odes of Horace* [New Haven, 1962], p. 132).

Yet at line 50 Gallus reaffirms that as a poet and lover he
will embrace his version of pastoral, living *inter spelaea
ferarum*, as if he were already poking fun at the rusticity of the
idea! In the meantime, not without the company of the
nymphs who might lend some sweet solace to the horrors of
such a transition, he will hunt and plunge into the wilderness
minus, of course, such curiosities as Pan and sheep which ill
befit the barren reaches of Maenalus, at least on this occasion.

The decision to hunt is short-lived. With line 60 comes another turnabout in Gallus' mood and resolution:

> . . . tamquam haec sit nostri medicina furoris
> aut deus ille malis hominum mitescere discat.
> iam neque Hamadryades rursus neque carmina nobis
> ipsa placent; ipsae rursus concedite silvae.
> non illum nostri possunt mutare labores,
> nec si frigoribus mediis Hebrumque bibamus,
> Sithoniasque nives hiemis subeamus aquosae,
> nec si, cum moriens alta liber aret in ulmo,
> Aethiopum versemus ovis sub sidere Cancri.
> omnia vincit Amor: et nos cedamus Amori.

As if this were a cure for my madness or that god could
learn pity for human ills! Now once more neither
Hamadryads nor songs themselves give us pleasure. Once
more farewell, even you woods. Our trials are not able to
change him, not were we to drink of the Hebrus in
weather most chill and brave Thracian snows during
wintry sleet, nor were we to drive the sheep of the Ethi-
opians beneath the star of Cancer when the dying bark
withers on the lofty elm. Love conquers all. Let us also
yield to love.

That such fluctuations are the lover's prerogative is one of the
lessons of *Eclogue* 2, but lines 60-69 in 10 make clear a final
difference between the two poems. Corydon is the shepherd

who returns to his country occupations after a bout with an unsatisfactory love. Gallus may pretend to embrace the pastoral spirit but his final decision is to renounce its aloofness and return to the battleground of love and war.

The shepherd's life, had it performed its part adequately, would at most have been a *medicina furoris*. Even this phrase is elegiac and reflects the truth of Gallus' mood. We need only refer to Propertius' comfortless words to his Gallus, faced with the possibility of falling in love with Cynthia in the fifth elegy of his first book (lines 27-28): "non ego tum potero solacia ferre roganti, / cum mihi nulla mei sit medicina mali" ("I will not then be able to bring comfort to you when you ask, since there is no cure for my own ill"). Propertius paved the way for this admission of his powerlessness in an earlier outburst (lines 3-4): "quid tibi vis, insane? meos sentire furores? / infelix, properas ultima nosse mala" ("What do you want, madman? To learn of my frenzy? Poor creature, you are hurrying to discover the worst of ills"). However extreme the remedy, the true god, *deus ille,* understands no gentleness toward the stricken lover. Were *Amor* to relent, Gallus might embrace a refined and restrained pastoral love.[36] But this is as impossible for the elegist as the discovery of a cure. Any interest in the Hamadryads or the sound of shepherds' songs must for the true elegist be only a passing affectation, embraced in a moment of escapism, but soon denied when the full meaning of the renunciation becomes clear.

The finality of *ipsae rursus concedite silvae* is undeniable. One is tempted to compare it with the cry of the shepherd, at line 58 in *Eclogue* 8, immediately before his suicide: "omnia vel medium fiat mare. vivite silvae." But the situations which elicit the two farewells are different. Gallus is returning to his wonted sphere of love by preference rather than relinquishing the bucolic life because of dissatisfaction. For him love is life

[36] *Mitescere* reminds us of many pastoral emblems, for instance the *mitia poma* which Tityrus offers to Meliboeus (*Ecl.* 1. 80).

with its sufferings and joys. For the troubled shepherd unrequited love pushed to an extreme spells suicide. A union of
rustic idealism with the world of affairs, with the day-to-day
concerns of the progress of history, may seem possible in the
fantasy of *Eclogue* 4. But when, as in *Eclogue* 10, Virgil
descends to actual cases to examine a situation in which he is
emotionally involved, he can only accept the final antagonism
that exists between "pastoral" (both as a poetic style and as a
mode of life) and the realities of the Roman social and creative world around him. The emotional tensions of elegy are
just as destructive to the idyl as the imposition of inimical
social forces, and when such tensions and forces are combined
in the figure of Gallus, the chances of his reconciliation with
the idyl seem distant. They grow even more remote once Virgil confesses the degree of his own emotional connection with
Gallus' words.

The verb *concedite* first suggests thoughts beyond the mere
withdrawal of Gallus. It turns our attention to the imperative
use of the same verb in line 1, as the poet craves Arethusa's
inspiration for one last song (*extremum concede laborem*).
It is noteworthy that in line 64, immediately after the implied
farewell of *concedite*, Gallus announces that his *labores* have
been unable to change the hard god of love. The juxtaposition
gives us reason to ponder the poem's first line yet again.

On the surface the line is Virgil's request for support from
his muse, but it is peculiar, as we observed earlier, that a pastoral poet, concerned with the uses of leisure, should demand
the bestowal of *labor*. When *labor* in whatever form, from
physical action to the subtlest spiritual trials, challenges *otium,*
it spells doom. The implication leads the reader one step further. If Arethusa does grant *labor*, especially one which is final
and conclusive, then there may be a sense of the sadness of departure, partially present in Gallus' *concedite*, in the poet's
initial *concede*. The *labor* may be the poem itself. More specifically, it may be the poem as a measure of Virgil's affection

for Gallus. The use of the word is, in fact, an admission, first of the difficulties of writing a poem which attempts to merge elegiac and pastoral elements, secondly of the trials of love which form the essence of Gallus' life, and which here seem to reflect the shepherd-poet's emotion as well. *Concede* is a prayer for inspiration which, because of the emotional similarities of Virgil's situation with that which causes Gallus to cry *concedite*, ultimately demands a withdrawal. But this is to anticipate for a moment.

Gallus tells us more of his *labores* in lines 65-68. These trials are not efforts to gain love but to bring about a forced oblivion. The lover may leave the elegist's natural surroundings for harsher scenery either with the hope of returning victorious, as does Milanion, or with the desire of escaping from love, as does Orpheus after the loss of Eurydice.[37] If Gallus at first deceives us (and himself) into thinking that the latter alternative is his reason for embracing a rural lot, we now learn otherwise. No shepherd's existence however extreme (be it hot or cold, dry or wet, north or south, summer or winter, and so forth) can replace the elegist's foreordained stance. Love and its imaginative vehicle, elegy, easily win the day over "pastoral." For Gallus there is no alternative.

Hence the famous line *omnia vincit amor* is only the terse pronouncement of the predestined.[38] The negative farewell to the woods and to the possibility of forgetting elegiac love in such a context yields to *Amor*'s expected triumph. It is the double victory of that *indignus amor* the elegist will always

[37] *G.* 4. 507-20.
[38] I cannot agree with Segal (*Tamen Cantabitis, Arcades*, p. 261) that, at this point in the poem, Gallus "would abandon Mars for a poetic Arcadia." Love's victory is over Arcadia as well as Gallus. It is also misleading to argue (as, for instance, does J. J. Wilhelm, *The Cruelest Month* [New Haven, 1965], pp. 42 and 215) that Virgil is here urging Gallus "to rise up and put love aside." Neither Gallus nor Virgil dismisses *amor* at the end of *Eclogue* 10. Virgil's point is quite the reverse.

feel for his girl and the *insanus amor* of war and the affairs of state. The combination, as we have seen, forms the physical and spiritual world of Gallus and forces a rejection of the pastoral myth.[39] The line may remind us of the shepherds in *Eclogue* 9, who are also *victi* because chance has overturned their whole existence (*omnia*). There, however, the shepherds stand alone against a ruthless power, which destroys the spirit by force of arms. *Eclogue* 10 is a special *tour de force* because the elegiac and pastoral worlds are juxtaposed in Gallus' purely mental conflict. The compliment to Gallus is as manifest as the outcome is predictable.

We have compared Gallus with Corydon, but the distinction between them may now be seen more clearly. Corydon's statement at line 62 in *Eclogue* 2—*nobis placeant ante omnia silvae*—should be contrasted with Gallus' renunciation—*concedite silvae*. Corydon easily returns to a sylvan life which can only prove unreal for Gallus. Though the result of Gallus' dilemma is easily anticipated, the evolution of his decision —and this is the core of the poem—certainly is not. In one sense he is part of Alexis' world in *Eclogue* 2, hostile to Corydon and his ways. But he is also held in affectionate esteem by Virgil, shepherd and singer of eclogues. And he is a poet himself, capable of formulating the most subtle intellectual problems. That Virgil's mind is the medium through which Gallus' thoughts are refined matters little in the evaluation of their expression.

As a vehicle for Gallus' emotions, then, the poem is a movement between two spiritual poles, each with its tangible attributes. We are now in a position to review the poem's various types of landscape in the hope of answering some of the questions projected earlier. At the center of the dream is the inner retreat of cool fountains and soft fields, of a love without care. Although Gallus imagines such a place in lines 37-43,

[39] On *vincere* see Pichon, *De sermone amatorio*, pp. 294-95. *Cedo* itself has elegiac overtones (see, e.g., Ovid *Am.* I. 2. 9-10).

and even imagines Lycoris into it, nevertheless it is different
from the chill and lonely slopes of Maenalus where Virgil
places Gallus. Such are the extremes to which he must submit as further *labores* to escape his love. There is pastoral love
in the bucolic world and elegiac love in Rome, but in the wild
landscape surrounding Maenalus and beyond, love is unwel-
come. Though this setting may challenge "pastoral," it is also
a stepping-stone into it, as Gallus says at the beginning and
end of his song. He too might have been a shepherd, drinking the Hebrus in winter or dwelling in torrid Ethiopia
where the dying bark withers on the elm.

To balance the setting, on the other side of true "pastoral" as
it were, is the reality of Gallus' life, the spiritual world
of elegiac poetry and the physical sphere of arms and warfare.
There is common ground between the two. As noted, one of
the *labores* to which he might fruitlessly subject himself in his
search for relief is to endure the cold, to drink the Hebrus
amid winter chills (*frigoribus mediis*), and bear the snows of
Sithonia (*Sithonias nives*). Yet one of the sufferings to which
Gallus really is subjected is the loss of Lycoris to another soldier
whom she has followed to the north, to the *Alpinas nives et
frigora Rheni*. It is ironic that she undergoes the same difficulties in escaping from Gallus with a new lover as he dreams
of suffering in attempting to escape from his liaison with her.
But the final victory of love over Gallus' contemplated withdrawal is the victory of endurance over escape. The backdrop
for this victory is provided by the actualities of Lycoris' north-
ern adventure, not the dream of an Orphic pose of renunciation which might have meant an acceptance of sylvan routine.

Each of these worlds, the wild and the civilized, the one in
which Gallus is placed by the poet and the other of which he
is ordinarily a part, is incompatible with the refuge of the poet-
shepherd. It is true that the scenery of Maenalus and Lycaeus
could lead into the pastoral landscape. The latter is Pan's
homeland and both are part of the traditional haunt of the

lovelorn swain, venting his sorrows to the wilderness. But Gallus is not like the Tityrus of *Eclogue* 8: he is looking from the outside in, contemplating an impossible dream, not rejecting a dream become a nightmare. Should his location on Maenalus draw Gallus into "pastoral," it would demand a spiritual conversion of impossible magnitude. Gallus' concluding cry is a return to life from death. The rigorous suppression of love's trials proves impossible.

We may appeal to Propertius for final clarification of the relationship between landscape and idea, setting and poetic form. In the eighteenth elegy of the first book he imagines himself as having escaped from Cynthia to a place where he can complain, alone and undisturbed, of his bitter griefs (lines 1-4):

> Haec certe deserta loca et taciturna querenti,
> et vacuum Zephyri possidet aura nemus.
> hic licet occultos proferre impune dolores,
> si modo sola queant saxa tenere fidem.

Here for certain is a lonely, quiet spot where I may lament, and the breath of the Zephyr is master of an empty grove. Here one may safely utter hidden griefs, provided the lonely rocks can keep faith.

If nothing else will prove his devotion to her, at least the trees will reflect it (lines 19-22):

> vos eritis testes, si quos habet arbor amores,
> fagus et Arcadio pinus amica deo.
> a quotiens teneras resonant mea verba sub umbras,
> scribitur et vestris Cynthia corticibus!

You will be witnesses, if trees have ever loved, beech and pine beloved of Arcadia's god. Ah, how often do my words re-echo beneath your soft shade, and how often "Cynthia" is written on your bark!

This, as we have seen, is a pastoral pose.[40] The words *vos eritis testes*, addressed to a beech or pine, echo the shepherd's lament in *Eclogue* 5—*vos coryli testes*—calling on hazels and streams to mourn Daphnis' death. The reference to the pine, sacred to Pan, with its suggestion of his unhappy love for Syrinx, also connects love with pastoral. *Resonant* is an ordinary verb to describe nature's response to a shepherd's plaint. And the carving of a lover's name into a tree is a commonplace. By the center of the poem, then, Propertius has made one of his typical jumps in thought. Though he starts by announcing that he is singing to lonely nature because it will keep faith and never reveal his sorrows, it is not long before he seems to embrace the quasi-pastoral pose of writing on trees and urging the words to echo his lament.

We feel for a moment that Propertius, like Gallus, could almost accept the bucolic mode as a relief for his sufferings. Yet it is at this crucial juncture that both Virgil's Gallus and Propertius choose the road of elegy. From now on Propertius' thoughts verge away from things pastoral and return to Rome and Cynthia's silent portals (*tacitis foribus*, line 24). He assures her that no other girl save herself has ever crossed his threshold. Finally the sheer loneliness of the sylvan setting overwhelms him again. Though his echo may continue, it reverberates in a landscape as deserted as he now feels. The *deserta loca* and *sola saxa* of the poem's opening seem a fit setting for lament and escape, but in the end they become something different. He had borne Cynthia's haughty commands with patience, Propertius affirms, but now (lines 27-32)

[40] On Propertius 1. 18 see Friedrich Solmsen, "Three Elegies of Propertius' First Book," *CP* 57 (1962): 73-88. Solmsen points out the similarity of the settings in *Ecl.* 2. 3ff. and 10. 52ff. (I do not see the resemblance with *Aen.* 6. 440ff.) He suggests that the *topos* may possibly have originated with Phanocles (frag. 1. 3f. in J. U. Powell, ed., *Collectanea Alexandrina* [Oxford, 1925]: σκιεροῖσιν ἐν ἄλσεσιν), but this does not necessarily demand the remoteness that figures in *Eclogue* 10 and Propertius 1. 18.

pro quo †divinit† fontes et frigida rupes
    et datur inculto tramite dura quies;
et quodcumque meae possunt narrare querelae,
    cogor ad argutas dicere solus aves.
sed qualiscumque es, resonent mihi 'Cynthia' silvae,
    nec deserta tuo nomine saxa vacent.

springs and chill rocks are mine and a hard slumber on
untrodden byways. And whatever my laments can tell I
am driven in my loneliness to utter to shrill birds. But,
whatsoever sort you are, let these woods re-echo "Cynthia"
for me, and do not let the deserted rocks lack your name.

Incultus implies lack of civilization, and *frigidus* and *durus*
offer full assurance that no love could exist in such a setting.
Dura quies, as noted before, suggests death as well as lack of
love.[41] Many of the words (*solus, deserta, saxa,* for instance)
have their counterpart in the opening lines, but here their
effect is more shocking as the poet realizes the extent of the
solitude such a return to nature would mean for an elegist.
It may be that the deserted landscape is only a symbol of his
unhappiness, and the rustic echo but a mockery of his sad affair with Cynthia. Propertius does not have the advantage of
being able to study his plight, as Virgil does Gallus', from
a supposedly unemotional point of view. By making Gallus,
premier elegist, realize the importance not only of the wild
setting of escape but of the inner pastoral dream as well, Virgil adds a dimension to his poem that is missing from Propertius' verses. Nevertheless—and this is the value of the Propertian parallel—like Gallus in *Eclogue* 10, Propertius, in an
attempt to forget his love, embraces at least partially certain
aspects of the pastoral myth only to realize the futility of such
a pose for anyone wishing to remain an elegist.

To return in summary to *Eclogue* 10, the victory of love

[41] This is the very opposite, say, of the *iucunda quies* of Propertius
I. 10. I.

means for Gallus a return to his ways of emotion and action, of process, physical and spiritual, antagonistic to the bucolic stillpoint of unconcern. In spite of Virgil's affection, Gallus' two lives cannot, should not, be reconciled with the shepherd's land. His sojourn therein could only be a temporary aberration.

Virgil's role in the poem is less open to analysis than Gallus'. Until the end of the elegist's song, the only word which reveals any particular involvement on Virgil's part with the subject of his song is the simple *meo* attached to the first appearance of Gallus' name in line 2. Otherwise, though his topic deals with *sollicitos amores*, the poet treats them like someone else's concern. Singer though he is, he remains apparently as aloof from the spiritual implications of his song as do the snub-nosed sheep.

The climax of the poem tells a different tale, however. Having finished a rehearsal of Gallus' song, Virgil turns, for the last time in the *Eclogues*, to the Muses of Pieria (lines 70-77):

> haec sat erit, divae, vestrum cecinisse poetam,
> dum sedet et gracili fiscellam texit hibisco,
> Pierides: vos haec facietis maxima Gallo,
> Gallo, cuius amor tantum mihi crescit in horas
> quantum vere novo viridis se subicit alnus.
> surgamus: solet esse gravis cantantibus umbra,
> iuniperi gravis umbra; nocent et frugibus umbrae.
> ite domum saturae, venit Hesperus, ite capellae.

This will be enough for your poet to have sung, goddesses of Pieria, while he sits and weaves a basket from slim hibiscus. You will make these most important for Gallus, Gallus, for whom my love grows hour by hour as much as a green alder shoots up in early spring. Let us rise. Shade is often oppressive to singers, the shade of the juniper is oppressive. Shade indeed harms crops. Homeward, goats, homeward, filled from browsing. Hesperus has come.

Eclogue 10

This is a renewal of Virgil's pledge of devotion to poetry and its patron divinities. He is their poet (*vestrum poetam*). We note also the pastoral stance of line 71 which is enriched by the words *divae Pierides*. As usual in the pastoral world, physical position reflects spiritual allegiance. Virgil is sitting, like Tityrus in the first eclogue, oblivious, it would seem, of external concerns, be they the disruption of the land's peace by outer forces or the violence of Gallus' love. And while he sits and sings, he plaits a basket—*gracili fiscellam texit hibisco*. This is an emblem of the poet's trade, a pastoral metaphor for the weaving of verses as they are sung. It is the manual counterpart of the *tenui harundine* upon which the poet "meditates" the pastoral muse at the start of *Eclogue* 6 or the *gracili avena* of what may have been the original line of the *Aeneid*.

The phrase also has a more specific purpose. It recalls the penultimate lines of the second eclogue. There, we remember, Corydon debates the best means of forgetting his love and makes a practical suggestion to himself: "quin tu aliquid saltem potius, quorum indiget usus, / viminibus mollique paras detexere iunco?" One way to become oblivious of the past is to attack the usual tasks. That Virgil is about such humble work as he sings the *sollicitos amores* of Gallus would seem to imply that he, too, is fully a part of the shepherd's world, that he is only the inspired vehicle of song—like Damon and Alphesiboeus in *Eclogue* 8—and in no way responsive to the cares of those about whom he sings.

The remainder of the poem proves such an assumption incorrect. Suddenly the apparent farewell to the Muses turns into a virtual command: "vos haec facietis maxima Gallo, / Gallo." The power of the repeated *Gallo* cannot be gainsaid. Virgil has had Gallus in mind all the time and his song, though it dealt with Gallus' loves, turns out to be a mark of his own affection as well.[42] The analogy Virgil uses to express

[42] This is the only use of the superlative of *magnus* in the *Eclogues*. The emotional force of this moment is even stronger than that of the *paulo maiora* of *Eclogue* 4.

his affection is forceful. His love for Gallus grows every hour as a green alder sprouts in early spring. The image is instinct with power. *Vere novo,* in fact, is the phrase which actually begins the main part of the first georgic (line 43), after the initial invocation. The farmer's life begins again as nature comes alive at the dawn of spring.

Hence the analogy of the growing alder, while betokening Virgil's own emotion, may anticipate his future poetic achievement. In so doing it draws the curtain down on the past. The image of growth is not common in the pastoral. Virgil put a version of it into Gallus' mouth at lines 54-55, and there is clearly a deliberate reference to this instance. He takes an elegiac conceit, applied by Gallus to Lycoris, and makes it a sign of his friendship for Gallus. He thus gives a signal that his own love also surpasses the bounds of "pastoral." From love as part of an essentially stable, unmoved and unmoving existence (exemplified by the sedentary singer weaving his basket), we pass, along with Virgil, to love as part of a life of change and process. Instead of rejecting Gallus when he has rejected "pastoral," the poet himself makes the burgeoning of love his final theme. In so doing he merges the emotion of Gallus' tale with his own, making the inner story part of the poem's outer frame. He thus concludes his *Eclogues* with a denial of part of the apparatus the other poems have always assumed.

The final lines repeat many of the same motifs. *Surgamus,* for instance, attaches to the specific pose of the pastoral singer, sitting as his flocks crop the grass, virtually the same metaphor as the verb *crescit* applies to the friendship of Virgil and Gallus. For the poet-shepherd, *surgamus* postulates the end of song just as *crescit* denies the stability of pastoral love.

The reason Virgil gives for ending the poem takes a markedly practical turn: it is shade (*umbra*). Although Gallus' involvement is stressed by the repetition of his name in lines 72-73, the word *umbra* is used three times with even greater emphasis. Shade weighs upon singers; the shade of the juniper is heavy; shade harms the crops. About the superstitious reasoning of the second instance, no convincing elucidation is forthcoming from the ancient sources. The first instance comes as a marked surprise because shade is essential for pastoral song as we have often seen. There are the *umbrosa cacumina* under which Corydon sings in 2; the shade where Daphnis urges Meliboeus to rest during the competition in 7; and the severe implications of the loss of shade by stripping the boughs of leaves in 9.

Hence, from a negative point of view, the unpastoral quality of the utterance comes as a shock. The emphasis, however, is reserved not for the harm shade may do the singer but for its pernicious effect upon the crops. The practical ring of the first and third suggestions, especially the latter, anticipates the *Georgics* as much as it denies the careless unconcern of the pastoral life.[43] It enlarges further on the hint which the words *vere novo* give. We might have anticipated such a conclusion from *haec sat erit* (line 70), a phrase which can apply not only to *Eclogue* 10 but also to the whole series of *Eclogues*. Hence the symbolism of the last line needs no further clarification. Night is falling and the well-fed sheep must make their way homeward as the evening star rises. The poet has sung all he wishes of pastoral song. His readers too, he assumes, have had their fill.

The conclusion of *Eclogue* 1 is similar.[44] There the fall of night seems to bring with it a certain peace and reconciliation. Tityrus' invitation to Meliboeus to share, for one last moment, the beauties of his land is complemented by the descent of

---

[43] See, e.g., *G.* I. 121; 156-57.

[44] The resemblance between the endings has been often noted. It is wrong, I believe, to dismiss these lines as less powerful than the conclusion of *Eclogue* 1 (as does, for instance, Albert Cook, *The Classic Line* [Bloomington, 1966], p. 183).

On the *topos* of shade see P. L. Smith, *"Lentus in umbra," Phoenix* 19 (1965): 298-304, esp. 303-4.

darkness which could tender at least a brief interlude before
the morrow's griefs. No such possibility is offered at the end
of 10. Virgil's lack of interest in further communion with "pastoral" is emphasized by one fact. In the first eclogue the poet
speaks through two voices to convey his intense feelings about
a situation which goes beyond the concerns of poetry to probe
the relationship of man and society and to seek a definition of
liberty. In the tenth, however, the same Virgil who at first
seems to tell only the tale of Gallus' woes, ends by involving
himself closely with the protagonist of his tale. (In this involvement he is unlike the aloof shepherds in *Eclogue* 8.) Virgil,
the poet, has spoken with his own voice before. But this is not
detached wonder at the mystical regeneration of nature through
history in *Eclogue* 4, nor is it the terse, impersonal announcement of a program of examples of a new poetic intention, as
at the opening of *Eclogue* 6. Rather it is both a personal dec-
laration of the poet's withdrawal from "pastoral" (but this
could have been done impersonally, had he followed the model
of *Eclogue* 1) and his acknowledgment of a degree of emotional attachment which is foreign to and destructive of
otium.

We have learned from Gallus' own words that for love, at
least the emotional tension of elegiac love, to grow mild is as
much an impossibility as for him to embrace "pastoral." Although we might expect the poet to keep himself divorced
from the song he sings, the opposite proves to be the case.
Not only do the pastoral Muses not work their charm over
Gallus, it is Gallus and love who win the day. The reader may
feel a sense of regret that Virgil compels himself to relinquish
"pastoral" at the same time Gallus does. Nevertheless it remains the poem's final irony that at the same moment as his
renunciation, Virgil proclaims in strong terms his affection
(*amor*, line 73) for Gallus, who shortly before had declared
omnia vincit Amor.

IT IS NATURAL that throughout the *Eclogues* the reader's attention should be focused on the problematical reaction of the shepherd to various crises forced upon him by internal and external pressures. We ponder the relationship of the shepherd to himself and to the life he leads. We are made to see the fatal conflict of his fragile myth with more potent verities. Though in the first five eclogues we are never allowed to forget that "pastoral" means the world of poetry and ideas, *Eclogues* 6 through 10 are specifically concerned with the power and meaning of bucolic poetry *per se*. The issue of *Eclogue* 9— whether poets, as symbols of human creativity and freedom, can survive when subjected to the consequences of human progress—was one which concerned Virgil for the rest of his career. The questions which *Eclogue* 10 raises are not so clearcut. Like its neighboring poems, it is a meditation on the substance and capacities of "pastoral." The sylvan world is once more integrated. Menalcas, the absent poet of the preceding poem, is back, the gods of the landscape are on hand, the poet-shepherd, this time Virgil in person, goes about his task in bucolic fashion with (apparent) unconcern for the strange state of his subject.

We find ourselves in a situation similar to, yet going beyond, that of *Eclogues* 6 and 7. The question of primary importance is not so much the suitability of Gallus' *sollicitos amores* as a topic for bucolic song (we have seen such a subject treated in *Eclogues* 2 and 8), but whether or not Gallus himself, in his own mind and from the viewpoint of those who gaze on him in astonishment, is a fit member of the shepherds' society. Again, it would be an oversimplification merely to ask if it is probable or even possible for a poet of elegy, who is also a soldier and statesman, to become a shepherd and singer of idyls. Nevertheless, from this basic question, readily as Virgil and his readers can divine the answer, stem further problems posed by such a juxtaposition.

There is the literary relationship with Theocritus' first idyl, making us ask what specific connection there might be, if any, between Gallus and Daphnis. Then what of the landscape? Is it suitable for elegy or pastoral, or both? We may first imagine that this wilderness, one step from the bucolic world, might purvey that beauty and refreshment which could cure the lovelorn Gallus. But to accept such a tempting escape would be, for Gallus, as lacking in courage as it would be untrue to himself. Nature may for a moment symbolize the dark night of the elegist's soul. To play at actually becoming part of the bucolic landscape is a flight of fancy for an elegist. For the pastoral poet, however, to read the lover's mind so well as to define in words the steps toward the inescapable decision is a notable accomplishment. It raises one last point.

The ninth eclogue depicts the death of the spirit. The land's inhabitants do not yield without suffering the maximum torture—the realization of what it means to lose the setting and inspiration for song. In *Eclogue* 10, quite to the contrary, the denial of pastoral song comes from within the poet himself and from an impulse which previously Virgil—or the voices of his songs, such as the shepherds in *Eclogue* 8—would have stoutly denied: the pull of emotional response. We might expect that any fusion between pastoral and elegy could not take place and that Gallus, the man of affairs, could not find peace in a *locus amoenus*. "Pastoral" assumes fulfillment and demands order. Suffering and lack of assurance are the stuff of elegy.

What we do not anticipate is the poet's own spiritual leave-taking. It is a compliment for his friend that Virgil depicts Gallus as fully knowledgeable of things rural, yet incapable of accepting a position in the bucolic world. It is a victory for Gallus that his departure not only signalizes the poet's own relinquishment of the pastoral form but also forces from him an acknowledgment that his affection for Gallus is the reason. No suicide here; that is the recourse of those for whom the destruction of happiness leaves nothing else. Rather the poet hints at new fields to conquer, new poetic forms to work with, and states, indirectly, that man must take responsibility for the world around him. The battles of life cannot be fought from the ivory tower of disengagement but from hand to hand combat with the enemy, be it the weeds which choke the weary farmer's field or the civil wars in which brother destroys brother in needless slaughter.

The lesson of the *Georgics*, disguised behind the mask of practicality, is essentially moral. The *Eclogues*, in a manner less pragmatic, present a vision which is hardly less civilized. It is the fantasy of a world of poetry which, if we interpret literally the perfection of bucolic leisure, on the surface seems a stranger to the human condition. We may likewise, for example, interpret literally, if we wish, and without grave injustice to the poems, the advent of the enemy in *Eclogues* 1 and 9, the birth of the boy in 4, the placing of Gallus in Arcadia in 10. But each of these teaches us, symbolically, a broader lesson. Though we seem to be dealing with an idealistic world aloof, its idealism is, in fact, much a part of life, the life of Rome, while being at the same time an emblem for the creative mind. This emblem in turn demands freedom, especially from the restraints with which human progress in space and time can narrow the boundaries of the spirit.

Whatever forms it may take, this idealism remained with Virgil throughout his career. In the *Aeneid* it has two partisans. Aeneas assumes the heavy burden of Rome's future history and ideology, and defends it almost to the end, against sallies of war and emotion, human and divine. Turnus accepts an equally vital mission. He is the champion of freedom for his land and people, the protector of his own against Aeneas' advancement toward his goal. The conclusion of the *Aeneid*, however, is not a conflict between two philosophies of life. In the end Aeneas' furious slaughter of Turnus makes him a victim of the emotionality which his opponent personified.

The end of *Eclogue* 10 has something in common with the

end of the *Aeneid*. Aeneas, the supposedly idealistic missionary, could, like the symbolic youth in *Eclogue* 4, become the motive force that reconciled and unified historical progress with the static abstracts of liberty and creativity. Instead he assumes Turnus' violence and kills him. Without losing sight of the great difference the two poems possess in terms of style, subject matter, and so forth, we may interpret *Eclogue* 10 on similar lines. There are the same grand tokens of idealism that Aeneas carries with him, this time the whole apparatus of "pastoral" from divinities to sheep to the shepherd, Virgil, who sings of it all. The poem is invaded by emotionality, in the form of the elegist-warrior Gallus who utters a speech beginning with a prayer for a love-death and ending, after a varied show of mental gymnastics, with an admission of love's power and an acknowledgment of the uselessness of the pastoral life. But this is not all. At the end, the poet Virgil, as idealistic a practitioner of "pastoral" as one may imagine, announces not only the end of his song, in an unwonted practical vein, but also his devotion to Gallus, partisan of an anti-pastoral art.

Nevertheless this action on Virgil's part is not the death of bucolic poetry, as in a sense Aeneas' killing of Turnus is an avowal of Rome's inability to combine empire and liberty. From Virgil, at the end of *Eclogue* 10, there is only a personal confession of the limited place of the pastoral myth in his present thoughts. This in no way lessens the value of the *Eclogues* as a superb testimony of the human spirit in its unceasing search for freedom, happiness, and beauty.

Index

Achilles, 142, 151, 156-57, 206
Acis, 348
Adonis, 354-55
adunaton, 51, 53-55, 185, 188, 264, 274, 276, 288
Aegle, 200, 220
Aeneas, 19, 78, 272, 276-77, 283, 362, 393-94
Afri, 54, 58, 63
Aganippe, 348
Alcaeus, 256, 260
Alexis, 46, 66, 82-119 passim, 132, 137, 208, 220, 226, 234, 246-47, 251, 263, 267, 289, 354-55, 365-66, 372, 381
Alfenus Varus, 161, 197-98, 239, 299, 309-10, 321, 330, 334, 343
Alphesiboeus, 187, 255-92 passim, 387
Alpheus, 344-45
Amaryllis, 22, 38, 40-41, 128, 137, 173, 209, 219, 247, 257, 278-89, 293, 304, 308, 315, 346, 365, 372
Ambarvalia, 187
Amphion, 97-98, 100, 102
Amyntas, 128, 135, 169-70, 187, 364-65
Anapus, 348
Antony, 143, 189
Apollo, 16, 106, 125, 132-35, 142, 145, 161, 167, 169, 177, 179, 184, 186, 189-90, 196-98, 201, 211-12, 217-19, 249-50, 252, 310, 315, 356, 358-60
Arar, *see* Saône
Arcadia, 3, 161, 328, 349-51, 353, 376, 393

Arethusa, 231, 240, 311, 342, 344, 348-49, 357, 379
Argo, 205-206
Argonauts, 151, 156-57, 206
Arion, 274-75, 277
Aristophanes, 373
Arnold, 4
Ascra, 211
Asinius, *see* Pollio
Astraea (Justitia), 140, 142, 154, 177, 190
Atalanta, 209-10, 270
Augustus, *see* Octavian

Bacchus (Liber), 125, 167-68, 174, 185-90, 199, 202, 220, 239, 248-49
Bavius, 130
Bianor, 327-28, 331
Boswell, 10
Britanni, 54, 58
Brundisium, Pact of, 143

Caesar, ix, 14, 61, 68, 78, 188-89, 318-21, 328-32, 334
Calchas, 217
Callimachus, 21, 196, 203, 213, 219-20, 373
Calliope, 161
Calypso, 167
Cartault, ix
Catullus, 7, 8, 11, 87, 112, 139-42, 144, 157-58, 163-64, 265, 269, 272-73, 312
Ceres, 150, 177, 185-86, 188, 190
Chaonia, 303, 312, 318
Chiron, 336
Cicero, 6, 7, 11, 69, 85, 87
Cinna, 274, 312-13, 337

Index

Index

Index